UNGUARDED BORDER

T0244316

WAR CULTURE

Edited by Daniel Leonard Bernardi

Books in this series address the myriad ways in which warfare informs diverse cultural practices, as well as the way cultural practices—from cinema to social media—inform the practice of warfare. They illuminate the insights and limitations of critical theories that describe, explain, and politicize the phenomena of war culture. Traversing both national and intellectual borders, authors from a wide range of fields and disciplines collectively examine the articulation of war, its everyday practices, and its impact on individuals and societies throughout modern history.

For a list of all the titles in the series, please see the last page of the book.

UNGUARDED BORDER

American Émigrés in Canada during the Vietnam War

DONALD W. MAXWELL

RUTGERS UNIVERSITY PRESS

New Brunswick, Camden, and Newark, New Jersey

London and Oxford

Rutgers University Press is a department of Rutgers, The State University of New Jersey, one of the leading public research universities in the nation. By publishing worldwide, it furthers the University's mission of dedication to excellence in teaching, scholarship, research, and clinical care.

Library of Congress Cataloging-in-Publication Data

Names: Maxwell, Donald William, author.
Title: Unguarded border : American émigrés in Canada during the
   Vietnam War / Donald W. Maxwell.
Description: New Brunswick : Rutgers University Press, [2023] |
   Series: War culture | Includes bibliographical references and index.
Identifiers: LCCN 2022037745 | ISBN 9781978834033 (hardcover) |
   ISBN 9781978834026 (paperback) | ISBN 9781978834040 (epub) |
   ISBN 9781978834057 (pdf)
Subjects: LCSH: Vietnam War, 1961–1975—Draft resisters—United States. |
   Vietnam War, 1961–1975—Desertions—United States. | Vietnam War,
   1961–1975—Protest movements—United States. | Americans—Canada—
   History—20th century. | Canada—Emigration and immigration—History—20th
   century. | United States—Emigration and immigration—History—20th century.
Classification: LCC DS559.8.D7 M39 2023 | DDC 959.704/3373—dc23/eng/20221220
LC record available at https://lccn.loc.gov/2022037745

A British Cataloging-in-Publication record for this book is available from the British Library.

Copyright © 2023 by Donald W. Maxwell
All rights reserved

No part of this book may be reproduced or utilized in any form or by any means, electronic or mechanical, or by any information storage and retrieval system, without written permission from the publisher. Please contact Rutgers University Press, 106 Somerset Street, New Brunswick, NJ 08901. The only exception to this prohibition is "fair use" as defined by U.S. copyright law.

References to internet websites (URLs) were accurate at the time of writing. Neither the author nor Rutgers University Press is responsible for URLs that may have expired or changed since the manuscript was prepared.

rutgersuniversitypress.org

For my families of birth and of choice, for their unflagging support

CONTENTS

UNGUARDED BORDER

UNGUARDED SCHOOL

INTRODUCTION

David W. Diamond graduated in the class of 1966 at Sherburne Central School in upstate New York. Like many young men of his generation, he went immediately to college. University life did not entirely suit him, however, and he was suspended during the middle of his sophomore year. He returned home to live with his parents, and although he attended a nearby community college, his life changed significantly.[1] For American men of Diamond's generation, flunking out of college even once meant they no longer would enjoy a deferment from the military draft during the Vietnam War era. Unless they could prove themselves unfit or unworthy for military duty, they were subject to conscription.

Six months and two days after his suspension from college, Diamond reported for induction into the U.S. Army. He attended boot camp at Fort Knox in Kentucky, then went to Fort Sam Houston in San Antonio, Texas, for medical aid training. One year to the day after Diamond was suspended from college, the U.S. Army declared him AWOL (absent without leave). While on leave after the medical aid course, Diamond and two of his barracks mates began traveling to Sweden to resist being deployed to Vietnam. Sweden was granting asylum on humanitarian grounds to American GIs, primarily military deserters who had left their posts in Europe and Asia. In seeking the shortest route from San Antonio to Stockholm, Diamond found himself in Canada.[2] Diamond likely could not have gotten to Sweden easily, but he did not need a passport to get into many Western Hemisphere countries. Among those countries during the Vietnam War, Canada was the only one that openly accepted deserters from the U.S. military, such as Diamond and his barracks mates, and draft resisters—men who did not report for induction when ordered to do so.

Diamond remained in Canada for nine years. In a diary entry he wrote in Montréal in the spring of 1975, he revealed the psychological toll the first seven years in exile had taken on him, admitting,

> I never have the nerve to go any where [sic] out of fear that there will be no place to return to. My father ... tried to convince me that things never change that fast on the earth but I seem to have it in my psyche that things can indeed change as rapidly as all that and faster. I could come home to my apartment and find it gone at the end of a long day of school and work and worse[,] I could have no place to turn for help, with the only real outside alternative to go to the states and to jail.[3]

For Diamond and other American men of draft age in the 1960s and 1970s, security about a place to belong was under constant assault. They faced the possibility of being drafted, the possibility of being told by their nation to spend two years of their youth in military service, the possibility of being a combatant in a war reviled around the world, the possibility of being wounded or killed, the possibility of a prison sentence for draft evasion or desertion, the possibility of feeling compelled to live in the underground to avoid criminal prosecution, the possibility of exile, the possibility of being extradited and deported from places of exile, the possibility of renouncing U.S. citizenship to resist fulfilling some of its duties, and the possibility of the United States reclaiming them under various schemes of the Gerald Ford and Jimmy Carter presidencies. These myriad possibilities gnawed at the psyches of young American men for over a decade. Those who most successfully negotiated these assaults often did so by identifying places in which they could live their lives on their own terms, usually by leaving the United States. It was in Canada, reached by a rather easy border crossing, that they could most easily find spaces in which they could pursue cosmopolitan ideals removed from the nation, yet to which they had easy access in their day-to-day lives. This study uses the definition of *cosmopolitanism* posited by the journalist Atossa Araxia Abrahamian: when "people want or need to belong to, or be accepted in, places they were not assigned to by the accident of birth, whether for economic, personal, or political reasons."[4]

Tens of thousands of people moved from the United States to Canada during the 1960s and 1970s. The number who were resisting the draft and deserting the military is difficult to pinpoint, because neither Canadian nor U.S. officials tallied people who cited such reasons for their immigration. Indeed, many émigrés feared that disclosure of their draft or military status would incriminate them. By taking up residency in another country, and in some cases renouncing their citizenship, U.S. émigrés pointed to new concepts of citizenship based less on the nation and more on the place from or to which they moved. The impact of the movement of émigrés was most felt in the *places* from which they left and in which they arrived, more so than the *nations* from which and to which they moved. Accordingly, this study focuses on individuals and grassroots efforts to aid (or hinder) their emigration from the United States to Canada.

Inescapable in the stories of these people is that they were still at the mercy of the laws of nations: immigration laws in both the United States and Canada and extradition laws of the rest of the world. Further, in the Vietnam War era, there was an ever-changing matrix of military conscription laws in the United States, laws designed to make more inclusive the United States's intensive, decade-long demand for military personnel, and reflecting the varying attitudes of the Lyndon Johnson, Richard Nixon, Gerald Ford, and Jimmy Carter presidential administrations toward military service, resistance, and desertion. Consequently, this book emphasizes the stories of young American men of draft age who were subject to those laws. While this study includes elements of cultural, military, legal, political, and diplomatic history, it is, at its heart, a social history—an immigration history—of U.S. residents who moved to Canada during the Vietnam War era and the Canadians among whom they moved.

To call these people immigrants is to acknowledge that national borders were crossed. Until the early twenty-first century, when strict post-9/11 passport restrictions came into play, the U.S.-Canadian border was a relatively easy one to cross physically, if not emotionally. In the second half of the twentieth century, the border could be crossed via many forms of transportation over 150 legal highway, railroad, and ferry crossings and over 5,500 miles (8,900 kilometers) of largely unguarded border. U.S. émigrés in Canada who had resisted the draft or deserted the military demonstrated a diminished sense of allegiance to the nation. Once they reached Canada, they were also often ambivalent about their new country of residence, feeling little kinship with fellow U.S. émigrés, and not forming strong expatriate communities.

In late 1974 David W. Diamond visited his parents at their home in upstate New York for the first time in six years, a visit that was legal due to a fifteen-day grace period during Gerald Ford's Presidential Clemency Program. With the war over and hoping to lure exiles back to the United States to perform alternative service or to seek exoneration, Ford allowed men to return to the

United States to discuss the possibilities with their families. Diamond was uncomfortable in his hometown and yet continued to feel like an outsider in Canada. He recognized the ambiguous place in which he resided, writing in his diary on New Year's Day 1975,

> Montreal isn't home to me either but I am not so uncomfortable here for I am not in the position of being somebody to the people around me. Here I have no history, and that more than likely implies that I have no future here either, and having no history I have no family history and therefore I don't have to act a part, don't have to be so much a symbol of the ambitions and strivings of all the people in the family both past and present and don't have to worry about being a disgrace; in this town no one cares because no one knows me.[5]

Many observers noted that U.S. émigrés did not seek each other out in Canada. A staff reporter for the *Los Angeles Times* newspaper observed in 1972 that émigrés were difficult to locate in Canada. As one twenty-six-year-old man acknowledged, "We're not glued together. We're all different, have different interests. The only cohesive force is that of the mind, the reason we came here. But as for being a close group—draft dodgers and deserters all buddies, that sort of thing; it just does not exist."[6] Michael Warsh, who immigrated to Vancouver in the late 1960s, noted that although émigrés gravitated toward immigrant aid groups when they arrived in Canada, they also quickly strayed away from them. He reflected that "there was a strong sense of denying one's Americanness and to stop being American. People became part of the woodwork."[7] Don Gayton, a draft resister who had been in Canada since the early 1970s, concurred, observing, "Expatriate Americans have a curious role in Canada. For the most part they try very hard to blend in. People of other nationalities tend to gravitate toward each other in specific Canadian cities and neighborhoods, but expat Americans do just the opposite. You will never find an ethnic enclave of Americans."[8]

U.S. émigrés in Canada often expressed an affinity for something beyond the nation. AMEX/Canada, an immigrant aid group for U.S. residents in Canada, surveyed subscribers to its publications in 1973 about their motivations for coming to Canada, their intentions to remain there, and their connections to the United States and other U.S. émigrés. To the question "What do you see as your primary identity?," some readers admitted ambivalence. For example, a Whaletown, British Columbia, resident responded, "I don't know—sometimes Canadian, sometimes American."[9] Others resisted labels that connected them to nations. A Drumheller, Alberta, man identified himself as "a citizen of the world, a member of the human race," while "Socialist human being of no nationality as primary identity" was the response of an Ottawa resident.[10] A Toronto man identified himself as "primarily religious; hence no need to have any citizenship," claiming that he could not give allegiance to any country because he had renounced his U.S. citizenship in 1970. He also allowed that he had little interest in meeting with others from the United States for social or political activities because "I feel no deep affinity with any-one on national or political grounds."[11] A London, Ontario, man admitted that "when I took what was then (1965) the extreme step of going to live in another country I never imagined that what I saw as a moral necessity would be less than a crime to other Americans. I accepted the legal price for what was essentially an individual moral action."[12] Similarly, a twenty-two-year-old man exiled in Canada in the late 1960s described the evolution of his feelings about nationalism to an interviewer: "During high school . . . I became interested in the war in Vietnam. I went to Europe when I was 18 and came back confused. I split with religion and nationalism, that is, God and country. I broke from materialism and felt detached from the U.S. I don't even consider myself part of the U.S. Politically, I am in no man's land. I am not accepted by anybody and I don't want to be."[13]

In a similar vein, in 1974, Bill King, a young American man exiled in Toronto, wrote to Gerald Ford to complain about the restrictions of the Presidential Clemency Program for draft resisters. His plaint articulated his worldview by pointing to the conceit of the Ford administration that U.S. residency was superior to exile in other countries and that draft resisters and military deserters would willingly surrender much to regain the freedom to legally return to the United States. He asserted to Ford that "As an American, born in Illinois and raised in the Minnesota middle class, I realize that it is difficult for most Americans to realize that non-Americans are equal human beings with as much talent, pride, morality, and dignity as those who happen to have been born in the U.S. I am a citizen of the world; all people are my brothers and sisters. Without the assumption that being American is some-how better than being human, your proposal makes no sense."[14]

Despite ambivalence about national allegiances and the lack of feeling kin-ship ties, the émigrés recognized Canada as a space in which they were free to shrug off the bonds of U.S. citizenship and to experience life more on their own terms. That often required exchanging nation for conscience. In Canada in the late 1960s and early 1970s, U.S. émigrés were able to embrace more cos-mopolitan ideals that helped them transcend nations and the obligations they placed on their citizens.

Canada was not bereft of internal political problems during the 1960s and 1970s. A political movement in the province of Québec matched opposition to the war in Vietnam in the United States. Adherents to this movement, who hoped to separate Québec into its own sovereign nation, escalated their protests throughout the 1960s. From 1963 to 1970, the FLQ (Front de libération du Québec, or, Québec Liberation Front) committed acts of vandalism, arson, and robbery during which members stole money and military equipment. The FLQ planted over eighty bombs throughout Québec and in the Canadian capital city of Ottawa, many of which detonated, killing at least four people and injuring dozens. During the "October Crisis" of 1970, cells of the FLQ kidnapped two government officials and murdered one of them, causing the government of Canada to enforce the War Measures Act, which put the country under martial law, suspending civil liberties for six months.[15] Police detained nearly five hundred people, including members of the FLQ and other individuals deemed subversive, including some U.S. émigré draft resisters and military deserters. The Canadian military deployed to protect various people and places in the province of Québec and nearby Ottawa. Groups aiding U.S. émigrés to Canada advised those who could not speak French not to move to Québec.[16] Such militarism in Canada was a deterrent to immigrants who hoped to go there and was a shock not only to Canadians, especially those in Montréal, but also to those from the United States who had immigrated to Canada in opposition to the militarism of their home country.[17]

Black draft-age men went to Canada, but the exact number of them is impossible to ascertain. Despite racism being as prevalent in the military as in U.S. society as a whole, Black men could gain some advantages in the military that they might have difficulty realizing outside of it, such as better food, shelter, and vocational training. As the journalist Myra MacPherson observed in *Long Time Passing,* her 1984 study of the impact of the Vietnam War on U.S. society, "During Vietnam, for some, it was the Army or jail; for others it was the Army or unemployment. Boredom and the lack of a future on ghetto streets played a part." Further, the historian Amy J. Rutenberg observed that minority and working-class men came from communities "that venerated the military values of 'brotherhood, team work, bravery and ruggedness' and that had strong traditions of military service during wartime." For this reason, those who sought to resist service often did so privately, avoiding, or being unaware of, antiwar organizations or draft counselors who could help them.[18]

Local draft boards, usually comprised of white, middle-aged businessmen and World War II and Korean War veterans, were more likely to conscript

Black and Hispanic men than white men. This race bias was criticized by many and led to the creation of a draft lottery in 1969, which randomized who was called up for potential military service among draft-age men. While racism was less of an issue for them, economically and educationally disadvantaged whites dealt with some of the same issues as Blacks and Hispanics. All were less likely than middle- and upper-class white men to be able to afford such professionals as attorneys, physicians, and psychologists who could help them resist the draft. For these reasons, Blacks, Hispanics, other minorities, and members of other disadvantaged groups were more likely to go to Canada in the Vietnam War era as military deserters than as draft resisters.[19]

Chapter 1 of this book describes a unique confluence of conditions in the late 1960s and early 1970s—the possibility of emigration, the proximity of Canada to the United States, and the Vietnam War—that propelled tens of thousands out of the country who resisted absorption into the U.S. military during the Vietnam War or who were uncomfortable with social conditions in the United States during that era. This emigration produced a set of events and ideas that transcended particular protagonists and locales, had links to émigrés from the United States from throughout its history, and had ramifications that reach into the twenty-first century. In chapter 2 I analyze print-based sources of information, especially magazine articles, travel literature, advice manuals for the military draft, and correspondence between (potential) émigrés and immigrant aid groups, that influenced young people from the United States to immigrate, especially to Canada. Such media painted generally positive portrayals of Canada and of U.S. immigrants who had gone there, thereby paving an attractive road north and out of the country for tens of thousands of others. Throughout the book I privilege these twentieth-century popular press accounts—and archival sources—to locate the voices of those who experienced this immigration. I incorporated few twenty-first-century primary sources such as interviews and correspondence.

In chapters 3 and 4 I analyze two manifestations of the affinity of those émigrés for a cosmopolitanism located in institutions that extend beyond the nation, but in which they could easily participate in their day-to-day lives, wherever they chose to live them: religion and postsecondary education. Churches and church groups in Canada provided humanitarian and pastoral aid to U.S. immigrants. Many men went to Canada not only to resist the draft but also to pursue undergraduate, graduate, or professional degrees. While émigrés tried to embrace cosmopolitan ideals, Canadian religious organizations hoped to attract the attention of the Canadian government and public with their good deeds. At the same time, many people in Canadian higher education looked to the government to staunch the flow of American men to Canadian graduate schools and to Canadian university faculties out of concern they would bring U.S. sensibilities and intellectual ideas to Canadian classrooms.

In chapter 5 I consider challenges to émigrés' assertions of cosmopolitanism posed by various schemes of the Canadian and U.S. governments in the 1970s to protect the sovereignty of their nations by trying to claim, reclaim, and redeem U.S. émigrés. Finally, in chapter 6 I consider the ways in which U.S. émigrés asserted their sense of cosmopolitanism to bring changes to the concepts of immigration, citizenship, compulsory military service, and identity, as asserted by such documents as passports, as they evolved in the late twentieth and early twenty-first centuries.

In this book I present a challenge to paradigms in the study of U.S. immigration history. No matter their disdain for the concept of nations in general, the modern geopolitical (and existential) reality is that these Americans had to live *somewhere*—in some country in the world. It would be easy to discount emigrants from the United States as members of another nation and therefore no longer a part of U.S. history. Those who leave the United States are often omitted from U.S. historical narratives out of anger, shame, confusion, or willful attempts to obscure the possibility that the United States is not a city upon a hill for all people.[20] This study rescues U.S. émigrés to Canada in the Vietnam War era from such ahistoricity. Following those émigrés out of the country and understanding the motivations for their departure and the extent to which they were able to start new lives in places outside the United States are compelling perspectives through which we can extend and enrich the history of the United States. More important, I assert that these émigrés, even as they moved from one nation to another, recognized a space that was beyond nations, with a prescience that points to a new paradigm—movement not between *nations* but between *places*—for understanding the history of immigration in the late twentieth century and into the twenty-first.[21]

1 · ESCAPING OVER THE BORDER

The Americans Who Went to Canada

It's not just the draft.
Nor is it that I particularly believe in...revolutionary ideas.
It's that every time I've crossed the Detroit River to Windsor,
I've had this feeling as if I'd escaped from a police state,
like over the Berlin Wall.
—anonymous Detroit resident and Vietnam War draft resister (1967)

One of the largest exoduses from the United States took place in the late 1960s and early 1970s, when over 50,000 men and women emigrated from the United States to Canada. They left either to resist being drafted into U.S. military service during the Vietnam War era, after going AWOL (absent without leave) from the military, in support of draft resisters or military deserters, or in opposition to U.S. foreign policy or domestic social conditions. The exact number of these emigrants is difficult to determine, since neither the U.S. nor Canadian governments tallied émigrés who cited draft resistance, military desertion, or war opposition as the reason for their immigration.[1] Use of the term "draft resister" in this book reflects a sentiment that men who found ways not to enter military service did so with conviction. Other terms, such as "draft dodger," appear in this book, but they are the words of others who used them colloquially, sometimes with the intention of using them pejoratively. Use of the terms "desertion" and "military deserter" echoes the U.S. government description of this action, as found in the Uniform Code of Military Justice.[2] The adjective "American" in this book is used to describe people from the United States, although anyone from anywhere in the Americas could claim the descriptor.

Although they were not required to serve in the U.S. military, women (often wives, girlfriends, mothers, and sisters) and other non-draft-age male family members accompanied resisting men to Canada or went there of their own volition. For example, the urban planner Jane Jacobs moved her family from New York City to Toronto in 1968, days before her oldest son turned eighteen, because she and her husband did not want their sons to serve in the military, or to go to jail for refusing to serve in the U.S. military during a war that they found "immoral, senseless, and cruel."[3] In other cases women moved to Canada alone, or in groups.[4] This book, however, is primarily concerned with American men of draft age, as they alone were subject to conscription and military laws of the United States in this era.

All of these émigrés' departures can be viewed as noncooperation with, or nonparticipation in, a U.S. society with which they felt at odds. The departures of draft-age men carried the added significance that they came in direct opposition to U.S. conscription laws and military policies. Such disobedience resulted in loss of full citizenship status in the United States, but movement to Canada opened new possibilities for a different type of citizenship, one less concerned with a young man's potential contribution to the military might of a nation and more concerned with the man's freedom of expression, which could include opposition to war.[5] This exodus of people sparked discussion not only in the United States and Canada but also around the world, and it was the subject of much press coverage in newspapers, popular magazines, association and religious publications, and underground press, as well as in books from commercial publishers and grassroots organizations.

The departures of tens of thousands from the United States forever changed the families, friendships, and communities they left behind, as well as the communities they entered or created in Canada. Thousands of people on both sides of the border were involved in grassroots efforts to counsel émigrés and would-be émigrés, providing them with food, shelter, and monetary, pastoral, and moral support. The laity and clergy of many churches and religious organizations in Canada and the United States—and worldwide—felt compelled to help them. The draft drained thousands of male graduate students away from U.S. universities, but those who moved to Canada had a chance to remain in school, where they had a profound impact on the university system and intellectual climate there. Presidents, prime ministers, U.S. cabinet officials, Canadian cabinet ministers, members of the U.S. Congress, members of the Canadian Parliament, and various state, provincial, and local officials on both sides of the border commented on and debated legislation concerning this large movement of people.

The military draft in the Vietnam War era laid bare citizenship requirements reserved for American men aged eighteen to twenty-six years, particularly in contrast to those for men outside that age range and women, just as it exposed racial and class inequities among the draft-age male cohort.[6] Draft laws in the United States were in constant flux from the end of World War II until the establishment of an all-volunteer military force in 1973, as the United States grappled with how to flex its military might in the Cold War era. The large influx of young men—and those who accompanied them—to Canada brought changes in immigration laws and citizenship requirements in both countries, contributing to the reframing of citizenship rights and responsibilities on both sides of the border. Reluctance to fulfill military obligations compelled some men not only to leave the United States but to renounce their U.S. citizenship.

Because Canada had no military draft at the time, having discontinued compulsory military service at the end of World War II, it would not extradite men who were in violation of draft laws of other countries. During the late 1960s, Canada went from passive to conscious acceptance of these immigrants. It did so in a couple of ways. In October 1967 the Immigration Branch of the Canadian government instituted a new system for evaluating potential immigrants to Canada. The new system was sympathetic to younger people, to those with more education, to those who could speak English, and to those who had the potential for holding down a job, particularly those with occupational skills in demand in Canada—all likely attributes of draft-age men from the United States.[7]

A second major change came nineteen months later. After months of parliamentary debate and pressure from many groups, the Canadian government, under Prime Minister Pierre Trudeau, announced on May 22, 1969, that it would treat draft resisters and military deserters as "ordinary" immigrants, meaning that Canada would admit them without any question as to their status with the U.S. Selective Service System (SSS) and would refuse to deport them, as long as they otherwise qualified as immigrants to Canada. The policy went into practice when Allan J. MacEachen, the minister of manpower and immigration, issued a memorandum declaring that

> membership in the armed service of another country—or desertion if you like, potential or actual—will not be a factor in determining the eligibility of persons applying for landed immigrant status in Canada, whether such persons apply from within Canada, at points of entry, or at Canadian immigration offices abroad. If a serviceman from another country meets our immigration criteria, he will not be turned down because he is still in the active service of his country.

Therefore, the selection criteria and requirements applying to him will be the same as those that apply to other applicants.

Our basic position is that the question of an individual's membership or potential membership in the armed services of his own country is a matter to be settled between the individual and his government, and is not a matter in which we should become involved.[8]

This clear assertion of policy encouraged thousands of Americans to emigrate from the United States to Canada over the next four-and-a-half years. Ostensibly, this could have applied to military deserters from any army in the world, but most significantly, it served as a green light for movement north over the U.S.-Canadian border.

The large movement of people from the United States to Canada was the result of a cultural opening created by immigration, the proximity of Canada to the United States, and the Vietnam War coming together in the 1960s and 1970s. People have always immigrated, usually deciding to move in an effort to improve—even save—their lives. The importance of Canada for the story that follows began in the late eighteenth century, when the United States began to exist as a nation, after some of the colonists of European descent who had settled in North America decided to rule themselves while others decided to remain subjects of the king of England, thereby splitting northern North America into two nations. The importance of Vietnam for this story does not develop until the mid-twentieth century, when its people struggled for independence (much like many British North Americans had in the late eighteenth century) rather than be ruled by France and Japan, which had colonized them over the previous century. The strong interest that the government of the United States took in the outcome of the ensuing civil war in Vietnam, 8,000 miles (13,000 kilometers) from Los Angeles, would propel this southeast Asian country into the consciousness of Americans, particularly those who would be affected by U.S. military involvement there.

People have always moved from place to place. Movement often comes as people seek economic, political, or social conditions that better suit them— and sometimes to save their lives. The traditional narrative of U.S. history emphasizes the influx of heroic people, especially those of European origin, to the United States, moving as "pioneering settlers who opened frontiers and constructed new nations, bearing individual initiative and progress to the cutting edge of world history."[9] Other people move because they are forced to—because their dislocation benefits their oppressors. In U.S. history such people have included aboriginals forced off land coveted by Europeans (who themselves had been immigrants to North America), as well as Africans brought to North America into chattel slavery. Later in this narrative come people of Asian and Eastern European origin, usually as laborers working on terms set by people descended from earlier waves of European immigration. More inclusive histories acknowledge people of European origin who moved to the United States from other places in the Americas, notably from its immediate neighbors, Mexico and Canada.

Although they tend to disappear from the traditional narrative of U.S. history, some people have left the United States. Social conditions brought them prejudice because of the color of their skin, their ethnicity, their gender, their sexuality, or their religious practices. In other cases, people from the United States determined they could practice their art, métier, religion, or personal or political beliefs more freely outside the United States. Such emigrants committed what some patriots believe to be, as the historian Roger Daniels characterized it, "the most profoundly un-American act that one can imagine" by leaving the United States.[10]

The perceived odiousness of expatriation from the United States can perhaps explain the paucity of scholarship on this sort of immigration. The U.S. government does not track expatriation, or if it does, it does not publish statistics on it. The U.S. government vade mecum *Historical Statistics of the United States* reports data collected by the U.S. Immigration and Naturalization Service on immigration *to* the United States but does not report data on emigration *from* the United States after 1957, aside from expulsions and deportations of aliens.[11] While this source reports data on U.S. immigrants to Canada, those data were collected by the government of Canada, not by the United States.[12] As the economic historian Richard Sutch once observed, "We have a lot of good data on how many people arrived, but very bad data on how many people left."[13]

There have been many notably large expatriations from the United States. Approximately sixteen thousand African Americans, liberated from slavery in the United States in the nineteenth century, were encouraged to enjoy that freedom in Liberia, which was not necessarily the place whence their ancestors came, rather than in the United States, the country in which most were born and raised.[14] Religious freedom has less often been the motivation for expatriation, but it was for adherents to Mormonism who left Illinois in 1846 with hopes that they would experience less oppression in Utah, which was, at the time, a part of Mexico. After the U.S. Civil War, Confederados, former Confederates who could not abide by the terms of Reconstruction, or who wished to continue an antebellum way of life, including slave ownership, moved from the United States to such places as Cuba and Brazil, where slavery remained legal until the 1880s.[15] In the twentieth century, many artists, such as the writers Gertrude Stein, Ernest Hemingway, and James Baldwin, the painter Mary Cassatt, and the performer Josephine Baker, chose to live and work in France.

Quite often Canada has been the destination of expatriates from the United States. The two countries share history, language, culture, and geography, differing primarily by when and how they separated themselves from Britain and how they govern themselves now. The relatively porous border between the two countries has allowed much movement in both directions for over two centuries. In the 1770s and 1780s, during and after the War for American Independence, 50,000 to 100,000 people, called United Empire Loyalists in Canada and Tories in the United States, quit the southern British colonies on their way to North American lands still under the control of the British Empire. They went primarily to what are now the Canadian provinces of Nova Scotia, Prince Edward Island, and Québec.[16] Others moved to British colonies in the Caribbean and Central America, as well as to Sierra Leone, India, Australia, and Britain itself. These émigrés included many enslaved Blacks who Loyalists moved to Canada, Native Americans who had aided the British during the war, and, presaging the movement of U.S. Vietnam War draft resisters and military deserters, Mennonites, Quakers, and members of other pacifist religious groups who refused to fight in the war.[17]

Another well-documented group of immigrants from the United States to Canada were people of African origin who had been held in chattel slavery in the United States and who escaped or moved to Canada in the nineteenth century. About two thousand African Americans moved to Canada—mostly to Nova Scotia—in 1814, during the War of 1812, when the British government offered them free transportation to a British North American colony as an inducement for them to desert the army of the United States.[18] After Britain abolished slavery in its empire in 1834, until the end of the U.S. Civil War, Canada West, or Upper Canada—now known as Ontario—was the primary destination of most of these immigrants since it was a place (along with Mexico and slavery-free European colonies in the Caribbean) to which Africans could move without the risk of falling into slavery again. The Fugitive Slave Act of 1850, which compelled all in the United States, north and south, to return suspected escaped enslaved people to their masters, was further incentive for free or freed Blacks to leave.[19]

During the Indian Wars of the late nineteenth century, after the U.S. Congress annulled treaties with Native Americans and left them bereft of trade goods and largely without access to game hunting, members of the Dakota tribe sought refuge from U.S. Army attacks by moving to Canada. In 1876 the Native American chief Sitting Bull (Hunkpapa Lakota) and three thousand other members of the Sioux tribe also retreated north across the "medicine line" that was the U.S.-Canadian border after killing Col. George Armstrong Custer and 264 other members of the Seventh Cavalry in the Battle of Little Bighorn. Sitting Bull remained in Canada for five years, and his presence there was a sore point between U.S. and Canadian government officials.[20]

An emigration rivaling in number that of Vietnam War–era draft resisters and military deserters was the movement of about 160,000 white and Black people from the U.S. Midwest to the western Canadian provinces of Manitoba, Saskatchewan, Alberta, and British Columbia from 1896 to the beginning of World War I. Canada wanted to boost population and productivity in that region, so government agents distributed promotional literature, gave lectures, and dispensed advice to U.S. farmers (and Canadians who had immigrated south) considering a move (back) to Canada. They sweetened the deal by selling land at cheap prices and providing cheap railroad fares to move farmers and their families, livestock, and equipment while shielding them from U.S. agents who tried to dissuade them from moving.[21]

Members of the Church of Jesus Christ of Latter-Day Saints not only tried to leave the United States by moving to Mexico, but two thousand or so of them also later moved from the U.S. West to Alberta in the late nineteenth and early twentieth centuries. Likewise, nearly two thousand Hutterites moved to Alberta and Manitoba in 1917 and 1918, due to persecution in the United States for their pacifism during World War I. They, along with smaller numbers of Mennonites and Doukhobors, were examples of religious minorities Canada accepted after making concessions to them (such as allowing Mormons to practice polygamy) in attempts to woo people to the Canadian West when the U.S. West often seemed a more attractive place to go.[22]

There is also a type of immigration seemingly for no apparent reason at all, characterized by a French expression, *fuite en avant*, translatable literally as "fleeing ahead," or, more figuratively, a headlong rush into a new situation. The French philosopher Henri Lefebvre's coining of the phrase—during the Vietnam War era, coincidentally—provides some psychological insight into what might seem to be an uncalculated jump into a new situation: knowing that little good awaits you if you stay where you are.[23] In this vein, in the United States of the Vietnam War era, draft-age men had to reckon with military service: U.S. society expected them to serve their country when they were called upon to do so. Men unwilling to fulfill these expectations often left the United States in an effort to wrest themselves from such responsibilities, unsure of where they would or could go, knowing only that they could not stay.

From 1955, just after the French left Indochina, to 1964, when the U.S. Congress passed the Gulf of Tonkin Resolution, leading to a steep increase in U.S. troops in Southeast Asia, the number of people who emigrated from the United States to Canada averaged around 11,200 a year. The number of emigrants nearly doubled over the next decade, with an average of 21,700 immigrating to Canada from 1965 to 1975, peaking at 26,541 in 1974. Among the countries of the world, the United States was the largest sending nation of immigrants to Canada in 1971 and 1972.[24] A public opinion survey conducted in 1971 found that 30 percent of college students were interested in leaving the United States to go to Canada, Australia, or western European or Scandinavian countries. Interest in emigration had doubled since 1959 and tripled since the end of World War II. A Gallup poll conducted that same year corroborated this, showing that one in eight people in the United States would have liked to emigrate, with Canada as émigrés' second choice of destination (behind Australia).[25] In the decade after the Vietnam War, interest in emigration cooled, with the number of emigrants from the United States to Canada averaging about 8,300 a year (Figure 1.1).[26]

Not all immigration from the United States to Canada in the 1960s and 1970s was out of resistance to military obligation. For example, many people moved from Texas to Alberta to meet the demand for expertise in the burgeoning Canadian petroleum and beef industries. Others went to Canada because they were transferred for jobs in U.S.-owned corporations with branches or subsidiaries in Canada.[27] Some left because they were disenchanted with life in the United States, citing such factors as racism, deteriorating cities, fear of violence, pollution, population increase, rapid pace of life, and rising corporatism, finding Canada an antidote for those societal ills.[28]

American émigrés in Canada recounted to journalists why they left the United States: "I couldn't take the hate people had for each other."[29] "Seeing the pollution, the crime, the anger, the people milling around . . . we couldn't handle it."[30] "I was sure tired of the States. Everything was so politicized and I felt immobilized. . . . There was a crisis every hour. . . ."[31] "It was a sense of impotence. I couldn't change anything."[32]

Some conservatives said they left because they were tired of the liberalism of the John F. Kennedy and Lyndon B. Johnson administrations.[33] Still others were displeased with the crackdown on liberal political and social

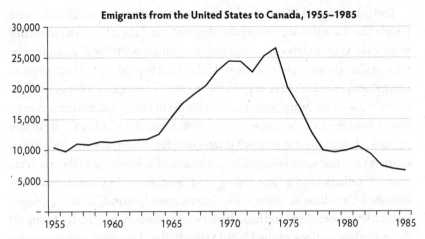

FIGURE 1.1. Emigrants from the United States to Canada, 1955–1985

expression of the 1960s and early 1970s, with many people citing the violence surrounding the 1968 Democratic National Convention in Chicago as the impetus for them to leave the United States to go to Canada.[34] Others saw the choice of nominees Hubert Humphrey, Richard Nixon, and George Wallace for the presidency in 1968 as "no choice at all," whereupon, as the *Los Angeles Times* observed, many "stuffed their disillusions in a suitcase and fled to Canada."[35] In the oversized pages of the pictorial news magazine *Life*, the Midwesterner Charlie Argast, who moved his family to Vancouver in 1970, explained the problems of being politicized during the more conservative Nixon presidency, complaining, "If you're against anything that's happening, you're stereotyped as a radical and no one listens to you."[36]

Other immigrants emphasized the psychological advantages they felt Canada had over the United States, saying such things as "it takes only four minutes to go through the tunnel from Detroit to Windsor but the emotional climate is so different on the other side you might as well have gone to another planet," and that crossing the border to Canada "was like coming in out of the rain."[37]

George A. Cohon, an attorney who moved from Chicago to Toronto to become president of McDonald's restaurants in Canada, cited social reasons for his move, telling *Business Week* in 1973, "I can't conceive of moving back. [Canada] is a better place to live and raise your children. The schools are better, the cities are cleaner, there's less hustle and bustle, and there's freedom to walk everywhere without fear of violence," adding, "Taxes are high, but not too high. Here you get value for what you pay."[38]

Émigrés weighed life in the United States against that in Canada, with people like the artist Art Green reflecting that some must have felt compelled to leave the United States because it was "profoundly politicized." In contrast he felt that Canada was a place where he "didn't have to produce so much negative energy" and "wouldn't have to go to the trouble of *caring* about things so damn much."[39] Likewise, Mary Anne Duffy indicated in the Canadian women's magazine *Chatelaine* that she had emigrated from Kentucky with her family in 1961 because "chances are just so much greater here for making life the way we want it. There's not that same feeling of hopelessness, of helplessness as there is in the States."[40] Others cited a "free feeling" and "gentleness" in Canada, and some described Canadians as "softer, more sincere, more humane." To them, Canada seemed less materialistic and had a better worldview because it had not adopted the militaristic outlook of the United States.[41] Tom Lawrence, a seminary student from California, explained to a *Newsweek* reporter in Vancouver in 1971 that "I came up here because I really believe in freedom of speech, justice and equality, all the good things that are not practiced in America right now."[42]

Some were attracted to Canada for reasons Frederick Jackson Turner canonically characterized in 1893: people from the United States thrived on opportunities that came from conquering frontiers.[43] Canada has long had more open land than the United States. That land has often been less expensive to purchase, and ownership gave many a sense of the frontier spirit they felt was missing in the United States.[44] One who saw such opportunities was Roger Davies, who grew up in Cleveland, Ohio, visited Québec and Ontario as a boy, and immigrated to Canada in 1967. As he thought about resisting the military draft, he weighed the options of going underground, becoming a conscientious objector, going to jail, or going to Canada. He opted for the latter because, as he reflected in the 1990s, "Canada had this romance about it. A place with the beautiful, wide-open wilderness and intriguing cities. I had a sense that Canada would be good for me and I would be good for Canada."[45] Similarly, an Oregon man told a *Minneapolis Tribune* reporter in 1972, "I prefer to live in Canada. It would be nice to go home and visit occasionally and see my parents, but Canada is a much more free, open and tolerant country."[46] An immigration official working at the Canadian consulate in New York explained that he thought some Americans were attracted to Canada because "there's room in Canada and they feel that it's getting crowded in the States. There's a certain amount of nostalgia for the way things used to be in a big, open country. . . . I think they just like the challenge of a new country. They want to take a chance. The Americans are risk takers, you know. . . . Maybe they're the last pioneers on earth."[47]

Likewise, the authors of *The Draft and the Rest of Your Life,* an American Lutheran Church–produced manual offering advice about dealing with the military draft, felt that some of the attraction of Canada came from "the image of a country with frontiers still to be pushed back."[48] The travel editor of the *Toronto Sun* newspaper noted the openness of Canada in a 1973 mass-market paperback travel guide, gushing, "There is ample opportunity. Less than eight per cent of Canada is owned. There couldn't be more freedom than this!"[49] Bob Proctor, a draft-age man who stood little chance of being drafted into the military because he had occupational and student deferments, nonetheless attempted to move to Canada in 1969 because he was fed up with institutions in the United States, was inspired by relatives who had homesteaded in Saskatchewan in the 1920s, and had "hippie dreams" of homesteading there himself and living off the land.[50] Likewise, Mark Vonnegut, in his 1975 memoir, *The Eden Express,* recalled reactions to his plans to move to rural British Columbia after his graduation from Swarthmore College in eastern Pennsylvania in the late 1960s: "Just about everyone, young and old, straights and freaks, wanted to stay up long into the night talking about that one. . . . What I find most amazing is how little argument we got from parents, professors, or anyone else. What few misgiving there were were vague, apologetic, and usually mumbled. I think the Kennedys, Martin Luther King, and war and assorted other goodies had so badly blown everybody's mind that sending the children naked into the woods to build a new society seemed worth a try."[51] In *Steal This Book,* his "manual of survival in the prison that is Amerika," activist Abbie Hoffman suggested Canada, especially British Columbia, as a place to acquire free land and to establish communities.[52]

Canada also loomed large for many young Americans in the 1960s and 1970s because its government had a different outlook on the Vietnam War. Canada did not send troops to Southeast Asia and was a member, along with India and Poland, of the International Control Commission, which was charged with overseeing the Geneva Accords of 1954 at the end of the First Indochina War of 1946 to 1954.[53] Passage of the Gulf of Tonkin Resolution in 1964 and the subsequent increase in the military draft and the escalation of U.S. bombing of North Vietnam made it clear that U.S. involvement in Southeast Asia had shifted away from aid and advice to South Vietnam toward a wider military effort to contain Communism in an ideological struggle with the Soviet Union and China. The political scientist Douglas A. Ross cited 1965 as a turning point in Canadian public, political, and bureaucratic support for U.S. conduct in Vietnam, observing that "more than any other single aspect of the war, the bombing of the north decisively alienated Canadian mass opinion from support for U.S. interventionary objectives." U.S. and Canadian perspectives on the war had become irreconcilable.[54]

Antiwar sentiment spread in Canada in the late 1960s. Academics called for a halt to U.S. bombing in Vietnam, if not an end to U.S. intervention all together. Thirty percent of the faculty of the University of Toronto signed a petition to call for the Canadian government to ask the United States to withdraw from Vietnam. Teach-ins and antiwar rallies took place on several university campuses. There were large antiwar demonstrations on Parliament Hill and in front of the U.S. embassy in Ottawa, as well as in the major cities of Vancouver, Edmonton, Winnipeg, Toronto, Montréal, and Halifax.[55]

The liberal religious community in Canada, spearheaded by J. Raymond Hord, secretary of the Board of Evangelism and Social Service of the United Church of Canada, worked to build public support for antiwar efforts. Hord made appearances on radio programs and at teach-ins and rallies and lobbied his fellow United Church clergy and the World Council of Churches to speak out against the war. He eventually convinced the Board of Evangelism and Social Service to provide financial support for Americans who were increasingly making their way to Canada to avoid the long arm of U.S. draft and military laws.[56] Soon, too, did the Canadian government begin to embrace draft-age U.S. émigrés, eventually admitting them to Canada while explicitly pointing to, yet disregarding, their status as actual or potential members of the U.S. military.[57] While Americans have emigrated from the United States to other countries for centuries, Canada has been the easiest place for them to get to geographically, as well as culturally and emotionally—qualities not lost on U.S. émigrés in the 1960s and 1970s.

The Vietnam in which young American men were being asked to fight in the 1960s and 1970s did not always exist. Further, it ceased to exist a few months after the draft ended. Young Americans called into military service in this era arrived at the end of nearly one hundred years of imperialism in Southeast Asia. The story began with the colonization of Vietnam, Laos, and Cambodia by France from 1884 to 1940. During World War II, the Vichy government of France acquiesced to Japan's demands to control the area. In the meantime, the Viet Minh formed in 1941, primarily to oppose Japanese occupation. Japan's surrender to the Allies in late summer of 1945 marked the beginning of a struggle between the Viet Minh and France, which was attempting to recolonize the area. Ho Chi Minh, the principal architect of an independent Vietnam, was inspired by the U.S. Declaration of Independence from Britain while writing his country's Declaration of Independence from France and approached the United States for support. It rebuffed him, choosing instead to support France, its World War II ally, prioritizing its interest in keeping Communism from spreading in Europe, and, by extension, in Asia. Ho then turned to China and the Soviet Union.[58]

The establishment of Communist governments in Eastern Europe in the late 1940s, the Democratic People's Republic of Korea in 1948, and the People's Republic of China in 1949 led the U.S. government to promote the "domino theory." It held that if one country in a region became Communist, then others around it would also "fall" to Communism, requiring the United States to intervene militarily—if necessary—to keep it from spreading. Three years of military combat on the Korean peninsula in the early 1950s ended in a frustrating stalemate for the United States, with a pro-Communist government remaining in place in the northern portion of the peninsula. In the meantime, the Vietnam in which France was trying to reassert colonial rule had much native support to establish a Communist government. And before the end of the decade, Cuba, less than 100 miles (165 kilometers) off the coast of Florida, would also adopt a Communist government.

The Viet Minh finally pushed France out of Southeast Asia after the Battle of Dien Bien Phu in the spring of 1954. The Geneva Accords of that year, overseen in part by Canada, divided Vietnam at the seventeenth parallel until elections could be held to determine the form of government an independent Vietnam would establish. Ho had already declared Communist rule in the Democratic Republic of Vietnam north of the seventeenth parallel. South of it, Ngo Dinh Diem declared himself president of the Republic of Vietnam after a controversial referendum in 1955 ousted Bao Dai, the emperor-turned-chief-of-state of Vietnam. The United States, which had been in Southeast Asia to support the French, remained there with hopes that its military and monetary support for the Republic of Vietnam would push Communism out of the region, something it had not succeeded in doing in Korea. This commitment on the part of the United States—which involved millions of troops—endured in various forms until 1975.[59]

A military draft was in place in the United States nearly continuously from September 1940 until July 1973, even when the United States was not involved in a formally declared war. The World War II–era draft ended March 31, 1947, and men began to leave the military at the rate of 15,000 a month, even as tensions of the Cold War began to heat up between the United States and Soviet Union. In response, a new draft began with U.S. congressional passage of the Selective Service Act in 1948. A military draft was in place through the Korean War of the 1950s, the Cuban Missile Crisis of 1962, and nearly all the Vietnam War.[60]

During the Vietnam War era twenty-seven million American men were of draft age, with nearly a third of them (8.7 million) serving in the military. Of those, about 3.4 million were deployed to Southeast Asia, with approximately one million serving in combat there, while 5.3 million served elsewhere in the world.[61] American men of draft age during the height of the Vietnam War were born during the Viet Minh's struggle to wrest Vietnam from French control. They were children and adolescents as the United States stepped up its commitment to keep Communism out of Southeast Asia. By the time that commitment escalated into war in the mid-1960s, they had become men—and they would be called upon, if not expected, to help fulfill their nation's aspirations for the area.

The decision about whether and how to serve in the U.S. military during the Vietnam War era was a major consideration for the generation of men who reached adulthood in the second half of the 1960s and early 1970s. Stephen Minot, a draft counselor, recognized the burden of the draft on young men in this era, remarking about one of his advisees that "some adults manage to get through a lifetime without being forced to tangle with the issues he is facing this afternoon."[62] Similarly, the journalist Chris Turner observed that draft-age Americans who resisted the draft by immigrating to Canada had to face a "gut check" before going there and "had to decide that their convictions were worth more than the comforts of home and family and career. If they weren't quite revolutionaries, they were in some sense pioneers, and if what they did was sometimes naive and foolishly audacious, it nonetheless took real courage."[63] The historian Michael S. Foley likewise noted that the Lyndon B. Johnson and Richard Nixon presidencies forced draft-age men to choose either to fight in a war that many considered to be illegal and immoral, to go to jail instead of serving in the military, or to find a way to avoid both war and jail. These choices, asserted Foley, "haunt many of that generation and . . . contribute significantly to the cynicism so many Americans have come to share about the faithfulness of their government."[64]

The qualms many American men had about being drafted into the military in the Vietnam War era stemmed from their distaste for the rationale and tactics of the war. In World War II the immediate threat to the sovereignty of the United States and its allies seemed clearer. In Vietnam, however, many felt that the United States was being imperialistic, trying to affect the outcome in a civil war in which it had no business meddling. They believed that U.S. involvement in Southeast Asia was unconstitutional and a violation of principles that emerged from war crimes tribunals in Nuremberg and Tokyo following World War II, the United Nations charter, and the Geneva Accords of 1954.

As the war wore on, Americans confronted news reports of increasing draft calls and casualty rates and encountered disenchanted veterans, while watershed events eroded public support for the war. The Tet Offensive of early 1968 demonstrated that the North Vietnamese and Viet Cong would not be easily dissuaded from trying to liberate South Vietnam from a U.S.-backed, non-Communist government. The violent clashes between demonstrators and police at the 1968 Democratic National Convention, where a peace plank for the party's platform was defeated, alienated many Americans. The atrocities at My Lai, committed by U.S. troops in 1968 but not disclosed to the public for twenty months, added further fuel to the fire of those opposed to U.S. actions. The U.S. invasion of Cambodia in April 1970 and the expansion of the war into neutral Laos angered still more Americans.[65] Opponents of the war, citing the forced relocation, imprisonment, napalming, bombing deaths, and executions of civilians, as well as the destruction of crops, livestock, and civilian structures, felt that U.S. actions in Southeast Asia were crimes against humanity. Draft resisters cited such inhumanity as a rationale for defying orders to join the military, feeling that military service in Southeast Asia would require them to commit immoral acts, and maintained that it was their patriotic duty to resist military service.[66]

The aims of a peacetime draft and the need for the United States to be militarily prepared during the Cold War were not transparent to all. Many young men implicated in the draft were often resentful of the obligations placed on them by their government to serve it in this way. A young man from the Bronx articulated this in a letter to the Vancouver Committee to Aid American War Objectors in 1969, saying, "I am very disturbed, distressed, and angered at the social and political climate of the United States. I believe it is a repressive society and rapidly becoming more so. It is a militaristic, violent society, and I am basically a pacifist. I am, in short, not proud of being an American."[67] In the late 1970s Jack Colhoun reflected on his opposition to the Vietnam War in an interview on Canadian television, saying,

I think it came more from a moral standpoint. I was raised in a very patriotic country and family, and roots trace back to the Mayflower. I was also raised in a religious way, and in the Boy Scouts, in addition to being an Eagle Scout I won the God and Country award. And it just seemed to me that what America was saying—all these great ideals were being totally contradicted in the most barbaric ways in Vietnam, and perhaps had I not taken what America was supposed to stand for so seriously I wouldn't have been so shocked.[68]

Similarly, David Harris, who went to prison for twenty months rather than be inducted into the military, told Canadian television viewers:

> I think what brought us [to the antiwar movement] was our belief in the school civics that we had been taught. . . . The notion of democracy that we had been presented in our childhood simply did not exist when we got out on our own. And I think that it was the recognition of that fact that was responsible for a great deal of the energy that went into the anti-draft and anti-war movement. We had been lied to. It wasn't true, it wasn't there. And now, I think that for me . . . part of the decision involved in resisting the draft was a much larger decision about who I was going to be. I felt very clearly that if the law was going to do the kinds of things that it was doing in South East Asia, then I wanted to be the kind of person that was against the war.[69]

In spring 1968, in Youngstown, Ohio, Sam Steiner was more demonstrative in his opposition to military service, sending his ripped-up draft registration certificate to the local draft board that would determine his eligibility for military service, along with a mimeographed statement titled "Why I Resist." He complained that because the Selective Service System forced men to kill, "It assigns itself an omniscience it has no authority to give. It usurps the human right to life. It bestows power it cannot. This is not 'service.' This is playing some kind of God. I will not play this role. . . . Thus I must say no to the Selective Service System. I must say no to the Draft." To drive his point home, he distributed copies of his statement, picketed with a sign that said "I MUST RESIST FOR I CANNOT HELP MANKIND BY DESTROYING IT," and refused to report for induction into the military.[70]

Richard Moore, of Houston, who deserted the United States Air Force in May 1969, reflected in his memoirs on his limited choices, typical for young men in that era:

> A number of things in my life brought me to a crisis three years after my graduation from high school. My Mom's death, my confusion about which major to take in university . . . and, of course the pressure of the Selective Service System. What I needed and wanted most in late 1968 was time to think, time to reflect and time to chart my course for the future.
>
> The policy makers of the U.S. government knew very well that they did not want me to have time to think. The people in charge of getting manpower for the war through the Selective Service System, through the draft, wanted my time.[71]

Similarly, David W. Diamond of upstate New York, who was exiled in Mon-tréal from 1968 to 1977, reflected in his diary in 1975,

The war pressed my nerve all the way from '61 on.

I watched that thing come forward and get worse and I thought maybe it would end before it got to be my turn to go in the service. I hoped it would end and that the draft would end and I could retire to the l[ei]sur[e]ly type of life I wanted when I was just finishing high school.

I wanted to just bum around for a little, see things and do things without the perpetual needling of the war and of the ambitions of others and the ambitions of personal pride to drive me forward in efforts to do things that in the end left me with no satisfaction really. . . . They had come to mean noth-ing to me but the means to the end of avoiding service and of avoiding Viet Nam.[72]

Diane Francis, who immigrated to Canada with her husband in April 1966, saw the contrast between what young American men wanted to be and what their government required of them, observing, "Basically they were just kids. They wanted to get laid. To get a job. They didn't want to think about the dom-ino theory or the Evil Empire [the Soviet Union]—they wanted to live their lives."[73]

Some men resisted military service or deserted the military because of stresses in their lives that had nothing to do with the war or their personal liberties. Drug abuse, illness in the family, pregnant wives or girlfriends, rela-tionship or marital problems, and the need to provide financial support to family members were among the concerns of young men who failed to fulfill their military obligations.[74]

In appealing contrast across the border, Canadian youth of this era had rel-atively carefree lives. Their country was not at war. There was no draft. Noting jealously that Canadians were "free to drop out with no fear of the draft," a U.S. draft resister in Toronto recalled meeting Canadian college students "who would just take a year off and go to Europe. Go to Cuba, and just do all these really groovy things, and then go back to school later. No hurry, no pressure."[75] Likewise, in 1975 the twenty-seven-year-old David Diamond observed that his teammates on a McGill University staff softball team were able to move into adulthood more easily because they did not have to deal with the uncertain-ties that resulted from anticipating military conscription: "Most of the guys . . . were younger than I am and most seem settled into a life style in a way I have not yet begun to dream of having. . . . All these important safe things they are doing. They belong somewhere, they know how to identify, who they are and why they are who they are."[76]

In a late 1972 diary entry written in Hamilton, Ontario, draft resister Steve Trimm reasoned why immigration to Canada was better than going to jail for draft resistance in the United States:

> You personally are free, you can still be heard, your presence in a friendly coun-
> try continually reminds the American people that there are countries in the
> world that do not wholeheartedly support US policy. Now a guy going to jail
> looks braver, but once he is in prison he is silenced. And prison can break him.
> Many antiwar guys have come out so broken in spirit that they never raised
> their voices again. . . . A guy in exile can set the terms of reference: he went into
> exile because of the war. Because he can still be heard thru print etc., his side is
> heard and he puts the govt. on the spot instead of vice versa. . . . You are better
> off in exile if you want to carry on any concrete work. In prison you are only
> making a principled point. That is always important, but sometimes not too
> useful.[77]

The Rebel, a Montréal newsletter for U.S. émigrés, also made a case for immigration, adding that it was important to build immigrant communities and observing, "One major failing of the 'We Won't Go' movement has been precisely that it hasn't dealt with . . . the question, 'What should one do after he refuses to go?'" Further, The Rebel opined that "a political movement which takes its most committed members and has them wind up in prison for five years or immigrating to another county to assimilate into that society is self-defeating. The only relevant option for the anti-war movement is the development of exile communities. A movement which merely depletes its country of its best activists or puts them in prison is ridiculous."[78]

Many other young Americans articulated their distaste for military service during the Vietnam War. When seeking advice on immigration to Canada from an Ottawa antiwar group, a Providence, Rhode Island, man wrote, "I, like many other young Americans, will most likely soon be faced with the alternatives of obeying what I consider to be immoral orders from my government, or refusing to obey those orders and thus subsequent imprisonment, or of leaving this country and entering Canada where I might be able to live a free life without having to take part in the mass genocide being committed by the U.S."[79]

A catalyst for making these three factors—immigration, Canada, and Vietnam—interact so strongly in this era was the influence of the New

Left—a broad social movement centered on social justice cast from a different mold than that used by traditional liberals. The New Left presented ideas that people could emulate as they negotiated the difficulties caused by U.S. involvement in Southeast Asia and other social issues of the era. The Port Huron Statement, written in 1962 by the activist Tom Hayden as the establishing document of Students for a Democratic Society, was widely read by youth—and others—interested in the New Left. The Port Huron Statement was a product of its times, and accordingly it condemned the Cold War, Communism and anti-Communism, the presence of nuclear weapons, and the attempts of imperialist countries to subdue wars of colonial independence.

Among the ideas expressed in the Port Huron Statement was that "men have unrealized potential for self-cultivation, self-direction, self-understanding, and creativity. It is this potential that we regard as crucial and to which we appeal, not to the human potentiality for violence, unreason, and submission to authority. The goal of man and society should be human independence." The Statement also asserted that a person should be able to attain "determining influence over his circumstances of life" to oppose "the depersonalization that reduces human beings to the status of things" and that "society [should] be organized to encourage independence in men." Such ideas supported the prerogative of a person to remove themselves from a place if its laws and customs took too much control of their lives from them. In the Vietnam War era the lives of draft-age men were controlled by the U.S. government, which reserved the right to direct them toward committing acts of violence in Southeast Asia and other places around the world.[80]

Another idea put forth by the Port Huron Statement was the idea of participatory democracy. There should be "individual participation" in politics where one lives. An individual should "share in those social situations determining the quality and direction of his life."[81] Such participation could happen through passive activities such as voting, sending letters, circulating and signing petitions, and signaling one's discontent through such activities as singing protest songs and raising a clenched fist. It was also rationale for such active protests as physically occupying spaces to the point of trespass in sit-ins and marches, confronting police, rioting, looting, and committing arson, which, in the Vietnam War era, could include burning military draft registration cards and records, which were technically U.S. government property.[82]

Mark Vonnegut reflected the New Left's rejection of old norms and the creation of new ones in that part of his rationale for moving to Canada was that "we expected to get closer to nature, to each other and our feelings, and we did. . . . We wanted to go beyond that and develop entirely new ways of being and experiencing the world. We had only vague ideas about the shape of these changes or when they would happen, but we looked forward to them eagerly. Since they would result from being free of the cities, of capitalism, racism, industrialism, they had to be for the better. It was a lot like taking some new drug and waiting for the changes."[83]

Amid the confluence of the historical, political, and social conditions that encouraged their emigration from the United States to Canada during the Vietnam War era, draft-age men faced an ever-shifting matrix of rules and regulations that determined who was subject to military conscription. Rules in place when a young man was fifteen or sixteen years old could change by the time he reached the draft age of eighteen. Men strategizing for their future could find their plans thwarted when the U.S. Selective Service System changed its rules in its attempts to increase the size of the U.S. military or to make the draft more racially and economically equitable. Indeed, the number of troops in Southeast Asia was 23,000 in 1964 before passage of the Gulf of Tonkin Resolution, increased eightfold to 184,000 in 1965, and peaked at 543,000 in 1969. The SSS, as the historian George Q. Flynn noted, had the power to "induce behavior" of draft-age men to fulfill all duties required of them by the complex and oft-changing draft law. Those failing to fulfill their duties were considered delinquent, and delinquents were first to be drafted.[84]

Draft-age men of this era faced myriad possibilities. They could volunteer for a branch of the military, its reserve, the National Guard, or ROTC (Reserve Officers' Training Corps). They could wait to be drafted and to serve as told. They could serve a prison sentence of up to five years. Or they could try to resist service by getting a deferment for being married, having children, being a minister or divinity student, being a conscientious objector, or attending college or graduate school. And they could fail the SSS physical and psychological examinations that determined fitness for military service—or get or act hurt in an attempt to fail them.

Men who were married before midnight on August 26, 1965, were deferred from military duty. The rule change set off such a flurry of weddings in the days before it took effect that a columnist for the *Los Angeles Times* derisively called it "the night of love among the draft-dodgers."[85] Fathers were deferred from service throughout the war.[86]

"Regular or duly ordained" ministers were exempted from the draft, yet the Reverend Billy Graham complained early in Richard Nixon's presidency that evangelical athletes in his Campus Crusade for Christ were being drafted because they were not ordained. Thousands of Jehovah's Witnesses went to jail rather than be drafted because the SSS did not exempt them.[87] Like ministers, divinity students were exempted if they were satisfactorily completing coursework "under the direction of recognized churches or religious organizations" or "in recognized theological or divinity schools."[88] One young man who had been admitted to a seminary in the fall of 1968 recognized, however, that "the main purpose of allowing the deferments of ministers is to preserve the image of the United States as a Christian nation. I cannot in good conscience allow myself to be used for this deception, and have decided that I cannot cooperate with the indenture system which is the selective service." Instead, he sought to immigrate to Canada to attend a seminary there.[89]

Those who were opposed to the actions of the United States in Southeast Asia could ask to be classified by the military as conscientious objectors. In the Vietnam War era the SSS usually only granted such appeals to men who were lifelong adherents to a peace-oriented church, such as the Religious Society of Friends (Quakers) or Mennonites. One's personal moral qualms about the unjustness of the war were usually not grounds enough to be excused from military service. Further, during the Vietnam War, U.S. courts upheld that the U.S. government alone could decide the justness of a war—not religious denominations, and not individuals.[90] Individuals could not define the moral grounds upon which their opposition to conflict in Southeast Asia was based. Voicing frustration with this attitude toward conscientious objection was Patrick Grady, an immigrant to Canada in 1968, who reflected that "I wasn't really a pacifist the way some people were. I didn't oppose war in general. That particular war I was opposed to. The vast destruction of a small country—I found it appalling."[91] Likewise, Stephen Eaton Hume did not apply for conscientious objector status during the Vietnam War because, as he recalled, "I had no compunction against killing. . . . At the time I was a hunter, had gone to a military academy, and was a member of the National Rifle Association. If it had been a different war, I might have enlisted, but I believed that doing so for this war would have made me no different than the 'good Germans' who fought for Hitler."[92]

In 1971 federal judges ruled that the U.S. military had to abide by the U.S. Supreme Court ruling in United States v. Seeger (1965), which deemed that potential servicemen could get conscientious objector status not only for being an adherent of an "orthodox religious sect" that espoused pacifism but also in any case in which they were a sincere pacifist. In Welsh v. United States (1970), the Supreme Court further ruled that a man whose belief system did not include a Supreme Being but whose pacifism "emanates from a purely moral, ethical, or philosophical source" should also be given conscientious objector status.[93]

During the Vietnam War era, undergraduate students were deferred from the draft if they were in school full-time at a four-year college, pursuing a regular degree, and in good standing at their schools.[94] Some universities refused to comply with the good-standing rule, however, and stopped ranking students or released grades to the SSS only with permission of the student.[95] Some men fulfilled the good-standing requirement by passing the SSCQT (Selective Service College Qualification Test) given by the SSS. When the SSS gave the exam in 1963, a year before the Gulf of Tonkin Resolution, 2,145 men took it. When the exam was next given three years later, 767,935 men sat for it to prove their good standing as college students.[96]

After passage of the Military Selective Service Act on September 28, 1971, Nixon began to phase out student deferments. Drafted men enrolled at a university could complete the semester and seniors could complete their degrees before being required to report for induction into the military. The chances of being drafted began to drop precipitously, however, starting in late 1971. While 94,092 men were inducted in 1971, only 49,514 were in 1972, and 646 in 1973, but only until June 20, when the last man was inducted.[97]

Male graduate students in U.S. universities enjoyed a deferment from the draft only until 1968. A law passed in June 1967 allowed the president of the United States to provide deferments from the draft only to graduate students "whose study, research, or other endeavors is found to be necessary to the maintenance of the national health, safety or interest." In February 1968 the National Security Council (NSC) advised the director of the SSS that deferments should only be offered to men studying medicine, dentistry, optometry, osteopathy, podiatry, and veterinary medicine, and that men who were in at least their second year of graduate school in any field and performing satisfactorily could earn deferments for up to five years.[98] Men who had declared their academic objective as a master's degree, not a doctorate, were likely to lose their deferment once they got the lesser degree.[99]

Two factors sank the graduate student deferment: the need for more men to fulfill draft quotas, and a desire for the population of draftees to more greatly resemble the demographics of the U.S. population. The intention of the latter was to reduce inequities in class and race that were extant in the draft system, but the resulting lack of opportunity for graduate study drew protest from many who otherwise might have been ambivalent about the war.[100] Because of the loss of deferment for graduate students, the probability that a college graduate would be drafted increased from three in ten in 1965 to six in ten in 1970.[101]

Further frustration came to graduate students because they were not eligible for deferments as teachers, even when teaching was a large part of their responsibilities and intellectual work at the universities they attended. SSS rules prioritized their status as students over their status as teachers.[102] Even so, some relief for graduate students came in September 1970 when men who had not requested a II-S deferment (for being an undergraduate student) since June 30, 1967, could request a 1-S(C) deferment for being a graduate student.[103]

Young men who wanted to pursue graduate degrees in something besides medical sciences needed to find a way to guarantee that they would be able to study without the interruption of their country's call to military service. This led many men to attend graduate school outside of the United States. Canada, with a largely English-language higher education system that meshed nicely with that of the United States, and with universities clustered within 100 miles (165 kilometers) of the U.S. border, became the primary receiving nation of many of those graduate degree–seeking immigrants.[104]

The U.S. military recognized that not every draft-age man was physically or psychologically fit for battle. Men called upon to serve their country were required to appear for an examination to assess their ability to serve in the nation's armed forces. Examining physicians were to adhere to the U.S. Army's *Standards of Medical Fitness,* a manual outlining physical, medical, and psychological standards deemed necessary for members of a peacetime army. Some physicians for draft boards looked askance at these standards in their attempts to help fulfill draft quotas. At the same time, the manual provided a list of conditions that draft-age men could try to document or affect, and that sympathetic doctors could diagnose for those they wanted to help save from military service.[105]

In the early 1970s, *Standards of Medical Fitness* listed physical characteristics that could earn a medical deferment from the draft. These included being under 5'0" (152cm) or over 6'8" (203cm) in height, being very underweight or overweight, lacking a ring, middle, or index (i.e., trigger) finger, or having obscene or multiple tattoos that could "significantly limit effective performance of military service." Medical conditions such as deafness, uncontrollable hay fever, asthma, and "frequent and incapacitating" migraines could also keep a man out of the military.[106]

Psychiatric disorders were also grounds for deferment and may well have been easier to assert or affect than medical ones. *Standards of Medical Fitness* cited a "history of psychoneurotic reaction which caused hospitalization," as well as personality disorders such as alcoholism, drug addiction, "frequent encounters with law enforcement agencies, or antisocial attitudes or behavior," that were "tangible evidence of an impaired characterological capacity to adapt to the military service," or "character and behavior disorders where it is evident by history and objective examination that the degree of immaturity, instability, personality inadequacy, and dependency will seriously interfere with adjustment in the military service as demonstrated by repeated inability to maintain reasonable adjustment in school, with employers and fellow-workers, and other society groups."[107] Unconventional sexual behavior, such as "overt homosexuality or other forms of sexual deviant practices such as exhibitionism, transvestism, voyeurism, etc.," could also earn a man a psychological deferment.[108]

The draft system was rife with race and class inequities. African Americans were disproportionately drafted and were more likely to serve on front lines. This was exacerbated by the near-absence of Blacks on the local draft boards that determined who would be drafted. In the Vietnam War era, draft boards were staffed by local veterans of World War II and the Korean War, as well as "middle-management leaders," who were generally white, over the age of fifty, and often "resented the entire youth culture arising around them."[109] African Americans were also less likely to attend college because they often could not afford tuition, so they were less often eligible for educational deferments.[110] Men from economically disadvantaged backgrounds, no matter their race, were also less likely to have access to, and to be able to afford, medical and legal expertise that might help them secure deferments that would keep them from being drafted.[111]

Early in his first term as president, Richard Nixon saw the political expediency of making changes in the draft and asked Congress for a lottery in a further attempt to reduce the socioeconomic and racial bias of the system, something advisers had been suggesting for years. The first lottery, conducted on December 1, 1969, determined the order in which men born between January 1, 1944, and December 31, 1950, would be called up for the draft.[112] The SSS last issued a draft call on December 7, 1972, and lost its authority to induct men into the military after June 30, 1973, but it conducted annual lotteries through 1975, implicating men born through 1956 in the draft.[113]

Rules for the lottery called for older men in the pool of nineteen- to twenty-five-year-olds to be drafted first. Universities and other groups petitioned the Department of Defense to spread the call for potential draftees among all seven age groups eligible for the draft in the lottery system (i.e., that a previously undrafted nineteen-year-old would be as likely to be drafted as a previously undrafted twenty-five-year-old). The government decided against making any changes to the order of call up, however, claiming that no alternative would work better. The rules for the lottery therefore propelled many recent college graduates and would-be graduate students to the top of lists to be called by draft boards for potential military service. Men who had already been eligible for the draft for seven years but had not yet been drafted were now the most likely to be drafted. There was further concern that the military would put these college graduates on the front lines of battle, not in positions that would make good use of their educations.[114]

The change to the lottery system prompted the Scientific Manpower Commission, a nonprofit organization concerned with recruiting, educating, and employing people in science fields, to issue a statement of complaint about such an "unselective random draft." Pointing to the need to train men in fields besides those in health professions, which would guarantee men a deferment as a graduate student, the Scientific Manpower Commission named, to no avail, other occupational fields in which men might be needed in case of major wars or disasters, such as food production, communications, and transportation, as well as occupations to anticipate and deal with the potentially catastrophic effects of late twentieth-century warfare.[115]

Another way men could resist the draft without having to leave the United States was to appeal their draft status. Weeks, months, and years could pass while men made various requests for changes and additions to their SSS records. If this failed, they could then make further appeals through the court system. Draft appeals were high during the Vietnam War, with 98 appeals per 1,000 draftees, compared to 47 per 1,000 in the Korean War, and 3 per 1,000 at the end of World War II.[116]

Some men kept their draft files on the move, requesting that they be sent, for example, from the draft board of their hometown to that of the town in which they were an undergraduate, back to their hometown, to their mother's town, back to their university town, to their father's town, to the town in which they were in graduate school, and so on—the aim being to keep them from being on anyone's desk long enough to be processed. The various appeals and other tactics could buy time away from military service until other deferments might work in their favor, such as being married, being a father, getting a job in a protected occupation, being too old to be drafted, or the war came to an end.[117]

Not only were draft-age men expected to fulfill all the requirements imposed on them by the SSS, but they were also discouraged from demonstrating against it. During the Vietnam War era, men found "interfering with the draft"—by picketing draft boards, turning in or burning their draft registration cards, and the like—were considered delinquent and therefore subject to immediate conscription. This attitude on the part of the SSS grew out of a sit-in demonstration at the draft board in Ann Arbor, home of the University of Michigan, in October 1965. The director of the Selective Service System in Michigan suggested to Lewis B. Hershey, the national director of the SSS from July 1941 to February 1970, that the protesters lose any deferments from the draft that they might have already been enjoying. Hershey agreed, a move that Flynn argued was the beginning of the end of the draft in the United States.[118] Such punitive reclassification of draftees was a threat to protesters for only a few years until the U.S. Supreme Court ultimately ruled that it was unconstitutional.[119] The damage to the institution of the draft was done, however, because Hershey and the SSS had so utterly blurred the line between punishment and service to the United States.

As options for resisting military service dwindled, men began to run out of options for staying in the United States and saw exile as a way to avoid that obligation of citizenship. Some men entered the military but later regretted it and chose to desert it. Others were unable to get deferments, could not face serving in the military, and could not handle a prison term. Members of all these groups felt compelled to go into exile and moved all over the world, including underground in the United States. Sweden and Canada were the best places for them to go, however. Sweden granted asylum on humanitarian grounds to about eight hundred men from 1967 to 1973, mostly military deserters who left their posts in Europe and Asia.[120] For men leaving the United States and military bases within it, Sweden presented geographical and language barriers. Canada was the better option. The Canadian government welcomed draft resisters and military deserters through much of the Vietnam War, refusing to extradite Americans who entered the country while in (potential) violation of draft laws or after having deserted the U.S. military. Canada was not that far away—one could get there easily by car, bus, train, plane, boat, or on foot. Language was not much of a problem. Most Canadians spoke English, even while French was the dominant language in the province of Québec and other pockets in Canada.

As U.S. involvement in Southeast Asia wound down, the United States ended the draft and changed to an all-volunteer force on July 1, 1973. Despite all the attempts to make the draft "fair," there were 570,000 draft offenders and 563,000 less-than-honorable discharges from the military during the Vietnam War era, in addition to the tens of thousands who left the country—some even giving up their U.S. citizenship—rather than serve in the military.[121] Although the United States has not had a military draft since that time, all men eighteen to twenty-five years of age have been required to register with the SSS since 1980. That change came during the Jimmy Carter administration in response to the Soviet invasion of Afghanistan. Ironically, Carter had provided an amnesty for Vietnam War–era draft resisters and military deserters just three years before.[122]

Adherence to the philosophy of the New Left caused many American men of draft age to be disinclined to serve in the U.S. military during the Vietnam War era and to seek to find a way out of it. To do so, they had to seize upon the cultural opening that occurred during the decade from the mid-1960s to the mid-1970s that came at the confluence of a civil war in Vietnam, the involvement of the United States in it, immigration as a way to resist military service, and Canada as a convenient and welcoming place to which Americans could immigrate.

The audacity of immigration to Canada by draft-age men and those accompanying them moved these people into a category outside the traditional narrative of U.S. history. These expatriates from the United States became a part of a small group that is understudied and misunderstood. We can rescue the history of these U.S. emigrants by placing them in the global context of people who moved to improve their social and political place in the world and people who moved to save themselves from the impact of war.

2 · THE WELCOME MAT IS SPREAD ALL ALONG THE BORDER

How Americans Found Their Way to Canada

In the 1960s and 1970s draft-age American men who resisted the requirement of the U.S. government to make themselves available for military service had many resources at their disposal to help them decide how they would comply with, and how to resist, their country's demands. Magazine articles and guidebooks abounded with advice for dealing with the draft and immigration to Canada and provided coverage of draft-age American men—and women—in their new lives in Canada. What young Americans may not have put together for themselves by reading travel guides and draft counseling manuals may have become more apparent while perusing magazines at newsstands or libraries or while waiting for the barber, doctor, or dentist. There, they might have encountered articles with titles such as "Why 'Good' Sons Become Draft Dodgers" or "Canada: Escape Hatch for U.S Draft Resisters." Further, grassroots groups in the United States and Canada published guides that provided advice on the draft and emigration and corresponded with those interested in immigrating. Collectively, this printed material served as an influential pull factor to attract U.S. residents to Canada.

"JOIN THE ARMY OF YOUR CHOICE": PUBLISHED GUIDES TO DRAFT LAWS

The demand for information about draft laws resulted in a small explosion of books and popular press articles whose authors attempted to provide answers for draft-age men, their loved ones, and draft counseling centers on both sides of the U.S.-Canada border. Among the guides published by commercial publishers was Arlo Tatum and Joseph S. Tuchinsky's 1969 *Guide to the Draft.* The authors noted on its first page that "it should be possible to go to a draft board and get a pamphlet fully explaining the regulations on deferments for men with dependents, on conscientious objection, on student deferments, or on physical standards, but no such publications are provided by Selective Service. Therefore, if you want to know your choices and rights, you must turn elsewhere."[1] In the absence of such a pamphlet, their *Guide* required nearly 300 pages to outline those choices and rights.

Similarly, David Suttler's 1970 pocket paperback *IV-F: A Guide to Medical, Psychiatric, and Moral Unfitness Standards for Military Induction* took 170 pages to outline ways to resist the draft legally. IV-F was the Selective Service System (SSS) code for "registrant not qualified for any military service"—the ultimate goal for those who wanted to resist military service with the blessing of the U.S. government.[2] Andrew O. Shapiro and John M. Striker's 1970 tome, *Mastering the Draft: A Comprehensive Guide for Solving Draft Problems,* required a whopping 626 pages to help readers interpret draft laws.[3]

Groups with an interest in the draft also published guides to assist young men in planning for it. The Scientific Manpower Commission published a thirty-page booklet called *The Draft Lottery and You* in 1970, urging an "in depth" analysis of the need for military personnel and the methods used to fill it.[4] The Central Committee for Conscientious Objectors (CCCO) published 385,000 copies of its *Handbook for Conscientious Objectors* in six editions and seventeen printings between 1965 and 1972.[5] The publishing arm of the American Lutheran Church published the one-hundred-page paperback *The Draft and the Rest of Your Life* in 1972, the authors of which were the director of the Emergency Ministry Concerning U.S. Draft Age Immigrants to Canada, an agency of the National Council of Churches of Christ, USA, and the director of the Office of Lutheran Selective Service Information of the Lutheran Council in the USA.[6] In 1968 the American Friends Service Committee, the peace- and social justice–promoting organization founded by the Religious Society of Friends (Quakers), published the eight-page, comic book–like "If the Army Is Not Your Bag!" and a leaflet called "Something's

Happening Here to the Draft," both of which described conscientious objection, going to jail, and expatriation.[7]

The activist Abbie Hoffman covered draft options in his 1971 book *Steal
This Book,* which he wrote in the Cook County Jail in Chicago while he was
being held for trial for conspiracy and inciting a riot during the 1968 Democratic National Convention. In a section called "Join the Army of Your Choice,"
Hoffman allowed that since rebellious American youths were in a state of war
with the "Pig Empire" (i.e., the United States), "we all have a responsibility to
beat the draft by any means necessary." For those men who wanted to resist
being drafted, he advocated a careful look at one's medical history for conditions that would potentially earn a medical deferment and recommended getting the advice of a local draft counseling center. He allowed, however, that his
specialty was giving advice for obtaining a psychological deferment, suggesting that affecting mental disorders could be particularly helpful in getting a
deferment, and providing ideas about the use of the psychedelic drug LSD in
doing so. The goal was getting committed to a mental institution for a night:
"In most areas, a one-night stand in a mental hospital is enough to convince
the shrink at the induction center that you're capable of eating the flesh of a
colonel. [Then,] see a sympathetic psychiatrist and explain your sad mental
shape. He'll get verification that you did time in a hospital and include it in his
letter, that you'll take along to the induction center."[8] Hoffman also recommended stealing Suttler's *IV-F,* Tatum's *Handbook for Conscientious Objectors,*
and the Toronto Anti-Draft Programme's *Manual for Draft-Age Immigrants to
Canada* for further ideas in resisting conscription.[9]

"HOW TO HELP YOUR SON FACE THE DRAFT":
POPULAR MAGAZINES AND DRAFT RESISTANCE

Reckoning with how and whether to serve in the military was such a wrack-
ing decision for many young men and their families that many popular
magazines such as *Time, Newsweek, U.S. News and World Report,* the *New
Yorker,* and even *Better Homes and Gardens* offered advice to draft-age men
and their families. While there was some negative stereotyping of draft resisters and military deserters, popular magazines tended to be neutral about the
immigration of draft-age men—and women—to Canada and generally seemed
to want to be helpful to them.

A number of popular magazines also provided fairly straightforward information about how to resist the draft. For example, in a March 1970 article,

U.S. News and World Report asked, "What are the choices for a man facing the draft?" and offered three alternatives: volunteering for a "ready reserve" unit such as the National Guard—which could reduce time spent in full-time active duty—or attending medical or divinity school.[10] This article did not mention the possibility of going to Canada.

A 1969 *Senior Scholastic* article outlined possibilities besides military service, including conscientious objector status, obtaining various types of deferments, serving a jail sentence, and leaving the country, specifically mentioning Canada.[11] *Senior Scholastic,* a news magazine for high school students, had a circulation of nearly three million at the time, putting it in the hands of one out of every seven high school students in the United States, thus providing a ready source of information to men of, or about to be of, draft age, as well as to their female peers.[12]

A short column in a March 1968 issue of *Time* called "The Draft: How to Beat It without Really Trying" described several ways to get a medical deferment.[13] *Newsweek* expanded this idea a bit in a 1970 article about legal and medical experts whose specialty was helping young men get deferments.[14] Interestingly, four articles—two in *Newsweek* and one each in *Time* and the *New Yorker*—mentioned that too many tattoos or an obscene tattoo could earn a man a medical deferment—a subtle hint, perhaps, that all a young man needed to do to resist having to bear arms in Vietnam was to get a profanity inked conspicuously on his own arm.[15]

Surprisingly, the most direct and concise information about alternatives to the draft in popular magazines came in a one-page November 1970 article in *Better Homes and Gardens* called "How to Help Your Son Face the Draft." Allowing that "there is no central source of information and advice on all the military options," the article listed nine possibilities "if your son's choice is to serve." These included several paths that could lead to military service but also mentioned conscientious objector status. The article listed five further possibilities "if your son does not wish to serve," including getting deferments and refusing to register for the draft or to serve if called up. ("This," the author warned, ". . . likely will result in a legal hassle which may adversely affect his future" and could also mean a prison sentence averaging three years.) The article suggested the possibility of the son being out of the country when he turned eighteen and not returning until after he turned twenty-six. Of the most interest here was the suggestion "Go to Canada. Getting into Canada is relatively easy and there are many groups which will help." This advice carried the caveat that the young man could be forced into "permanent exile" because returning to the United States at that time carried the risk of arrest.[16] *Better Homes and Gardens* may seem like an odd venue in which to find an article on resisting military service, but the magazine was directed toward middle-class homemakers and handymen—people likely to be parents of draft-age men. Further, with 7.8 million subscribers in 1969, the magazine had the sixth-highest circulation in the United States, arriving in about one in seven U.S. homes each month.[17]

The persevering reader of popular magazines could find other hints about ways to resist military service. In 1970 *Newsweek* reminded its readers that the SSS used a manual bookkeeping system in the 1960s. Men could resist military service by exploiting loopholes in the system.[18] The article "The Magical Mystery Great Lakes Express," in a special September 1968 college section of the men's magazine *Esquire*, described a system of moving men from Detroit to Canada via sailboats on lakes Erie and Huron operated by students from the University of Michigan.[19] An October 1968 *U.S. News and World Report* article pointed out that no passport was necessary for entrance to Canada and that aid groups to draft resisters and military deserters in Canada provided free room and board for penniless émigrés.[20]

"ENTER FIRST AS A TOURIST"

It is useful to look at the immigration of people from the United States to Canada in the late 1960s and early 1970s through the lens of travel or tourism. This is not to suggest that U.S. émigrés to Canada were tourists, but rather that tourism within North America made the idea of emigrating from the United States to Canada a comfortable one for many classes of Americans and helped pave the way for many who felt compelled to leave the United States. Travel outside of one's home country implies a rejection of that country—temporarily, as a traveler or tourist, or permanently, as an immigrant. Travel can be a countercultural activity in that being in places beyond one's home can give a person new perspectives, just as the use of drugs or alcohol, sexual experiences, and listening to music can. Jack Kerouac's 1957 popular semiautobiographical novel *On the Road* made a case for travel, with characters driving, riding buses, and hitchhiking coast to coast across "the groaning continent" several times, as well as to Mexico and back, working temporary jobs, having extramarital sex, drinking alcohol, smoking marijuana, and listening to various kinds of music. Kerouac's description of travel, "when all the golden land's ahead of you and all kinds of unforeseen events wait lurking to surprise you and make you glad you're alive to see," captured his beatnik characters' sense of adventure and recklessness and piqued wanderlust in many young people in the 1960s and 1970s.[21]

The sociologist Marie-Françoise Lanfant asserted that tourism has potential to change the cultures and the futures of societies that allow it. Tourism is one way in which a place can connect itself to the global community. Lanfant believed that planning for tourism is related to such empire-building activities as exploiting lands, occupying territories, and conquering resources. A large industrial country could plan for tourism as a way of dealing with identity "in regions of depopulation."[22] In the 1960s and 1970s Canada was trying to assert its culture and sovereignty in a North America dominated by the United States. Many parts of Canada were sparsely populated. In endeavoring to attract tourists (and emigrants) from the United States, Canada sought to conquer resources in the form of U.S. residents—and U.S. dollars.

Lanfant further described the use of stereotypical yet flattering images of a place as a part of tourism intended to create a respectable identity of natives, draw the interest of outsiders, "praise the idea of the nation," and "reinforce national cohesion." Nations do this to try to assert regional autonomy.[23] In the case of Canada this could include the use of such images as uniformed members of the Royal Canadian Mounted Police (popularly known as "Mounties"), moose, beavers, and maple leaves to attract the interest of Americans and to remind them in pleasant ways that Canada was different from the United States. For Americans to embrace such images and what they symbolized marked a victory for Canada over the United States, which was often at odds with the interests of Canada.

The geographer John A. Jakle has examined tourism in the United States and Canada and has provided further rationale for asserting that tourism has an influence on immigration. In particular he pointed to the rise of use of the automobile as a provider of unprecedented social mobility. Unlike trains and buses, which travel on set routes and schedules, automobiles allow drivers, as Jakle put it, "to validate the world around them: a world increasingly of their own making." In their own cars travelers could travel on their own routes, on their own schedules, and at their own speed. This sort of freedom was particularly liberating for working-class people, because they could escape the places where they were workers, see the larger world, interact with the non–working class, and be less limited in the roles they could play.[24] Jakle observed that decisions to travel, as well as the destinations of that travel, would usually be based on advice from friends, as well as on scenes viewed in geography classes, on television, in films, and in advertisements and articles in the popular press.[25] Jakle ultimately believed, however, that twentieth-century

Americans and Canadians did not travel to view landscapes. Instead, they pursued "packaged and standardized tourism" that offered glimpses of stereotypes akin to the flattering images of a place that Lanfant described. Further, tourists did not choose destinations critically. They did so out of "locational need."[26] To many U.S. tourists, Canada was—and is—a conveniently located destination for foreign vacations, and it was a convenient place for Americans to go to escape obligations of military service in the 1960s and 1970s.

The historian Karen Dubinsky supports Jakle's view of the democratizing effects of tourism, noting that after World War II, the working class, with increased leisure time and more disposable income, was able to join the middle and upper classes in tourism and travel. She saw that tourism was not some plot foisted upon an unwitting public, but rather that the public recognized tourism as a democratic institution open to nearly all who wished to participate in it, either as tourists or as tourism entrepreneurs. In Canada this was fueled by recognition on the part of its tourist industry that although fewer than 7 percent of U.S. tourists left the United States, 80 percent of those tourists came to Canada. Consequently, in the 1950s and 1960s, the industry endeavored to make Canada more attractive to Americans.[27] Within Canada, Dubinsky says "tourism was sold as a public good . . . and the American tourist especially acquired a special kind of reverence."[28] Evidence of this reverence was that, remarkably, the federal government of Canada spent 100 percent of its travel promotion budget in the 1950s and early 1960s on advertising in the United States, ignoring non-Americans, even Canadians, in its promotion of Canada. In addition, plans to improve Canadian highways, lodgings, and restaurants, and to train tourism workers to be more professional, represented efforts to make travel in Canada more pleasing to U.S. tourists.[29] After World War II, North Americans could travel to Europe more easily, so Canada was competing with much of the Western world for U.S. tourists.[30]

Compelling evidence of the relationship of tourism to immigration is that the government of Canada, for a time, seized upon the idea of tourists as potential immigrants. From 1966 to 1972, a time span largely coincident with most Vietnam War–era immigration from the United States to Canada, people who entered Canada describing themselves as visitors could, upon having a good look around, apply for landed immigrant status from *within* Canada.[31] They would not have to return to their home country and apply at an embassy or consulate there. People with landed immigrant status—similar to those having a "green card" in the United States—were allowed to stay in Canada indefinitely if they possessed the right combination of age, job and language skills, education, and personal qualities. Some organizations in Canada that counseled (potential) U.S. émigrés to Canada advised them to use this law to their advantage. For example, a July 1970 memo from the Winnipeg Committee to Assist War Objectors advised, "EVERY potential immigrant should enter first as a TOURIST, and contact a Canadian group for counselling: When asked [by border officials] if he is immigrating, the answer is NO. He must be counselled here [in Canada] about the [immigration] application, local policy, etc., and he should look for a job offer in Canada before applying."[32] Likewise, the Toronto Anti-Draft Programme, through its *Manual for Draft-Age Immigrants to Canada,* advised, "We recommend that all prospective immigrants come in as visitors and consult with us."[33]

Though it was an era of easy automobile travel, the 1960s also ushered in an era of jet airplane travel. Compared to propeller planes, jets could deliver twice the number of passengers to a spot across a continent or over an ocean in half the time. So, while many people in the United States were within a day's drive of Canada, others from around the world could arrive at a Canadian airport in the same amount of time. Indeed, the number of airplane passenger arrivals in Canada nearly quadrupled from 4.6 million in 1958, the year of the first commercial jet airplane flight, to 18.1 million in 1972.[34] Canada, with its generous policy of admitting visitors as landed immigrants from within the country, was now hours away, not just from the United States but from most of the world. The huge number of arrivals in Canada in the late 1960s and early 1970s, the number of appeals from people resident in Canada but unqualified to remain there, and the impact on employment rates would force the hand of Canadian officials to change immigration policy. As we will see later, U.S. émigrés to Canada would get tangled up in this change, and the era of relatively easy immigration to Canada would come to an end.

"HEADING NORTH IS SO EASY": CANADIAN APPEALS TO YOUNG PEOPLE

On May 22, 1969, the Canadian government, led by Prime Minister Pierre Trudeau, announced that it would treat draft resisters and military deserters as "ordinary" immigrants, meaning that Canada would admit them without any question as to their status with the U.S. Selective Service System and would refuse to deport them, as long as they otherwise qualified as immigrants to Canada.[35] This clear articulation of immigration policy served as a green light for border crossings from the United States to Canada.

If the idea of tourism could convince Americans that Canada was a place not only to visit but perhaps also to immigrate to, they had to learn about Canada. Articles about Canada published in U.S. popular magazines, as well as in travel guides about Canada published in the United States or Canada, provided assurance of what American travelers would encounter at their destination. As the historian Daniel J. Boorstin observed in the early 1960s, twentieth-century tourists did not go to undiscovered lands: "People go to see what they already know is there. The only thing to record, the only possible source of surprise, is their own reaction."[36] By planning travel based on descriptions and advice found in travel guides and articles, tourists, particularly those who would become immigrants, had a better idea of what to expect in their destination and could ideally make their travel and/or immigration more pleasant and successful. Such travel planning by many Americans going to Canada in the 1960s and 1970s is akin to the findings of the historian John Bodnar in his study of nineteenth- and early-twentieth-century immigrants to the United States: people did not move randomly but rather from specific places to other specific places at specific times. To succeed in the new place, immigrants with few resources at their disposal had to concentrate on "that portion of their world in which they actually could exert some power and influence: the family household, the workplace, and the local neighborhood or community."[37] In the late twentieth century, travelers and immigrants could assure success at the end of their journey through consultation with relevant print literature.

Popular magazines were an important source of information for potential draft resisters and military deserters, primarily because of their pervasiveness in the United States in the Vietnam War era. Another measure of the popularity of an individual title was whether it could be found in public, high school, or university libraries, the likelihood of which was increased by the periodical's inclusion in *Readers' Guide to Periodical Literature,* an index to articles in magazines readily available to middle-class consumers in libraries and on newsstands.[38]

A young man in the United States of, or close to, draft age in the mid-1960s may have learned, through the popular press, about Canada as a possible place to live or at least to resist the draft, even if he had not seriously thought about his options. Perhaps he had learned about Canada in school. If a teacher drew lesson plans from an April 1965 issue of *Scholastic Teacher,* the teacher's supplement to *Senior Scholastic,* he may have learned about the easy accessibility of, and job opportunities in, Canada and that it was an overnight train ride from much of the United States. *Scholastic Teacher* described Toronto,

Canada's then second-largest city, as "a new city . . . a clean city . . . a city on the way up, and frankly . . . most exciting," where one could see "all the new factories lit up in colorful display . . . along the highways at night."[39]

Two years later *Scholastic Teacher* reminded educators—on the occasion of Canada's centennial celebration—that the United States and Canada "live in trust and harmony" along the longest border in the world, and a relatively unguarded one at that, adding the encouragement that "the welcome mat will be prominently spread all along our 3,534-mile border."[40] *Scholastic Teacher* exhorted instructors to teach their students more about Canada, "a country whose future is closely linked to our own" and that was "*here,* right at our doorstep. . . . American students need not limit their learning to passive reading and note taking—they can readily visit Canada, meet its people, and experience the Canadian way of living firsthand."[41] A 1967 *Saturday Review* article on Canada's centennial also reminded readers of the long, "peaceful and undefended border," reassuring them that "[Canadians] are, generally speaking, remarkably like [their] counterparts to the south," and enticing them by characterizing Canada's largest urban areas as "the peer of those anywhere in the world" and as "swinging cities today by any standard."[42]

A young man might also have encountered information in magazines intended for teenaged women. Perhaps a friend, a sister, or a cousin of a draft-age man subscribed to *Seventeen,* which described itself as "Young America's Favorite Magazine." The magazine had more than 1.5 million subscribers in 1969, putting it in the hands of one out of every six women aged fifteen to nineteen in the United States. *Seventeen's* May 1969 issue featured Canada and would have arrived in the mail and appeared on newsstands at about the same time as the Trudeau government's announcement that Canada would welcome—and not extradite—draft resisters and military deserters. The issue emphasized the ease of travel to major cities, saying, "Ways to get here: by air from many United States cities, by car . . . from Buffalo. Any way you go, go pronto, it's Toronto."[43] A column called "Teen Travel Talk" advised that "heading north is so easy. If you're a citizen or permanent resident of the United States, you can cross the border either way without difficulty or delay." It also suggested an alternative to driving across the border: ferries in Washington State that transported passengers between the United States and Canada.[44] A full-page advertisement for Air Canada extolled the airline's half-price fares for flights to and within Canada for youths under twenty-two years of age. "Come on up to Canada," the ad enthused, for "tuned-in cities" and "swinging discotheques."[45] Perhaps this was simply a way of attracting young tourists to Canada (and selling plane tickets), but if there was any controversy about attracting men who might be in violation of U.S. Selective Service System regulations, Air Canada, the national airline of Canada, did not seem to take heed. Readers of *Seventeen* who were sensitive to the plight of male peers looking for a way out of military service might mention the Canadian alternative to them, especially if they were aware of Trudeau's announcement. More than twenty-six thousand women immigrated to Canada between 1965 and 1974.[46] Presumably they, too, were favorably impressed by the picture of Canada painted by such articles.

Even the conservative *Reader's Digest* hinted at the desirability of moving to Canada for escape. An article condensed from the travel magazine *Holiday* retained a passage quoting a young Dutch man working at a bar in Banff, Alberta: "I came here five years ago because I was fed up with army service. I chose Canada rather than the United States partly because of the fuss about entering the States—the forms, the questions and all that—but chiefly because there is more scope for the individual in Canada.... Here life is open. You can be anything."[47] The article's author further opined that in Canada "the individual is freer and has a better chance in a country that is still being opened up."[48]

"YOU NEED NO SHOTS AND NO PASSPORT": TRAVEL GUIDES TO CANADA

A second form of useful travel information was travel guides about Canada published in the United States or in Canada for a U.S. audience. Familiar themes in these guides were the ease of entry into Canada from the United States, the gracious welcome Canadians would give Americans, and the enjoyment that Americans, particularly young people, could find in Canada. Guides stressed the cultural familiarity, yet political distinctiveness, of Canada, as well as the attractiveness of Canada as a place to live—permanently. In *Young Americans Abroad,* journalist Robert A. Liston characterized reasons why U.S. youths traveled in the early 1970s, citing "gaining independence," "escaping parental controls," "having a fling and seeing the world before settling down to a job or career," "taking a breather from college," and "seeking easy access to marijuana, narcotics and drugs." He noted other motives, such as "expressing political and social dissent against the United States Government and society in general," "avoiding law enforcement officials at home," and "escaping the draft," that suggested expatriation more than travel.[49] Although his descriptions applied primarily to travel in Europe, they could apply to Canada as well.

Travel guides to Canada painted an attractive picture for potential visitors—temporary or permanent. Many stressed the ease of entry into Canada. As one 1964 guide promised, driving into Canada "couldn't be simpler at any of the 138 border crossing stations along the frontier," and a 1972 guide promised that "red tape and regulations have been kept to a minimum."[50] The *Manual for Draft-Age Immigrants to Canada,* which the Toronto Anti-Draft Programme published in six editions between 1968 and 1971, reinforced this by advising that a car was the best means of transportation for getting to Canada from the United States.[51]

The open arms of Canadians was another theme of travel guides. The author of a 1972 guide provided assurance that "Canadians are genuinely glad to see visitors. They love their land and its great beauty and want you to enjoy it as much as they do. Your appreciation gives them pleasure."[52] Likewise, *So You're Going to Canada,* a forty-eight-page publication of the Canadian Government Travel Bureau in the early 1970s, assured potential visitors that "Canadians are proud of their beautiful, spacious country, and love to share its attractions with visitors. Whether you wish to visit the modern, sophisticated cities, the elegant vacation centres or the many areas of natural unspoiled beauty, everywhere you will find the friendliness and hospitality for which Canadians are known around the world."[53]

The 1971 book *Young Person's Guide to Canada,* by the college students Howard Cohen and Charles Greene (the son of Lorne Greene, a Canadian-born actor in the popular 1960s television western *Bonanza*) was not intended specifically for use by young American men going to Canada to resist military service, but it provided some reassurance for those who were considering making such a move. In addition to describing the youth scene and mentioning the presence of draft resisters in Vancouver and the number of cars crossing the Ontario border "loaded with youngsters and crammed with camping gear and tow[ing] and/or carry[ing] canoes and boats of all shapes and sizes," the authors emphasized that "the food won't disagree with you, the water won't make you ill, the plumbing is fine. . . . You need no shots and no passport," and they added that "although you may encounter the exception, we found the people of Canada to be warm and hospitable."[54]

In the Yorkville neighborhood of Toronto, Canada's largest English-speaking city, Rochdale College was created as supplemental housing for the burgeoning baby boom generation heading to Toronto's universities. Rochdale provided cooperative living space more relaxed in nature than that operated by universities, offered noncredit classes distanced from the lecture format and sprawling research centers of the University of Toronto, and included a cinema, a library, a newspaper, literary presses, a medical clinic, restaurants, and bars.[55] Black and women's liberation groups operated from the building, and a Hare Krishna community existed alongside Christian communes.[56] Though the idea of an alternative university was barely achieved, a large countercultural community formed at Rochdale, attracting "a wildly heterogeneous collection of people, for reasons as diverse as utopianism, homelessness, boredom, and mere convenience," creating, as the historian Stuart Henderson saw it, "a culture of Otherness, an unaccountable space in which the pursuit of random experience was the preferred ambition." Henderson posited that residents of Toronto came to see the Yorkville area "as a distinct local-foreign land" that invited "the curious to come and partake."[57] In short, if one needed a place to stay—and potentially to hide—in Canada, but be somehow apart from it, the crowded, high-rise Rochdale College, in the heart of Toronto, had great appeal to many in the counterculture, including draft resisters and military deserters from the United States.

The Rochdale College building and its residents generated a lot of press in Toronto and beyond, which, while mostly negative, served, Henderson believed, as "a hip advertisement" for young people who sought "an authentic countercultural experience."[58] Several editions of the *Manual for Draft-Age Immigrants to Canada* mentioned it, with one describing its community as "split between students and drop-outs who are 'doing their own thing.'"[59] A brochure intended to attract residents to Rochdale addressed stereotypes of Canada held by many Americans: "Forget Sergeant Preston. Toronto weather is similar to New York's. No snow and ice during the summer." It further outlined the accessibility and desirability of Toronto for young people (and its distance from demonstrations that had occurred in many cities in the United States and other countries in the 1950s and 1960s):

> Toronto is an attractive city of two million people, only four hours from Montreal by train, only an hour from New York by air, twelve hours from Boston via Sherman tank . . .
>
> Like any other city, Toronto has museums, a zoo and planetarium, legitimate and experimental theatres, traditional and new wave film houses, too many psychedelic topless go-go girls and **PEOPLE!**—English, French, Scots, Irish, Hungarians, Ukranians [sic], Jamaicans and Draft Dodgers.
>
> No riots, everyone lives together. Peaceful.[60]

What Every American Tourist Should Know about Canada, an eighty-page, pocket-sized souvenir book published for Expo 67, the 1967 world's fair in

Montréal, played up Canada's desirability as a vacation destination, asking, "When you told your relatives, friends, neighbors, that you were making a trip into Canada, just what did they say? We'll bet that those who had been up in this part of the continent were full of enthusiasm . . . and they told you Canada was a friendly place." The guide also connected tourism and immigration by citing the number of arrivals to Canada, adding that "a leading Canadian observor" [*sic*] had written that

> Canadians have always encouraged the newcomer to join them, and have been eager for him to find the roominess of life that Canada offers. This is a land where every man and every woman can find a place in society suited to his or her inclinations and capabilities. It is a country where the ordinary citizen, no matter how humble, has a chance to better his life. . . . There has always been a major participation in Canadian development by Americans—even though it began as a flight to sanctuary in revolutionary days, and later gold and then free land and now opportunity.

Authors of the guide also felt that every American tourist should know that "Canada has played a major role in NATO—sending men and material to every trouble spot," but added conspicuously that "Canada has no commitments in the current war in Vietnam."[61] Stanley R. Tupper and Douglas L. Bailey's Canadian centennial-themed *Canada and the United States—The Second Hundred Years*, provided a brief history of U.S. immigration to Canada, mentioning Loyalists and enslaved people on the Underground Railroad as well as twentieth-century farmers, skilled laborers, scientific personnel, professionals, and "'entrepreneurs' planning to invest in Canadian business or open new enterprises." In the same breath, the authors mentioned draft resisters, tacitly connecting them to the heroic immigrants of previous centuries.[62]

The 1973 mass-market paperback *A Guide for Travellers in Canada* also played up the ease of travel in Canada. A section titled "Information for American Tourists" observed that "in no other vacationland, covering an area as vast as Canada, is the American so at liberty to travel. One language—English—will open the door to near total involvement in the nation's life. . . . You will be received as friendly neighbors and few adjustments will have to be made." Another section of the book, "Border Procedures," winked at Canada's policy of admitting draft-age American men into the country by indicating that a draft card was among the acceptable forms of identification for gaining admission to Canada, and that after a few questions "you will be waved along in friendly fashion."[63]

FIGURE 2.1. Illustration from Norman Reader and Jerome E. Klein, *Canada* (1967).

A 1967 geography book intended for school libraries called simply *Canada* emphasized the many tourism opportunities available for Americans but noted that surpassing them was "the communal bond which has existed between our two countries for more than a century," adding that "our borders remain unfortified and peaceful . . . and our common affection warm." A photograph in this book showed a young, smiling, ostensibly American heterosexual couple arriving in Canada by automobile and encountering a pleasant border guard, while its caption promised that "the friendly smile and cheery greeting of a Canadian customs official make crossing the border into Canada a pleasure. Formalities between Canada and the United States are almost non-existent" (Figure 2.1).[64]

A 1972 publication called *Handbook Canada* described a Canadian federal government program that sponsored stays in 130 hostels throughout the country, charging travelers no more than fifty cents a night and providing free meals. Having lured young people to Canada with the promise of low-cost lodging and free food, the guide blurred the line between tourism and immigration by describing the steps necessary for immigration to Canada and listing the many aid centers in the country that provided assistance to émigrés.[65]

The inaugural U.S. and Canada edition of Harvard University's *Let's Go* student budget travel guide series promised that getting into Canada was generally a "cinch" and noted that ferries between Maine and Nova Scotia were an especially hassle-free way to enter the country. *Let's Go* also pointed to Vancouver as "a cosmopolitan haven for the student" and an easy place to get help with "problems of any kind—concerning food, clothing, and/or transportation."[66]

Likewise, the YMCA (Young Men's Christian Association) and the Addiction Research Foundation, an Ontario provincial government agency, funded publication of *The Toronto Survival Manual: A Practical Guide to Better Living & Psychological Survival for Young People Who Have Just Left Home,* a free twenty-four-page publication (printed on presses at Rochdale College) to help youth from all over the world, but especially U.S. exiles. In 1973 the Church of the Holy Trinity in Toronto published the *Toronto Survival Guide,* an inexpensive 250-page paperback, with analogous intentions to assist newcomers to Toronto. The guide played up the compassion of Torontonians, intoning, "Theoretically, using the information within these pages, it is the last 50¢ you will ever have to spend. . . . Remember what the city lacks in social services, and what the social services lack in quality and dignity, can be found from the people of Toronto themselves."[67]

Despite the author's attempts to be sardonic, the Canada chapter of the 1968 guide *Student Travel in America* offered a further incentive for a move to Canada: cultural familiarity. "Much of Canada is a carbon copy of the United States. . . . [Canadians] watch American television and movies, listen to American records and buy products from branches of American companies." Readers also might have appreciated the guide's take on Canada's less political nature: "Some smugly point out that Canada has successfully avoided most of the political, military and social excesses of the U.S." The advantages of Canada's less militaristic nature were couched as travel advice: "It might also be advisable to avoid discussions about . . . why Canada takes U.S. draft dodgers with no questions asked or why Canada doesn't support the U.S. in Vietnam."[68]

Similarly, readers of *Canada: Wonderland of Surprises,* a 1967 geography book for high school–aged readers, would have learned that "young people come expecting to see Eskimos or Indians but, instead, see other young people who dress, talk, and look exactly as they do—and sing the same songs, watch the same movies, read the same comic strips, drive the same makes of cars, drink the same brands of pop, and scream over the same singing groups." Again, the book implied the possibility of immigration of Americans to Canada by concluding with a description of immigrants who had already come to Canada with "skills . . . energies, and their keen desire to build a good life" in a place that promised "justice and fair play."[69]

"THE STRANGE AND WONDERFUL THING IS THAT IT ISN'T STRANGE AT ALL": AMERICANS ADJUST TO CANADA

Benedict Anderson, in *Imagined Communities*, his classic examination of nationalism, posed as a test of membership in a community whether one would willingly die for it.[70] In the Vietnam War era, many could not imagine themselves as a member of the community that was the United States, preoccupied as it was with controlling the outcome of a civil war in Vietnam, and could not imagine risking their lives in Southeast Asia. With knowledge of U.S. conduct of the Vietnam War, knowledge of their options within the U.S. military's draft system, knowledge that expatriation was a possibility for resisting the draft, and knowledge that Canada was one place to which they could easily immigrate, many Americans began to take a serious look at the possibilities of moving there. While they may have recognized that Canada was a place they could go, and despite Canada's concerted efforts to attract Americans as tourists or immigrants, they may not have known much about the place as a potential home. Despite Canada's proximity to the United States and its openness to U.S. émigrés during the Vietnam War era, it remained a mystery to many young men from the United States. "For most Americans, the border is the backdoor" is the apt observation of the geographer Randy William Widdis. The U.S. psyche is centered in a mythical, geographically transcendent heartland, away from the U.S.-Canadian border. However, because most Canadians live within 50 miles (80 kilometers) of the United States, the border is a major part of the Canadian psyche.[71]

The geographical proximity of Canada to the northern United States played a major part in the movement of Americans there (Figure 2.2). From 1966 to 1972, 74.4 people per 100,000 population emigrated from the United States to Canada. Eight of the eleven border states were in the first quartile of sending states. Montana was the leading sender (338.6 per 100,000 Montanans went to Canada), Washington second, Idaho fifth, Alaska sixth, Vermont seventh, Maine eighth, New Hampshire eleventh, North Dakota thirteenth, and Michigan fourteenth. Relatively few from southern states went to Canada. Alabama was least likely to send immigrants (9.6 per 100,000 Alabamans went to Canada), followed by South Carolina, Mississippi, Arkansas, Georgia, West Virginia, Tennessee, North Carolina, Kentucky, Louisiana, and Virginia.[72]

Many American men admitted they knew little to nothing about Canada before going there. The expatriate Howie Prince recalled that he had been

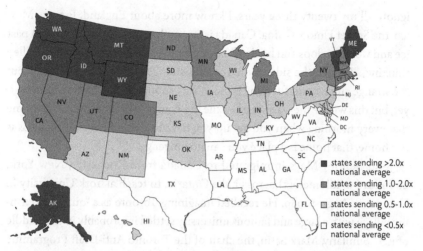

FIGURE 2.2. Likelihood of U.S. residents to go to Canada, 1966–1972, by state (national average was 74.4 residents per 100,000 U.S. 1970 population). (Source: Created by author based on table that appears in the Appendix.)

taught that Canada "was a pretty strange place" because it had been "host to the bad guys" (the British) during the War for American Independence and War of 1812 and had given refuge to Loyalists and Tories (and later, Native American Sioux after the Battle of Little Big Horn of 1876 and Communists during the First Red Scare of the early twentieth century). Canada, therefore, was quite foreign because the Founding Fathers of the United States "didn't particularly like what Can[ada] did."[73] When Tom Engelhardt of New York City felt certain that he was going to be drafted, he went on an exploratory trip to Canada. He recalled thinking, "I didn't know what I was going to do. Canada felt like another land and I felt so deeply American I couldn't imagine going there."[74] Bill Wittmeyer, a Vietnam War veteran and expatriate in Montréal, noticed that many Americans were ignorant about Canada, saying they think "there's nothing up here but little villages and snow and ice. They don't know enough about Canada, like even my mother thought that I was ruining my life by coming up here, and she's even been here. They don't realize that you can do the same things here that you can do down in the States."[75]

Jack Todd grew up in Nebraska, deserted the army while stationed at Fort Lewis, near Seattle, and moved to Vancouver, British Columbia, in 1970. In his memoirs, he recalled his impressions of Canada upon his arrival there: "In the distance you can see the Coast Mountains where the Cascades soar on north into Canada, into this big, wild, cold country I have managed to ignore all my twenty-three years. I know more about England, France, Mexico, the Soviet Union, China. Canada is a complete mystery once you get past ice and wolves, igloos and hockey." Yet, upon arriving in Vancouver he recalled thinking, "I watch the side of the road for strange and wonderful things, but the strange and wonderful thing is that it isn't strange at all. I haven't fixed on it yet, but this will be the warp of it—exile in a country that is so much like home that every morning when you get up you have to remind yourself that this is not home, that home is a place you can no longer go."[76]

John Bentley Mays immigrated to Canada from Rochester, New York, 20 miles (30 kilometers) across Lake Ontario, to teach at York University in Toronto in August 1969. He recalled imagining Toronto as a "quaint old fishing village with a large and famous university settled improbably in the middle of it."[77] Similarly, Mark Satin, the chair of the Toronto Anti-Draft Programme in the late 1960s and editor of early editions of the Programme's *Manual for Draft-Age Immigrants to Canada,* told a writer for the *Los Angeles Times,* "Before I came [to Canada] I thought there were log cabins and igloos in the middle of town."[78] Dick Perrin, who grew up in Vermont, and who also went to Canada in 1969, after deserting the military in Europe and living for a time in Paris, recalled his first impressions of Canada after flying into Montréal: "It didn't look an awful lot different than the United States—same housing, convenience stores on the corner, shopping malls. But it still amazes me that a young man who grew up about 100 miles south of the Canadian border could have known so little about that country. In those days, the salient image I had of Canada was from an old TV series about Sergeant Preston of the Yukon."[79]

STRAIGHT DRESSERS AND THE ARMY OF THE UNSCRUBBED: ÉMIGRÉS TO CANADA IN POPULAR MAGAZINES

"Graduate students and high school dropouts, Christians and nonbelievers, track stars and acid heads, radicals and hippies; they are all there, linked by a stubborn independence [and] a common revulsion against their country's war in Vietnam," wrote John Cooney and Dana Spitzer in the September 1969 issue of *Trans-action.*[80] Bill Davidson, in the *Saturday Evening Post* in January 1968, painted a similar composite portrait of Vietnam War–era draft resisters in Canada, writing, "The draft evaders, or 'non-cooperators,' as some like to call themselves, vary tremendously in background. They are simple Mennonite farm boys . . . scholars with Ph.D.'s . . . Negroes from the ghettos . . . [and]

boys from America's richest families."[81] Oliver Clausen, in a May 1967 issue of the *New York Times Magazine*, came to the similar conclusion that "the variety of draft-evader types makes a composite portrait impossible."[82]

Beyond such admissions that draft resisters and military deserters were difficult to categorize, popular magazines of the late 1960s and early 1970s tended to emphasize four themes in their articles about them: their appearance, education, and family background; descriptions of their politics (or absence thereof); their attitude toward the United States; and their comfort level in Canada.

Popular magazine portrayals of life for draft resisters, military deserters, and other émigrés in Canada had great potential to influence Americans who were considering going to Canada to resist the draft—or for other reasons—during the late 1960s and early 1970s. Indeed, emigration from the United States to Canada from 1965 to 1974 was 95 percent higher than it had been in the previous decade.[83] Popular magazines helped connect young Americans to the wider world.[84] Not under consideration here are alternative or underground publications that published information about draft resisters and military deserters. Those sorts of publications are admittedly another form of popular press, and they would expand the portrayal of this group of men, but of greater interest here are mainstream publications that may have influenced young Americans who were not attuned to more radical print media.[85]

One major preoccupation of the popular press was the superficial characteristics of the men. Their hair and clothes, intelligence and educational attainment, and family backgrounds warranted frequent mention, often as a way of suggesting their normality or deviation therefrom. For example, a 1966 *U.S. News and World Report* article characterized most émigrés (and potential émigrés) as "just ordinary Americans from middle-class backgrounds," and the *Christian Century* described them in 1968 as "white middle class, liberal and college oriented."[86] In *The Reporter*, Edmond Taylor concurred, characterizing one such man as "a quiet, earnest-looking 19-year-old former university student."[87] In "Boys without a Country," published in the *New York Times* in 1967, Clausen described most draft resisters in a Toronto group as "articulate and well-educated," with one having "a surprisingly babylike face" and a "thick Bobby Kennedy–style head of hair." Another was a "22-year-old piano student" with "a neat beard" and "natural self-assurance . . . who married a pretty Canadian girl this spring." A third, a "bright 20-year-old from a small Ohio town," wrote "highly promising, sensitive" plays.[88]

A column by Stewart Alsop in a July 1970 issue of *Newsweek* described one draft resister as "a good Catholic . . . [who] cuts his hair and dresses straight."[89]

In the magazine *Ladies' Home Journal* in 1967, Gail Cameron gushed about a man who had moved from Hartford, Connecticut, to Toronto, describing him as "a soft-spoken, remarkably contained young man. . . . He graduated 19th out of a class of over 400, [and] picked up five prizes in chemistry and physics."[90] Similarly, Cooney and Spitzer described a nineteen-year-old draft resister whose clothes "followed the styles advertised in *Sports Illustrated*" and whose hair "grew only to his ears." He was an active member of his church, "a fair athlete," "always among the top in his high school class," on the dean's list at Stanford University, and the son of "an engineer for General Electric."[91]

In *Ladies' Home Journal* Cameron characterized the variety of draft resisters positively, suggesting that "contrary to popular assumption few U.S. draft dodgers in Canada are flag-burners, draft-card-burners or hippies. In fact, most of these flamboyant front-page dissenters look down on the boys who have gone to Canada for 'opting out on peace.' For the most part, these boys are well educated (most of them college graduates), from good, middle-class homes, raised by conscientious, loving parents. For many, this is the first rebellious act of their lives. They are all aware of the implications of their decision, and none of them has made it lightly."[92]

Other journalists described émigrés more derisively. In one 1966 *U.S. News and World Report* article, they were construed as an "army of unscrubbed . . . a flow of young drifters—of the long-haired, bearded, beatnik variety—moving from city to city in Canada. . . . Many are U.S. citizens who hide their identity by melting into the jungle of Canada's own unscrubbed youth."[93] In *Newsweek* in 1970, Alsop derided their clothing as "the uniform of the radical young—lots of hair, granny glasses, unwashed feet, poor-boy costumes for the boys, either micro-minis [dresses] or sweet-little-girl costumes for the girls." He allowed, though, that many émigrés were "obviously highly intelligent."[94] Clausen felt compelled to describe one young man as a "long-haired 20-year-old from Milwaukee," baiting readers for his description of a second, similarly coiffed youth, this time adding, "He also looks and sounds just like a boy many a citizen of [his home town] would love to give a good spanking to."[95]

Alsop saw the less conventional dress of some draft resisters as intentionally politicized. He called one draft resister, Ted Steiner, "a highly intelligent and articulate young man, who affects the uniform of 'The Movement.'" He was the "son of a decorated ex-marine, now a successful businessman," who was "suburban" and "middle-class." Alsop saw Steiner, however, as "needing" to hate and full of loathing for his father's lifestyle.[96]

Authors of popular magazine articles about draft resisters and military deserters may not have been far from the mark in noting that some young men had short hair and conservative dress. They may have preferred that style for any number of reasons, one of which may have been to follow the advice of the *Manual for Draft-Age Immigrants to Canada* and similar literature. Early editions of the *Manual* advised those applying for immigration to Canada: "Get a good night's sleep, bathe, shave, and get a haircut. You must appear neat. Applying for [landed immigrant] status is a suit-and-tie affair, even in 100-degree weather. The applicants who are most successful present themselves as good middle-class persons, determined to work hard and be a credit to their new country."[97] Clausen, despite his disdain for expatriates, quoted this advice to the potential benefit of future émigrés, while a 1968 *U.S. News and World Report* article paraphrased it: "Also to be avoided is: 'hippie type' regalia. . . . Long hair, beads, unkemptness make it hard to enter the country and more difficult to obtain a job."[98] Likewise in *Steal This Book,* Abbie Hoffman encouraged potential immigrants to have "a stereotyped middle class appearance and life-style."[99] In its March 1970 publication, "Notes on Immigrating to Canada," the Alexander Ross Society, an immigrant aid group in Edmonton, Alberta, advised that "the smoothest way to handle immigration involves entering Canada as a visitor, checking with the committee nearest your destination, getting a job offer, and returning to the border to immigrate. People entering as visitors should look and act like conventional, respecta[b]le tourists planning to stay for a few days."[100]

Ultimately, popular magazines could not agree on a single description of the appearance, background, and education of resisters and deserters. As a cross-section of American youth, they were impossible to identify based on their origins or superficial characteristics.

A second major theme in the articles was the politics of draft resisters. Oliver Clausen was quick to find their politics on the fringe of the mainstream. He stereotyped draft resisters and military deserters as representative of "a half-digested kind of New Left idealism, attracted by the hip glamour of being political refugees from the United States militaristic dictatorship or whatever" and described others as Maoists hoping for victory for the Communists in Vietnam and anarchists calling for a revolution in the United States. Clausen observed that one long-haired young man had "a yellow button announcing DISSENT in the lapel of his rumpled jacket" and seemed surprised to find that another was "an anarchist even though he is absolutely neat and clean-cut."[101] Clausen, in his response to a letter to the editor about the article, showed his hand by admitting, "I find it hard to side with anyone who refuses his nation's call to fight expansive totalitarianism today."[102]

Cooney and Spitzer had a different take on the politics of draft resisters. They described some in Canada as having "antipathy towards their government's involvement in Vietnam" while describing a group of military deserters in Mon-tréal as simply apolitical.[103] Renée Kasinsky, a sociologist who studied U.S. refugees in Canada from 1969 to 1975, entered into a dialogue with Dana Spitzer through letters to the editor of *Trans-action*, arguing, "I strongly dis-agree with Spitzer's contention that draft resisters in Canada are political while deserters are apolitical," adding that she found "deserter groups more politi-cal and the men personally more radical in many ways than the resisters."[104] Spitzer replied that he expected the whole community of draft resisters in Canada would be radical. Radicals were indeed there, but he allowed that "so were many others, ranging from the left to right on the American political spec-trum."[105] Bill Davidson also saw more variety, describing military deserters as ranging politically "from Maoists to Bobby Kennedy Democrats to Goldwater Republicans." He further categorized some as pacifists having a "nonideologi-cal, live-and-let-live attitude."[106]

As a part of an August 1969 special issue called "American Militarism," the large-format general-interest magazine *Look* examined the state of military conscription in the United States and attitudes toward it, finding that "an unpopular war and a capricious method of conscripting men to fight it have produced uncountable numbers of . . . young men hostile not only to the military but to the whole Government in which they once expected to par-ticipate." In the article, John Poppy, a *Look* senior editor, reported on a study conducted in the psychology department at the University of California–Berkeley that contrasted twenty ROTC (Reserve Officers' Training Corps) cadets with eleven convicted draft "refusers." The study characterized the ROTC cadets as "typically violently aggressive," "hyper-masculine and hard," and viewing themselves "morally as pawns." In contrast, the composite por-trait of draft resisters was men who felt they should be held accountable for their actions, and who were "more softly masculine."[107]

While the authors of some articles tacitly approved of immigrating to Canada, others found fault with such a move. Leaving the United States when many wanted changes in the country's draft laws and an end to the Vietnam War did not fulfill the tenets of participatory democracy. The *Saturday Eve-ning Post* printed a letter to the editor from an Odon, Indiana, man who com-plained, "It takes courage for someone to stand up for what he sincerely believes . . . but there is no courage in going to Canada or to jail merely to avoid going to Vietnam."[108] Similarly, the folk singer Joan Baez, the one-time wife of David Harris, who went to prison for twenty months rather than be drafted, was outspoken on the subject of immigration to Canada. Clausen quoted her as contending, "These kids can't fight the Vietnam madness by holing up in Canada. What they're doing is opting out of the struggle at home. That's where they should go, even if only to fill the jails."[109] Clausen also opined, "Many evaders unquestionably are cowards pure and simple, hiding behind pretensions of idealism, afraid either to go to war or to take the consequences of their refusal."[110] Draft resister and émigré Mark Satin responded to Clausen in a letter to the editor: "I have been counseling draft resisters for two months now and have not met one of Mr. Clausen's 'cowards pure and simple.' To grow up in the United States as a dissenter takes courage. To give up the fruits of the richest country on earth, for an idea, takes far more courage than to accept the status quo. The real cowards are those who cannot tolerate ways of life that challenge their own."[111]

John M. Swomley Jr., a professor of social ethics and philosophy of religion, argued in the *Christian Century* against the views of Baez (and others): "No adult can indict these young men as lacking understanding or courage or loyalty. At 18 or 20, these qualities are at a different level than at 35 or 40. Exile today may be a mistake, but on the other hand it may be the door of opportunity and service, as it was for many Europeans in the 18th and 19th centuries who came by faith and necessity to an unknown land."[112]

Just as it had been difficult for them to predict who would be a draft resister or military deserter based on appearance and background, so did journalists have a difficult time predicting the political ideology of expatriates. A young man's politics, whether leaning to the left or the right, or toward Communism, socialism, or capitalism, did not always predict his willingness to adhere to the call of the United States to serve in its military during the Vietnam War.

A third theme in popular magazines was the attitude of draft resisters and military deserters toward the United States. Articles portrayed them as being everything from apolitical to anarchists. In *Ladies' Home Journal* Gail Cameron related the ambivalence one young man from the U.S. Southwest had about his home nation:

Vietnam is just a symbol of the real sickness that affects this whole country— it's a lust for power. I hate America right now, but really it's more of a love-hate thing, because I love it, too. I believe in America and the principles it was founded on; but *because* I know what it really could be and I see what it has become, that I *had* to leave—that, along with the draft, of course, which was going to catch up with me soon anyway. I worry about the United States, I guess, because I am really an American deep at heart and always will be—and if I could return someday, I would, and try to change it from within.[113]

Cooney and Spitzer found many "deeply committed" to the United States and wanting to continue to play a part in whatever was happening there. They hoped to affect change despite being physically isolated from the United States, despite the pleas of Baez and others to try to do so from within the United States, and despite very few of them feeling "remorse at the prospect of not being able to return home."[114]

Edmond Taylor suspected in *The Reporter* that some of the exiles in Canada were there "less to protest against the war in Vietnam than to exploit Canada's traditionally easygoing hospitality," but he allowed that they may have been doing so "in pursuit of their own unending war against what they call the 'system'—i.e., the entire American society on which they have turned their backs."[115] Bill Davidson reported on even stronger feelings in the *Saturday Evening Post:* "Most of the draft resisters . . . have turned against their country completely." One young man asserted, "They ought to tear down the Statue of Liberty because it doesn't mean anything any more [*sic*]." Another, named Stuart Byczynski, "a thin, intense, balding young man who wears glasses," told Davidson: "I believe in the freedom of the individual, [but] big government in the United States is taking away all our freedoms." After complaining about taxes, legal driving and drinking ages, and "forc[ed] artificial racial equality," he returned to the theme of individual freedom—his own. "Even while I was still in high school, I decided no government was going to tell me I couldn't pursue my chosen profession and would have to sleep on cots with a lot of other people." He added, "My sole reason for going to college was to avoid the draft as long as possible with a 2-S student deferment."[116] Byczynski lost his deferment due to poor grades in college and expatriated to Canada in 1967.

Taylor profiled expatriates in Toronto outspoken about the race situation in the United States of the late 1960s, as well as about U.S. imperialism, writing, "activist émigrés here, along with their Canadian fellow revolutionaries, began to shift the emphasis of their permanent Hate America campaign from Vietnam to Latin-American themes." Further targets of these activist-revolutionaries, as Taylor saw them, were the "American military-industrial complex" and "racial fear of yellow men in Vietnam and black men in the United States."[117]

Stewart Alsop's July 1970 *Newsweek* interview with Ted Steiner uncovered the most anti-U.S. venom. Alsop quoted Steiner as perceiving "the lies and deceptions" and "the terrible hypocrisy" of the "American dream" and as seeing the United States as "a very rotten and very imperialist society." Alsop decided that "to Ted Steiner, America is 'the beast.'"[118] Alsop immediately followed his description of Steiner with that of a clinic in Toronto for drug users—managed by a U.S. military deserter—apparently equating draft resistance and drug use as criminal activities. Steiner's mother presented a different view of her son a few weeks later in a letter to the editor:

> I have just returned from a seven-day visit to Toronto. . . .
>
> I passed the time becoming familiar with the beauty of Toronto and its friendly people.
>
> None of the boys, including Ted, think of America as the "beast"; they are simply saying "No" to war and are genuinely saddened by the many sicknesses threatening our country today.
>
> Many brave boys have sacrificed their lives supposedly to keep America safe from an outside threat and these boys will sacrifice America and their homes for the rest of their lives to protect it from an internal threat. Which is better? Killing mankind or trying to improve it?[119]

Elsewhere in his article, Alsop balanced his account of émigrés by quoting Stan Pietlock, who had noted the inextricable relationship of the United States and Canada in an editorial for *AMEX/Canada,* a magazine published in Toronto for Vietnam War resisters. "Is it enough to have refused to go? Is it enough to be merely an expatriate and 'Canadianize' oneself, forgetting about the U.S. forever? We are hardly free of the United States up here, and as the U.S. is the oldest and closest enemy of Canada perhaps it is our role to lead the fight, physically, against the U.S. from our exile."[120]

On the other hand, the *Saturday Evening Post* writer Bill Davidson saw that some U.S. émigrés to Canada did indeed feel powerless to effect change in the United States. To that end, he observed that some draft resisters and military deserters returned to the United States "in order to make a less comfortable, more forceful protest." Davidson interviewed a young man who, despite facing prison time for draft evasion and international flight to avoid federal prosecution, returned to the United States voluntarily because, as he put it, "I felt impotent in Canada. Being up there just created tension for me, because all of us in Toronto were out of the mainstream of protest. I want to preserve my conscience, so I am ready to go to prison."[121] Articles in *Time, Senior Scholastic, U.S. News and World Report,* and *Better Homes and Gardens* also discussed the prospect of prison for those who resisted the draft or simply refused to serve.[122]

As was the case when they tried to predict the likelihood of a young man becoming a draft resister or military deserter based on his appearance, background, education, or politics, journalists found it difficult to predict whether a young man would expatriate based on his allegiance to the United States. Anarchists left the United States alongside patriots and men whose sentiments toward their country were more ambivalent.

"THE DUSTY ROOTLESSNESS" OF LIFE IN CANADA

The fourth major theme in popular press articles was the comfort level of U.S. émigrés in Canada. Authors of popular magazine articles portrayed the plight of those men in Canada in sympathetic yet sometimes apocalyptic terms, presupposing that U.S. émigrés would feel a great sense of alienation and loss in Canada.[123] For example, Bill Davidson saw émigrés as "choosing to live as aliens and to cut themselves off from friends and family and all things familiar," describing one young man who "genuinely grieves about his permanent exile from the United States."[124] The 1968 *U.S. News and World Report* article "For Americans: An Easier Life in Canada" suggested that "the biggest stumbling block to adjusting by the deserters is separation from home and family."[125] Oliver Clausen described a young man he interviewed as having "a suppressed sob in his voice when he spoke" of the United States, adding, "There are many such individual tragedies in Canada's colonies of draft resisters."[126] Predictably, Stewart Alsop painted a dismal picture of life in Canada, describing "the emptiness, the dusty rootlessness, of the life of a man without a country."[127]

Taylor also painted a grim portrait, suggesting, "Living conditions aren't too pleasant, but mainly it's the loneliness that gets you," adding a caveat about employment: "Jobs are very hard to find if you're an American draft resister in Canada."[128] Clausen claimed, too, that "it is risky for a young man with a marked American accent to turn up for a job interview."[129] *U.S. News and World Report* added in 1968 that "small employers throughout most of [Canada] are generally sympathetic and will hire [U.S. émigrés] if they can," yet warned, "Finding employment in Canada, despite help, is not always easy. . . . This is a period of increasing unemployment in Canada. Often draft evaders have to take lower-status jobs and less pay than they could expect at home. Some have been unable to get work, and have returned to the U.S."[130] Cooney and Spitzer characterized a twenty-seven-year-old man as "well-groomed and wearing a brown business suit," who nevertheless allowed that his job prospects in Canada were not good. "Many [prospective employers] feel I'm too educated for the jobs they have open," he declared, adding, "With a masters degree in history I've got no special skills."[131]

The preoccupation of the popular press with employment was well founded. Draft resisters and military deserters had to be employed in order to apply for landed immigrant status. Once accorded this status, they could not be deported, except in certain extreme circumstances, such as committing criminal or drug use offenses, becoming a political subversive, a chronic alcoholic, a public charge, or mentally or physically defective, or falsifying information on an immigration application.[132]

The *Manual for Draft-Age Immigrants to Canada* may have failed many immigrants on this count. Early editions of the manual painted a positive picture of employment in Canada. The second edition (1968) included an essay by Robert D. Katz, identified as "employment counsellor, [Canadian] Department of Manpower and Immigration," and Naomi Wall, director of American Immigrants Employment Service in Toronto, titled "Jobs Are Available," that included such optimistic observations as, "If you have a trade or profession it is likely that you will be able to transfer it to Canada with little difficulty"; "If your [bachelors] degree is in a field such as chemistry, physics or engineering your opportunities are excellent"; "For any B.A., teaching is a possibility"; "There are jobs available to high school graduates in banking, accounting, retail trade, and the food industry"; "For those who have a trade, or are semi-skilled, there are a good number of jobs available"; and "If you appear at Immigration with well-defined occupational goals you will be likely to receive landed immigrant status with no difficulty."[133] Another section of the second through fourth editions (1968–1969) of the *Manual for Draft-Age Immigrants* quoted Katz opining that "I am not suggesting that every company in Canada will hire draft resisters, but most companies will."[134] An appendix listed several dozen "occupations in strong national demand," including teachers at all levels, from nursery school to trade school to universities, as well as social workers, psychologists, librarians, salesmen, farm hands, production workers, and mechanics.[135]

The third through fifth editions (1969–1970) of the manual replaced the Katz-Wall essay with one more pragmatic, allowing only that "job opportunities in Canada vary tremendously from province to province. Employment is scarce on the west coast and only slightly better in the mid-west. The maritime, or eastern provinces, offer very little for the professionally skilled, who seem to do much better in the larger cities such as Toronto, Montreal (if you can speak French), Hamilton, Windsor, and Ottawa. Semi-skilled and unskilled labour opportunities are good in many of the smaller cities in southern Ontario. . . . Teaching opportunities are good throughout the country." It tempered the optimistic "no difficulty" claim of the second edition with "If you appear at Immigration with well-defined occupational goals, you will be likely to receive landed immigrant status with *little* difficulty" (italics added). The third and fourth editions repeated the list of "occupations in strong national demand," with the fifth edition allowing that no more recent information was available.[136] The sixth (and last) edition (1971) of the manual omitted both the essay on jobs and the list of occupations in demand. Describing itself as completely revised and edited by the staff of the Toronto Anti-Draft Programme, it noted the high unemployment rate in Canada, coupled with rising resentment toward U.S. émigrés, and warned that there was "an increasing unwillingness among employers to hire American immigrants of draft age, regardless of whether they are landed and merely need a job, or need not only a job but a written job offer as well."[137] Another section of this final edition of the *Manual for Draft-Age Immigrants* observed that

> things have changed here since the first wave of mid-60's draft dodgers arrived. Businesses in Canada by and large are either owned or dominated by U.S.-based corporations. Estimates run as high as 60–80% U.S. control over the Canadian labor market. Increasingly, these businesses are refusing to hire American immigrants of draft age. The excuses vary, but the end result is a lack of job possibilities for you. At the same time, Canadians are reacting to this American takeover, both in business and in the universities. A backlash has been created, showing itself most strongly through the increasing reluctance of Canadians to hire immigrants while so many Canadians are out of work. In the cultural and educational fields, a sense of national pride has lead [*sic*] to decisions to increase the percentage of [employed] Canadians by hiring only people of Canadian origin.
>
> What does this all mean to you? It means that finding a job becomes more difficult, and finding one in your field becomes an even harder task. This automatically makes immigrant status harder to obtain.[138]

"WELCOME! I SYMPATHIZE WITH YOU. I HOPE YOU LIKE IT HERE!": URGING AMERICANS OVER THE BORDER

For Americans who wanted or needed specific advice concerning immigration, there were many sources to provide it, from publications of small presses, commercial publishers, and the Canadian government, to advice dispensed by immigrant and draft aid groups on both sides of the U.S.-Canada border. Several commercially produced draft counseling books provided advice about immigration. For example, Richard L. Killmer and Charles P. Lutz's 1972 book *The Draft and the Rest of Your Life* outlined motivation for immigration, citing "hatred of the Vietnam War and a refusal to participate in it," the sense that going to jail would be useless, if not intolerable, a refusal to "play the games" necessary to get conscientious objector status or various other deferments, and "the belief that the political situation generally in the U.S. is beyond hope." Killmer and Lutz discussed the possibility of going to Great Britain, Denmark, Japan, and Germany, but ultimately allowed that Sweden and Canada were best for U.S. expatriates. They reinforced geographical proximity, similarity of culture and language, and "the openness of its immigration law" as primary reasons young Americans went to Canada, yet warned that "Canada is no utopia" and mentioned repressive measures employed by the Canadian government during the "October Crisis" of 1970, when cells of the Front de liberation du Québec kidnapped two government officials and murdered one of them.[139]

Leslie S. Rothenberg's chunky, 350-page pocket paperback, *The Draft and You: A Handbook on Selective Service,* warned against *fuite en avant*—fleeing ahead over the border—by encouraging readers to give serious consideration to moving to Canada, asking, "Who will you be leaving behind in the way of family, friends, girlfriends, and others who are meaningful to you? How deep are your roots in the United States, and do you feel that you can readjust elsewhere, in another society? How much do you know about Canadian life and society?" Rothenberg went on to advise:

> Canada, for example, is in many respects similar, especially in its large cities, to the United States, but some Americans who have emigrated there have found it difficult to make the transition to Canadian life and to accept the long-term implications of their decision. Some had difficulty finding jobs at times when unemployment was high in many Canadian provinces; an undetermined number have returned to the United States, either to face prosecution and prison sentences for refusing induction or to attempt to evade arrest by the FBI while living the life of a fugitive, even if only psychologically. Loneliness seems to have stimulated many returns from Canada.[140]

Abbie Hoffman's *Steal This Book* provided rather straightforward advice for immigration for when "you've totally fucked up your chances of getting a deferment or already are in the service and considering ditching." Hoffman suggested that the safest places to go would be countries "with which Amerika [*sic*] has mutual offense treaties such as Cuba, North Korea and those behind the so-called Iron Curtain," but he offered more practical advice about Sweden and Canada. He advised leaving the United States via Montana, described the immigration procedure at the border, and also warned against *fuite en avant* by encouraging potential émigrés to learn as much as possible about Canada before going, and to "pose as a visitor" when crossing the border. Hoffman also put a negative spin on expatriation, saying, "We feel it's our obligation to let people know that life in exile is not all a neat deal, not by a long shot. . . . Most people are unhappy in exile." Hoffman cited the distance from the ideological "struggle" in the United States, difficulty in finding employment, and culture shock as reasons why people returned to the United States and ran the risk of arrest for draft evasion.[141]

In contrast, in "Leaving to Avoid the Draft," chapter 16 of their *Guide to the Draft*, Arlo Tatum and Joseph S. Tuchinsky described the general situation for expatriation and the implications of renunciation of U.S. citizenship, emphasizing that, although some people who expatriated later regretted it and returned to the United States, most people were happy in their new lives outside the United States, adding that if they were not entirely happy, they would "rather have their dissatisfaction than a prison term." Tatum and Tuchinsky also allowed that Canada was the destination most expatriates chose, explaining, "Its extradition treaty does not include draft offenses. It is English-speaking, economically and culturally similar to the United States in many areas, and an attractive land with attractive people and a liberal government. It has no draft. And it is in need of more people with education and job skills, so it readily grants 'landed immigrant' status to those who meet its standards."[142] Chapter 17, "Emigration to Canada," included a description of the Canadian system for determining who was eligible to be an immigrant, adding the encouragement that "most draft emigrants should meet these standards with little difficulty."[143]

Tatum, who was also editor of the seventh through twelfth editions (1965–1972) of *Handbook for Conscientious Objectors*, published by the Central Committee for Conscientious Objectors (CCCO), discussed immigration to Canada, noting its accessibility and calling it "the principal haven for a number of reasons." The tenth edition, published in late 1968, before Canada's May 1969 statement about the admissibility of draft-age immigrants, mentioned Canada's "accessibility and an official desire for immigrants," whereas the twelfth edition, published three and a half years later, tempered its description, allowing that Canada has a "willingness to admit employable immigrants" while advising that a move there should be "well planned" because of the high unemployment rate.[144]

The CCCO offered other books of advice concerning Canada. Its 168-page pocket-sized book *Advice for Conscientious Objectors in the Armed Forces* reminded enlisted men that their military status had no bearing on their admissibility to Canada and noted that several thousand other Americans, many self-described as conscientious objectors, already lived in Canada. The guide acknowledged that deserters could not be extradited from Canada but allowed that they would be guilty of desertion, for which there was no statute of limitations, and warned that "it is not always easy for a person who wishes to leave the military to settle [in Canada]." The CCCO covered similar ground in shorter publications, such as its 1969 memo, "Emigration to Canada: Notes for Draft-Age Men," which reminded readers that young men usually decided to leave the United States because they could not "conscientiously take part in the American military," a choice with many parallels in western history: It was "like the decision made by many of our ancestors to leave countries where they faced a system of conscription they found objectionable and to come to the United States." The memo touted Canada as a place to avoid military service by pointing out, in its last paragraph, "It is nearby, accessible, mostly English-speaking, and culturally similar to the United States. Above all, Canada is one of the few countries which has no draft and welcomes immigrants."[145]

A widely distributed 1969 CCCO memo titled "Immigration to Canada and Its Relation to the Draft and the Military" outlined Canadian immigration laws, procedures, and various types of immigration status, and provided contact information for dozens of agencies in Canada that could assist potential U.S. émigrés. The memo emphasized, on the first of its nine pages, in all capital letters, the potential attractiveness of Canada to a young man with his back against the wall concerning his draft status: "AN AMERICAN WHO IS CLASSIFIED I-A, WHO HAS RECEIVED AN ORDER TO REPORT FOR HIS PHYSICAL, WHO HAS RECEIVED AN INDUCTION, WHO HAS REFUSED INDUCTION OR HAS JUMPED BAIL, OR WHO HAS SERVED TIME ALREADY FOR NON-COMPLIANCE, HAS NO GREATER DIFFICULTY—FORMALLY, AT LEAST—IN ENTERING, AND REMAINING IN CANADA, THAN DOES ANY OTHER AMERICAN."[146] A fourth CCCO memo was a gushingly positive two-page document published in July 1970 called "Going to Canada: A Personal Account." In it, a deserter from the U.S. Army related his experience in applying for landed immigrant status in Canada, describing immigration officers as "business-like and polite" and "very pleasant and cordial," and the response of their new Canadian neighbors in an unnamed, "small, very conservative city" as "Welcome! I sympathize with you. I hope you like it here!" The émigré concluded his account by exclaiming that "the people are friendly and the opportunities are present" and that "my wife and I love it here."[147]

The Winnipeg Committee to Assist War Objectors distributed a four-page document in 1971 called "Canada As an Alternative" that emphasized the welcome given to immigrants to Canada. "Canadians are friendly people," the committee reassured. "Their attitude to draft evaders and deserters is generally one of apathy or curiousness, rather than hostility." In addition to summarizing procedures for immigrating to Canada, the document extolled the advantages of Winnipeg in particular, allowing that while there were tens of thousands of U.S. émigrés living in Canada, "a massive amount of people" had gone to the major cities of Vancouver, Toronto, and Montréal, taxing the ability of those cities to provide assistance and employment. Winnipeg had advantages, too, including "a warm atmosphere" for a city of its size, cultural and recreational opportunities, a low unemployment rate, and immigration officials who "treat people fairly. They are business-like or sympathetic toward Americans rather than hostile." Furthermore, Winnipeg was in the province of Manitoba, controlled by the left-leaning New Democratic Party, which had taken a stand against the Vietnam War, whereas all the other provinces were run by "traditional parties."[148]

The frequency with which the Toronto Anti-Draft Programme's *Manual for Draft-Age Immigrants to Canada* was cited in popular magazine articles and books suggests that it may have been the most commonly used source of information about emigrating to resist military service.[149] It was certainly the most complete. The manual contained basic information on centers in Canada that provided immigration and draft counseling, drop-in centers and coffeehouses that would appeal to young U.S. émigrés, as well as prospects for housing, employment, medical assistance, and education. It also included information on Canada's history, politics, culture, and climate to help émigrés assimilate, along with advice on applying to become a student or landed immigrant in Canada. Further, it contained information about extradition and deportation, mobility within Canada and abroad, and how to renounce U.S. citizenship.[150]

The records of the Toronto Anti-Draft Programme (TADP) indicate that between 1970 and early 1972, it sent copies of the *Manual for Draft-Age Immigrants to Canada* in bulk to universities, bookstores, public libraries, student groups, draft counseling centers, draft resistance centers, law firms, and Quaker and other church groups in the United States, and to immigrant aid groups throughout Canada.[151] Notes kept by the TADP in the draft lottery era also show evidence of *fuite en avant* on the part of many émigrés. A mission statement of the TADP from the early 1970s noted, "Many men falsely assume there is no alternative to the draft except Canada, and base their flight on this assumption. We see 18-year-olds who panic when they receive a 1-A notice and dash to Canada before they find out their lottery number will not even be determined for another year." The TADP felt it was necessary to try to advise men of all their options while they were still in the United States, because by the early 1970s, émigrés to Canada were hampered by increasing unemployment, increasing reluctance of Canadian employers to hire young Americans, and a "rising backlash against Americans."[152]

Young American men in military service or traveling in Europe may have encountered publications of the London-based War Resisters' League. Similar in name and scope to guides published by the Toronto Anti-Draft Programme, the attorney-authored, sixteen-page booklet *Manual for Draft-Age Americans in Europe* covered the general obligations and options for draft-eligible men.[153] Another War Resisters' League booklet, *American Deserters,* addressed immigration directly in a section called "US Deserters Abroad," describing the advantages of various countries (Great Britain, West Germany, France, Japan, and Sweden) that were receptive to the immigration of U.S. draft resisters and military deserters, and allowing that the reason so many American men went to Canada was "the practicability of the 'escape.' GI's who desert or go AWOL in USA find it easier to go to Canada than anywhere else. With the largest number of US deserters and draft resisters, Canada has been called their heaven. Language is another strong factor which makes this country an obvious first choice."[154]

Similarly, the American Friends Service Committee in Madison, Wisconsin, addressed *fuite en avant.* In an eight-page mimeographed document called "Is Immigration to Canada the Answer?," the committee asked potential émigrés whether they had considered alternatives to the draft, whether they had "personally investigated vocational or academic opportunities in Canada"—as opposed to relying on hearsay—whether they had considered that a move to Canada might mean they would never again be able to enter the United States legally again, and whether they had weighed the emotional effects of permanently breaking their ties with family and friends.[155]

Besides the Toronto Anti-Draft Programme, the Winnipeg Committee to Assist War Objectors, and the Alexander Ross Society, other groups from coast to coast in Canada and the United States tried to provide assistance to immigrants from the United States through their publications.[156] Authors of articles, books, brochures, memoranda, and the like could only hope that the information in their publications was reaching its intended audiences. In addition to their publishing programs, Canadian immigrant aid groups often fielded written inquiries from potential immigrants. Such correspondence provided answers to specific questions and is another record of the fears, hopes, and misgivings individual Americans had about their situation.

One such local draft counseling group in the United States was the Draft Counseling and Information Center (DCIC) in Madison, Wisconsin, the home-away-from home of thousands of draft-age men attending the University of Wisconsin. Typical of the advice dispensed by these draft information groups was that which DCIC counselor Bob Tabak gave in a letter to a young man 300 miles (500 kilometers) away in Ashland, Wisconsin, a Lake Superior town with a population of 9,600. Tabak outlined what he thought were the five options for draft-age men: going into the military, gaining conscientious objector status, obtaining a deferment, resisting the draft (and risking a jail sentence), or immigrating to Canada or another country. While "we do not advocate any of these options," he noted, "we have detailed information on all of them."[157]

Correspondence between DCIC counselor Joe Chandler and a young couple in Oshkosh, Wisconsin, warned against *fuite en avant*. Chandler sent them a copy of *Manual for Draft-Age Immigrants to Canada* and warned them: "READ IT IN ITS ENTIRETY BEFORE YOU LEAVE FOR CANADA. . . . It is much better to wait a while longer and make sure you understand precisely everything there is to know about immigrating than to rush north and be rejected for some technical reason. The border is relatively wide open, you need only have a good understanding of the immigration procedures, money, and the correct attitude."[158]

Another aid group that conducted correspondence with Americans was the Ottawa Committee for Peace and Liberation. Much of the mail sent to the committee in the late 1960s was answered by Goldie Josephy, the committee's correspondence secretary, who had immigrated with her husband and two children from England to Canada in the mid-1950s. To a young man who had handwritten a letter that said, "Rather than go to jail I would like to become a Canadian citizen," Josephy sent reassurances. "Provided your papers are in order and you have no criminal record," she wrote, "the Canadian authorities will not stop you entering the country as a visitor—they are officially not interested in your draft status."[159]

A New York City man who had managed to delay his induction into the military on various appeals and technicalities wrote to the Ottawa Committee in early September 1967 seeking encouragement to go to Canada. He had already spent some time exploring largely French-speaking Montréal but did not want to stay there because "I don't want to add a language barrier to all the other problems of settling in a new country." Josephy advised him, "If you are coming to Canada, I would strongly advise you to do so before the cold weather starts (around Nov.). . . . What most boys do, is find a temporary job as a dish-washer etc. which is easy, and then look around for something more suitable. As long as you look reasonably conventional (this does help) and are healthy and prepared to work, you should have no difficulties in settling down. Quite a few people are arriving, and it helps to keep in touch with one another, otherwise it can be rather lonely at first."[160]

Many correspondents asked for information about employment in Canada, perhaps knowing that they needed a job offer in order to get landed immigrant status. Typical of Josephy's pragmatic responses was one she sent to a twenty-two-year-old college graduate from Minneapolis who, naïve about the enormity of Canadian geography, requested employment information for all of Canada: "You obviously are a well educated boy—I can see this from your letter, and part of education is learning to stand on your own feet. With your qualifications, all you need to do is come to Canada and look around for yourself—no-one else can do this for you, or should be expected to! This is quite a civilised country! . . . Your best plan is to get up here and look around—you will find Canadians very fair-minded and tolerant—provided you are the same."[161]

Josephy offered similar advice to a Philadelphia man two months from earning a B.A. in English: "I am always constantly amazed by the number of people who write and ask me to find them jobs—and before they get here. Canada is a free country—you don[']t live far away—and if you applied for a job anywhere, you would have to go after it yourself. The same rules apply here. I can only say that any qualified, sensible person has very little difficulty, if they get up and get on with it themselves. No-one can do it for you."[162]

Josephy showed less patience in dealing with U.S. graduate students who wrote for assistance. She told a man about to graduate with an M.A. in history from the University of Illinois who had written for employment help, "You know you are one of the lucky ones—the boys who really need help are people with no education, no money and sometimes no papers! For people of your type, it really is up to you to make a serious decision and then get on with it. We are very overworked and must concentrate on helping those individuals who have really serious difficulties."[163] To a Phi Beta Kappan from the University of North Carolina, who was in his first year of graduate school in psychology at Brown University, she intoned, "Under the most normal circumstances employers like to see who they are getting—and unfortunately we have neither facilities nor the desire to act as an employment agency."[164]

Reflecting on her own assimilation into Canada a dozen years before, Josephy was pragmatic about the amount of time it might take to feel at ease in a new country. To a young woman who had written from Yellow Springs, Ohio, she advised, "You must be prepared to paddle your own canoe—no-one can do more than give you a helping hand . . . but that is the price you have to be prepared to pay, it is no good expecting things to be easy."[165] Similarly, she advised a Memphis, Tennessee, man moving to Canada to marry a Canadian citizen, "Provided you are willing to work hard and take anything (even dish-washing) in the beginning, you should be O.K. Being an immigrant is always tough—but we think it was worth it."[166]

The Toronto Anti-Draft Programme fielded many letters as a result of its publication of the *Manual for Draft-Age Immigrants to Canada*. David Hughey of Columbia, Missouri, asked for advice for the dilemma he faced, with his military training, his newfound philosophy toward the Vietnam War, and the imminent loss of his student deferment:

> I'm a grad student at U. of Missouri and am in the advanced program in ROTC here, scheduled to be commissioned as a 2nd lieutenant in the army the first week of June. I have in the last few months come to consider the war in Vietnam as completely unnecessary . . . and thus atrocious in its destruction and death.
>
> I don't hate the U.S., but cannot participate in this war. I hope to play some part in the anti-draft movement, but will obviously be unable to do so once I am sucked up in June.
>
> I would appreciate very much your sending me any information you might have [that] I need to know in order to gain immigrant status in Canada, for I've decided to make the trip within the next six weeks, if possible. . . .
>
> What are the opportunities for furthering graduate school education—assistantships, etc.? (in psychology)[167]

The TADP also fielded letters from men who were looking for advice about the practicality of leaving the military and moving to Canada. One correspondent wrote on U.S. Army stationery from Fort Bragg, North Carolina, to explain,

> My problem is a simple one—I'm in the United States Army and want out—How can I get out of this mess and still go to Canada and gain citizenship[?] I have strong convictions about the United States that begin with Vietnam and end with community and domestic problems. I am discontented and frustrated with the war in Vietnam . . . the crime in our streets, the general disrespect for

the law, the racial unrest, the higher tax rate, inflation, the soaring coast [sic] of living and the declining morality. I have lost all trust and confidence in my leaders, in the public and private institutions, and in the traditional values this country has so long held.

My dissent has led me in a definite direction—away from the United States, forever. Although, this may very well be a retreat rather than an advance, may be cowardly rather than courageous, I firmly believe this is the only sane decision.

I . . . have visited your country many times. I contacted your office just last month to obtain information on obtaining citizenship status—your assistance is still appreciated. However, I came back to the United States to report for my induction at the insistance [sic] of my parents. Now, three weeks later I find myself regretting the decision, I write to you in hope you can give me some information on how to get out and still be able to live as a citizen of Canada.[168]

J. McRee Elrod, who had moved with his family from the United States to Vancouver in July 1967, used print media to give immigration advice in another way. A few months after his arrival, Elrod wrote letters to the editors of several mainstream publications encouraging people to write to him if they had questions about immigrating to Canada. The *Christian Century* and the *New York Review of Books* published his letters.[169] Elrod fielded dozens of letters similar to those received by the Ottawa Committee for Peace and Liberation and the Toronto Anti-Draft Programme with questions about employment prospects, crossing the U.S.-Canadian border, safety from arrest by the FBI (Federal Bureau of Investigation), and transferring to Canadian universities. Several correspondents were interested in moving their families because they had sons who were, or were about to be, of draft age.

Elrod also received letters describing situations common for young men in the United States in the Vietnam War era, but with a surprising twist. A student at the University of California–Berkeley, who was about to graduate with a bachelor's degree in civil engineering, wrote to say that the army was forcing him to "fight in an immoral war. And my conscience does not allow me to do this." The young man was Vietnamese, with a visitor visa from the U.S. government, on a training program of the South Vietnamese ministry of education, who added, "All my friends who have been forced to come back to South Vietnam are now carrying arms to fight and kill their own country-men." He asked, as did so many other men in U.S. universities, "Can you give some information about how to go to Canada and stay there as an immigrant? . . . Your help will greatly affect my future and my conscience."[170]

A few months later another Vietnamese student at the University of California, who was to graduate in December 1972 with honors with a bachelor's degree in chemical engineering, wrote, "I would like to say straightly, shortly, and firmly that I do not want myself as well as my energies and talents to be 'mis-used' on returning to Saigon by this time. Chemical engineers and chemists are so famous—and so blamed, too—for their chemical weapons. Therefore, I wonder if you can help me get landed in Canada legally for a few years."[171]

Popular magazines and books of the late 1960s and early 1970s were a valuable source of information for young American men interested in exploring options beyond required military service. Magazines did not hesitate to publish information about ways to resist military service, including advice about immigrating to Canada. Travel guides and magazines portrayed Canada as an accessible and pleasant place to visit—or live. Draft manuals and popular magazines portrayed a wide range of possibilities for complying with—or defying—the military draft. Unflinchingly portrayed in many print sources were Vietnam War–era draft resisters, military deserters, and others who had exiled themselves in Canada. Readers could find everything from neutral, descriptive portrayals to those rife with stereotypes and expressions of pity and/or anger. Taken as a whole, many writers of print media accounts depicted draft resistance and military desertion in a way that demonstrated their tacit support of immigration to Canada to resist military service. They certainly did not go out of their way to condemn it.

Given the pervasiveness of popular press in homes, libraries, waiting rooms, newsstands, bookstores, and other public places in the 1960s and 1970, the press had great potential to influence not only draft-age men but also their parents, wives, girlfriends, children, and other family members, and others who moved to Canada with them or of their own volition. Print media also connected young Americans to a wider, more cosmopolitan world beyond their home towns. Draft and immigrant aid groups in Canada and the United States also corresponded directly with potential immigrants, providing specific answers to queries and creating another print source through which we can view the plight of many Americans in the Vietnam War era.

3 · RELIGION AND POLITICS AT THE BORDER

Canadian Church Support for American Vietnam War Resisters

> For I will take you out of the nations;
> I will gather you from all the countries
> and bring you back into your own land.
> —Ezekiel 36:24

In May 1971, in the Admiral's Room of the Detroit Metropolitan Airport, 12 miles (20 kilometers) from the U.S.-Canadian border, delegates to a joint conference of the Canadian Council of Churches and the U.S.-based National Council of Churches closed their meeting by speculating whether the groups' cooperation on the handling of draft resisters and military deserters who had left the United States for Canada during the Vietnam War could act as any sort of model for U.S.-Canadian relations in general.[1] This was a particularly prescient concern about which to speculate. The resister-deserter issue had been a sore point between the two nations for the past several years, particularly the previous two.[2] Church groups in Canada and elsewhere in the world, even the United States, had provided financial support, shelter, and various forms of counseling to American men in Canada, thus providing strong pull factors to bring U.S. émigrés to Canada. The U.S. government was not pleased with this help to these men, not surprisingly, and neither was the majority of the Canadian public. How was it, then, that the leadership of so many churches and church organizations in Canada justified providing aid to resisters and deserters?

The success celebrated in Detroit was the result of more than a year of cooperation between the Canadian Council of Churches and the National

Council of Churches at the height of U.S. troop involvement in Southeast Asia. The groups had begun planning for it in a December 1969 meeting a dozen miles away in Windsor, Ontario, across the Detroit River and across the U.S.-Canada border, outlining in a joint statement pastoral reasons for assisting U.S. émigrés in Canada: "As churchmen who have helped raise up many of these men whose conscience now rejects participation in the war, violations of due process, and brutalization in military life, we must not abandon them in their hour of critical need. As citizens of two countries which have proud traditions of welcome to immigrants escaping oppressive military service in their homeland, we should continue to honor that traditional liberty of conscience."[3]

Religious publications and records of religious groups on both sides of the U.S.-Canadian border show that there was genuine interest in helping U.S. émigrés as newcomers to Canada. As the sociologist and legal scholar John Hagan posits, the Canadian government, with support from prominent religious groups in Canada, made émigrés "unexpected symbols of Canadian sovereignty."[4] Resisters and deserters were of value to churches—especially the United Church of Canada—as they attempted to prove their vitality to Canadians and their government. The émigrés themselves enjoyed a form of cosmopolitanism in that no matter from where in the United States they came, they were assisted by church groups in Canada that were in turn aided by church organizations from throughout the world in a system that transcended nations.

The U.S.-Canadian border is a site from which U.S. history can be explored or retold, but often is not. The historian William Westfall has observed that "while American religious history has celebrated all those who have come to America seeking freedom, the religious journeys of Americans *leaving* the United States rarely appear (if at all) in the standard accounts of American religion. American religious history seems to presume that when Americans leave the United States they leave American history altogether, lost forever in the black hole that begins on the other side of the border."[5]

It was not necessarily for religious reasons that young men left the United States during the Vietnam War era, but religious groups often aided immigrations. Major religious periodicals in the United States often pointed to Canadian disapproval of U.S. military intervention in Vietnam. For example, in 1967 the liberal-leaning *Christian Century* observed, "By and large Canadian opinion of U.S. policy toward southeast Asia and toward Vietnam specifically is highly critical. Denunciation of U.S. intervention even extends to the highest reaches of church and government in Canada." Suggesting that the Canadian government was reticent to criticize the United States because the Canadian economy was "beholden" to the United States, the *Christian Century* reported that J. Raymond Hord, an official of the United Church of Canada, called Canadian prime minister Lester B. Pearson "a puppy dog on L.B.J.'s [U.S. President Lyndon B. Johnson's] leash." When rebuked by the United Church for his statement, the official revised it to say that Pearson was "a puppy dog on Washington's leash so far as American policy in Vietnam is concerned."[6] The revision was certainly no retraction, and it certainly also was not the last bold statement from the United Church concerning U.S. military activity in Southeast Asia in this era.

At the other end of the political spectrum, the conservative-leaning *Christianity Today* complained in 1972 about a statement made by another representative of the United Church blaming "the American political and national ego" for "the deaths of thousands of human beings and the wasting of an entire subcontinent." *Christianity Today*'s questioning of "the propriety and usefulness of a Canadian churchman's indulging in self-righteous denunciation of American policies" makes it obvious that Canadian opinion about U.S. involvement in Vietnam was strong enough to merit comment by a religious magazine south of the border.[7]

Fueled by anti-U.S. and pro-Canadian sentiments, leaders in the Canadian government, as well as in Canadian churches, found in U.S. draft resisters and military deserters a way to exert some independence from the United States: opening doors to its exiled sons and their families. As we have seen, American men could go to Canada largely without fear of extradition back to the United States after the Pierre Trudeau government declared in May 1969 that Canada would consider draft resisters and military deserters to be "ordinary" immigrants, would admit them no matter their status with the Selective Service System in the United States, and would not deport them if they were qualified to have permanent immigrant status in Canada.

Many immigrant aid groups were funded and supported by religious groups in Canada. The Canadian Council of Churches funded much work throughout Canada in myriad ways. With this financial assistance, refugee aid groups found in major Canadian cities provided basic humanitarian aid to émigré draft resisters and military deserters. Nearly all groups provided counseling on immigration, the draft, employment, and legal matters. Many provided food and shelter in hostels, private homes, or local churches. Several groups provided clothing, noting that men who moved to Canada during the warmth of summer often later needed coats and thermal underwear to endure Canada's colder winters.[8]

For example, in September 1971 the Canadian Council of Churches gave a grant to the Vancouver-based Committee to Aid American War Objectors, which had noted that it aided thirty-five to forty new military objectors a month, many of whom were supposed to be at Fort Lewis, Washington, 135 miles (220 kilometers) away, to be processed for deployment to Vietnam.[9] The Alexander Ross Society in Edmonton helped with creature comforts such as bus fares, phone calls, laundromat money, cigarettes, and medicine.[10] The Winnipeg Committee to Assist War Objectors secured the services of a medical clinic that could provide physical exams.[11] The American Refugee Service in Montréal offered French classes to ameliorate language difficulties for English-speaking Americans in French-speaking areas of Canada and conducted workshops to give émigrés woodworking skills.[12] The Toronto Anti-Draft Programme arranged for housing, loaned money, and ran an employment service.[13] Aid groups did not confine their activities to draft-age male émigrés. They also helped women, non-draft-age men, men who were "unlandable" (i.e., inadmissible as immigrants to Canada), and refugees from Vietnam.[14]

In some cases, local religious groups provided assistance to immigrant aid centers in their communities. For example, the Victoria Committee to Aid War Resisters received aid from Catholics and Unitarians in that city—a two-and-a-half-hour ferry ride from Seattle.[15] Likewise, the Vancouver Committee to Aid American War Objectors received donations from the Vancouver Unitarian Church, and local congregations of the United Church of Canada gave money directly to individual émigrés.[16] The Winnipeg Committee to Assist War Objectors indicated that it received 60 percent of its financial assistance from local Unitarian and United churches in addition to funds from the Canadian Jewish Congress.[17] The Nova Scotia Committee to Aid American War Objectors received support from the Halifax Society of Friends.[18]

The Canadian Council of Churches' Ministry for Draft-Age Americans in Canada did not act in total isolation. From within Canada the ministry received funds from the United Church, the Lutheran Church of America–Canada Section, the Mennonite Central Committee, the Presbyterian Church in Canada, and the Anglican Church of Canada. It also received money from church organizations around the world, including the U.S.-based United Church Board for World Ministries, the Church of the Brethren, the First Methodist Church, the United Methodist Church, the United Presbyterian Church, the Disciples of Christ U.S.A., the Protestant Episcopal Church, the United Church of Christ, the National Council of Churches, and Clergy and Laymen Concerned About Vietnam (CALCAV). The Canadian Council of Churches also received money from Danchurchaid in Denmark; Cimade in France; Brot für die Welt, Diakonisches Werk, and Lutherischen Weltbund in Germany; and Mennonites and Stichting in the Netherlands.[19] The monetary support of church groups large and small and from Canada, the United States, and Europe was evidence of the concern of religious groups around the world about the plight of young men who felt compelled to leave the United States rather than participate in a war in which they did not want to fight.

There are two interrelated explanations for why Canadian church groups were so keen on helping fugitives from the United States settle in Canada: humanitarianism on one hand, and a combination of Canadian nationalism and anti-Americanism on the other. Proof of the humanitarian interests can be found not only in the actions of churches but also in religious periodicals of the era. For example, a column in the *United Church Observer,* the official organ of the United Church of Canada, indicated that aid was given because "once they are here it is irrevocable. They can't go home. They are homeless, jobless, and in some cases, in deep mental distress."[20] In August 1970, when the *Christian Century* reported on the appeal of the World Council of Churches (WCC) for funds to support the "program of pastoral care" for draft resisters and military deserters started by the Canadian Council of Churches, it quoted Alan Brash, the head of the WCC's service division, who stressed, "These men are refugees and we do not make any judgment on the rightness or wrongness of their decision. We help them as human beings whom the churches in Canada are trying to assist."[21] A few months later, in a similar vein, the *Christian Century* described the work of the Canadian Council of Churches on refugees' behalf as "*ministry* to people in need, not support for draft evasion," adding, "we long for the day when the transcendent fact of human identity will be honored by national governments above the peculiarities of legal identity."[22] The debate about the refugee status of these men was taken a notch higher in an article on a meeting of the central committee of the WCC the next year in Addis Ababa, Ethiopia. In it, the *Christian Century* described draft resisters and military deserters as "political refugees— in the same category as the countless refugees of Africa, Asia and Europe" and linked them to Jews prevented from emigrating from the Soviet Union to Israel as "particular cases of human misery" of the early 1970s.[23]

Beneath the surface, however, motivations appeared more political than humanitarian for church aid to draft resisters and military deserters. When the Canadian Council of Churches' Ministry for Draft-Age Americans in Canada was formed in February 1970, one of the tasks it set out to accomplish was to "encourage the American religious community to discover together what it can learn from the experiences of the deserters and resisters" to "assure that the motivations of these young men will be reported and the life they face in Canada will be described to the American public."[24] The Canadian Council of Churches and the U.S.-based National Council of Churches wanted to be sure that the world heard the stories of resisters and deserters in order to broadcast that their choice to live in Canada was an alternative to—and an improvement over—the life they might have in the United States. The groups were not questioning why men immigrated to Canada; rather, they were questioning the U.S. government for pressuring these men to be in military service in a controversial and unpopular war. They wanted people in the United States, Canada, and the rest of the world to know that Canada was the better nation for having admitted those Americans as immigrants. Further, while the Canadian Council of Churches respected the sovereignty of the U.S. government in determining whether draft resisters and military deserters would be eligible for amnesty, it hoped that that government would respect the resisters' civil rights and grant them a nonpunitive amnesty for civil or military laws they may have broken. The council hoped, however, that even when the United States might be open without legal jeopardy to returning American men, they would choose to remain as émigrés to Canada.[25]

Another political aspect of Canadian support for draft resisters and military deserters was the Canadian government's funding of the Canadian Council of Churches. *Christianity Today* reported in 1972 that the Canadian International Development Agency gave $12 million to the Canadian Council of Churches. Ironically, there was also indirect U.S. government funding for U.S. émigrés. *Christianity Today* also reported that the U.S. Agency for International Development gave $11.2 million to the National Council of Churches. Since the latter was also a sponsor of the Ministry for Draft-Age Immigrants in Canada, U.S. draft resisters and military deserters received aid funded, in part, by the U.S. government once they became émigrés in Canada.[26]

A further indication of the political nature of Canadian church aid to U.S. émigrés came when the Canadian Council of Churches named Robert Gardner as the head of the Ministry to Draft-Age Immigrants in Canada. Gardner acted as a liaison between churches, aid groups, and émigrés. The forty-nine-year-old American World War II veteran and former chaplain at Michigan State University attested that he felt "rising furious indignation over" U.S. involvement in Vietnam.[27] Early in his tenure, Gardner wrote a strongly worded position paper encouraging repatriation—letting men return to the United States without punishment for violating Selective Service System or military laws. The paper appeared in *Amex: The American Expatriate in Canada* (later known as *AMEX/Canada*), a magazine for Vietnam War resisters in Canada, while a toned-down version appeared in the United States in the liberal-leaning magazine *New Republic*.[28]

On the United States and its presence in Vietnam, Gardner inveighed, "The American dream has been punctured. The nation has lost its innocence. The greatest military power in history has been ground to a stalemate by revolutionary insurgents. The crew-cut, clean-limbed American boy next door is a rapist and a murderer. A generation of presidents and national leaders have been proven liars and inept fools. The economy doesn't work. The cities are unliveable. . . . The land of the free and the home of the brave has killed, crippled, jailed and exiled thousands of its young."[29] Gardner presaged "Vietnam syndrome" and an era of economic imperialism by writing, "It is difficult to imagine the U.S.A. losing empire with grace. The psychological convulsions the U.S.A. will go through during the remainder of the century will be frightening to behold. . . . It will sling its economic power about ruthlessly. It will exercise its infinite capacity for repression. It will harden itself in every reactionary manner against the reality of its new destiny. It could be that the U.S.A. may begin to be a sane place in which to live sometime early in the next century when it has settled back into being a second-rate power once again."[30]

Gardner went beyond anti-U.S. statements to make some pro-Canadian ones as well. "Canada is beginning to wake up. It is trying to put some distance between itself and the U.S.A. It is seeking a multiplicity of international ties lest it be irretrievably bound to a debilitating continentalism (otherwise known as Uncle Sam's rip-off). Hopefully, Canada could be North America's second chance and model of social democracy."[31] While Gardner's statement was not official policy, there could be no mistaking that the man leading the Ministry for Draft-Age Immigrants to Canada for the Canadian Council of Churches had profoundly anti-U.S. attitudes.

Humanitarian and political motivations also manifested themselves in the activities of the United Church of Canada in the late 1960s and early 1970s. The United Church of Canada is a uniquely Canadian denomination, formed in 1925 as a union of Presbyterian, Methodist, Congregationalist, and other small denominations. In the Vietnam War era it was the largest Protestant denomination in Canada, with about 3.7 million adherents in a country of twenty million people.[32] The historian Phyllis D. Airhart noted in the late twentieth century that "key leaders of the United Church have been so involved in movements of social reform that its national agenda is sometimes assumed to be coterminous with the Social Gospel critique of existing social arrangements."[33] Airhart cited the journalist Ron Graham, who described the United

Church as "the most Canadian of churches, and like Canada, its strengths may be the same as its weaknesses: diversity, tolerance, compromise, humility, practicality, and niceness. . . . Some jocularly call it the 'Church of Christ Sociologist.'"[34]

Publications of the United Church during the Vietnam War era reveal the social reform aims of the church. In 1963 the Department of Religious Education of the Anglican Church in Canada commissioned the journalist—and agnostic—Pierre Berton to write a book critiquing organized Protestant denominations in Canada. The resulting volume, *The Comfortable Pew*, fueled a nationwide discussion of religion in Canada, was a surprise best seller, and was reprinted in several editions, including ones intended for British and U.S. audiences. A second volume, *The Restless Church*, published a year later, allowed people from within and without the Anglican Church to respond to questions raised by Berton.[35]

The moderator of the United Church subsequently commissioned the books *Why the Sea Is Boiling Hot* and *Peace, Power, and Protest* as contributions to the public debate on Canadian international relations.[36] The 1965 self-study *Why the Sea Is Boiling Hot: A Symposium on the Church and the World* took up a challenge posed by newspaper columnists for the United Church to be involved "in the vital issues of the day."[37] The study repeatedly called the world a revolutionary place and called for the United Church to experiment and to "take the Gospel as it is to the people where they are, and speak in contemporary terms to contemporary needs."[38] It suggested work in slums, with poverty, and with such people as "the trouble-makers, the snarling switchblade flashers, the drunks, the prostitutes, the pimps, the money-grabbers, [and] the marriage wreckers."[39]

The 1967 volume *Peace, Power, and Protest* was specifically concerned with the roles Christians could play in world affairs, such as questioning the causes of war and participating in movements for peace.[40] Donald Evans, the editor of the volume, a United Church minister and a professor of philosophy at the University of Toronto, set the tone for the volume by examining the role of God, religion, and the church in foreign relations. Though he observed that "God is at work in the complex processes of human history," he warned that "it was another thing to try to derive political decisions from this. . . . We want to be 'with it,' and what could be more gratifying to our pride than an 'it' which combines the inexorable stream of history with the infallible will of God?"[41]

The involvement of the United States in Vietnam weighed impressively in *Peace, Power, and Protest*. Evans observed the dilemma of Canadian foreign relations as it pertained to U.S. military actions in Southeast Asia, asking, "Is it best to go along with them on most things, occasionally using quiet diplomacy to give the American war machine a gentle nudge when it veers too close to the brink of world war? Or should we take an independent line on many important issues, publicizing our stand and braving the wrath of most Americans while strengthening the moderating hand of others?"[42]

Evans presaged the United Church's attempts to advance church policy as well as the debate that took place within the church between laity and clergy over providing aid to U.S. émigrés to Canada. He asserted that the "general public has a right to participation and to protest in matters of foreign policy" and saw statesmen—perhaps the United Church's Board of Evangelism and Social Service—as having dual roles: "advocating policies in the hope of *changing* the existing views of the general public" and making decisions that should "*represent* the existing views" of the general public.[43]

Evans speculated that while the Canadian government could have done little to restrain U.S. military escalation in Vietnam, the Canadian people could engage in other activities to bring about change, particularly when they were motivated by moral concerns and inspired by efforts to promote peace.[44] By suggesting that Canadians could take action in resisting "any demand for unconditional loyalty ('My country right or wrong')," in "desanctifying" the nation-state and revising government policy to meet human needs, and in demonstrating that "*all* killing in war is morally evil," Evans outlined a philosophy that Canadians could adopt to help relatively powerless young Americans by helping them escape from the immorality that may have resulted from their required service in the military.[45]

Other United Church publications put forth similar challenges. In June 1969 the *United Church Observer* wrote admiringly of progressive church programs of the Holy Trinity Anglican Church in Toronto: "It bursts with life and activity—a noon-time restaurant, a professional theatre, a teens drop-in centre, a 24-hour telephone Distress Centre, an AA (Alcoholics Anonymous) group, art therapy classes, a seminar on urban problems, numerous discussion groups 'religious' and otherwise, a psycho-drama group, poetry readings. For awhile [sic], part of the nave was a haven for draft dodgers." A member of the Holy Trinity congregation stressed the contemporariness of the church's activities, much in the way advocated by *Why the Sea Is Boiling Hot*: "We are like first century Christians seeking to find the meaning of the Church for us, in our time—as they did before all the laws and doctrines were written down and solidified."[46] An article in an October issue of the *United Church Observer* described the thousands of dollars being spent by churches on community programs in Vancouver: legal advice for the poor, a mobile drop-in center for teenagers, and English classes for Italian immigrants, in addition to money for draft resisters. It also boasted of money spent on a home for juvenile delinquents in Hamilton, Ontario, and a "haven for detached young people"—the hippies of Toronto's Yorkville neighborhood.[47]

The debate about the role of the United Church of Canada in aiding U.S. draft resisters came to a head in the fall of 1967 when the Board of Evangelism and Social Service (BE&SS), chaired by J. Raymond Hord—who earlier in the year had controversially called Canadian prime minister Lester Pearson a "puppy dog" on U.S. president Lyndon B. Johnson's leash—passed a resolution noting that many young Americans were "objecting for reasons of conscience to the Viet Nam War," that the Christian church had, for centuries, recognized conscientious objection as "a valid position . . . to state policies," and that historically, Canada had often provided political asylum to émigrés. For those reasons, much in the way *Why the Sea Is Boiling Hot* suggested, the BE&SS encouraged Canadians to provide expatriate Americans with shelter, jobs, and other support and encouraged those expatriate Americans to become landed immigrants (to have permanent residency) in Canada. Most controversial in the board's resolution was the provision of a $1,000 grant to support Canadian volunteer groups that provided such assistance.[48] As there were already seven to ten thousand U.S. émigrés in Canada in 1967, the grant money was barely more than symbolic, as it could have provided only ten to fifteen cents per person.[49]

A week later, the executive committee of the General Council of the United Church rescinded the grant, complaining that the BE&SS acted outside its authority and was overzealous in publicizing its decision. The General Council was also reeling from implications that the United Church—as a denomination—condoned aid to draft resisters and so feared a drop in donations to the church. In its defense, the General Council reasserted that it had already "strongly criticised" the Vietnam War and was supportive of those who were conscientious objectors. Further, the executive committee felt compelled to confirm that the United Church was "willing to minister to human need, of draft dodger as of any other person, wherever need exists," yet added, "The United Church does not consider it the province of Canadian citizens to proffer incitement or encouragement for young Americans to break the laws of their own country."[50]

The BE&SS's proposed grant and the General Council's rescission of it ignited quite a debate within the United Church. The church's offices received dozens of letters, many vocally against the resolution, others in praise of it. The pages of the *United Church Observer* were filled with articles, editorials, and letters to the editor over the matter. Opponents of the resolution and the grant felt that the United Church should not be involved in international politics and should not meddle in the affairs of the United States. They felt that such aid was unlawful, that it was morally wrong or un-Christian, and that it would have an unduly positive influence on people who were unworthy of receiving it. For example, U.S.-born J. Soderling of Clarkson, Ontario, a World War II veteran with a son who he said would soon register for the draft in the United States, complained that "if the Church of my attendance condones the [BE&SS's] ridiculous position on something that is none of their business, my meagre contribution for five-hundred dollars a year to the Church will find its way to more Christian causes."[51] Likewise, H. A. Lee of Port Credit, Ontario, was "amazed the executive board of the United Church has nothing more important to do than interfere with the policies of a neighbor nation" and was surprised that the United Church would "abet" U.S. citizens to break U.S. laws.[52] Doug Orchard of Haileybury, Ontario, accused Hord of "encouraging treason of another country's citizens" and demanded, "Why do you select the United States only?" and not draft resisters from Israel, China, and the Soviet Union?[53] R. C. Patterson of Markham, Ontario, wrote that elected representatives of the U.S. people were more capable than the BE&SS in deciding the proper course for the United States.[54] From Fonthill, Ontario, 11 miles (18 kilometers) west of Niagara Falls, W. G. Rivers complained to Hord,

> For several years I have been trying in my own small way to get our American friends to realize the short-sightedness of interference in Canadian affairs. Therefore you may appreciate the extent of my astonishment and downright annoyance when you, the head of the Evangelical side of my own United Church of Canada, took it upon yourself to instigate a $1000 contribution towards an organization which openly encourages or at least openly assists young men from the U.S.A. to come to Canada to avoid the draft in their own country. This isn't even common sense let alone being Christian.[55]

D. M. Sennett wrote to Hord from Port Credit to opine, "How any responsible organization can deliberately set out to aid citizens of another democratic country to evade the laws of that country is something I cannot understand."[56] In Ottawa, World War II and Korean War veteran R. J. Hauser, describing himself as "no casual adherent of the Church," found the resolution "an extremely dangerous one which should be publicly retracted as soon as possible," adding, "It falls neither within the purview of evangelism nor social service, and is completely undemocratic in that it affects the entire church membership, and can be considered as meddling in national and international political matters."[57]

Many correspondents wrote to question the efficacy of immigration as a protest technique. For example, Wray Hagerman wrote that the elders of Applewood United Church in Cooksville, Ontario, felt it was morally wrong that the United Church was assisting U.S. residents to break the laws of their country by giving them "comfort and financial assistance," while Mrs. W. I. Reid of Brampton, Ontario, suggested that U.S. émigrés should be considered lawbreakers, not conscientious objectors, as the resolution had called them: "Objectors, yes, but conscientious, no! Were they conscientious, they would stand up and make their views known to their Draft Boards and Government. Instead, they prefer to flee here where a few misguided individuals will assist them in finding an easy out."[58] D. L. Aiton of Oakville, Ontario, wrote to ask, "Why do they not join the peace corp, the red cross, the medical corp [sic], or a similar organization and do their best to promote peace? I do not approve of Cassius Clay but he appears to back his conviction and is willing to accept the consequences of his actions. Instead of standing and being counted, these people run away; to me they are spineless."[59] Similarly Jean Conquergood of Toronto wrote Hord to suggest that American men who asserted themselves as conscientious objectors and defended their point of view in court, or refused to be inducted into the military and serving a jail sentence, were doing something "more honorable than running away."[60] MacGregor W. Sinclair of Toronto intoned that "if they are conscientious[,] there is ample opportunity for them to serve some honourable cause in their homeland, in and out of the military."[61]

Others expressed their sentiments more bluntly. A woman from Saskatchewan wrote to the *United Church Observer* that draft resisters and the churchmen who helped them should be "loaded on a cattle boat and shipped to Russia, or better, sunk on the way," and a woman from Winnipeg suggested to the *Observer* that "they should get what they would get in North Viet Nam—the firing squad."[62]

Several others felt U.S. émigrés were a class of people unworthy of monetary church aid. The Reverend George D. Watt of St. Paul's United Church in Oakville, Ontario, asserted in a letter to Hord that if draft resisters were able-bodied enough to be drafted, they should also be able to support themselves financially. Church aid would be wasted on "people who are not real conscientious objectors but young people unwilling to accept responsibility for the total society in which they live."[63] Similarly, from Sunnybrook Hospital, a

Toronto medical facility for veterans, Andrew Stevens opined in a letter to the editor of the *Toronto Daily Star* that "so long as there is one hungry young belly, one helpless old person in need, I see nothing humanitarian in the United Church donating $1,000 to feed healthy young men."[64]

Similarly, the *Christian Century*'s Canadian correspondent, in a 1971 article called "Canadian Christians Primed for Ministry to U.S. Draft 'Refugees,'" obliquely questioned the target of some Canadian church aid, observing that if U.S. war resisters were considered refugees, then "the problem of whether U.S. refugees ought to have priority over refugees from the Third World will have to be faced soon."[65] The magazine's reference to the "Third World" and the word "refugees" in quotation marks in the article's title point to the irony some felt about assisting youth from a "first world" country.

Doug Orchard thought other people in Canada were more deserving of help, mentioning Italian families with language difficulties, Black orphans in need of adoption, and members of First Nations tribes.[66] W. H. Tester of St. Catherines, Ontario, wrote to Hord "to take violent exception" to the offer of financial assistance to U.S. émigrés, complaining that "many of these are types that our country can well do without, much less help them financially to become bums."[67]

In defense of the BE&SS resolution, Hord wrote back to Tester to contend,

> We should realize that the U.S. draft laws are very tough and that it is difficult to secure C.O. status. . . . The penalty for evading the draft is five years in jail or to come to Canada. I don't believe that we Canadians should suggest that young Americans go to jail for five years[,] nor do I believe that we should encourage them to come to Canada, but certainly when they take the crucial step of giving up their American citizenship and coming here as landed immigrants, we should "welcome these strangers within our gates." You will note that our action was taken on compassionate grounds and in the light of historic Christian teaching.[68]

In response to a similar complaint from the Reverend Donald W. Laing of Regina, Saskatchewan, Hord pointed out that the BE&SS gave $6,000 a year for the United Church's Lodges for Alcoholics, which served only a few dozen men a year, adding, "If there are some 10,000 young Americans who have come across [the border,] $1,000.00 does not seem to be a large contribution. . . . Surely a statement on this matter would help our people to keep things in proportion."[69]

Even so, the United Church offices received dozens of letters praising the BE&SS's promise of money, with some correspondents sending even more funds to be distributed to draft resisters and military deserters.[70] The vice chairman of the Canadian Peace Congress wrote to the General Council of the United Church to chastise it for reversing the actions of the BE&SS: "Our executive [committee] has asked me to write to you to express our deep concern over and disapproval of your attitude toward Dr. Hord and the Board of Evangelism and Social Service for their support of young men coming from the United States to avoid being sent over to kill their brothers. Indeed, if the Church had taken a strong stand much sooner, we might not now be facing the horror of World War III. How dare we pretend to be followers of Christ? We mock all His teachings."[71] Claire Agranone of Toronto wrote to ask, "As a Christian who helps 'man' what better opportunity do you have, now, to support those who obey the commandment 'THOU SHALT NOT KILL'?"[72]

The Reverend Bev Johnston assured Hord that Grace Church in Saskatoon, Saskatchewan, saw the $1,000 grant as a "symbol," yet one that could be "a significant, and powerful sign that the United Church is prepared to place its money where its resolutions are." Further, Grace Church felt that the action did not meddle in U.S. affairs because "the issue is larger than that. This is one world, and the war in Viet Nam affects each nation. Therefore each nation, and each Church has the right to do the truth as it sees the truth."[73]

In 1967 a group of women writing from the edge of Yorkville—a "hippie" enclave in Toronto and home to Rochdale College, the controversial high-rise cooperative housing unit and free university—countered the argument that draft-age American men were undeserving of humanitarian aid, writing, "Our family appreciates very much Rev. Ray Hord's efforts to aid intelligent boys from [the] United States, who do not wish to kill in Vietnam, to come to Canada. They will make a real contribution to our country as refugees usually do."[74] In a similar vein, the Reverend Ronald R. Clark of Macklin, Ontario, observed, "The 'conscientious objector' has two alternatives—a jail sentence in the prisons of his own country or a jail sentence in Canadian hide-outs. Human need is indeed the issue at stake. Defectors from the [Lyndon B.] Johnson 'Gestapo,' if they have to spend time in concentration camps in Canada, should have support of the Church here."[75] Harold Barker of the Toronto suburb of Scarborough also equated the United States with Nazi Germany, writing that draft resisters "should be treated with as much respect as Jews fleeing Hitler's Germany. Let us show, also, in as many ways as we can that we dislike wars made in the U.S.A."[76] Edna Hahn of Toronto felt the BE&SS grant was warranted by "belief in the simple doctrine of the brotherhood of man" and was "like a sweet-smelling fresh breeze into a cold musty cellar."[77]

Many other people wrote in appreciation, echoing *Why the Sea Is Boiling Hot,* by calling the BE&SS "prophetic" and "relevant." For example, the Reverend Bruce Cameron, from Nanaimo, British Columbia, on Vancouver Island, sent a "note of appreciation for all your endeavours on behalf of all of us to make our church prophetic, alive, & relevant."[78] The Reverend Ross E. Readhead of the Paisley Memorial United Church of Guelph, Ontario, wrote, "It is significant to me that there are so few church leaders who speak out prophetically today. It is rare to be able to quote a positive and unambiguous statement from church leaders on most of our contemporary problems that people are seeking answers to. . . . Thanks to leaders such as yourself our United Church is in the forefront of public service."[79] From Downsview, a suburb of Toronto, the Reverend G. M. Paterson wrote with "my highest regard and respect for the style in which you have grappled with some of the enormous issues of our day" and echoed his colleague Readhead by saying, "The church has so often shielded itself behind a screen of respectability that it is heartening, even moving, to observe the verve with which you and your colleagues have spoken and acted in the areas of social justice and concern."[80] The Reverend Alex Cowan of the Canadian Bible Society wrote with the encouragement that "I appreciate the leadership you are giving the church & beyond the church, in the vital area of the impact the gospel must & should make on the major areas of the life of our world. Specifically I say you are both Christian & relevant in the matter of support for young Americans who in personal loyalty to their conscience, being free to come to Canada, choose this among the narrow range of alternatives open to them" and noted that ministers "are charged by the church to provide such a cutting edge of leadership in these dangerous & challenging times."[81] The Reverend K. Teddy Smits of Toronto, himself an immigrant to Canada from the Netherlands, wrote, "I am more than pleased that you are waking the church up to a social conscience. A church is more than the display of some piety on Sunday, and Jesus took issue with so many things."[82]

The pages of the *United Church Observer* reveal more debate within the United Church of Canada about draft resisters in the late 1960s and early 1970s. In light of the BE&SS–General Council tussle over funds for draft-resister aid groups, the *Observer* editorialized in late 1967 that "the United Church has a serious problem here."[83] The *Observer* saw that the "ultra-conservative" church hierarchy and the "left-winging" BE&SS largely agreed that war resisters were in need of assistance but disagreed on the role of the church in providing it. In an editorial that pointed to the dissonance within the church and that supported the call for more radical work, the *Observer* wrote that "[the church] wants to have prophets who are far-seeing, bold, and right, who are alert to the great issues in the modern world, and speak up so the world listens and the people follow. But many of the most effective prophets aren't like that. They are often shrill, irritating, unpopular, sometimes even wrong—but they do shout loudly on the great moral issues of our time."[84] In a letter to the editor of the *Observer*, a United Church minister wryly commented on the church's infighting, observing, "The executive [committee] said in effect we are willing to minister to young war resisters, except where their need exists.... The executive seems to have presumed it was speaking for all in the United Church—and here it showed how wrong it can be."[85]

South of the U.S.-Canadian border, the *Christian Century* reported the disappointment of Rev. Hord in the failure of the United Church to take liberal action: "When we need men of action like [Martin] Luther, our church is casting her leaders in the mold of Erasmus, who said: 'I should not have the courage to risk my life for the truth. I follow the just decrees of popes and emperors because it is safe.'"[86] (Coincidentally, Pope Paul VI denounced U.S. draft resisters a few weeks later while calling for a worldwide observation of peace on New Year's Day 1968.[87])

The cover story of the September 1, 1968, *United Church Observer*, Robert Marjoribanks's "Draft Dodgers: What Makes Them Run?," let U.S. draft resisters and military deserters explain to United Church adherents why they left the United States. Their stories echoed anti-U.S. sentiments, citing the immorality and unjustness of the Vietnam War, opposition to U.S. foreign policy and imperialism, and disgust with U.S. political and social conditions. In making such connections between anti-U.S. attitudes and immigrants in Canada, the article suggested irreversibility both in political thinking and of immigration: draft resisters and military deserters shared the views of many others in Canada *and* could not go back to the United States without the risk of being arrested for violation of selective service or military laws. As Marjoribanks had concluded, "By the time he gets to Canada—if he decides to come to Canada—he ought to know what he's doing. There's no going back."[88]

In early 1970 the *United Church Observer* printed an article written by the conscientious objector (CO) John C. Lott. Despite declaring CO status, Lott was forced to go through six weeks of basic training and ten weeks of medical support training and believed that he still faced a 90 percent chance of going to Vietnam. Lott ultimately realized that "being a conscientious objector in the military is the ultimate hypocrisy. A CO simply cannot be a soldier. The fact that he doesn't carry a weapon is irrelevant. He is still a soldier, and as

such, he assumes just as significant a role in the war machine as do infantry-
men and bomber pilots." Unable to bring himself to serve in the military any
longer, Lott considered turning himself in to face a potential court martial and
a prison term. He learned, however, about the option of going to Canada
(from television news in the United States) and realized his options were "Viet
Nam . . . jail . . . or Canada. So Canada seemed to be the obvious choice." Lott
went to Canada with his wife, writing, "Perhaps someday I will feel that I could
have better witnessed for my Christian convictions by going to jail. But we had
to risk." In going to Canada, Lott felt he followed Jesus, whom he called "perhaps the greatest radical in history." Lott dared readers to take similar action,
saying, "As followers of Christ, I believe we too must be radical."[89]

Lott met some of the challenges the more liberal factions of the United
Church posed in that he not only promoted progressivism but went beyond it
to advocate radicalism. As the Marjoribanks article had done, Lott portrayed
immigration to Canada not just as an irreversible move, but more construc-
tively as a place to go for redemption from participation in the militarism
of the United States and as a better place to fulfill one's Christian convictions.

In another article about a conscientious objector that appeared in 1970 in
the United Church Observer, a mother described as "providential" the opportunity she and her husband had to support their son financially and morally
when he decided to immigrate to Canada. Like Lott, she lamented the U.S.
treatment of conscientious objectors but refrained from further anti-U.S.
rhetoric. Instead, she had a more pacifistic message, hoping "all countries will
weigh more seriously the decision to become involved in a war, just as young
people of all countries are questioning the rightness of automatically accepting a call to fight and kill others."[90]

The debate in the United Church over treatment of American émigré draft
resisters and military deserters was aptly summarized by Marjoribanks in his
September 1968 United Church Observer cover story: "Some Canadians who
have never met them call them 'scum,' 'cowards.' Other Canadians admire
them, helped them to come to Canada and find jobs and a place to live." He
finally conceded, "Most Canadians are mixed up and uncomfortable about
these latest immigrants."[91]

A June 1969 editorial in the United Church Observer pointed to the ambivalence of the United Church toward U.S. expatriate draft resisters and military
deserters, noting, "Some Canadians believe they should be kept out. They
may be right, although the Church . . . [has] pointed out that Canada has a
long tradition of asylum for men from many lands escaping forced service in

foreign wars. But the point is that public law must not be negated by bureaucratic regulations even for desirable purposes. If we believe deserters don't make good Canadians, our law should say so."[92] Canadian government officials and the leadership of some churches in Canada had indeed used the openness of Canadian law and changes in it in the late 1960s as rationale for allowing U.S. expatriates in Canada. Admitting American men to Canada, especially potential soldiers, was one way for Canadian government and church leaders to express criticism of the involvement of the United States in Vietnam and elsewhere in the world and to wage an ideological battle against it.

It may have seemed that Canada opened its arms wide to accept draft resisters and military deserters, but that was not entirely the case. A majority of clergy were in favor of supporting U.S. émigrés to Canada—61 percent in a 1968 poll in the *United Church Observer* and 74 percent in a 1969 poll in the *Christian Century*—but a sizable minority of laypersons were opposed to supporting them: 43 and 48 percent, respectively. Church and government leaders exploited Canadian law to admit them anyway.[93] These leaders were motivated by a sense of anti-Americanism, owing to negative public opinion about the Vietnam War and to perceived U.S. economic and cultural imperialism over Canada.

Generally, adherents to organized religion in Canada were motivated by a genuine sense of humanitarianism. They truly wanted to minister to those who were exiles from another country. Many cared not from where draft resisters and military deserters came. Adherents of the United Church of Canada were also motivated by a sense of wanting to be more radical—wanting to appear to be more vital and relevant in a world in which religion, especially organized religion, seemed to be less relevant. U.S. draft resisters and military deserters were an unusual class of needy. They were literate, educated, employable North American men in the prime of their lives and not likely to be much of a burden on social service agencies. They held more potential value for Canada than did some of the usual recipients of church aid: people in poverty, alcoholics, criminals, and exiles from non-English-speaking countries. As an administrator for the Toronto Anti-Draft Programme observed, U.S. émigrés "will add to Canada's stock of creative, interesting people. They fit right in, require no retraining, no special orientation. We're getting a lot of high-status people and we're not spending much money to attract them."[94]

John Hagan's thesis that "the grievances of American military resisters . . . were framed as symbolic of Canadian sovereignty" holds up to data found in religious publications on both sides of the U.S.-Canadian border, as well as to records of the Canadian Council of Churches.[95] In aiding U.S. émigrés, Canadian churches hoped to increase church membership rolls by demonstrating greater relevance of religion to Canadians and, perhaps more important, to enhance their position in the eyes of the liberal government of Canada, a government eager to distinguish Canada from its neighbor to the south.[96] This was a government that was unable to stop U.S. involvement in Vietnam but had found a uniquely Canadian way to oppose that involvement, a way that strongly capitalized on the not impenetrable membrane that constitutes the 5,500-mile-long (8,900-kilometer-long) border between the United States and Canada. Canada demonstrated its might in the world by accepting potential soldiers and other citizens of the United States. By opening its borders to immigrants, yet closing them to extradition, Canada showed the strength of its position concerning the war in Vietnam and its version of North American nationhood while pointing to the weaknesses of the same in the United States.

4 · "KNOWLEDGE HAS NO NATIONAL CHARACTER"

Americans in Canadian Universities and the Movement of Ideas over the U.S.-Canada Border

dear john has gone, he's parting | we both know he's starting |
dear john has gone to mend his life as best he can...
dear john has gone, we're sorry | we all know this story |
dear john has gone, to spend his life a lonely man
　　—song lyrics by David W. Diamond, writing as Colin Pacquettes (1972)

In his diary in the summer of 1975 in Montréal, David W. Diamond reflected on his days as an undergraduate student eight years before: In 1967 he was attending summer school after his first year of college at the University of Denver, hoping to avoid being put on academic probation. If he failed to keep his grades up he could lose his student deferment and would be more likely to be drafted into the military. Nonetheless, he set himself up for academic failure by deciding to take a difficult science class.

All my problems depended from my unwillingness to be in school in the first place. I had not wanted to go to school since the third day of kindergarten. I had rather do most any thing other than go and be bored in school. I had day dreamed my way through all of my grade and high school years and had continued on to college mainly because it was the thing to do to satisfy expectations and to make my parents happy in the knowing that I would make a better life and that they had not tried in vain.[1]

Earlier in the year, Diamond had given further thought to the ambivalence he had about college:

> The classes I attended were uniformly dull and the kids at school seemed all resigned to the living death rather than the real one in Nam. I knew which was the lesser evil so I kept my marks at what was a passing[,] if not an achieving[,] level[.] I felt that as long as . . . I had a C the school would have no reason to make me lose my II-S and I could continue on my scholastic way until the war ended or my junior year arrived . . . and I would have to start worrying about med school or grad school. . . .
>
> If I could have been given four years after high school free from worry about service and war and the like I might have gone to school without thinking twice for I would then have seen more of life and have been more able to support the meaninglessness I found in life at that age. But as it was[,] I searched for a reason to do what I was doing.[2]

Diamond expressed what surely was the desire of many people of his generation: to take some time to determine what he wanted to do with his life, including doing nothing if he wanted to. Young American men in the 1960s and early 1970s often did not have that opportunity. Their choices were limited. Diamond realized that an easy way to avoid military service was to stay in college, but college, under that sort of pressure, was of little interest to him.

> By the time I had come to be in university, all my values had become so turned around and the press for grades, instead of learning what I wanted to learn[,] had so turned me off to learning that I expended only the amount of energy I felt was necessary to get me past the bench mark indicating another distance travelled along my way to somewhere I did no longer want to go. I was trapped and the war had trapped me. It was pushing me up against what should have been the most carefree and happy years of my life, which I felt I should be passing enjoying my studies, instead of rushing from one thing to the next at a pace designed to program[,] not educate.[3]

The traditional time to begin a college education is immediately after high school. In the United States, beginning in the late nineteenth century, institutions of higher education had grown more numerous and flourished. Accordingly, the number of people attending college increased steadily throughout the twentieth century. In 1941, when the United States entered World War II,

8.4 percent of people aged eighteen to twenty-four years went to college, 58.3 percent of them men. By 1950 the rate had increased to 14.3 percent, 68.4 percent of them men. In 1963, a year before the U.S. Congress passed the Gulf of Tonkin Resolution, the rate had nearly doubled to 27.7 percent, 62.0 percent of them men. By 1970, at the height of U.S. involvement in the Vietnam War, 35.8 percent of eighteen- to twenty-four-year-olds were pursuing a college education, two-thirds of them full-time. The percentage of college students who were male had slipped to 58.8 percent.[4]

The Selective Service System (SSS) had, during the early years of World War II, deliberated over which—if any—students deserved to be deferred from military service. Generally, local draft boards protected students because they were reluctant to draft men under the age of twenty-one. They were also concerned about protecting talented and well-educated men and desired to keep colleges and universities from going bankrupt if too many of their students and faculty were called to war.[5] But by 1943, in the depths of the war, only a small number of men—approximately 579,000—were enrolled in college.[6]

After the war, the SSS operated a peacetime draft, and students once again merited special consideration. Men who performed well in college continued to be deferred from military service, even during the Korean War. By executive order in September 1951, President Harry S. Truman permitted men to defer military service if they were in the top half of their class or if they scored well on the Selective Service College Qualification Test (SSCQT). Men could be deferred for a total of eight years to earn undergraduate, master's, and doctoral degrees.[7] The effect was that a class bias began to be built into the draft, benefiting men whose families could afford to send them to college and who could survive several years without gainful employment.

In a trend parallel to the rise in university enrollments, there was also a rise in the number of men who received the II-S deferment from the military for being undergraduate students. In January 1952, at the height of the Korean War, approximately 210,000 men were classified as II-S. In May 1965 there were over 1,650,000, and by the end of the year the number had grown to over 1,830,000, which was roughly 10 percent of all draft registrants. By that time, draft calls by the Pentagon were sufficiently high that the SSS felt compelled to make II-S deferments more difficult to attain and maintain.[8] Male undergraduate students were deferred from the draft if they were in school full-time, making steady progress on a bachelor's degree, and kept their class rank high.[9] And, as was the case during the Korean War, men also could prove their good standing as students by scoring well on the SSCQT.[10]

Male graduate students enjoyed the deferment that had been created for them during the Korean War until 1968, when that deferment was rescinded due to the high demand for military manpower and in the face of charges that the draft showed class bias favoring men more likely to go to college and graduate school. Only graduate students in medicine, dentistry, optometry, osteopathy, podiatry, and veterinary medicine would receive a deferment, as could men who had already completed a year of graduate school, but only until they received a master's degree or had satisfactorily completed five years of graduate school, whichever came first.[11] Men who wanted to complete advanced degrees in non-medical fields and who were unable to get a deferment from the military had to find a way to attend without the risk of being drafted. One solution was to go to Canada, which was easy to get to and culturally quite similar to the United States. Further, nearly all of Canada's English-language universities were within 100 miles (165 kilometers) of the U.S. border and would admit qualified American men as students. Although some universities in Canada are funded by local, state, and/or federal governments, they operate largely independently of them. This gave draft-age American men access to a form of cosmopolitanism akin to that which they were able to experience with church-based aid.

David Diamond did not succeed in bringing his grade point average to acceptable levels and was suspended from the University of Denver in December 1967. He returned to his parents' home in upstate New York and commuted to Utica College, 35 miles (60 kilometers) away. His attendance at Utica suggested he was dedicated to earning an undergraduate degree and was a gamble that his draft status would not be changed from II-S to I-A. As he recalled years later in his diary,

> The courses were alright for my purposes and I found I did not really mind living with my parents and going to school.... The school demanded little of me and I had sufficient interest in the subjects to remember most of the matter on the first acquaintance.... But all the time I was going to Utica I knew this would probably be the outcome of my suspension from the U of D and my loss of defferment [sic], still I persisted in the quiet life as long as I could[,] knowing full well that it would be the last I would know.[12]

In April 1968, the month Martin Luther King Jr. was assassinated and Pierre Trudeau became prime minister of Canada, Diamond's draft board changed his draft status from II-S (deferment for a college student) to I-A (available for military duty). The next month Diamond received a draft notice and reported for a pre-induction physical examination. Hoping that he could appeal reinstatement of his II-S deferment because he was in school, Diamond consulted with his draft board. His efforts were futile. "They told me tough luck[,] but one chance was all one got and then it was in you get and they told me to pack my bags[,] for it would not be long before I would be on my way."[13] Diamond realized, "This was the beginning of the process that would bring me eventually to Canada."[14] On June 17, 1968, twelve days after the assassination of Robert Kennedy, David Diamond was inducted into the U.S. Army.[15]

Young American men in the Vietnam War era had two basic options: go to college, or face potential induction into the military. Psychologists have identified characteristics of the postsecondary/late adolescent/young adult years, the ramifications of which could be problematic for those with such limited options. The psychologist Erik H. Erikson observed in 1968 that the pressure to create an identity in modern societies necessitates what he called a psychosocial moratorium, that is, a period of adolescence during which responsibilities are kept to a minimum so that young people can establish an identity without having to make life-altering decisions. This is sometimes done by allowing adolescents to be in school, a period that is extended for those who want to attend college and graduate school.[16]

Further, in the Vietnam War era, psychologists studied college-age men and characterized a type of identity that they termed "alienated achievement" formed by some in late adolescence. Men with such an identity expressed a lack of "occupational commitment" with great conviction, suggesting that their ideological commitments precluded any occupational commitments. Men with such an identity would seem unlikely to want to make a commitment to the military and would perhaps seek a psychosocial moratorium of the sort characterized by Erikson.[17]

Some men were not even sure that they wanted to attend college at this point in their lives. Recall David Diamond's reflection, "If I could have been given four years after high school free from worry about service and war and the like I might have gone to school without thinking twice for I would then have seen more of life and have been more able to support the meaninglessness I found in life at that age."[18] Richard Moore, who deserted the military in 1969, had felt a similar ambivalence in the months before he entered the military, recalling, "What I needed and wanted most in late 1968 was time to think, time to reflect and time to chart my course for the future. The policy makers of the U.S. government knew very well that they did not want me to have time to think. The people in charge of getting manpower for the war through the Selective Service System, through the draft, wanted my time."[19]

Similarly, the psychologists Lawrence Kohlberg and Carol Gilligan posited—during the Vietnam War era—that there were three levels of moral reasoning, the most advanced of which was postconventional moral reasoning, realized in late adolescence or early adulthood. In reasoning at this level, people see societal norms as relative, not absolute, and not definitive. Further, they will call those norms into question should they conflict with such principles as justice or the sanctity of life.[20] Indeed, many young American men who found military service undesirable or the war immoral rebelled against the societal norm that was the military draft of the 1960s and 1970s. Limiting the choices of young adults did not contribute positively to the morale of men who were forced to be in the military and no doubt was a factor in misconduct, unauthorized absences, and desertion. In addition, those who were committed to earning postsecondary degrees and/or who were in any way aware of their need or desire to delay the responsibilities of adulthood must have felt particularly constricted by the lack of choices given them by the Selective Service System. It is not surprising that many young men unable to deal with such a lack of choices expatriated from the United States, and that many did so with the intentions of furthering their educations.

A survey conducted in the early 1970s by Daniel Yankelovich, Inc., for John D. Rockefeller III's JDR 3rd Fund measured a revealing shift in the attitudes of U.S. college students from the mid-1960s to the early 1970s that demonstrated the influence of the New Left. Many more students were interested in the less tangible benefits of a college education. To this group, which Yankelovich termed "post-affluent," "self-expression, self-fulfillment, self-actualization, and societal change" became more important, as the post–World War II values of good careers, good income, and good social stature, though still relatively important, took a back seat.[21] The Yankelovich survey found that such students were far more likely than "career minded" students to approve of such protest tactics as burning draft board records, holding sit-ins, blockading buildings, assaulting police officers, and shielding political prisoners. The post-affluent were half as likely as the career minded to view nationalism as an important personal value and to view leaving the country in resistance of the draft as morally wrong.[22] While a larger number of young people were interested in pursuing college degrees, many of them were also likely to hold values that justified more radical means to protest that which displeased them in the world, as well as to be so unpatriotic so as to leave their country if they did not want to answer their nation's call to military duty.

A Gallup poll taken in April 1970 showed a similar disparity between the values of students and adults. When given four possible responses to the question "If a young man refuses to be drafted, which one of these things do you think should be done?," students (41 percent) were more likely than adults (26 percent) to "make him serve on special civilian projects here at home" or to suggest (29 percent to 8 percent) "no penalty—let him go back to his usual work." They were far less likely (7 percent to 17 percent) to "send him to jail for a term."[23]

Many American men considered Canada a place to attend college or graduate school. The sociologist Renée Goldsmith Kasinsky surveyed U.S. draft resisters and military deserters in Vancouver, Toronto, Ottawa, and Montréal in 1970 and found that 80 percent of those men indicated that they wanted to further their education in Canada.[24] For example, Steve Wohl, a twenty-five-year-old draft resister from Brooklyn, New York, who had earned a bachelor's degree in mechanical engineering and had been pursuing an M.A. at the University of Massachusetts, was motivated to expatriate to continue his education. When his draft board rescinded his II-S deferment in 1966, he was ordered for induction into the army. After considering various legal options, Wohl decided to go to Canada. He admitted, "I had the choice of going back to school and waiting to be dragged away, or battling the thing in the courts, which seemed quite closed." Wohl ultimately attended McGill University in Montréal.[25] Similarly, a twenty-six-year-old man from Evanston, Wyoming, told Kasinsky that the termination of his II-S deferment was one of his primary motivations for leaving the United States. He ended up in Vancouver, with two university degrees and the hopes of entering a Ph.D. program at the University of British Columbia.[26]

The Ottawa Committee for Peace and Liberation received several letters from men seeking advice for moving to Canada due to interruptions in their graduate school careers caused by the draft. Herbert Ford of Bethlehem, Pennsylvania, had hoped to do graduate study in the United States in the fall of 1968 but changed his plans when deferments for graduate study disappeared. Conceding that "for three years I had hoped there would be no need for this letter," he admitted, "I must now ask what universities ... in your area offer graduate work in History? When is the deadline for applying for fall '68 and winter '69?"[27]

In March 1968, in his first year in the master's program in social work at Tulane University, Steven C. Wood received notice that he was to be inducted into the military before he could complete the semester. Wood wrote to the Ottawa Committee to ask for advice on schools of social work in Canada because he wanted to be able to finish his degree.[28] Likewise, Joel Kestenbaum of Brooklyn, New York, who had been admitted to medical school in the United States, was worried that his admission would be withdrawn because he was eligible for induction in the military. He asked the Ottawa Committee for assistance in identifying Canadian medical schools, "in case I am definitely not allowed to study in the U.S.A." Hoping also to get information about employment opportunities, he revealed how well-educated he was, how dedicated to education he was, and how talented Canadians might have seen him as an immigrant: "I am willing to do most any kind of work. I am in reasonably good health and have an M.S. & B.A. in math and chemistry. I would be willing to farm, fish, do construction, teach. . . . Any help or advice that you can offer would be sincerely appreciated."[29]

Similarly, John W. Perry, a senior at Fordham University in the Bronx, New York, wrote to the Vancouver Committee to Aid American War Objectors in late 1969. Citing the United States as "repressive," "militaristic," and "violent," he sought counsel about moving to Canada, which he saw as "romantic and dynamic" and, notably, full of "new ideas and new ways to discover." He, too, expressed interest in attending graduate school in Canada.[30]

Americans considering university study in Canada could find encouragement to do so from many groups. The Canadian Department of External Affairs, analogous to the Department of State in the United States, distributed such publications as *Notes for the Guidance of Students Concerning University Study in Canada* and *Canadian Colleges and Universities* through Canadian embassies and consulates throughout the world. The Canadian Department of Manpower and Immigration issued the publication *Admission of University Students to Canada*, which allowed that "during their stay in Canada, foreign students help to broaden the intellectual atmosphere of Canadian universities" and dangled the possibility of immigration to Canada in front of them by adding that "if a university student, after successfully completing his course decides that he would like to make his permanent home in Canada, the local Immigration Officer may accept his application."[31]

Manuals that counseled men on the range of possibilities for their draft-age years often mentioned educational opportunities in Canada. Editions of the Toronto Anti-Draft Programme's *Manual for Draft-Age Immigrants to Canada* published in 1968 through 1970 provided a detailed description of Canada's university system, including a comparison of U.S. and Canadian undergraduate education, graduate schools, and scholarships. The manual was careful to note at which of Canada's universities student activists, left-wing students, and U.S. émigrés would feel most comfortable.[32] (In a reflection of the increasingly chillier climate for U.S. émigrés in Canadian universities, such information did not appear in the sixth [and final] edition of the *Manual for Draft-Age Immigrants to Canada* in 1971, however.[33]) In their *Guide to the Draft* Arlo Tatum and Joseph S. Tuchinsky acknowledged the possibility of attending college in Canada, and they outlined steps young people could take to change their status from visitor to student to permanent resident without having to leave Canada: "You can stay in Canada as a visitor for a maximum of six months. You can't go to school unless you change to student admission status (which can be done from within Canada). . . . If you decide to stay in Canada after graduation, you can apply for landed immigrant status from within Canada."[34]

Armed with a letter of admission, an American student headed for a Canadian university then had to prove he had enough money to pay for his tuition and living expenses without needing to work once he entered the country. (Permission to work in Canada was difficult to secure and could only be officially given by a Canadian immigration officer.) Students received a "Student Entry Certificate," which got them into Canada—and, importantly, out of the United States. Similar to getting II-S status in the United States, the student certificate was only good for a year at a time.[35]

At the same time that many men and women were leaving the United States to go to Canada to resist military conscription or to leave behind a country, the citizenship requirements, social conditions, or politics with which they did not agree, Canada was experiencing a surge of nationalism. Canada had received nationhood from Great Britain a century earlier but had kept close ties to its powerful mother country. Proof of this affinity was that most Canadians claimed Britain as their country of origin until 1951.[36] Canada sent troops to fight in World War I at the behest of Britain and then volunteered to do so in World War II. Britain conducted Canada's foreign relations until 1931 and controlled its constitution until 1982. When the balance of world power shifted after World War II, Canada found itself sharing a 5,500-mile (8,900-kilometer) border with the country that had succeeded Great Britain as the most powerful in the world. Canada and the United States had long been each other's largest trading partners. They were founding members of the North Atlantic Treaty Organization (NATO) in 1949 and had blurred the sovereignty of their nations' defenses by forming NORAD (North American Aerospace Defense Command) in 1958 in an effort to detect Soviet missile attacks on North America over the sparsely populated Arctic region of Canada.

In the 1950s and 1960s, Canada grappled with the extent to which it wanted to be a nation independent of influence by the United States, with the mid- to late 1960s bringing many events to Canada to boost its national pride. In February 1965 the now-familiar maple leaf flag was inaugurated as the official flag of Canada. The centennial of Canada's confederation sparked a massive celebration throughout 1967, which, along with the twenty-nine-nation, Olympic-style Pan American Games in Winnipeg and the Expo 67 world's fair in Montréal, gave Canadians multiple opportunities to celebrate their "Canadianness." As the official guide to Expo 67 promised, "visitors to any part of Canada in 1967 will find some manifestation of the Centennial." The celebration included a fifteen-car train and eight seventy-six-foot-long (twenty-three-meter-long) tractor trailers carrying "the story of Canada's development from earliest man to the present," as well as a traveling military tattoo, naval assemblies, a 3,500-mile (5,800-kilometer) canoe race, arts performances, memorial buildings, exhibits, celebratory bonfires, and special stamps, coins, films, and radio and television programs.[37]

In *1967: The Last Good Year*, his history of Canada's centennial year, Pierre Berton linked the pro-Canadianness of the national celebration with anti-Americanness, observing, "Months of enthusiastic flag waving had helped turn the eyes of the nation inward. After a long dry period of war, depression, and reconstruction, the new nationalism was making itself felt, and the old queries were being asked again: How cozy should we get with the Americans? . . . How much of the country's resources can we afford to peddle to foreigners? How can we accept Yankee dollars and Yankee institutions and still retain a measure of independence?"[38] Similarly, the Canadian journalist Oliver Clausen observed in the *New York Times Magazine* that "Canada is celebrating its centennial of nationhood on a nationalist binge," with Canadian political parties benefiting by "turning nationalism against the United States 'capitalist domination.'"[39]

A turning point in the sentiment of Canadians and their government toward U.S. involvement in Vietnam had come in 1965, amid rumors that the United States was supplementing its conventional bombing in Vietnam with nerve gas and napalm. Canada's diplomatic contacts in the Soviet Union and Eastern Europe, fearing that North Vietnam would be driven into closer relations with China, thus complicating Soviet-Chinese relations, hoped that Canada could talk the United States into cutting back its offensive in Vietnam.[40] Accordingly, Lester B. Pearson, the prime minister of Canada from

1963 to 1968 and recipient of the Nobel Peace Prize in 1957 for his idea of using neutral, multinational peacekeeping forces in Egypt to promote regional stability during the Suez Crisis of 1956–1957, attempted, albeit in a backhanded way, to convince the United States to check its aggression in Vietnam. In an April 2, 1965, speech at Temple University in Philadelphia, where Pearson was accepting the university's World Peace Award, he suggested that the United States temporarily suspend bombing in Vietnam as a way of testing whether North Vietnam would be interested in diplomatic talks. In doing this, Pearson was the first head of government of a NATO member nation publicly to ask the United States to restrain itself in Vietnam.[41] Paul Martin Sr., Canada's secretary of state for external affairs, and others in his department felt the speech would not positively influence U.S. president Lyndon B. Johnson. Canadian ambassador to the United States Charles Ritchie also advised against it. Pearson opted not to give an advance copy of the speech to the White House.[42] Johnson greatly resented Pearson's speech, especially since it took place on U.S. soil, reportedly complaining, "You don't piss on your neighbor's rug."[43]

The next day Johnson and Pearson met at Camp David, the presidential retreat in Maryland, where Johnson berated Pearson, out of earshot, but not out of sight, of the two executives' handlers. In 1974, a year after the deaths of both Johnson and Pearson, Ritchie recalled the encounter in the Canadian news magazine *Maclean's*:

> [Johnson] strode the terrace, he sawed the air with his arms, with upraised fist he drove home the verbal hammer blows. He talked and talked . . . expostulating, upbraiding, reasoning, persuading. From time to time [Pearson] attempted a sentence—only to have it swept away on the tide. . . .
>
> [Several minutes later, Pearson], only half seated, half leaning on the terrace balustrade, was now completely silent. The President strode up to him and seized him by the lapel of his coat—at the same time raising his other arm to the heavens.[44]

Pearson tried to make amends but felt compelled to write to Johnson that his hands were tied, that there was "a quite genuine feeling [in Canada] that current U.S. policy in Vietnam is wrong and heading for trouble," and that he could not shrug off the feelings of Canadians as unimportant.[45] Nonetheless, in the summer of 1965, Johnson decided to send large numbers of ground troops to Vietnam, thus "Americanizing" the war and stirring up more anti-U.S. sentiment in Canada.[46]

Despite Pearson's reservations, his administration did not impede the flow of war matériel produced in Canada to the United States and on to Southeast Asia. The historian Luke Stewart pointed to the inextricable political, security, and economic relationship of the United States and Canada, observing that "while Canada could be a middle or second-rate power on the world stage, it was partner number one when it came to supplying the U.S. empire with necessary raw materials." Of particular note in that trade was the U.S. purchase of useful military materials such as uranium, iron ore, nickel, asbestos, and platinum from Canada. Further, there was much U.S. direct investment in Canada, U.S. industries set up branch plants in Canada, and the two countries' militaries became more connected. Various Defence Production Sharing Agreements between the two countries had been in place since 1956, calling for a balance of defense-related purchases. U.S. purchases of such things as napalm, Agent Orange, and hardware expanded quickly with the U.S. military buildup in Vietnam, doubling between 1964 and 1966 and totaling $2.47 billion between 1965 and 1974.[47] The diplomatic historian Robert Bothwell observed that "the Canadian government did not ask where or how the Americans intended to use what they bought, though it was obvious that some commodities . . . were destined for Southeast Asia."[48] It seemed that as long as the Canadian government kept quiet about the war and with commodities and investments crossing the border freely, the U.S. government could put up with draft resisters and military deserters in Canada.[49]

Canada's wariness of its southern neighbor was nothing new in the 1960s. In the years following World War II, the Canadian government scrutinized outside influences on its culture and economy. In 1949 the governor general of Canada appointed the Royal Commission on National Development in the Arts, Letters, and Sciences, popularly known as the Massey Commission, headed by the statesman Vincent Massey. The commission's mandate was to study the state of culture in Canada, particularly the institutions "which express national feeling, promote common understanding and add to the variety and richness of Canadian life."[50] The commission's findings spawned a new national cultural policy, which brought about a renewed commitment to extant government agencies such as the National Film Board of Canada, the Canadian Broadcasting Corporation for radio and television, the national library and archives, national museums, historic sites and monuments, and the funding of Canadian universities, undergraduate and graduate students, and artists.[51]

The commission's final report made oblique references to cultural influences from outside Canada, particularly those of the United States, by saying

that Canadians should have the confidence to "nurture what we have in common and resist those influences which could impair, and even destroy, our
integrity."[52] It also made direct references to the United States, noting that
many teachers in Canada were educated in the United States and lamenting
that "this training may be excellent in itself, but it is surely permissible to
wish that men and women who are going to exercise such a powerful influence on Canadian life should meet and work in some institution which, however international its staff may be, could put Canadian interests and problems
in the first place."[53] The commission asserted that Canadian universities
should carry some of the load for promoting Canadian culture, observing,
"There is probably no civilized country in the world where dependence on
the universities in the cultural field is so great as in Canada. It is impossible to
imagine the gap which would exist if the universities were to disappear or
even if their activities in this field were to be curtailed."[54]

Canonical books published in the 1960s attest to the great amount of public debate over the influence of the United States on Canada. Chief among
those was 1965's *Lament for a Nation: The Defeat of Canadian Nationalism,* by
George Grant, a professor of philosophy of religion at McMaster University.
Grant observed that the Canadian government, under Prime Minister John
Diefenbaker from 1957 to 1963, was perhaps the last that espoused full cultural
and economic autonomy for Canada. Diefenbaker had been critical of U.S.
investment in Canada, of U.S. treatment of Cuba in the years after Fidel
Castro came to power, and of U.S. obstruction of (Communist) China's
admission to the United Nations.[55] Most notably, Diefenbaker had been
reluctant to allow U.S. nuclear warheads to be placed on Canadian soil and
had held firm to this stance, even in the months immediately following the
Cuban Missile Crisis of 1962. Amid overwhelming public and media opinion
in favor of allowing nukes in Canada, the Diefenbaker government lost a parliamentary vote of confidence in April 1963, forcing an election that put Diefenbaker's Conservative Party out of control of Parliament.[56]

In Grant's view, the Diefenbaker government was brought down because it
stood up to the United States. Grant's lament was that Canada could not survive as a nation in an age of liberalism, in an age of progress, and especially not
"on a continent we share with the most dynamic nation on earth." After the
world wars of the early twentieth century, the rise of power of the United States,
coupled with the collapse of the British empire, left no "alternative pull in Canadian life."[57]

Despite his aspirations, Diefenbaker, in Grant's eyes, was not sure about
what he wanted Canada to be, could not articulate his ideas to others, and

failed to appreciate that Canada's élite did not want such strong national-ism.[58] Grant felt that the Liberal Party, which took control of Parliament after the 1963 elections, was too selfishly concerned with its own ambitions, so Canadian sovereignty, as espoused by Diefenbaker and the Conservatives, was dead. Liberalism in the world was leading to internationalism. In Canada that primarily meant continentalism—that is, close ties with the United States. Because of its military and economic strength, the United States would continue to exist as a formidable political entity in an international world, but Canada would be reduced to a "branch-plant satellite" and would be culturally and economically absorbed into the United States.[59]

Grant's arguments about Canadian sovereignty struck a chord with many Canadians and inspired them to seek other ways to retain distinctiveness from the United States. *Lament for a Nation* spurred so much new debate about nationalism in Canada that the topic became the subject of teach-ins, art, creative writing, and intensified study.[60] A succession of collections of essays followed *Lament for a Nation*. In *The New Romans: Candid Canadian Opinions of the U.S.*, fifty intellectuals, journalists, politicians, novelists, and poets were asked to answer such questions as "Do we really *like* Americans as individuals and as a people? Do Canadians feel that the U.S. is pursuing a just and honourable policy with its military presence in Southeast Asia? . . . Do Canadians feel that the U.S. is using . . . power badly or that it does more harm than good in the world today?," with the book's editor and publisher hoping the responses would provide a boost for Canadian sovereignty.[61]

The University League for Social Reform (ULSR), a group of young fac-ulty members in the fields of history, philosophy, English, economics, politi-cal science, and sociology from the University of Toronto, nearby York University, and other Canadian and U.S. universities, along with invited dip-lomats, politicians, businessmen, media officials, athletes, and journalists, compiled several volumes during this era. The goal of the group was to make foreign policy concerns understandable to the general public in order to spark grassroots discussions that would "break the vicious circles which have been paralyzing thinking on Canadian foreign policy."[62] The ULSR's 1968 *An Independent Foreign Policy for Canada?* contained several essays about the state of Canadian relations with the United States.[63] Its 1970 *Close the 49th Par-allel etc.: The Americanization of Canada* collected twenty essays that articu-lated problems in Canada resulting from U.S. "corporate imperialism" and "permissive" Canadian policies that allowed imperialism to thrive.[64]

Likewise, the independently published *Star Spangled Beaver* contained two dozen essays, again by an array of scholars as well as labor leaders, politicians, and diplomats. The volume examined "the overwhelming dominance of the United States as seen by Canadians," especially in the realms of academics and foreign affairs.[65] In 1971 the historian Ramsay Cook charged in *The Maple Leaf Forever*, still yet another collection of essays about Canada's place in the world, especially next-door to the United States, that "nothing more effectively discredits the United States in the eyes of the world than that dirty little war," adding, "Canada should exert whatever small influence she possesses to encourage the United States to hasten its withdrawal from Viet-Nam."[66]

The ULSR should have been pleased. The debate about U.S. influence in Canada indeed reached the public, largely through the popular press. For example, in early 1969, *Canadian Forum*, a left-leaning cultural and political magazine, invoked the historian Frank Underhill, who gave Canadians credit for the genesis of anti-Americanism: "We are . . . the first anti-Americans, the primeval anti-Americans, the anti-Americans with the longest experience— indeed, the archetypical anti-American, the ideal anti-American in the mind of God. There are those who believe this is the first article of our citizenship: to be distinguished as Canadians for the reason of our stubborn resolve not to be Americans."[67]

In 1969, in the left-wing *Canadian Dimension*, which described itself as "an independent journal of fact and opinion," the political scientist James Laxer criticized the Liberal Party's move toward "a rational continentalism" because "the implication is that Canadians should not expect to make fundamental decisions regarding their own society. [Canadians] should operate on the margin of the United States as a pressure group on Washington." Laxer further observed the hazards of the economic relationship of Canada with the United States, warning, "It is in the interest of North American capitalists to weaken the Canadian state and to limit it to the passive function of maintaining a peaceful and secure climate for investment."[68]

In May 1970, Robert Fulford, the editor of *Saturday Night*, a popular weekly Canadian general-interest magazine, recalled the "Old anti-Americanism" of the 1940s and 1950s as based on the simple proposition that England was cultured and good, that the United States was uncultured and bad, and that "Canada, being an extension of England, was therefore better than the United States." In contrast, Fulford defined the "New anti-Americanism" of the early 1970s less as a comparison of the United States to Great Britain and more a vilification of the United States, based on the premise that "the United States is a colossal empire and a corrupt one, and that its imperial designs are forcing its corrupt nature on us, crushing the Canadian Spirit."[69] A year later Fulford took up the theme of anti-Americanism again in the pages of *Saturday Night*, complaining about both British and U.S. imperialization of Canada, observing that "just as our schools once taught us that literature was something written by dead Englishmen, so our media now teach us that important events are things that happen to Americans or are caused by Americans. In both cases the result is to cut us off from our own reality."[70]

As the debate about nationalism raged in Canada, often taking the form of anti-Americanism, the place of Americans in higher education in Canada came under great scrutiny. Men and women were moving from the United States to Canada at the rate of hundreds a month, many of them interested in pursuing higher education, while others took jobs on university faculties. The acceptance of draft resisters, military deserters, and other émigrés into the higher education community created a dilemma for Canadian nationalists. On one hand, if Canadians denied entry to these men and women because of their own anti-Americanism, they would be keeping others out of Canada who also potentially had anti-U.S. sentiments, as demonstrated by their emigration. On the other hand, by admitting those Americans to Canada, paradoxically it would be admitting people who could potentially exert cultural and political influence on Canada by suggesting *how* to be anti-American.[71]

In an effort to educate potential U.S. emigrants about the Canadian self-image, the Toronto Anti-Draft Programme addressed the topic in the sixth edition of its *Manual for Draft-Age Immigrants to Canada*. Citing the dominance of the United States on the Canadian economy, mass media, trade unions, education, and professional sports, the manual warned, "When you consider the considerable degree to which Canada's character has become somebody else's, then you can appreciate the crisis which this creates in the thinking of Canadians. And when you consider the role of America in this process, it is understandable that Canadian nationalists should single out America for their hostility."[72]

After museums and art galleries, universities received the most attention from nationalists concerned about Canadian culture.[73] This was because, as the historian Ryan Edwardson saw it, those places, along with mass media, were sites where "the lives of . . . middle-class participants are often intertwined with the ebb and flow of cultural activity. It is here that one finds canaries in the coal mine of nationhood."[74] The sociologist Jeffrey Cormier also saw the nationalist movement centered largely in Canadian universities, with their increasingly larger, working-class, and more socially responsible student populations, along with their parents, most likely to wave the maple leaf flag.[75] Canadian graduate students unsuccessful in finding employment after graduation were also unsurprisingly drawn to the movement.[76]

Future Canadian leaders were often educated in Canada's colleges and universities. To preserve that which was uniquely Canadian, nationalists wanted students to learn Canadian perspectives on the humanities and social sciences from scholars who were also Canadian. Nationalists feared that scholars from outside Canada would promote the state of their fields from their native country's point of view. Canadian students would learn too much from those outsiders and would not be able to sustain the quantity and quality of Canadian culture necessary to fend off foreign culture, especially that from the United States.[77] Edwardson also felt that U.S. academics teaching in Canada were unwittingly caught by the double standard of having the gravitas that could contribute to nation building (or as nationalists may have seen it, nation destruction) while also being independent-minded and not susceptible to "politicized interests."[78]

The higher education system in Canada expanded greatly in the 1960s. As was the case in the United States, a university education in Canada was no longer only for the élite, and, by the end of the decade, the baby boom generation was of college age.[79] Further, as the University of Toronto economist Melville H. Watkins observed, college-age Canadian youth were not as likely to be siphoned off into working in the burgeoning military-industrial complex as were U.S. youth, nor were young Canadian men absorbed into a military draft.[80] The number of full-time students attending undergraduate or graduate school in Canada nearly tripled in the 1960s, increasing from nearly 114,000 in 1960 to over 309,000 by 1970.[81] Canadians overwhelmingly supported spending more money for higher education.[82] More than a quarter of Canada's eighty universities were established (or gained autonomy from larger universities) in the period from 1959 to 1970. The operating budgets and capital expenditures of Canadian universities increased more than sixfold in the 1960s, from $262 million to $1.616 billion.[83] The number of full-time faculty members tripled during the 1960s, expanding from 7,760 in 1960 to 24,733 in 1970.[84] Canada had too few people to hire as qualified faculty members.[85] The number of doctorates earned in Canada expanded from 306 in 1960 to 1,625 in 1970—a fivefold increase, but a quantity still inadequate to supply the booming Canadian higher education system.[86] As Canadian institutions looked for qualified scholars for their universities, a natural place to find them was south of the border.

Whereas Canadian universities sought faculty members to teach a burgeoning student population but were awarding doctorates only in the hundreds each year, tens of thousands were earning doctorates every year in the United States.[87] Many Canadian universities with open faculty positions did not even advertise for scholars in Canada, opting to contact the large academic community in the United States directly.[88] As was the case in the United States in the same era, university department chairs often used the "old boys' network"—contacting their alma maters and asking for the names of recent or imminent graduates who could fill open positions. If the chair were from the United States and had attended a U.S. university, chances were that the new hire would also be American.[89] In the late 1960s James Laxer observed that "American professors in many instances outnumber the Canadians" teaching in some Canadian universities and felt that they had "little concern for the maintenance of the cultural integrity of Canada," complaining, "Canada has been reduced to playing the dual role of consumer market and resource base in an emerging liberal empire whose centre is the United States."[90]

Spearheading the scrutiny of U.S. scholars in Canadian universities were the English professors Robin Mathews and James Steele of Carleton University in Ottawa. In late 1968 the pair presented a memorandum to their Carleton colleagues providing evidence that the proportion of Canadians on Canadian university faculties was rapidly diminishing because as Canadian universities expanded, they were hiring a large number of foreign academics. Further, they proposed that Carleton adjust its hiring practices to assure that its faculty was two-thirds Canadian, that its administrators were Canadian citizens, that the university advertise its openings in Canadian publications, and that the university work with the Canadian Association of University Teachers to assure the collection of accurate statistics on the nationalities of university faculty in Canada.[91] Mathews and Steele connected the situation at Carleton with that of Canadian universities in general, and with that of Canada as a whole, suggesting that "this problem facing Canadian universities is only one aspect of a much larger crisis which Canada is now undergoing."[92]

Bruce McFarlane and Dennis Forcese, members of the sociology department at Carleton, presented a petition in opposition to the memorandum of Mathews and Steele. They argued that the faculty support instead "the principle of an academic community of excellence, dependent upon criteria of professional and academic performance, and not criteria of race, gender, nationality, or any like basis."[93] The debate was on, and it radiated out to the Canadian academic community and beyond.

Robin Mathews was adept at media relations, especially with newspapers and magazines. Consequently the internal debate at Carleton attracted a great amount of external attention from popular press and its readers. Columnists and writers of letters to editors extended both sides of the Carleton argument, while many university faculty and students corresponded with Mathews and Steele.

So much material had been generated by the summer of 1969 that Mathews and Steele were able to compile *The Struggle for Canadian Universities*, a book that chronicled the first few months of the intense debate over non-Canadians in the Canadian academy and pushed the discussion out for consideration by the general public.[94]

In *The Struggle for Canadian Universities*, Mathews and Steele warned that if the influx of foreign scholars into Canadian universities went unchecked, "The Canadian university will become a truly 'alien' university, for it will be staffed by an increasingly large majority of scholars whose primary community is not the Canadian community; whose primary national experience is not Canadian; [and] whose primary interests do not merge with and show respect for the seriousness of Canadian problems."[95] They suggested that the many non-Canadians on Canadian university faculties gave Canada a colonial status: "The influx of foreign scholars does not merely imply that Canadian matters will be taught by scholars unused to them, unable to recognize avenues of analysis which are of peculiar relevance to the community. No. We observe that Canadian matters are pushed aside and considered parochial, or are sometimes examined confidently with instrumentalities forged in other nations to meet non-Canadian needs."[96]

Mathews's and Steele's detractors felt that Canada should have a more global higher education system, or at least one that included more Americans. Mathews believed, however, that the search for "a truly cosmopolitan intellectual community" in Canada was ultimately "neo-colonial," as it would inevitably draw primarily on U.S. influences. Such cosmopolitanism regarded the United States as "superior, desirable, central, inevitably expansionist, and right," whereas it regarded Canada as "inferior, parochial, and inept."[97]

In the pages of *Maclean's*, the prominent Canadian news magazine, the political scientist–politician Pauline Jewett noted that while Canada was educating an increasing number of Canadians as academics, "our universities have taken practically no advantage of it," theorizing, "There has always been a tendency in Canadian life toward a kind of intellectual colonialism, a reluctance to use one's own talents if other talents are available. For a long while our universities looked to Britain. Have they now simply shifted to the States? . . . In short, have our universities taken little advantage of Canadian talent because they have been indifferent to Canadians? Because they have had a decided preference for others?"[98]

Melville Watkins also perceived the Canadian university system as colonial. He felt the Canadian élite, whom he viewed as always having been "timid and colonial-minded," had neglected the system in deference to British influences and to keep themselves in power. That the Canadian university system should be susceptible to U.S. influence in the 1960s was a reflection of its subsidiary role to the United States: It produced "branch plant intellectuals—people capable of rationalizing the system while having the technical skills needed for its smooth operation." He sardonically suggested that the best way to produce these intellectuals was to "Americanize" Canadian universities.[99]

Similarly, the political scientists Charles F. Doran and James Patrick Sewell observed in late twentieth-century Canada that Canadians who worked in the corporate hierarchy of U.S.-owned businesses were frequently unable to advance in their jobs. The lack of mobility for those Canadian workers was a further contributor to anti-U.S. sentiment.[100] The political scientist Howard H. Lentner made similar observations in 1970, complaining that since so many mining and manufacturing businesses in Canada were owned by U.S. firms, the leadership of labor unions was also concentrated in the United States and was therefore less responsive to concerns of Canadian workers.[101]

In contrast, Watkins advised that Canadian universities should not gaze too inwardly, as universities around the world could provide useful lessons for them. Observing that "across the globe, the university has become a battleground to expose the contradictions and the repressiveness of corporate capitalism," Watkins saw Canadian universities as potential sites from which Canada could wrest control of its culture from U.S. influence.[102] Lewis Hertzman, professor of history at York University, founded in 1959 outside of Toronto, feared that Canadian universities had deteriorated so much that they were lucky to attract *any* highly skilled foreigners. He warned that universities would severely decline if they were not "in immediate contact with the streams and currents of the entire intellectual and scientific world." As had Watkins, Hertzman recommended that Canadian universities look to "the non-U.S., English-speaking world" for examples of cosmopolitanism that could assist Canadians in recognizing models of nationalism that would help their country evolve better than the model of sovereignty and "autarchy" proposed by Mathews, Steele, and their allies.[103]

While he asserted that there was a problem in the demographics of Canadian university faculties, Mathews had difficulty articulating what it was that non-Canadians should not teach. Even as late as 1971, he only could manage this plaint: "We discover that some of the most exciting, complex, instructive material available in Canada—knowledge that cannot be duplicated anywhere in the world, Canadian knowledge—is ignored in most Canadian universities. That statement is true not only of rare and unusual knowledge necessary to a fundamental truth about Canada, in history, literature, economics, politics, art, to mention only obvious areas of extreme neglect."[104] H. Blair Neatby, professor of history at Carleton, contributed to the debate about the definition of Canadian knowledge by allowing, in a broadcast of the Canadian Broadcasting Corporation in January 1969, that "it would be more constructive if we concentrated on defining what is uniquely and distinctively Canadian about our universities. Most of the American professors that I know would lean over backwards to respect our identity if we could tell them what it is. If our universities become American, it will be because we don't know what makes them Canadian."[105] Similarly, G. C. Andrew, the executive director of the Association of Universities and Colleges of Canada, admitted that the debate would be more productive if the educational philosophy of humanities and social science fields such as Canadian literature (in both English and French), history, and political science was studied and defined.[106]

Pointing to the hazards of nationalism in a university setting, Herbert Lefcourt, a U.S.-born professor of psychology at the University of Waterloo, founded in 1957 in Ontario, observed in a letter to the editor of *Saturday Night*, "Accidents such as citizenship cannot become primary concerns without the risks of mediocrity and insularity."[107] Likewise, Bernard H. Gustin, a Canadian sociologist teaching at the University of Chicago, wrote to the *Globe and Mail*, the Canadian newspaper of record published in Toronto, to argue against linking the nationality of instructors with the techniques they used in their fields: "Frightened talk about 'national character' is simple muddle-headed hocus-pocus that confuses academic disciplines with the phenomena they study. There is no such thing as Canadian sociology as distinct from Cuban sociology as distinct from American sociology." He added, "Unlike folk songs and apple strudel, knowledge has no national character."[108]

Natalie Zemon Davis, a U.S.-born scholar of French history teaching at the University of Toronto, was disheartened by the jingoism of the nationalistic movement in Canadian universities. She likened it to other forms of discrimination she had experienced, asking, "I've been a woman, a Jew and now I'm an American, what's next?"[109]

Some *were* able to define what made Canadian universities distinctly Canadian, and, by extension, potentially difficult for non-Canadians to teach in. Unlike the United States, Canada did not rebel against Britain, and so therefore it did not feel compelled to discard European cultural and educational traditions as the United States had. Canadians also included many descendants of the French who had colonized North America in the seventeenth and eighteenth centuries, who had, in their own way, asserted their nationality boldly through French-language institutions in a predominantly

English-language country.[110] And, as the National Conference of Canadian Universities posited in a brief to the Massey Commission of the late 1940s, no other country could cultivate "the rare creative minds, the future Canadian writers, musicians, artists and architects. . . . There are no alternative nurseries of a truly Canadian culture."[111]

Canadian nationalists frequently scorned U.S. draft resisters and military deserters who attempted to enter the Canadian higher education system. Robin Mathews pulled no punches in expressing his contempt for U.S. émigrés in Canadian universities, even when addressing them directly in *Amex: The American Expatriate in Canada*, a Toronto-based magazine for U.S. émigrés (later called *AMEX/Canada*). In a June 1970 guest column, he asserted that Americans in the Canadian university system were bent on a cultural takeover of Canada, saying, "They often claim to be universalists. . . . They think they bring a better culture. For that reason they think they have a right to all and any positions in Canadian culture." Mathews warned draft resisters and military deserters that they spoke "to the Canadian ear, with same accent as all the U.S. citizens who have taken positions in Canada that should have gone to Canadians." Mathews particularly resented the influence of dissident U.S. émigré youth on Canadian youth, complaining that Canadians were airing grievances that were U.S. in nature and irrelevant to Canada, such as police brutality, poor race relations, the military draft, and the Vietnam War, arguing that if Canadian youth were to protest something, it should be U.S. imperialization of their country.[112]

James Laxer made an argument similar to that of Mathews's, objecting in *Canadian Dimension* that the New Left in the United States had too much influence on the left in Canada and had distracted it from issues more pertinent to Canada. Laxer felt the Canadian left should support *Canadian* organizations, particularly those that strengthened Canadian culture. To do otherwise would result "in a further softening-up of this country for American takeover."[113] In retrospect, however, it was in the 1960s and early 1970s that Canada made several social changes that distinguished it from the United States throughout the rest of the twentieth century: the development of an extensive welfare state, the establishment of the New Democratic Party, with strong ties to the left and to labor, and the official recognition of a hybrid English-French culture.[114]

Some Americans did experience or witness prejudice in Canadian universities because of their nationality. Richard Lemm, an American who moved to Canada to resist being drafted, met several other Americans in Canada who had excellent, even superlative, grades from U.S. universities but who were rejected by Canadian schools. Lemm himself had a high grade point average at San Francisco State University and was admitted to an honor society at the University of Victoria, in British Columbia, but was not admitted to the university itself. Simon Fraser University, founded in 1965 in Burnaby, British Columbia, did admit him, and there he finished his undergraduate degree. Lemm felt that older Canadian universities held bias against Americans in general, or were less likely to admit more "radical" students, and that "new" universities—of which there were many in the 1960s—were more accepting of them.[115] Stephen Eaton Hume, who had been admitted to graduate school at both the University of Chicago and the University of Toronto, opted to attend the latter starting in 1969. He felt proud of himself for expatriating, particularly since he had been an active protester of U.S. actions in Vietnam. He recalled that officials at Toronto were not impressed by his move, saying, in effect, "Who do you think you are, you chauvinistic American? We don't owe you anything. We don't even like Americans."[116]

There were many Canadians who saw positive aspects of Americans moving to Canada. Many saw the influx of Americans as a welcome reversal of a "brain drain." Rather than have its talent and youth drawn away to the United States, as had been the case for decades, Canada was now receiving promising new residents and potential citizens *from* the United States.[117] Robert Adolph, a U.S.-born professor teaching at York University, asserted that not all U.S. émigrés to Canada were agents of United States imperialism. Like many immigrants throughout time and throughout the world, Americans living in Canada were often eager to "learn the ways of their adopted land."[118]

Many saw admitting Americans to Canada as a way to assert Canadian nationalism. Recall that Oliver Clausen observed in the New York Times Magazine in 1967 that "most draft resisters are unquestionably quite sincere in wanting to remain [in Canada] as Canadians, and in many ways they are immigrants of the kind that Canada wants. This is one reason why the Government has made it plain that it will take no action against the draft dodgers."[119] Similarly Roger Williams, a U.S. exile living in Montréal, posited in the American magazine New Republic in 1970 that "the draft dodger question and now the deserter issue seem to be ready-made pegs on which Canadians can hang their anti-Americanism," adding, "conservatives and liberals use the deserter-resister issue to assert Canadian independence. They smile and point out that nothing in Canadian law prevents their nation from accepting servicemen still in the active service of their respective countries."[120] The journalists John Cooney and Dana Spitzer observed in 1969 that there was in

Canada "a strong anti-Americanism that makes it easier for the war resisters to cope once they arrive. Generally, those Canadians who resent the economic and cultural domination of their country by the United States are the ones most friendly to American exiles, often giving moral support and financial assistance."[121]

In 1968, poor grades for David Diamond spelled the end of his II-S deferment for being an undergraduate student, as well as the freedom to go to college without the increased risk of being drafted. After six months in the U.S. Army, he deserted it and moved to Canada, restarting his undergraduate studies in the fall of 1969 at McGill University in Montréal. At McGill, Diamond attended school for a few months, dropped out, was allowed to return, flunked out, and was allowed to return a second time. Tellingly, rather than trying to fulfill what he thought were his parents' or others' ambitions by pursuing pre-med studies, Diamond shifted his studies from the science classes he took at the University of Denver and Utica College, to become an art history major at McGill.[122] He finally graduated in 1974, at the age of twenty-six, a few months before Richard Nixon resigned from the U.S. presidency.

By September 1974, the same month President Gerald Ford offered a limited clemency to draft resisters and military deserters, David Diamond was still in Montréal, attending graduate school at Université de Montréal. The young man who had expressed such ambivalence about attending school "since the third day of kindergarten" was now quite enthusiastic about it, embracing the opportunity to study what he wanted: English literature, in a mix of courses on Canadian, American, and British topics. Perhaps exile from the United States allowed him to be an intellectual and had relieved him of pressure—real or perceived—from his parents, society, and himself to be career minded. Years later, as he reflected about graduate school, he recalled fondly, "One or two nights a week I did attend [school] for about six hours straight and got home about eleven on the bus and that was a little straining on my patience but it was all right when the alternative was not attending. And I knew I wanted those classes."[123]

Diamond got a job as a lab technician in a medical center at McGill University in order to support himself in graduate school. The science classes of his early undergraduate career paid off while he worked toward an M.A. in a humanities field at Université de Montréal. He was thrilled to get the job and felt pity for anyone who was not attending the classes they wanted.[124] He was a U.S. military deserter living in French-speaking Canada, attending graduate school and working at a second university of which he was an alumnus. He had been admitted and re-admitted to Canadian universities four times in five years. If there were anti-U.S. sentiments in Canadian universities, Diamond certainly did not seem punished by them.

In March 1967 a group of students at the University of Windsor, a campus relocated in 1963 to the foot of the Ambassador Bridge connecting Windsor, Ontario, with Detroit, Michigan, proposed that their student council spend funds to advertise at Michigan universities to provide information about Canada that would encourage American men to immigrate there. The group, called Info 67, a play on Expo 67, the name of the world's fair to be held in Montréal later that year, felt the military draft in the United States was unjust and was critical of the punishments meted out to those who resisted it. Put to a campus-wide vote, however, Info 67's proposal was soundly defeated.[125]

Student groups at other universities were more successful in supporting U.S. émigrés. In September 1967 students at the University of Toronto voted to make $250 available to U.S. émigrés, stressing that while Toronto students might have varying opinions about the Vietnam War, they thought they "should help those who desire to live without participating in any war."[126] Three months later, a "Faculty Committee on Vietnam" at Toronto issued a press release encouraging Canadians to welcome U.S. émigrés "with friendly assistance, an unhesitant welcome, and perhaps above all, a chance to prove themselves." The committee echoed their students and those at the University of Windsor by asking, "Is it not difficult to reconcile the idea of liberty with the practice of compelling young men to kill against their will?" The committee asserted, "There are many reasons for helping these youngsters who, rather than blindly follow the orders of their government, have sought refuge here. . . . They will doubtlessly make a valuable contribution to our society, particularly because many of them are motivated by idealism and compassion."[127] Further, several administrators from Simon Fraser University wrote to Prime Minister Pierre Trudeau in 1969 to express that they felt that the Canadian government should admit U.S. "political dissenters" arriving there because doing so upheld the United Nations' Universal Declaration of Human Rights of 1948, to which Canada was a signatory.[128]

Many émigré Americans noted the assistance they received upon arriving at Canadian universities. For example, the draft resister Steve Wohl said that after driving north from Amherst, Massachusetts, to Montréal, he arrived just as classes were starting at McGill University. "I spoke to various people, and within two days I was a graduate student and bonafide [sic] teaching assistant at McGill, pretty much the same kind of position I had had [at the University of Massachusetts]—I fell right into things here."[129] Similarly, the military deserter Dick Perrin stated in his autobiography that he was hired as a teaching assistant for a first-year psychology course at the University of Saskatchewan, with a high school diploma as his only credentials. Further, he received emotional and financial support from other University of Saskatchewan faculty members.[130] Christopher Clausen was a draft-age American who attended Queen's University in Kingston, Ontario, during the Vietnam War but was never drafted. He recalled that "Canadians, particularly Canadian academics, greeted me as a refugee from oppression and sympathized vastly with all I had suffered," never mind that as a non-enlisted man he was free to come and go from the United States, despite his opposition to the war.[131]

Through her surveys of U.S. draft resisters and military deserters, Renée Goldsmith Kasinsky communicated with a Davenport, Iowa, man exiled in Vancouver, and a Boston man in Ottawa. Both men were in graduate school, aspired to become college professors, and had received fellowships from their Canadian universities.[132]

The nationalist movement in Canada also enjoyed some success in the 1970s as a result of the reaction to the influx of U.S. émigrés to Canadian universities in the 1960s. The movement begun by Mathews and Steele in late 1968 gained enough legitimacy that by 1977, Canadian universities were required to advertise open positions within Canada. That accomplished little, as universities were still free to hire from outside Canada. The federal government of Canada changed the law in 1981 to require that Canadian candidates for open positions be interviewed before the positions could be advertised outside of Canada. Further, Jeffrey Cormier believed that once the nationalist—or Canadianization—movement began to carry some weight in the Canadian academic community, networking among Canadians began to counteract the U.S.-based "old boys' network."[133] While universities could still reject Canadians as unqualified, they did so under greater scrutiny from the federal government.[134]

The Canadian government also took steps to promote Canadian humanities and social sciences both within and outside Canada. The Department of External Affairs had many years of experience organizing traveling exhibits, musical acts, and academic lectures, along with student exchange programs. In the mid-1970s, the department stepped up such efforts, supporting Canadian studies programs by encouraging universities and other institutions to make Canada an object of study not only in Canada but also in the United States and Great Britain, as well as France, Japan, Belgium, Italy, and Germany.[135]

The concern about the number of U.S. students in Canadian universities was not borne out by statistical data collected by the government of Canada.

In the 1960s and 1970s this information was scattered across several publications, but one can see that U.S. students never constituted a numerically large percentage of postsecondary students in Canada. In the 1960–1977 era, the total number of students in Canadian universities increased by 146 percent, averaging 135,600 a year from 1960 to 1964, 241,100 from 1965 to 1970, and 333,900 from 1971 to 1977. The number of non-Canadian students in Canadian universities increased by 278 percent, from an average of 8,300 a year in 1960–1964, to 14,500 in 1965–1970, and to 31,400 in 1971–1977. The number of U.S. students increased by a more modest 136 percent, averaging 2,800 a year in 1960–1964, 4,000 in 1965–1970, and 6,600 in 1971–1977. As a percentage of postsecondary students in Canada, Americans constituted only 1.88 percent throughout the 1960–1977 period, peaking at 2.27 percent in 1973.[136]

In 1970–1971, the first year that statistics for undergraduate and graduate students were reported separately, 2,221 American men were enrolled full-time as undergraduates in Canadian universities. Those numbers hovered around 2,400 in the mid-1970s before dropping to about 1,800 by 1980, averaging 0.72 percent of the undergraduate student population in Canada in the 1970s. The number of American male graduate students peaked at just over 2,000 in 1973, declining to 1,075 in 1980. In that decade, 4.44 percent of graduate students in Canada were from the United States. The greater percentage of advanced students is an indication of the deferments available for undergraduate students in the United States that were lacking for graduate students in many fields.[137]

Choices for draft-age American men during the Vietnam War were limited. The acceptance of émigré Americans by many Canadians, especially government and church leaders, along with the possibility of emigration from the United States to Canada, provided relief for those who could not accept their limited options within the United States, or its military. Canada, with a university system similar to that of the United States and dozens of English-language institutions clustered near the Canadian-U.S. border, was a refuge for Americans whose intellectual aspirations could not be fulfilled in their home country.

Like the unique, yet fleeting, confluence of historical conditions of the late 1960s and early 1970s—immigration, Canada, and the Vietnam War—that caused many Americans to leave the United States, the relief was temporary. Late in the war, Canada underwent a nationalistic period that began to limit possibilities for émigré Americans, even in the realm of higher education. Despite the claims of many that there was little room for the nation in the more cosmopolitan, universal, and international world of higher education,

Canada ultimately imposed limitations on the hiring of scholars from outside Canada to work in its universities.

Some émigré scholars, such as David Diamond, were able to succeed because they found the right time in their lives and the right place in the world to fulfill their intellectual aspirations and potential. For those scholars who were also draft resisters or military deserters, and who did have some measure of academic success in Canada, the importance of the nation could impose itself in other ways.

As President Gerald Ford grappled with how to reclaim men who had left the country in opposition to fulfilling their military obligation, he allowed them to return to the United States without risk of arrest or detainment for a fifteen-day grace period in late 1974 and early 1975. The intent of the grace period was to allow men to consult with their families and legal and other counsel to decide whether to accept a conditional clemency offered by the Ford administration. Some returned to the United States for a few days in order to rally against the conditions of the clemency, while others visited family and friends, often with no intention of following through with an application for clemency.[138] David Diamond took advantage of the opportunity, returning home to Sherburne, New York, legally for the first time in over six years. After the visit home he returned to Montréal and to graduate school, and he reflected on his sense of statelessness because he felt compelled to live outside of the United States as a fugitive:

> I wasn't really home. I was just at the place where home had been when I left it years ago. Nothing had changed there. . . . It was me that was changed. . . . It all looked the same but my heart had moved, moved almost completely out of the picture and the time frame was definitely past retrieving. . . . Montreal isn't home to me either but I am not so uncomfortable here for I am not in the position of being somebody to the people around me. Here I have no history, and . . . I have no future here either. . . . In this town no one cares because no one knows me.[139]

Diamond had not only become painfully aware of his sense of statelessness but also seemed to surrender to the forces that worked around him, and sometimes against him, for nearly a decade. In March 1975 he reflected, "I was at one time bitter about my exile . . . but now I am less bitter and find that what has happened to me is caught up in something much bigger than only my life or the war or the state of the nations."[140]

As a military deserter, David Diamond was in the group most unforgivingly treated by the U.S. government. The Nixon administration refused to offer any sort of consideration to the group. The Ford administration offered a conditional clemency that could have required Diamond to perform perhaps as much as eighteen months of alternative service as a condition of his return to the United States. Diamond did not accept Ford's clemency because he felt it required him to admit that "I was completely wrong while the gov[ernment] was completely right."[141]

In September 1977 Diamond accepted the terms of an amnesty that President Jimmy Carter's administration had offered to military deserters in April 1977. Diamond was allowed to return to the United States, but his discharge from the U.S. Army was under "other than honorable conditions" because he had deserted. Diamond was not successful in his appeals to upgrade his discharge status. He returned to his hometown, where he spent most of the rest of his life writing, helping in his family's business, and caring for his parents until his death—by suicide—in 1988.[142]

5 · "THESE ARE THE THINGS YOU GAIN IF YOU MAKE OUR COUNTRY YOUR COUNTRY"

Defining Citizenship along the U.S.-Canada Border in the 1970s

In the Vietnam War era the military draft drew a great amount of scrutiny for the peculiar citizenship requirements it imposed on young American men: that they make themselves available for military service, something that was not required of women or older men. The system that allowed men to serve, defer, delay, or even resist military service was difficult to comprehend and was often skewed on socioeconomic, if not racial, grounds. Draft regulations shifted throughout the era, inserting great uncertainty into the lives of young men at the same time they were attempting to start adulthood, attend college, and start careers and families. Many of those men, along with other Americans of all genders and ages, felt compelled to leave the United States because of their discontentment with the war, as well as with U.S. policy overseas and social conditions in their homeland.

Draft-age exiles seeking alternatives to residency in the United States and to U.S. citizenship were on the leading edge of a concept of U.S. citizenship that was evolving in the increasingly globalizing and cosmopolitan world of the late twentieth century. Although men resisted the draft by going to many places in the world, including underground in the United States, their best bet was usually to go north to Canada. There they could escape some of the responsibilities of U.S. citizenship while enjoying benefits of residency in, or legal immigration to, another country that was linguistically, culturally, and geographically similar to the United States and that generally welcomed them.

In the 1920s the historian and diplomat Hugh Ll. Keenleyside recognized the unique quality of the U.S.-Canadian border, observing, "Geographically the United States and Canada form a single unit; politically and to some extent socially they are divided and unique. The international boundary, cutting laterally through the continent, has in physiographic terms no logical or rational explanation; it is a thoroughly human product."[1] More recently, Lauren McKinsey and Victor Konrad, the editors of the Borderlands Project at the University of Maine, asserted that "North America runs more naturally north and south than east and west as specified by natural boundaries, and that modern communication and efficient transportation help to blur distinctions between regional neighbors."[2] The forty-ninth parallel, which forms much of the border between the United States and Canada, is, as Canadian writer Douglas Coupland opines, "the stupidest way possible" to divide two countries.[3] The historian John J. Bukowczyk observed of the U.S.-Canadian border that "de jure political boundaries are not necessarily the same as de facto economic or cultural ones," while the historians John Herd Thompson and Stephen J. Randall characterized it as "more a symbol than a barrier to the movement of ideas, goods, people, and capital."[4]

The travel writer Porter Fox has noted the quiet significance of the U.S.-Canada border, observing that "politicians, federal agents, pundits, and most Americans focus on the line with Mexico, even though its northern cousin is more than twice its length and many times more porous." Nine times more U.S. Customs and Border Protection agents patrol the Mexican border than the Canadian border, yet, Fox adds, the only known terrorists to cross into the United States by land came from Canada, and tens of billions of dollars of drugs and ten thousand illegal immigrants enter over that border every year.[5] The political scientist James Laxer, though, saw the U.S.-Canadian border as psychologically emblematic of international boundaries that allow people to escape from governments and their laws, observing, "Having a border handy to allow for flight has always been valued by freedom seekers (and by criminals) the world over."[6] Tens of thousands of Americans recognized cultural connections between the United States and Canada and that the countries' shared border was largely unguarded and was more a symbolic than physical barrier for movement. In the Vietnam War era, a short trip across the border could take American men a long way toward acquiring citizenship rights and duties that were more consistent with their values.

While it was generally easy to move from the United States to Canada in the Vietnam War era, American émigrés still had to deal with the matrix of laws concerning immigration that were in place in the two countries in the 1960s and 1970s. Canada was one of few places in the world where American men could go without risk of extradition to the United States. Americans could drive, take a bus or train, fly, bike, canoe, walk, or hitchhike to Canada. When they got to the border they did not need a passport to gain entry into Canada. Canada was an encouraging place to go, not only because of its proximity to, and cultural similarities with, the United States—qualities promoted heavily in tourist literature of the era—but also because of an apparently unique law on the books in Canada from July 1967 to November 1972, a time span largely coincident with the Vietnam War. During that time, people who entered Canada describing themselves as visitors could thereafter apply to be an immigrant from *within* Canada.[7] They did not have to go to any expense, risk, or effort to apply to immigrate from a consulate or embassy in their home countries. With this law, the Canadian government affirmed that a good citizen could be someone who showed interest in Canada by traveling there and who made an effort to acquire legal immigrant status while there. Canada particularly viewed Americans as potential, good, new Canadian citizens.[8] While the immigration act passed in October 1967 attempted to make a potential immigrant's race and gender irrelevant, it underscored the sentiment that a good, new Canadian was between eighteen and thirty-five years of age, had at least a high school education, could speak English, and was likely to find and hold down a job—all likely attributes of draft-age American men.[9] Officially, the door was wide open for many draft-age Americans to become new Canadians. More important, unlike the United States, Canada did not require its young men to serve in the military. It made no different demands on them than it did on its other adult citizens.

As more Americans made their way into Canada, inconsistent enforcement of Canadian immigration policy became problematic, and public debate over the matter was reflected in the popular press, parliamentary debate, and much hand wringing by the Canadian Department of Manpower and Immigration.[10] Prior to January 1968, Canada generally did not admit people known to be in active military service as immigrants. The practice changed to allow people in active military service for another country to apply for landed immigrant status if they applied from within Canada. On July 29, 1968, the rules changed to make it possible for people in active military service to apply to immigrate to Canada at the Canadian border or at a Canadian immigration office outside of Canada, but only at the discretion of the agent considering the potential immigrant's case. While the Canadian government officially supported U.S. immigration to Canada, individual immigration officers had wide latitude to interpret and enforce laws as they wished, often taking matters into their own hands by refusing to provide necessary forms, breaking and making up rules to exclude Americans, or trying to talk Americans out of immigrating. Officers—often immigrants themselves and/or World War II veterans—told Americans that immigrants from other countries were more worthy than they were. Some officials felt that people caught up in other crises of the era were more deserving of admittance as potential immigrants to Canada. Officials berated émigrés with comments such as, "I hate the son of a bitch who refuses to serve his own country" and asking, "What are you scum coming up here for, anyway?"[11] Those responsible for enforcing Canadian immigration law also found less concrete clauses in it as grounds for excluding foreigners, such as "peculiar customs, habits, modes of life or methods of holding property," "unsuitability . . . to the climatic, economic, social, industrial, educational, labour, health or other conditions," and "probable inability to become readily assimilated or to assume the duties and responsibilities of Canadian citizenship within a reasonable time."[12] This led to a difference in treatment of applicants for immigration to Canada, depending on whether they were applying from within or outside of Canada. Officials felt compelled to establish a policy that was in conformity with the 1967 immigration law and "based on the principles of nondiscrimination and universality."[13]

In May 1969, Allan MacEachen, the minister of manpower and immigration, made an announcement that "membership in the armed service of another country . . . will not be a factor in determining the eligibility of persons applying for . . . immigrant status in Canada. . . . If a serviceman from another country meets our immigration criteria, he will not be turned down because he is still in the active service of his country."[14] Further, Canada would refuse to extradite U.S. draft resisters and military deserters, because it did not want to put itself in the position of interpreting or enforcing U.S. laws.[15] While this announcement might have seemed like an inevitability, considering the modifications in immigration regulations in the previous year, a confidential memorandum showed that the Department of Manpower and Immigration had considered suggesting that Parliament pass a law *excluding* people in the military of other countries from immigrating to Canada.[16]

After men made their way to Canada, it looked hopeless that they would ever be able to return to the United States. Many had not been able to abide by a requirement of U.S. citizenship enforced by the Lyndon B. Johnson administration in the mid- to late 1960s that young men had to serve in the U.S. military in Southeast Asia or wherever else it had a military presence in other parts of the world. Enforcement of that requirement did not waver with Richard Nixon in the White House. Nixon commented frequently on draft resisters and military deserters while seeking reelection as president in 1972. Whereas Democratic Party presidential frontrunner George McGovern advocated an unconditional amnesty, Nixon took a different tack, telling CBS television news correspondent Dan Rather in January 1972, "We always . . . under our system, provide amnesty. . . . I for one would be very liberal with regard to amnesty, but not while there are Americans in Vietnam fighting to serve their country and defend their country, and not while POW's are held by the enemy. After that, we would consider it."[17] Later in the summer Nixon hardened his stance. In an August 29 press conference in his hometown of San Clemente, California, he said, "It is my view, and I hold it very strongly, that those who chose to desert the United States or to break the law by dodging the draft have to pay the penalty for breaking the law and deserting the United States before they can obtain amnesty or pardon, or whatever you want to call it. . . . I say: Pay a penalty; others paid with their lives."[18] Later in the campaign season, Nixon said that to offer amnesty to resisters and deserters would have made a mockery of those who served: "It would not be fair," and it could be "no greater insult to the memories of those who have fought and died, to the memories of those who have served."[19] Ultimately Nixon viewed unwillingness to serve in the military as emblematic of national weakness, making this analogy clear in a campaign stop in Greensboro, North Carolina, the Saturday before the election, when he strung together the following three sentences: "We stand for peace with honor versus peace with surrender. We stand for a strong America versus a weak America. We stand for no amnesty for draft dodgers and deserters."[20] Even after his reelection Nixon further asserted that if he gave an amnesty, there could be no viable armed forces in the United States in the future.[21] Nixon said several times that those who had served or died or were prisoners of war in Vietnam had paid a price for their service and that those who resisted service had to pay a price: "not a junket in the Peace Corps, or something like that," but "a criminal penalty for disobeying the laws of the United States." While Nixon asserted that draft resisters and military deserters had a price to pay to the nation, he was unwilling or unable to articulate what it would take to be a citizen again, saying only that "if they don't want to return, they are certainly welcome to stay in any country that welcomes them," thus leaving thousands of American men in the limbo of self-exile.[22]

Meanwhile in Canada, immigrants were arriving from all over the world at the rate of thousands a week, not declaring their intention to immigrate until they reached the border—as the law allowed them to.[23] While many of the new arrivals would not be admissible as immigrants to Canada, due to such factors as their age or medical condition, they were allowed to remain there while they appealed their case.

In the summer of 1972, Bryce Mackasey, the minister of manpower and immigration from January to November of that year, noted the reasons for, and problems with, the immigration policy that had been in place in Canada since 1967. The regulations had been intended to boost the economic and cultural growth of the country and to eliminate "what may have been unintentional discrimination under the earlier systems" that might have weighed a potential immigrants' race, color, creed, or gender against them. The problem with the policy, as Mackasey saw it, was that "no one could have forecast the tremendous impact jet-age world travel would have on Immigration," which had led to an unexpectedly high volume of immigrants and an inability to cope with the accompanying high number of appeals from people deemed ineligible to remain in Canada—about 13,500 people in June 1972.[24] The debate about immigration procedures and plans to introduce new immigration legislation in the next session of Parliament sparked an uptick in immigration to Canada, particularly from the West Indies and India, in the summer and fall of 1972, with 4,500 potential immigrants arriving in the Toronto airport in just one October weekend.[25]

By autumn 1972, the nine-person immigration appeals board faced a backlog of twenty thousand appeals that looked to take seven years to clear up.[26] The Liberal Party government, under Pierre Trudeau, was taking a beating over its liberal immigration policy, particularly amid rising unemployment.[27] On November 3, 1972, four days after parliamentary elections narrowly returned Trudeau for a second term as prime minister—but without a majority for his Liberal Party—and four days before Richard Nixon was elected in a landslide to a second term as president, the Canadian government rescinded its policy of allowing applications for immigrant status from within Canada.[28] Thousands of U.S. draft resisters and military deserters, and others from around the world who were in Canada but had not yet declared their intention to immigrate there, were plunged into further legal ambiguity. People who wanted to immigrate to Canada now had to apply at the embassy or at a consulate or apply in writing to the immigration department in Ottawa. A personal interview, which had yielded immigrants vital points in the past, was no longer a part of the process, so the applicant had to have a very good occupational and/or educational record. A response could take up to a year to arrive. This could be a long wait for a person uncomfortable about being in their home country and was untenable for a young man with a notice for induction into the U.S. military in hand.[29]

While the Trudeau administration had defended its liberal immigration policy as "typical of the Canadian concern for people of other lands," it lamented that its end was brought about by "too much faith in human honesty" and the abuse of "decent and generous legislation."[30] Opponents of the policy change complained that it was racist and was intended to target immigrants from Africa, Asia, Latin America, and the Caribbean.[31] Lincoln M. Alexander, a Progressive Conservative Party member of Parliament whose parents were born in the Caribbean, complained about "the government's lack of interest in the area of immigration," noting that in the Liberals' eleven years of control of Parliament, there had been ten different ministers of immigration. Further, Alexander viewed the Canadian immigration appeals court's backlog of cases as inept as the worst courts in the Jim Crow U.S. South.[32]

Amid complaints and fears that the unexpected change in immigration policy left émigrés to face strife if they were forced to return to their native countries, religious groups, immigrant groups, and U.S. exiles appealed to the Canadian government to get those people out of limbo.[33] On opening day of the newly elected Parliament in January 1973, 150 opponents of the rule change picketed on Parliament Hill in Ottawa and presented members of Parliament with a petition with two thousand signatures.[34] Typical of opponents' sentiments about the change were those of members of the Quaker Social Concerns Committee of Vancouver, who wrote to Trudeau on behalf of U.S. draft resisters and military deserters, imploring, "These young men share our language, much of our culture and our values. Their unwillingness to kill in a war which they—and many others around the world—view as brutal and unjust should surely not prejudice their eligibility for Immigrant Status in Canada.... Is it logical to deny Immigrant Status to English[-]speaking young Americans who have opposed, at great personal cost, what they sincerely believe to be the gross misuse of American military power in the Third World?"[35] Similarly, the National Interreligious Service Board for Conscientious Objectors and the Canadian Coalition of War Resistors warned that the new immigration rules would force many U.S. draft resisters and military deserters to go underground in Canada out of fear they would be discovered and deported.[36]

The Canadian government acceded to such concerns, allowing anyone who had arrived in Canada before November 30, 1972, and who did not have proper legal papers to come out from underground during a sixty-day grace period during the fall of 1973 (Figure 5.1).[37] Canada reserved the right to block the immigration of people such as the sick or disabled, members of subversive groups, people leading lives of moral turpitude, and the like, who would not have been admitted under Canadian immigration regulations had they presented themselves at the border as immigrants rather than tourists. Because of such restrictions, some participants in the program were fearful of being deported. There was no right of appeal, so much was at stake when they applied. However, Robert Andras, immigration minister since November 1972, reassured resisters and deserters that their reasons for coming to Canada would not be held against them, saying in an interview, "We don't want roundups. We don't want appeals. We want to see people get landed," and in a press release, "I hope you will take my word for it that we have no intention whatever of being punitive. We want the people involved to come forward, not so that we can 'get our hands on them,' but rather so we can give them a proper start in Canada and relieve them of the doubts and anxieties under which they must now be living." Other immigration officials hinted at the compassion they would show to those who had come to Canada by admitting to the press, "If they're breathing, they're in!"[38] AMEX/Canada, the immigrant aid group for Americans in Canada, recognized that high unemployment since 1970 had made immigration to Canada difficult for many. The group was confident about officials' promises and cautiously encouraged American men in Canada to participate in the Canadian government's immigration status adjustment plan (Figure 5.2).[39]

The Canadian Department of Manpower and Immigration, with the aid of the Canadian Coalition of War Resistors, an amalgam of U.S. émigré aid groups, launched a massive public relations campaign to alert illegal aliens to the immigration adjustment program.[40] The group operated counseling offices in Vancouver, Calgary, Edmonton, Regina, Winnipeg, Toronto, Ottawa, Montréal, and Halifax. Staff members distributed leaflets and appeared on radio and television. They created a sixty-second public service announcement for television featuring the Canadian folk singer Ian Tyson. They ran

COP.CA.MP.972
Copy 2

MP 23

FIGURE 5.1. The Canadian Department of Manpower and Immigration created posters, such as this one with tear-off coupons, along with brochures and newspaper advertisements, as part of a major public relations campaign to alert illegal aliens to its 1973 immigration adjustment program. © Government of Canada. Reproduced with the permission of Library and Archives Canada (2022). (Source: Library and Archives Canada/OCLC 1007197837.)

FIGURE 5.2. Mark Satin (far left) counseling Americans in offices of the Toronto
Anti-Draft Programme (TADP) in August 1967. The TADP was Canada's largest
organization providing pre-emigration counseling and post-immigration services to
American émigrés in Canada in the Vietnam War era. Photo by Laura Jones.
(Courtesy of Laura Jones and Bennett Jones Phillips, Baldwin Street Gallery,
http://www.baldwinstreetgallery.com)

advertisements in nearly a hundred mainstream and underground newspapers in Canada. They contacted agencies, such as hostels and shelters for
youth and transients, that might communicate with U.S. émigrés.. Evoking
the train and tractor trailers traversing Canada during the centennial celebrations of 1967, staff members drove a bus with signs reading "LAST CHANCE
FOR LANDED IMMIGRANT STATUS" painted on its sides, stopping in over fifty
towns and cities between Toronto and Victoria, British Columbia, focusing
on places frequented by transient youth, to draw attention to, and to distrib-
ute information about, the upcoming change in immigration laws.[41] Officials
placed ads on mass transit vehicles and distributed materials at the Canadian
National Exhibition fair in Toronto through an exhibit by CHIN, a local mul-
tilingual radio station.[42] The Toronto Anti-Draft Programme published a
short manual and posters and revised its sixth (and last) edition of *Manual for
Draft-Age Immigrants to Canada* with information about the sixty-day grace
period, warning it "could be your LAST CHANCE TO GET LANDED INSIDE OF
CANADA. However, it's tricky and not that simple and WILL not affect every-

one the same. So, SEE US FIRST before applying during this 60-day period of grace."[43]

During that period, church groups renewed their support for U.S. émigrés (Figure 5.3). The Canadian Council of Churches produced public service announcements for radio and television featuring the musicians Jesse Winchester (who had moved from the United States to Canada to resist the draft), Ian Tyson, and Joan Baez.[44] Steve Trimm of upstate New York, living in Hamilton, Ontario, was attracted to the immigrant program after the Canadian folk singer Buffy Sainte-Marie lent her 1965 song "Welcome, Welcome Emigrante" to the campaign. Trimm recalled that "when I heard her voice on the radio, saying, in effect, that it was safe for illegal immigrants to step out of hiding, this is what tipped the scales for me. Sainte-Marie's politics were my own. She would not vouch for the Canadian government's promise of a safe haven unless she believed it. With this song, I decided to come up from the underground."[45]

The United Church of Canada, which had been so active in welcoming and accommodating U.S. émigrés to Canada, supported the sixty-day grace period, naturally. N. Bruce McLeod, moderator of the United Church, reflected the position of the church by enthusing in a press release, "While the new provisions apply to persons from many countries who are staying in Canada illegally, we are delighted that they apply to American war resisters who, in most cases, have made a fine contribution to Canadian life."[46] In the United States, the National Council of Churches assured its contacts of its continuing interest in U.S. émigrés in Canada and that it would enthusiastically contribute money to the efforts to contact them about the grace period, stating, "The funds which have been given by the churches for this program have come from the Emergency Relief / Refugee type of funds. This is where big money is to be found within the churches which can be released fairly quickly . . . as the proper church bureaucrats were convinced that this program was essentially a program to ease the plight of a group of refugees." Further, the council wrote letters to editors of newspapers and magazines to publicize the program, urging readers to contact U.S. émigrés in Canada to encourage them to legalize their status with the Canadian government. The council's suggestion that alerting American men to the program would be "a true service to the prospect of peace with ourselves" reveals its ongoing interest in helping the United States heal from the internal conflicts that resulted from its decades-long involvement in Southeast Asia.[47]

In print publicity such as posters and newspaper advertisements, concerned groups extolled the many benefits of staying in Canada, emphasizing, "These are the things you gain if you make our country your country." Émigrés could

FIGURE 5.3. The Yellow Door in Montréal was one of many religion-based organizations in Canada that endeavored in various ways to alert illegal immigrants, including U.S. Vietnam War draft resisters and military deserters, to Canada's 1973 immigration adjustment program. Jack Pocock Memorial Collection, Thomas Fisher Rare Book Library, University of Toronto.

easily convert their status from illegal immigrant to welcome newcomer. They would have better job opportunities, as well as the right to remain with their families and in their communities. They would eventually have the right to vote and to travel the world on a Canadian passport.[48] From the perspective of exiled U.S. draft resisters and military deserters, such assurances held greater promise than returning to the United States, where they would face the possibility of a jail sentence or a less-than-honorable discharge from the military. In Canada, U.S. émigrés would regain rights and freedoms lost upon exit from the United States. The message continued to be that a good new Canadian citizen could be anyone who had made an effort to get to Canada. In the fall of 1973, adherence to rules during the grace period seemed more important than one's motivation for being in Canada.

As was the case in the late 1960s, the Ministry of Manpower and Immigration sought to clarify that Canadian immigration laws applied to U.S. draft resisters and military deserters in the same ways that they applied to other immigrants to Canada. In an August 30, 1973, memorandum to Prime Minister Pierre Trudeau, immigration minister Robert Andras opined that such Americans were not refugees as defined by the United Nations' 1951 convention relating to the status of refugees and its 1967 protocol, to which Canada had been a signatory since 1969. But because Canada had treated those Americans as an exceptional case during most of the Vietnam War era, they would be accorded the same treatment as all other illegal immigrants under the rules of the adjustment of status program.[49]

Yet there was much distrust of the adjustment of the status program, borne out of fear that it was designed to flush out illegal immigrants in order to prosecute, imprison, or deport them. For draft resisters and military deserters from the United States, this distrust was perhaps a reflection of the many changes in Canadian immigration laws in the previous five years. Late in the sixty-day program, leaders of the Vancouver Committee to Aid American War Objectors wrote to Andras to air their many concerns:

> We are dealing with people who for many reasons have lived in secrecy, fearing that if the government discovered them they would lose their freedom, merely for attempting to make a new life in their chosen country. The fear of exile or prison is a strong one, one that does not disappear merely because the sources of that fear say, "We are forgiving." What a leap of faith that asks. . . .
>
> They do not trust your department, your advertisements. They . . . are afraid to come forward; afraid even to call the Immigration Department to discover whether they qualify.

It seems impossible to find, inform and convince these illegal immigrants fearfully hiding in the two-week period remaining. . . .

Yet the consequences to these unfound, unconvinced human beings are dreadful. If they do not come forward by October 15, they are deported and have no appeal. No Special Inquiry Officer has the discretionary power to allow these people to stay even where the most compelling humanitarian grounds exist. They will never reach the Immigration Appeal Board[,] which has this power.

No matter what deadline is placed on coming forward, some will not have heard and so will be deported when found. . . . As it stands now, there is the risk that more people will be caught than will have come forward.[50]

At midnight on October 15, 1973, despite the concerns of the Vancouver Committee and many others, Canada ended its immigration adjustment program, having admitted nearly forty thousand official newly legal immigrants, some of whom had entered the country as early as 1906.[51] Roughly 30 percent of these new immigrants came from the United States.[52] Anyone without papers now ran the risk of deportation if they were discovered. For U.S. draft resisters and military deserters, that would have meant being sent back to a country that viewed them as criminals.

SELLING AND BUYING THE IDEA OF AN ALL-VOLUNTEER FORCE

The U.S. military realized the folly of conscription during the Vietnam War in its own way. The President's Commission on an All-Volunteer Armed Force, chaired by Thomas S. Gates Jr., U.S. secretary of defense from 1959 to 1961, recognized in 1969 that the authority of the military to draft U.S. citizens for military duty, as derived from the concept that a citizen's moral responsibility was to serve his country, was passé. The fifteen-member commission was unanimous in its belief that "the nation's interests will be better served by an all-volunteer force . . . than by a mixed force of volunteers and conscripts."[53] The commission's report was notable in that it recognized the complaints of many young people about the military draft and suggested that a change to an all-volunteer force would minimize "government interference with the freedom of the individual to determine his own life in accord with his values."[54] Further, the commission recognized reasons that a military draft had seemed appropriate in the past but had become anachronistic:

However necessary conscription may have been in World War II, it has revealed many disadvantages in the past generation. It has been a costly, inequitable, and divisive procedure for recruiting men for the armed forces. It has imposed heavy burdens on a small minority of young men while easing slightly the tax burden on the rest of us. It has introduced needless uncertainty into the lives of all our young men. It has burdened draft boards with painful decisions about who shall be compelled to serve and who shall be deferred. It has weakened the political fabric of our society and impaired the delicate web of shared values that alone enables a free society to exist.[55]

The commission concluded, much in the way many young Americans had already determined for themselves, that "compelling service through a draft undermines respect for government by forcing an individual to serve when and in the manner the government decides, regardless of his own values and talents."[56]

William C. Westmoreland, who had commanded U.S. troops in Vietnam from 1964 to 1968 and had been the U.S. Army Chief of Staff from 1968 to 1972, validated the findings of the President's Commission in an address to the Army Commanders' Conference in the Pentagon in 1970, observing, "Today our society is . . . more informal and more oriented toward personal free-dom." He felt the military needed to recognize this trend because it was powerless to change it. To that end, Westmoreland felt the army might have greater appeal to young people if it could better fulfill their aspirations by providing opportunities for "responsibility, respectability, challenge, and adven-ture." The army needed to be "more enjoyable, more professionally rewarding, and less burdensome in its impact on our people and their families." If the army would replace policies that treated "a man like a juvenile" with some that treated "a young soldier like a responsible man," Westmoreland believed, "he will act like one."[57]

In anticipation of an all-volunteer army, the military turned to ideas from the consumer market to fill its ranks. It hired major national advertising agen-cies to develop advertisements to be placed in print media and on radio and television for a campaign, as historian Beth Bailey observed, for "an unpopu-lar 'product' that seemed to be in the midst of a controversial internal transfor-mation."[58] For the U.S. Army the ad men of N. W. Ayer developed a campaign driven by "the perceived 'needs' of American youth." Westmoreland, Secre-tary of the Army Robert Froehlke, and George Forsythe, special assistant for the modern volunteer army, accepted Ayer's pitch, despite their discomfort with the tenor of the campaign, with Ayer executives reminding them that the ads were not meant to appeal to generals but to gain the attention and interests of contemporary youth.[59] Bailey also noted that the military accordingly altered its appeals from those of "public portrayals of shared sacrifice and obligation" to those of "a language of consumer dreams and images of individual opportunity."[60] Young men were no longer pawns of the state. Those who had interest in military service could voluntarily devote themselves to supporting the state in that way. Those who did not were free to choose another path.

EARNED REENTRY, HOPE, HARD WORK, AND MUTUAL TRUST

U.S. involvement in the Vietnam War had ended on March 29, 1973, with the withdrawal of the last U.S. troops from South Vietnam. A year later, a U.S. House of Representatives subcommittee held hearings to determine how to act on ten resolutions regarding amnesty for persons violating the Selective Service Act during the Vietnam War era. The subcommittee heard testimony from dozens of people, including representatives of the military, veterans groups, federal government units, groups advocating amnesty, and religious groups.[61] One surprise of the hearings was the admission of Robert F. Froehlke, Richard Nixon's secretary of the army from July 1971 to May 1973, that "all draft evaders should be given blanket amnesty. I readily concede that it would be 'nice' if we would only grant amnesty to those who fled for moral reasons and not to those who fled for selfish reasons. Unfortunately, in my opinion, it is impossible to determine intent. Therefore, the amnesty for draft evaders must be blanket."[62]

While amnesty supporters emphasized compassion and forgiveness and the difficulty and expense of determining amnesty on a case-by-case basis, legislators seemed more swayed by arguments of the U.S. Department of Justice that Congress was not permitted to legislate amnesty, and of the U.S. Department of Defense that amnesty for deserters was bad for morale and "would establish an undesirable precedent" for any future military drafts.[63] The U.S. military may have been no longer involved extensively in Southeast Asia, but the hearings proved the debate about the citizenship status of draft resisters, military deserters, and veterans with less-than-honorable discharges was not over. None of the ten measures passed. The hesitation of Congress to resolve the issue, along with President Nixon's refusal to grant any sort of amnesty, left the citizenship status of tens of thousands of American men uncertain.

Froehlke's stand on amnesty elicited complaints from many who were disturbed by the notion that men would emigrate rather than fulfill military obligations. The audacity of such a move, according to some, should not be rewarded with an amnesty that would allow a return to the United States. A Florida woman complained to Froehlke, "Upon 'copping out' of their obligations & privilege, they gave up all rights to our country. And it's [sic] benefits. Let them stay where they are, as our great country doesn't need any more 'gutless wonders.'"[64] Similarly, a New Jersey man opined that "one must always pay the consequences of his shortcomings even after forgiveness. These who left their country because they felt it was not worth defending have no business coming back to reap the fruits of a land which is not good enough for them."[65] From Nebraska came the invective, "Let's keep our country for the people who care and who appreciate our way of life well enough to fight for it, whether in battle or just defending her verbally."[66]

From the summer of 1974 to the beginning of 1977—a period of just over twenty-eight months—the United States had three different presidents. Three administrations grappled with the fallout of the failure of the United States to fend off a Communist government in Vietnam. One particularly difficult aspect of this failure was the creation of a policy to deal with men who left the United States rather than serve in its military—men who asserted that the United States was wrong in its actions in Southeast Asia or wrong in its expectations of its young men. Five months after the House subcommittee hearings on amnesty, Gerald Ford succeeded Richard Nixon to the U.S. presidency after Nixon resigned because of his involvement in the Watergate scandal. Ford endeavored to distance himself from Nixon in many ways, one of which was to offer a limited form of clemency to fugitive draft resisters—but not to military deserters. Ten days into his presidency, in his first trip outside of Washington as president, Ford announced his plan in Chicago to an astonished assembly at the seventy-fifth annual convention of the Veterans of Foreign Wars (VFW).[67] While Ford prefaced his remarks by saying, "I [have] stated my strong conviction that unconditional, blanket amnesty for anyone who illegally evaded or fled military service is wrong. It *is* wrong," he called expatriates and those who had gone AWOL (absent without leave) among the "casualties" of the Vietnam War, because they were outside of "the real America." In expressing that "I want them to come home if they want to *work their way back*" and that he saw their return as an "earned re-entry—*earned* re-entry—into a new atmosphere of hope, hard work, and mutual trust," Ford began to articulate something his predecessor was not able to: the price émigrés would have to pay to regain their U.S. citizenship rights. They would have to abide by new requirements for men of draft age in the Vietnam War era despite the draft and U.S. involvement in the war having ended.[68]

The day after Ford's address, the VFW passed two unanimous resolutions against an unconditional amnesty for draft resisters and military deserters. One resolution reaffirmed the group's "total opposition to general and selective 'amnesty' for draft dodgers and military deserters" and called for the resisters to stand trial and pay penalties for their crimes. The other resolution called for the 1.8 million members of the VFW to promote their opposition to an amnesty to members of the U.S. Congress and the U.S. public.[69]

Ford was unswayed by the VFW's resolutions. Four weeks later, in a proclamation formally announcing his clemency program, he made clearer the requirements for expatriates to reclaim the perquisites of U.S. citizenship and residence in the United States: draft resisters had to perform up to twenty-four months of alternative service that "shall promote the national health, safety, or interest," and they had to acknowledge "their allegiance to the country and its Constitution."[70] Ford's program was unwieldy. Three different agencies were to consider, on a case-by-case basis, the applications of the 113,000 men eligible for the program. The U.S. Department of Justice handled the cases of draft resisters, and the U.S. Department of Defense handled military deserters. Recognizing how little support he had for his program, even from his own White House staff, Ford created the temporary Presidential Clemency Board to consider the cases of those who had already been convicted and punished for draft-related offenses, including those who had been court-martialed for desertion or who had undesirable discharges for going AWOL.[71] Chaired by former New York senator Charles Goodell, the program would give qualified applicants "official forgiveness for designated draft or military offenses, restoring all Federal civil rights lost."[72] Successful applicants did not earn veterans' benefits, but neither were they given felony convictions.

Under Ford's clemency plan, the definition of citizenship for young American men became partially disengaged from the duty of military service. Many men who had moved to Canada during the Vietnam War applied for clemency through the program. Profiles of their cases found in the records of the Presidential Clemency Board reveal not only their interest in reconciling their status as citizens of the United States but also that their motivations for moving to Canada were often related to frustration with the draft and/or the U.S. military during the Vietnam War era. For example, after dropping out of high school, a Southern California man enlisted in the Marine Corps in 1970 for a three-year term, serving only seven months of it before moving to Canada to avoid being sent overseas for combat duty. After three years in Canada, he contacted the Marine Corps about returning to the United States because his father was gravely ill and could no longer take care of the family. Upon his return stateside, he was given a dishonorable discharge and sentenced to ten months of hard labor. When the Presidential Clemency Board was created a year later, he applied for an upgrade of his military discharge status.[73]

Similarly, a Washington State man, who was also a high school dropout, voluntarily joined the military but felt that recruiters had lied to him about his job possibilities within the U.S. Army. As he began to question the involvement of the United States in Vietnam, he reconsidered his enlistment. Denied consciousness objector status, he moved to Canada, where he lived for fourteen months. Upon his return to the United States he was given a bad conduct discharge in a general court martial and was sentenced to nine months of hard labor and forfeiture of his pay. Four years later, when the Presidential Clemency Board was formed, he, too, applied for an upgrade of his discharge status.[74]

As another example, a man from Santa Cruz, California, applied for conscientious objector status but was denied it because "he lacked sincerity." After twice failing to report for induction, he fled to Canada and enrolled at the University of Ottawa. He was apprehended when he tried to return home for Christmas. Ford's clemency program commuted his fifteen-month prison sentence to ninety days, with eighteen months of probation, during one year of which he was to work in the interest of the nation.[75] A Colorado man who dropped out of high school but attained the certification for academic skills comparable to a high school education through the GED (General Educational Development) tests, received conscientious objector status. He agreed to do twenty-four months of alternative service but refused to alter his clothing and hair to satisfy his supervisors and was chronically late for work. Within a year he was convicted of failing to complete alternative service and was sentenced to two years in prison. He failed to turn himself in and moved to British Columbia, where he lived for three years. He applied to the Presidential Clemency Board from Canada for a commutation of his jail sentence.[76]

A Texas man who was in the fourth generation of a family opposed to war, but "not officially a Quaker," had earned bachelor's and master's degrees and had begun work on a doctorate when his draft induction notice came in 1968. No longer eligible for a student deferment and denied conscientious objector status, he moved to Europe, then to Canada, where he lived for five years.

After he lost vision in one of his eyes in an automobile accident, he returned to the United States knowing he would fail a preinduction physical. Still, he was arrested and convicted for having failed to submit to induction in 1968. He was sentenced to three years in prison but was released on furlough by the Presidential Clemency Program.[77] Similarly, a college graduate with a degree in electrical engineering who had lived in Canada since 1968 and had started graduate school there was ordered for induction into the military in 1970. In April 1972, a few days after his twenty-seventh birthday, he was indicted for failure to report for induction. A year later he was arrested when trying to cross the border back into the United States. He explained that his failure to appear was borne out of deep-seated opposition to the Vietnam War— opposition that was more morally based than religiously based. Nonetheless he was sentenced to five years in prison, which the Ford clemency program was willing to suspend, provided he served three years' probation, during two of which he had to perform civil work in the national interest.[78]

The introduction to the final report of the Presidential Clemency Board expressed the primary reason it had been formed: "Something had to be done to bring Americans together again. The rancor that had divided the country during the Vietnam War still sapped its spirit and strength. The national interest required that Americans put aside their strong personal feelings."[79] In marked contrast, the clemency program seemed only to fuel that rancor. Very few seemed to approve of the program, with draft resisters, military deserters, veterans, liberals, and conservatives all voicing criticism of it.[80]

While the requirements of citizenship changed slightly with Ford's clemency program, it was not enough to satisfy a huge number of those whom it was intended to help. Eighty-one percent refused to participate in it, electing to remain outside of the nation. The foremost criticism of the clemency continued to be that the Vietnam War had been unjust and that Americans had the responsibility to protest and resist participation in such a war.[81] In an advertisement in the *New York Times,* the publishers of *AMEX/Canada* explained their displeasure: "We broke Selective Service and military laws because the Indochina war was and is illegal and immoral, believing that loyal Americans had a duty to disobey the illegal orders that made this war possible."[82] Gerry Condon, a former Green Beret, echoed *AMEX/Canada,* telling the *Washington Post,* "We are definitely being asked to pay a penalty. It is too much to ask. It is our right and responsibility to resist illegal wars."[83] Charles Stimac, a Michigan man who had moved to Toronto to resist service in the Vietnam War, complained to the *New York Times* that Ford's clemency program was unduly punitive. "It is based on the erroneous assumption that the

Vietnam war was fair and legal," he stated, "and that we did something wrong by opposing it."[84]

Richard Moore, living in Burnaby, British Columbia, complained the day after the official announcement of Ford's clemency that it was "nothing more than a façade behind which lies a trap for all war resisters" and that it would simply "set up prison-work camps for those men who turn themselves in expecting 'mercy.'"[85] Col. Jack D. Kaufman, state director of the Selective Service System in Maryland, thought it was unreasonable "to expect these people to turn themselves into fine upstanding citizens and take a low-paying job for two years."[86] In a postcard to Charles Goodell, a veteran from Baltimore intoned that "draft evaders deserve americas [sic] cheers for pointing the way in the idiocy of Vietnam war."[87] In a letter to the editor of the *Toronto Star*, Norman Lewis of Lake George, in upstate New York, asked, "Can any right-minded person blame those fine young men who feel outraged by President Ford's ambivalent offer?" and opined, "I personally feel that Canada will be the gainer by their permanent residence in that country and that these young men are fortunate to have such a second country, which their children will consider their first."[88]

Members of Congress, too, voiced displeasure with Ford's plan. Robert F. Drinan of Massachusetts, a member of the U.S. House of Representatives subcommittee that conducted hearings on Ford's clemency plan in August 1975, questioned "why any person who opposed the war for reasons of conscience should be required to undertake [alternative] service."[89] Similarly, Rep. Andrew Young, from Georgia, spoke on behalf of the Congressional Black Caucus, encouraging Ford to grant an amnesty—not alternative service—"for those who refused to participate in the saddest spectacle of our history."[90]

Not lost on many advocates of a full, unconditional amnesty for draft resisters and military deserters was the irony of Ford's September 8, 1974, "full and absolute pardon" of Richard Nixon for his role in the Watergate scandal. As an attorney in Arkansas opined in a letter to the Ford administration, "If we can forgive a president for the abuse of the public trust, we can forgive those thousands of young men who refused to participate in a war that we all now agree was wrong from any of point of view."[91] Vernon E. Jordan Jr., the president of the National Urban League and a member of the Presidential Clemency Board, similarly implored, in a keynote address to the 1975 annual conference of the league, that Ford should show the same compassion he had shown Nixon to "those who were right about an evil war and those whose service for their country has resulted in the unfair, lifelong punishment of a bad discharge."[92] Jordan resigned from the Presidential Clemency Board when the Ford administration ignored his recommendations for improving the program.[93]

At the urging of Attorney General William B. Saxbe, the Ford administration made an act of contrition a condition of earning clemency.[94] Many draft resisters and military deserters who went to Canada felt they had found moral high ground concerning the war before most of the rest of the country. Accordingly, they resented having to take an oath of allegiance to the United States and its Constitution, feeling it forced them to admit that the actions they took during the Vietnam War era were wrong or constituted taking some of the blame for the war. The draft resister William Meis expressed such a sentiment in an appearance before the Presidential Clemency Board in 1974, saying, "President Ford's proposal . . . fills me with anger and great sadness. The President demands that I, and thousands like me, be punished for refusing to participate in the Vietnam war, even though that war is now universally regarded as our greatest national tragedy. The President demands that I reaffirm my allegiance to America, even though I have never been disloyal. He demands that I perform involuntary servitude, even though the Constitution clearly prohibits such treatment. I cannot accept these proposals."[95] A deserter from New Jersey complained, "It sounds like he wants us to crawl back on our hands and knees. He is saying: 'You're going to have to say I'm sorry to us.' Instead, they should be the ones saying they're sorry."[96] Another critic from Arizona wrote to Goodell to say, "The American people realized much too late the immorality, illegality and injustice of our involvement in Vietnam. I question therefore whether it was wise to punish those who, at least in their majority, recognized this earlier than the civilians, largely untouched by the war, by the heavy requirements [Ford's] executive order places upon them as condition for their reentry into the U.S. society."[97] Charles Stimac further complained, "[The clemency] tries to shift the blame for the war onto us, and we are penalized." Mark Davies, an Illinois man living in Toronto, agreed, saying, "I don't believe I did anything wrong. The President's offer makes us look like criminals," while the editors of *AMEX/Canada* observed, "Ford's program leaves no room for principled objection to the Indochina War, and in fact, penalizes war resisters for it."[98] In a letter from Toronto, Bill King told Gerald Ford, "If you want an apology you can go to hell."[99]

Echoing the criticism by U.S. exiles was Henry Schwarzschild of the American Civil Liberties Union (ACLU), who called the program "unsatisfactory," "cumbersome and confusing," "useless, punitive . . . inequitable," and "stigmatizing."[100] The ACLU and the National Council of Churches agreed that it was worse than having done nothing at all.[101] The journalist James Reston Jr. recognized the direct opposition of émigrés to the U.S. government, noting that "much time, thought, emotion, and considerable misery has gone into the exiles' course of action. To force a public display of contrition is to add insult to injury."[102]

Over one hundred organizations, including such peace groups as the American Friends Service Committee, Catholic Peace Fellowship, Central Committee for Conscientious Objectors, Clergy and Laity Concerned About Vietnam, Jewish Peace Fellowship, Vietnam Veterans Against the War, Women Strike for Peace, and the Women's International League for Peace and Freedom, as well as groups of U.S. exiles such as AMEX/Canada and Vancouver American Exiles Association, along with the National Conference of Black Lawyers and the American Civil Liberties Union, banded together as the National Council for Universal and Unconditional Amnesty (NCUUA). The NCUUA encouraged activists to bring awareness not only to draft resisters and military deserters but also to the plight of the millions of U.S. residents being held legally liable for acts of resistance during the Vietnam War, including veterans with less-than-honorable discharges and civilians arrested and convicted for war protests.[103] These offenses included desertion and absence without leave, naturally, and also such offenses as burning draft cards, "enticing desertion or harboring deserters," and desecrating the U.S. flag. The day after Ford formally announced his clemency program, the NCUUA issued a statement in which it declared that it "totally reject[ed] this fraudulent program and call[ed] upon the American people to join us in demanding universal and unconditional amnesty for all those who courageously opposed the military machine in the Vietnam era."[104] The NCUUA continued its criticism of Ford's proposal through such publications as the pamphlet "Have You Heard the Joke about President Ford's Clemency Program?," the booklet "Amnesty for Vets Too!," and the bimonthly newsletter *NCUUA Amnesty Update*, published from April 1974 to August 1977.[105]

As we have seen, churches and other religious groups had long been advocates of American exiles in Canada. Dozens of U.S. church denominations had issued statements in the early 1970s encouraging amnesty.[106] Not surprisingly, many religious leaders expressed their disappointment with Ford's clemency plan. For example, representatives of the Mennonite Central Committee and the Church of the Brethren suggested that "the inequities that were operating in the Selective Service System need to be clearly understood before a just decision can be arrived at concerning the fate of draft exiles in Canada, those who went 'underground,' etc."[107] The American Friends Service Committee issued a statement the day after Ford's announcement to suggest, "The requirement of two years of forced labor on top of the years of distress already endured totally ignores the history of the Indochina war and the rejection of that war by the vast majority of Americans" and that "to require a pledge of allegiance of these alleged offenders is degrading to them and to the United States. These are American citizens who rejected an immoral and unpopular war, not their country."[108] William P. Thompson, a high-ranking administrator of the United Presbyterian Church, opined that while alternative service seemed equitable, it merely repeated the inequities of the military draft: "The vast majority of young Americans were not called for military service either through privilege or chance. Rather than requiring the few to pay the price of being readmitted to society, the General Assembly [of the United Presbyterian Church] has expressed its view that service freely given to the nation is vastly to be preferred to labor exacted to avoid further punishment. Let us invite them rather than compel them."[109]

American exiles and liberal groups found strange bedfellows among those who also criticized Ford's clemency plan. Charles Goodell reflected several years later that not only were the Department of Justice and veterans groups against it but also it was likely that no member of Ford's staff agreed with it.[110] Many echoed the concerns of Nixon and the Department of Defense that clemency for draft resisters would be an insult to veterans and to the families of those who died in the war.[111] Dozens of decorated veterans returned service medals and certificates in protest of Ford's plan, with one intoning with calculated irony that he had "no more pride in this medal than I would have for a bus ticket to Canada."[112]

Prompted by Ford's clemency plan, a debate about the meaning of U.S. citizenship raged in letters to Ford, his administration, U.S. exile groups, and other amnesty proponents, as well as in the press. Ford's supporters echoed his sentiments that "these Americans should have a second chance."[113] From Scarsdale, New York, came the reassurance that "there is a large, compassionate body of citizens who look forward to a true amnesty as another refreshing breeze of post-Watergate air."[114] The chancellor of the University of Wisconsin–Stevens Point noted that with an amnesty, "we have a chance to show this great American heart."[115] A veteran of the Vietnam War asserted, "Not only should they be pardoned but I think they deserve some special recognition, having been prisoners of war, exiled from their own countries. They are vetrans [sic] of the Viet Nam war the same as I. . . . Welcome home[;] it was wrong for you to be away so long. I think we owe these people an apology, a pardon, and a 'Yes you were right all along, it was a stupid war.'"[116]

In contrast, clemency opponents often expressed qualms about the program through criticism of those who sought its benefits. They defined what they felt were qualities of citizenship, albeit in negative terms. To be a good citizen, a young American man could not accept the material blessings of the United States without accepting its responsibilities.[117] He could not choose the laws he wanted to obey or the wars he wanted to fight in.[118] He could not decide for himself which wars were just or unjust.[119] In such definitions of citizenship, clemency opponents presaged the writing of Benedict Anderson, who posited that a willingness to die for one's community was a true test of one's membership in it.[120] Draft resisters and military deserters rejected membership in American society during the Vietnam War era and faced much scrutiny while trying to regain participation in it.

To many, American draft resisters and military deserters in Canada did not deserve to be readmitted to the United States because they were, as one Boston man viewed them, "yellow bellied" cowards.[121] Others disapproved of exiles' nonconformity to traditional standards of masculinity. From a Pennsylvania man came the criticism of draft evasion that "it wasn't the manly thing to do by any standards."[122] The mother of several veterans complained in a letter to AMEX/Canada—handwritten on stationery bordered with roses—that draft resisters "weren't men enough to serve there [sic] country. We need men in this country[,] not draft dodgers and deserters, not cowards and evaders!"[123] A woman from outside of St. Louis, Missouri, berated, "LIVE UP TO YOUR RESPONSIBILITY and BE A MAN and not a weakling who goes and hides."[124] Another correspondent complained to AMEX/Canada, "The weakening fiber of America is so evident everywhere you look. We do not want weak men in this country. Stay where you are and weaken the other countries with your selfishness and softness."[125]

Some attacked the countercultural affectations of some of the exiles. To one Virginia man, most American expatriates in Canada were "dirty hippies completely lacking in patriotism."[126] A Florida family felt it was wrong to expect men who had fulfilled their service obligations to "kow tow to these louzy [sic] long haired slackers that run to foreign land[s]."[127] Likewise, a Pennsylvania correspondent complained that if Ford's clemency was not "understood and accepted by you and the rest of you who fled, with your long uncombed hair and beards and disheveled dress . . . then by all means you should remain in Canada."[128]

Returning to the United States under Ford's plan was not an attractive option for many. Not only did they find the act of contrition distasteful, they also rejected the possibility of having to perform many months of poorly paid alternative service. Henry Schwarzschild of the ACLU asked, "why should they . . . come down here to move bed pans for $50 a week when they have been proven correct? The war was a travesty, it was immoral, unconstitutional."[129] Similarly, James Reston Jr. urged the Ford administration to "imagine the headaches of any hospital administrator or inner city Vista superviser [*sic*] who has a grudge-bearing exile on his hands for two years."[130] Katie McGovern, a spokeswoman for the Toronto Anti-Draft Programme, called Ford's clemency "a farce" and "punishment thinly disguised as amnesty."[131] A correspondent from Rhode Island correctly predicted that few would return to the United States under the "devastating" conditions of the program, to be "condemned to cleaning latrines and carrying bedpans for two years because you dared have a conscience."[132] Charles Goodell warned Ford in a memorandum on New Year's Day 1975 that such an admission of guilt on the part of clemency program participants "puts anyone in extreme jeopardy if their alternative service experience is unsatisfactory, and it makes the program clearly punitive."[133]

Gerald Ford's Presidential Clemency Program was a failure. Deserters who fulfilled the alternative service option earned a "clemency" discharge from the military. Such a discharge carried no greater benefit than the undesirable discharge they would receive—or had already received—for doing nothing to reconcile their status with the U.S. military.[134] A stumbling economy, coupled with unemployment that had soared to 9.1 percent in early 1975, made jobs for clemency program participants difficult to secure—a fact not lost on detractors of the program.[135] "Jobs are getting hard to get in [the] USA," exclaimed a Connecticut man, "so do we want rotten apples like you [to] come back and give competition to good men[?]"[136] The program was to have lasted only four months, but it was so underpublicized and so unappreciated that it was extended twice to encourage greater participation.[137] Only 21,729 of the 113,337 eligible men, or 19 percent, participated in the clemency program by its end on March 31, 1975.[138] Not knowing when the war would end or whether they would ever be allowed to return to the United States without having to fulfill some sort of obligation for military service during the Vietnam War, they had gotten on with their lives, finishing college, attending graduate school, getting married, starting families, and starting careers. Those who had been in Canada for more than five years were eligible to apply for Canadian citizenship.[139] Perhaps the only success of the clemency program was to alert influential people to the dilemmas many young American men faced concerning their status with the Selective Service System after the

Vietnam War.[140] While the program endeavored to offer wider citizenship options to those men, those options were still quite limited and still on terms set by the U.S. government, not those demanded by men who had rejected their government's call to military service—a group largely resolved to remain outside of the nation.

From March 1975 through 1976 (a U.S. presidential election year), the possibility of an amnesty for such offenses as draft resistance, military desertion, draft card burning, and other protests seemed remote. Advocates continued to rally for an unconditional amnesty, but Gerald Ford was disinterested in extending or expanding his plan. Vernon E. Jordan Jr., the director of the National Urban League and a member of the disbanded Presidential Clemency Board, helped keep the debate in the eye of the public by reminding readers in his syndicated column "To Be Equal" in November 1975 that "most [offenders] were individuals who were caught up in the snares of a giant bureaucracy and, rightly or wrongly, chose to escape their situation in ways that the law defined as illegal." He noted that many cases handled by the Presidential Clemency Board involved conscientious objectors not given their rights, desertion for reasons not deemed valid by commanding officers, or men who never should have been drafted, allowing that "the conventional image of the spoiled rich kid who ran away to Canada to beat the draft just didn't hold true for most cases." Jordan felt that the case-by-case treatment of men by the Presidential Clemency Board did not work and that the U.S. government should "wipe the slate clean and end the War still being waged against the draft resisters and offenders." In Jordan's eyes, the more than 200,000 men who had less-than-honorable discharges were assessed "penalties absurdly inappropriate to the real or imagined offences, often minor, . . . that would earn no penalty at all in a civilian setting" and that were often imposed for "racially-inspired reasons." Without an amnesty, these men would be punished for their rest of their lives because they would not be eligible for veterans' benefits and could be barred from government and private sector jobs.[141]

"WHAT YOU DID, WHETHER IT'S RIGHT OR WRONG, YOU ARE FORGIVEN"

The day after Christmas 1976, Philip A. Hart, a U.S. senator from Michigan, died of cancer. Fellow Michigander and former congressional colleague President Gerald Ford telephoned Hart's widow, Jane, that day to offer his condolences. In their conversation Jane Hart asked Ford to reconsider his stance toward Vietnam War–era draft resisters and military deserters and to give those men an amnesty. Twenty-four days later, on the last full day of his presidency, Ford made clear his unwavering attitude toward amnesty. In a public letter to Jane Hart, he wrote, "I know how firmly you and Phil and your children have felt about Vietnam amnesty, and I respect that feeling and belief. However, I also have a strong personal belief that earned clemency was the right approach to healing our country's Vietnam wounds and to creating a mutual understanding among all those individuals and families who were personally involved in the Vietnam war, from those who felt they could not serve to those who lost a child, a husband, or a father. I thus have decided to maintain my position on earned clemency and hope you will understand."[142]

The next day, Philip and Jane Hart's daughter Laura wrote to the newly inaugurated president Jimmy Carter with her own plea for amnesty, saying,

> As you may know, in his last months my father mentioned often that amnesty was one thing that he wanted to see carried out, and was sad that he could not. A year and a half ago the doctors discovered his cancer. Since then our family has learned, or come to understand better, the importance, and the necessity, of a family. It is, as a matter of course, a tragedy that so many families are going to be forever apart because one or more member was killed in the Vietnam War, but compared to this, by keeping families apart that could be together is equally tragic. Mr. Carter, only you can heal this tragedy, and I am writing with sincerest hopes that some day you will, that some day you can be thanked for the love that, until now, has been unable to be expressed—the love that your family and mine know so well. Please consider these thoughts—in your heart as well as your mind.[143]

The Harts' entreaties to Ford and Carter were examples of the perseverance of advocates of a broader amnesty for legal violations during protest of the Vietnam War era in the United States. When Ford's clemency program ended, there seemed little chance that anything would be done to extend a broader amnesty during the remainder of his term. Members of the NCUUA resolved to press the issue with candidates for the presidency in the 1976 elections. They urged those in favor of amnesty to be sure that the candidates were "confronted with the issue of Universal, Unconditional Amnesty on the campaign trail," because they felt that the candidates "would prefer to avoid this unpleasant reminder of the war."[144]

The NCUUA drew massive attention to its cause at the Democratic National Convention in New York City in July 1976 by getting podium time for Louise Ransom, a Gold Star mother and an affiliate director of the NCUUA in New York, to nominate Fritz Efaw as the party's vice-presidential candidate. Efaw had been in exile in London for seven years to resist military service and risked arrest when he entered the United States as a convention delegate for Democrats Abroad. Efaw's nomination was seconded by Ron Kovic, who had been paralyzed below the waist by enemy gunfire during the Vietnam War and who had become an antiwar activist after his return to the United States.[145] In his speech declining the nomination, Efaw articulated the need for an amnesty, saying,

> The legacy of the war remains.
>
> Over one million Americans continue to be punished for their acts of opposition to the war and to the arbitrary nature of the military system during the war....
>
> The Democratic party can now confront the divisive lingering problems of the Vietnam era with a truly broad amnesty which includes all the war's victims: civilian and military resisters, deserters, and veterans with less than fully honorable discharges—over one million in all....
>
> The burdens of the war fell unequally on different people in our nation. The wounds of war can only be healed if President Carter proclaims an equal amnesty for all the war's victims.
>
> I am proud to come to this convention to represent war resisters. The risk involved in coming before you was certainly worth taking. I respectfully decline nomination for Vice President of the United States. I seek no office, and no further recognition.[146]

The nomination gave Ransom, Kovic, and Efaw control of the microphone to make the case for a universal, unconditional amnesty more widely known, not only to delegates at the Democratic National Convention but also to a large nationwide television audience and to readers of print publications covering the convention.

In the months leading up to the 1976 U.S. presidential campaign, the Democratic Party had been divided about whether to extend pardons to draft resisters and military deserters, with many presidential candidates outspoken against doing so. When Jimmy Carter became the party's frontrunner, his advocacy for a pardon for draft resisters and a case-by-case consideration for military deserters made its way into the party's platform, perhaps as its most controversial plank.[147] Recognizing that Gerald Ford's clemency program had been a failure, Carter, a veteran of the U.S. Navy, had outlined the different approach he would take toward U.S. Vietnam War exiles early in his campaign. Carter established that he recognized who had borne the burden of combat for the United States during the war, allowing, in a March 1976 interview with the *Washington Post,*

> In the area of the country where I live, defecting from military service is almost unheard of. Most of the young people in my section of Georgia are quite poor. They didn't know where Sweden was, they didn't know how to get to Canada, they didn't have enough money to hide in college. They thought the war was wrong. They preferred to stay at home, but still they went to Vietnam. A substantial . . . proportion of them were black. They've never been recognized for their service to the country. They've often been despised, characterized as criminals, they were never heroes, and I feel a very great appreciation to them. They were extraordinarily heroic . . . even if they didn't have the appreciation of their fellow citizens and even if they thought the war was wrong. It's very difficult for me to equate what they did with what the young people did who left the country.[148]

Pointing to the loss of the advantages of life in the United States that exiles had already endured, however, Carter acknowledged, "I cannot equate the actions of those who went to Vietnam . . . with those who thought it was wrong and defected. But exile for this long a period of time is adequate punishment."[149] He further allowed that he found the motives of those who protested the Vietnam War from within the United States to be more heroic than those "who went and hid in Sweden," but explained, "I'm not capable of judging motives, so I'm just going to declare a blanket pardon."[150] R. D. "Bulldog" Smith, the newly elected commander-in-chief of the Veterans of Foreign Wars and a fellow Georgian, scoffed at Carter's proposal, complaining, "Changing the word 'amnesty' to the word 'pardon' doesn't fool us for one moment and I don't believe it will fool the American people."[151]

On the campaign trail, Carter promoted his plan for a pardon, daring to assert it in late August at the American Legion national convention, much in the way that Gerald Ford had sprung his amnesty plan on the Veterans of Foreign Wars meeting in Chicago two years earlier. Carter's announcement that "I do not favor a blanket amnesty, but for those who violated Selective Service laws I intend to grant a blanket pardon" brought fifteen thousand legionnaires and their wives to their feet, shouting "No!" and booing for three minutes. Carter attempted to disarm his detractors with his smile, but only when the legion's national commander gaveled to bring order back to the proceedings did the expression of dissent end.[152] Carter continued, defending his plan by adding, "It is time for the damage, hatred, and divisiveness of the Vietnam War to be over."[153] The next day, Kansas senator Robert J. Dole, Gerald Ford's running mate, took the podium and echoed Ford's campaign position: "No blanket pardon, no blanket amnesty, no blanket clemency." The American Legion applauded Dole, but it was Carter's statement that was in the headlines of newspapers that day, garnering the interest of those outside the convention hall who wanted a resolution to this lingering aspect of the Vietnam War.[154]

In contrast to Ford's punitive clemency of 1974, Carter advocated that a pardon would help the nation reclaim American exiles, explaining in his September 23, 1976, presidential debate with Gerald Ford that "what you did, whether it's right or wrong, you are forgiven for it" and adding that his version of a pardon would be a way to "bring about an end to the divisiveness that has occurred in our country as a result of the Vietnam war." In the debate Ford held his ground on his clemency program, saying, "I think we gave them a good opportunity. I don't think we should go any further."[155]

Forty days later, Carter won the election and delivered on his campaign promise unflinchingly by pardoning draft resisters in his first act on the first full day of his presidency.[156] The full benefits of U.S. citizenship were again open to American men who had left the country rather than cooperating with the military. Many people praised Carter. Claiborne Pell, a U.S. senator from Rhode Island, immediately wrote to assure Carter that his amnesty was "a correct, courageous and compassionate action."[157] A Korean War veteran from New York City wrote, "I applaud your courage. I salut [sic] your love. . . . You made me proud of you . . . and of us. Today we behaved like we should."[158] A Maryland man wrote to the editor of the *Washington Post* to say, "President Carter's pardon of draft evaders from the Vietnam war is unfair to those who obeyed their country and fought in it; however, it was unfair of the United States to draft men when our security was not being threatened."[159]

Not surprisingly, the Carter administration also took a lot of heat for the pardon, especially from conservatives and veterans groups.[160] For example, the New Hampshire House of Representatives passed a resolution "expressing disapproval of blanket amnesty."[161] The Oklahoma House of Representatives passed a resolution "urging the president of the United States to refrain from granting a pardon to deserters from the Viet Nam War," observing that "in the face of this nation's greatest need, many selfishly turned their backs and fled" and that "this nation cannot and will not allow our boys to have fought and died in vain."[162] The U.S. Senate considered a resolution "urg[ing] the President not to issue a general pardon for Vietnam-era draft or military law violators," but it was tabled before it came to a final vote.[163] A Memphis woman pulled no punches, exclaiming in a letter to the editor of her city's newspaper, the *Commercial Appeal,* that "[Carter] insulted the dead military men of all the wars of this nation. He insulted the wounded and the basket cases in our veterans hospitals. He insulted the fathers, mothers, wives, children, brothers and sisters of the missing in action. He is a traitor to the whole history of these United States."[164] A California man complained that "the tinsel is really off the tree out here with this damn pardon thing. Someone back there seems to have forgotten that there were a hell of a lot of guys that didn't think anymore of the fiasco in Viet [sic] than you and I did, but they accepted our participation as the law of the land."[165]

As had been the case during the Nixon and Ford administrations, there were many who believed that pardoning draft resisters or military deserters would make it difficult for the United States to have a viable military in the future. Smith of the VFW speculated, "Does this leave the door open for young men to say, 'This is enough—I want to go home,' when they are fighting?"[166] Charles J. Reynolds of the Ohio American Legion complained to his U.S. congresswoman that Carter's amnesty would make a "mockery of our service as well as discouraging future military service, encourage future draft dodging and wholesale desertions without fear of punishment, reduce our standing among world powers, and reward deserters for dodging their responsibility as citizens."[167] Carter defended himself in addressing a query from the actor John Wayne, saying, "I would not expect this pardon to have ill effect on future troop strength or commitment in the event of war, since our involvement therein would have the backing of Congress and the American people—which, as you know, was not the case with Vietnam."[168] And, as the magazine *New Republic* suggested to readers in a late December 1976 editorial, "A wise and compassionate pardon cannot attempt to hedge against national security requirements of future wars. The circumstances next time (should there be a next time) will inevitably be as different from Vietnam as Vietnam was from World War II. A sweeping pardon or unconditional amnesty would not diminish a citizen's responsibility during a time of war, for the nation's resolve in a time of crisis does not derive from legal precedent."[169]

Carter also took heat from liberals and others who complained that he had done nothing for military deserters, whose full citizenship status he had not restored. Carter had said throughout his campaign that he would not issue a blanket pardon for deserters but would consider exonerating them on a case-by-case basis.[170] In the weeks before the presidential election Carter described his attitude toward deserters, "Somebody who goes into the military joins a kind of mutual partnership arrangement.... Your life depends on other people, their life depends on you. So I don't intend to pardon the deserters."[171] Carter had correctly observed that many of those drafted into military service in the Vietnam War were poor and/or Black, but he did not outwardly recognize that members of these same groups were among the many who had deserted the military.[172] His detractors pointed out that many deserters had left the country because of the extreme punitiveness, rife with class and race bias, of the U.S. military. As Leon White, a Korean War veteran and the commander of an American Legion post in Brooklyn, New York, complained in the *New York Amsterdam News,* a newspaper primarily for an African American audience, Carter's pardon "was a victory for the rich boys and a slap in the face to Blacks and poor whites responsible for [Carter] being President.... Now those who sat on the sidelines as cowards can return home and take my job; or else the one I was denied because of color."[173] Race and class issues were also motivation for Charles B. Rangel, a U.S. congressman from New York City and also a Korean War veteran, to write to Carter to encourage him to extend an amnesty to men who received less-than-honorable discharges: "Many of these men, as you have noted several times[,] are poor and black. Clearly it would be a graver injustice to subject these men to a permanent badge of dishonor for their actions, which could have possibly been prevented if they had been able to afford proper counsel before entering the service."[174] Peter Salerno Jr., the secretary of the Emergency Ministry for Veterans Services of the United Presbyterian Church, upheld this point of view when he wrote to church members, "The core of the matter is racist. The upper and middle class are free. The poor, the black, the brown, and the disadvantaged now must carry the totality of the suffering of the war and the very division which Mr. Carter seeks to heal now is set permanently. It is a sad day for all of us."[175]

A group of Vietnam War–era exiles that met in Toronto shortly after Carter's inauguration saw the president's amnesty as creating two classes of war resisters, differentiated only by when they asserted their dissent from the war.[176] Veterans, many with less-than-honorable discharges, who attended the meeting expressed outrage that Carter's pardon had excluded deserters, many of whom were poor and from minority groups. As Leon White had done in the *New York Amsterdam News,* they pointed to the irony that Carter had campaigned for the presidency as a friend of these groups. The veterans called for an unconditional amnesty, not only for draft resisters and military deserters but also for veterans with less-than-honorable discharges and civilians with convictions resulting from Vietnam War–era protests.[177] At the Toronto meeting, Louise Ransom outlined offenses that were not covered by Carter's amnesty, saying,

> We are those who felt constantly in the center of a recurring nightmare in which a mighty locomotive was roaring down the tracks with innocent people in its path and all we could do was to run out and try to stop it with our bare fists.
>
> So we broke some laws, some of which were bad laws, like the draft laws, or absurd laws, like some in the Uniform Code of Military Justice, or small laws like trespass, or big laws like damage to property or person. The laws were different but the frustration was the same—so great that we had to resort to lawbreaking to force the actions of the country we love to become more lawful.[178]

Pat Simon, the coordinator for Gold Star Parents for Amnesty, also spoke at the Toronto meeting, rejecting the "bitter kind of honor" that Richard Nixon had promoted in his refusal to grant amnesty to draft resisters. Such honor, she complained, "places war before peace and death before life" while asserting that "I know our sons would be alive if our government had listened to what the resisters were saying and had stopped the war."[179]

Patricia Schroeder, a U.S. congresswoman from Colorado, made similar observations about race and class among those excluded from Carter's amnesty, observing in a letter to Carter that "many are people who did serve honorably before running afoul of military officialdom. During the war the administrative discharge system became an easy way for the military to unload hundreds of thousands of young service people onto civilian society with . . . a permanent scar on their records. Many should have never been in the military to begin with. Many are minorities or come from low income backgrounds. . . . The less than honorable discharge is now one more hobble." Schroeder felt that a general amnesty would suffice "because we are considering a pardon, not beatification."[180] Robert C. Macek, a Buffalo, New York, man who had worked as a draft and military counselor in the 1960s and later as an attorney for men with legal problems stemming from the military draft, wrote to the Carter administration in February 1977 to encourage a pardon for military deserters, saying that "without such relief, the domestic bitterness and frustration of Viet Nam will not recede into our past." Macek not only noted the stigmas faced by men with less-than-honorable discharges but also promoted the advantages of readmitting them more fully as citizens of the United States, observing, "Many of these men are publicly useful, responsible and prosperous individuals, whose ability to travel on business, and otherwise to visit this country or to reimmigrate here, would benefit the United States.... [They] can be greater assets to the community if released from those bonds."[181]

In a February 10, 1977, meeting, leaders of groups concerned about the lack of a pardon for deserters articulated their concerns to Margaret "Midge" Costanza, Carter's assistant for public liaison. In the meeting, Louise Ransom noted that deserters were often "unsophisticated persons with pre-existing problems" who could not find other ways to resist the draft that often led them to receive less-than-honorable discharges upon their release from the military. Such discharges often put these veterans at an extreme economic disadvantage because employers were less likely to hire them. Tom Wynn, the national coordinator of the National Association of Black Veterans, pointed to racism in the military, with cultural differences contributing to white supe-riors being more likely to give less-than-honorable discharges to Black ser-vicemen. Further, the group expressed concern about the treatment of men who had served honorably in Southeast Asia and who sometimes had "severe readjustment problems" upon returning to the United States, which also resulted in less-than-honorable discharges.[182]

Finally, on April 5, 1977, the Carter administration relented and directed the Department of Defense to operate a special discharge review program, which gave deserters the opportunity to apply for a possible upgrade of their less-than-honorable or general discharge status "in the spirit of compassion and forgiveness in which the President has sought to bind up the divisions of the Vietnam war"—something the Ford administration had not permitted. Once again this was done on a case-by-case basis, potentially duplicating the folly of the Selective Service System in the 1960s and the Ford clemency program in 1974 and 1975. However, rather than punish men for certain kinds of behavior in the military, the new program widened the parameters of citizenship for draft-age men of the Vietnam War era, rewarding many for a variety of sacri-fices and positive actions during the Vietnam War era, such as successfully completing a tour of duty in Southeast Asia or other places in the world in support of military operations in Southeast Asia, being wounded during mili-tary service, receiving a military decoration besides a service medal, receiving an honorable discharge from the military at any point in the past, satisfactorily completing twenty-four months of military service, or completing alternative service or being excused from it as a part of the Ford clemency program.[183]

For three years the peculiar citizenship requirements for young American men abated. There was no draft. Draft resisters and military deserters of the Vietnam War era had the opportunity to be readmitted to the United States as citizens, although few took advantage of the offer.[184] Although the Carter program for review of Vietnam War–era discharges used a case-by-case method, it upgraded most less-than-honorable discharges. Many military deserters had their discharge status upgraded but were not eligible for veterans' benefits.[185] Ironically, on July 2, 1980, in the face of renewed Cold War tensions with the Soviet invasion of Afghanistan in late 1979, the Carter administration felt compelled to reinstate draft registration for American men eighteen to twenty-six years of age and born in 1960 or later—a law that remains in effect into the early twenty-first century.[186] On July 1, 1980, the day before reinstating military draft registration in the United States, Carter had signed the Vietnam Veterans Memorial Bill into law, authorizing the construction of a Vietnam Veterans Memorial in Washington, D.C. In his remarks at the bill-signing ceremony in the Rose Garden of the White House, Carter noted that "for too long we tried to put that division behind us by forgetting the Vietnam war and, in the process, we ignored those who bravely answered their Nation's call." In this he echoed his rationale for his pardon of Vietnam War–era military service resisters in his September 23, 1976, presidential debate with Gerald Ford—that the divisiveness of the war should be put in the past.[187]

Jimmy Carter does not mention the amnesty program in his presidential museum in Atlanta, nor did he mention it in his presidential memoirs or his published White House diary. Carter's silences are not surprising. By dealing with the lingering problem of amnesty for draft resisters on the first day of his presidency, he seemed determined not to let the Vietnam War, which had ended two years before, intrude upon his administration, as it had those of his predecessors. Thus, in his efforts to discuss "themes that are still pertinent" in the early twenty-first century, it is conceivable that any references to his amnesty would be a part of the three-fourths of the diary he excised for its 2010 publication as a monograph. He did mention it in his 2015 memoir, *A Full Life: Reflections at Ninety,* saying only that "my first official act was to pardon the draft evaders from the Vietnam War."[188] He declined invitations to discuss the amnesty for this book.

Approximately half of the men who went from the United States to Canada in the 1960s and 1970s were still there in the mid-1990s.[189] Their ambivalence is notable. Although they lived in a world that assigns nationality and citizenship to nearly everyone, young Americans were in a unique position to choose between two very similar countries that made distinctly different demands of them. Young men living in the United States lived in a country that ascribed and denied them citizenship rights based on their demonstration of allegiance through fulfilling military duty, yet thousands of those men challenged such claims through noncooperation with, nonparticipation in, or expression of opposition to the U.S. military during the Vietnam War era. Canada, in contrast, projected an image of a country that welcomed new residents, forgave their transgressions, and would go out of its way to provide them the freedom to enjoy life as they wanted to enjoy it. During the Vietnam War era, Canada opened its borders to young U.S. residents as immigrants, yet closed them to extradition. Canada had tried diplomatic means to influence the United States to lessen its involvement in Southeast Asia. Largely unsuccessful in this, Canada created policies actively to encourage Americans to immigrate to Canada.

Many young American men recognized the porousness of the U.S.-Canadian border and crossed it, recognizing that a move to Canada would give them the opportunity to acquire citizenship rights that better reflected their values and worldview and to leave behind a world in which duty required them to fulfill the needs of others. Young Americans were well educated, spoke English, and were usually employable in the Canadian economy. Many were, after all, a few steps away from being (or recently had been) soldiers in the military of a world superpower.

U.S.-born men who reached adulthood in the late 1960s to mid-1970s weighed definitions and offers of citizenship from both the United States and Canada. Despite being the subject of much public debate about their admissibility as residents or citizens of the United States or Canada, the voices and the actions of those men reflect ambivalence about citizenship. These men did not necessarily adhere to requirements of citizenship of any country, in particular, but saw themselves more as citizens of the world at large.

6 · AMERICAN VIETNAM WAR–ERA ÉMIGRÉS AND THE BLURRING OF BORDERS

I had spent a whole day and asked everybody I could find but no one seemed to know how to leave the country. Not only that, but nobody had even thought about leaving the country. I guess everybody just assumed they were American because they had been born that way and that being American or whatever was part of what you were. Maybe they never thought about who they were. Maybe they thought that they were secretaries or bus drivers or Americans instead of thinking that they were their own selves being secretaries and Americans.

—Allen Morgan, *Dropping Out in 3/4 Time* (1972)

As a way to learn the political geography of the United States, children are sometimes given a jigsaw puzzle with each piece of the puzzle in the shape of one of the fifty states. The pieces are placed into a frame in the shape of the (continental) United States. (The non-continental states of Alaska and Hawai'i are usually squeezed onto the puzzle out of place and out of proportion in size to the rest of the states.) Some versions of this puzzle suggest that the United States borders other nations, with fleeting indications that Mexico lies to the south and Canada to the north. Other versions show the United States in no geographical context, as if the nation were floating in space or bordering nations constituted some sort of terra incognita.[1] When the puzzle/map is complete, its pieces fit together perfectly, they do not overlap, and all the space on the puzzle grid is filled.

Benedict Anderson describes this phenomenon as a "map-as-logo" or "logo-map" and notes how such maps can remove "all explanatory glosses," including references to geographical features, place names, latitude and longitude, and neighboring countries. These maps become "pure sign, no longer compass to the world" and are reproduced in all sorts of two-dimensional media to the extent that the logo becomes "instantly recognizable, everywhere visible . . . penetrat[ing] deep into the popular imagination, and forming a powerful emblem."[2]

While they can provide lessons about geography, maps—whether they are an interactive tool, such as a puzzle; are posted on classroom walls; or are illustrations in books, magazines, and the like—can be deceptive in their suggestion that that which is represented on the map is stable. Political boundaries in and of the United States—the lesson to be learned from such a puzzle map—have remained stable since the early twentieth century, with the shape of the continental United States having been locked in place since 1853, which only furthers the deception that there is stability throughout the area represented on the map.[3] Maps can exert the same sort of psychological power often attributed to books, plays, and films. They can dehumanize a landscape in their representation of geographical space by not acknowledging inhabitants of a mapped area. Ultimately maps have the power, according to the geographer J. H. Andrews, to "disapprove as well as approve" and to "criminalize as well as legitimatize."[4]

To extend the metaphor of the child's puzzle/map of the United States, consider the dilemma faced by many young Americans in the 1960s and 1970s who may have learned from this sort of educational tool and were inculcated into such dehumanized and (de-)legitimizing geographical thinking as they grappled with the limits of their options in the Vietnam War era. None of the pieces/states offered escape from obligation to the military. All required adherence to a national order. There was nowhere on the map to go. The only escape was to abandon the puzzle/nation altogether and go to the periphery that was the terra incognita.

In reality there is no terra incognita. Émigrés had to go to some other country in the world when they left the United States. As the philosopher Kwame Anthony Appiah has observed, "All individuals in the world are obliged, whether they like it or not, to accept the political arrangements of their birthplace—however repugnant those arrangements are to their principles or ambitions—unless they can persuade somebody else to let them in."[5] Tens of thousands of American residents in the latter third of the twentieth century found compulsory military service for, or social conditions in, the United States repugnant and succeeded in persuading someone else to let them in: the Canadian government and a large number of Canadian people.

COMMANDING ALLEGIANCES

Among such commonplace metageographical divisions as continents, cardinal directions, and First and Third Worlds, nation-states are universally recognized political subdivisions of the world—but they are unique in that they have armies to enforce their political points of view.[6] Armies can enforce the sovereignty of nations and can command the allegiance of those within its borders, yet nations are rarely challenged when they assert the right to prevent individuals from crossing their borders to enter the country.[7] At the same time, individuals are usually able to exercise their universal right of movement within, and exit from, their home countries.[8] The Peace of Westphalia of 1648 essentially locked the idea of international borders into place in the imaginations of the world's governments. The world would thereafter be a system of nation-states, each with equal sovereign rights.[9] Policies regarding emigration and immigration, passports, and border controls became important to nations as they attempted to control the movement of people over those borders. Nations reserved the right to determine who constituted its population as a matter of self-preservation.[10] From the late nineteenth century forward, it would seem impossible for there to be enough immigrants to arrive in a place to constitute an invasion of it, so immigration, as the historian Mae M. Ngai saw it, must be more "a matter of escape than one of conquest."[11]

Along the 5,500-mile-long (8,900-kilometer-long) United States–Canada border throughout most of the twentieth century, and certainly during the Vietnam War era, armies, police, and border guards were present to keep undesired people out of the United States. Although border guards were likely to apprehend military deserters if they tried to reenter the United States, they were not there to keep Americans from *leaving*, not even men with military obligations to fulfill to their country. In the same era, the Canadian government enforced its immigration legislation in a way that encouraged those same émigrés to enter Canada. It actively sought to admit young, educated, English-speaking people without regard to their status with the military in their countries of origin. Military might, as measured by the number of soldiers and workers at a nation's disposal, the willingness of an entire nation to become socially mobilized by identifying with and supporting those who served militarily, or the willingness of a soldier to die for the nation, became less important in the late twentieth century.

After World War II, with the founding of the United Nations and its condemnation of war, peace became the raison d'être of international relations. An interest in economic growth, which determined a nation's ability to stockpile military supplies and equipment, train professional military specialists, and accumulate allies, replaced mobilization for war as a basis of national cohesion.[12] American men who resisted the military draft during the Vietnam War presaged such a change in their conception of U.S. citizenship. Because a nation had less to prove to other nations by conscripting people to increase the size of its army, compulsory military service became outmoded as an obligation of citizenship. The United States responded to this change by turning to an all-volunteer military, but not until the end of its involvement in Vietnam—too late for draft-age men of that era. Yet the United States was one of the first nations to discontinue military service as a condition of citizenship. Tellingly, Canada had been among the very first, discontinuing it at the end of World War II, whereas most European nations continued the practice until the 1990s or early twenty-first century—if they have ended it at all.[13]

American men of the Vietnam War era also anticipated the changing relationship of nations to their citizens. The original foci of citizenship were duties, responsibilities, and obligations to the nation. Recognizing that the price of extracting some duties can outweigh the benefits of them, nations became more liberal, bestowing more rights on their citizens in an effort to promote social stability. A dilemma can result when nations try to require new duties of their citizens, or by requiring old duties of them again—military service chief among such requirements.[14] In the past two centuries there has been "powerful belief" in both individuals and nations, which, as the historian Adam M. McKeown has observed, chafe "against each other in their striving for autonomy, precedence and survival." Disagreements over the optimal proportion of individual rights and preservation of national identity have created, as McKeown puts it, "endlessly innovative struggles" in the modern world, as expressed in such debates as the rights of man versus national self-determination, immigrant rights versus national interests, and universal human rights versus citizenship duties.[15]

American Vietnam War–era draft resisters and military deserters pointed to such tension between their rights and duties. Beyond rejecting the call of their nation for military service, they asserted their right to protest wars they felt were immoral and their right to do as they wanted with their lives. Many people in late adolescence in the late 1960s and early 1970s wanted to avoid, postpone, or redefine occupational commitments and other responsibilities of adulthood. They wanted to pursue a postsecondary education and to engage in other activities of self-fulfillment and self-expression. At the same time, the federal government of the United States asserted its own prerogatives, chipping away at such assertions of rights and interests by continuing to require men to fulfill a military duty to their country, even when many young people did not agree with the nation's military objectives in Southeast Asia and other places in the world.

In the late twentieth century, full citizenship was enjoyed by more people than ever, because constitutional governments had replaced authoritarian governments in many parts of the world. Subjects had become citizens. In more liberal countries, former second-class citizens—primarily women and ethnic minorities—asserted that they deserved equal rights and were able to attain full citizenship.[16] In the United States, for example, young adults eighteen to twenty-one years of age shed their second-class status when they received the right to vote in 1971, owing in large part to the demands of the student movement and Vietnam War protests in the 1960s and 1970s.

Part of such liberalization was a greater recognition of the multiple identities of citizens. Gender, race, ethnicity, age, religious beliefs, business and professional contacts, and ties to other nations and to globalization could contribute to multiple political citizenships, thereby undermining the sovereignty and cohesiveness of nations.[17] Post–World War II power blocs, residing in alliances of capitalist and Communist countries, contributed to a sense of regional identification that distracted some from national allegiances.[18] People could have multiple identities and multiple allegiances of various scopes and intensities, with varying impact on their lives. Ease of global movement owing to the rise of multinational corporations, more guest worker programs, recognition of the plight of refugees, speedier global transportation and communication networks, and greater travel and educational opportunities contribute to a greater sense of multiple identities and can cause people to have allegiances beyond those to the countries in which they were born or live. The historian Linda K. Kerber saw the dissipation of national allegiances and the rise of multiple political and social allegiances as akin to a sense of statelessness viewed in the positive light of "cosmopolitanism, flexible citizenships, [and] multiple citizenships," all of which help to "sustain a dream of unboundedness."[19] Similarly, the journalist Atossa Araxia Abrahamian has asked, "What does citizenship become when it becomes detached from any kind of civic engagement and political identity—when it is a matter of convenience, not community? What are the stakes when members of a community no longer feel a particular kinship or loyalty to any particular place?"[20]

Vietnam War–era émigrés from the United States recognized, sometimes consciously, sometimes not, the possibilities of multiple political citizenships based on various global, regional, religious, or ethnic ties, human rights concerns, or connections to transnational corporations and chose citizen-ships beyond those they were given by virtue of their birth in the United States. Further, these émigrés recognized similarities between the United States and Canada while exploiting differences between the two countries to improve their personal situation. This is not to assert that Vietnam War–era émigrés to Canada felt a Canadian identity so much as that they felt a regional or North American one, or a global identity. Whether they were aware of the benefits of Canadian residency before or after their immigration, American émigrés recognized that differences between the United States and Canada were usu-ally minor and, for many, could be easily overcome. Through small geograph-ical movement, they could realize significant social gain: no expectation to serve in the nation's military.

Although the physical movement of these émigrés was relatively small, the emotional shift could be enormous. An examination of the changing mean-ings of borders, the sovereignty of nations, and citizenship of the late twenti-eth century into the early twenty-first century reveals the presaging of such trends in the movement of Vietnam War resisters to Canada. U.S. law con-cerning passports—the documents necessary for the movement of people between countries—brings further complexity to the study of emigration from the United States to Canada.

AUTHENTIC PROOF OF NATIONAL CHARACTER

Definitions of national boundaries, sovereignty of nations, and citizenship take on new meanings when they are challenged by people who want to move from one nation to another. To control such movement, nations have come to rely on passports: identification papers based on physical characteristics (a photograph of the bearer in the modern era) and indicating age, gender, date and place of birth, and, most important, nationality, of the traveler. The traveler must present his or her passport upon arrival at or in a country—at the frontier when arriving by land, at a port when arriving by ship, or at a passport control area when arriving by airplane. The right to be in a country is enforced not only at entry points but also by mobile patrols of immigration officials in the interiors of countries.[21]

A major factor contributing to the ease of movement of Americans from the United States to Canada during the Vietnam War era was the long-standing *lack* of a passport requirement for travel from the United States to other places in the Western Hemisphere. The liberal attitude of the U.S.

government toward expatriation can be traced to the founding fathers Samuel Adams, Benjamin Franklin, and Thomas Jefferson, who espoused emigration as a natural right—an idea they later expanded as the right for Britain's North American colonies to be independent.[22] During the Napoleonic Wars of the early nineteenth century, the British royal navy impressed American sailors on its ships, asserting that those born in North America under British rule still owed allegiance to Britain. The United States argued that former British North American subjects had the right to become citizens of their own newly created country instead. Tension over this matter contributed to the War of 1812 between Britain and the young United States.[23]

During the U.S. Civil War of 1861 to 1865, the U.S. Department of State restricted exit from, and entry into, the United States through seaports, along the U.S.-Canadian border, and along the lines of the Union army for reasons of national security and to control the desertion of soldiers and the entrance of mercenaries that might aid the Confederacy.[24] Only later in the nineteenth century did the State Department legally articulate the right of Americans to travel out of the United States freely. Earlier fears of emigration linked to feudalism—that people were bound to a place and that such a connection could not be broken—began to be supplanted. By the late nineteenth century, emigration became more connected to such tenets as freedom of movement and freedom of trade.[25] By 1888 the U.S. Department of State was not only supportive of foreign travel by U.S. citizens but also advised those traveling outside of the United States to carry passports in order to avoid "serious inconvenience if unprovided with authentic proof of their national character."[26] A decade later U.S. Secretary of State Richard Olney reiterated the belief that Americans should be able to travel freely, informing President Grover Cleveland that "the tendency of recent years has been towards freer and less hampered travel" throughout much of the world and that it was a "wise precaution" for the U.S. government to issue passports to its citizens so that they could travel as freely as possible in the world, no matter the passport requirements of other countries.[27]

In December 1915, in response to the chaos caused by the Great War in Europe, U.S. President Woodrow Wilson issued an executive order requiring anyone leaving the United States to be in possession of a passport issued by the U.S. Department of State.[28] During the First Red Scare (widespread fear of the rise of Communism in the United States), this became law in May 1918, giving the president the authority to prevent departure from, or entry into, the United States during times of war, particularly out of concern that spies would take national intelligence out of the country with them.[29] The next year, with the war over, the law was revised, allowing restrictions on the movement of immigrants into the United States at any time.[30] This law remained the backbone of U.S. immigration law throughout the rest of the twentieth century.[31]

At the Second International Conference on Emigration and Immigration in Havana, Cuba, in 1928, while most of the forty-one participating countries were primarily interested in discussing their rights as recipients of immigrants, the U.S. delegation was asserting the long-standing U.S. State Department view that countries no longer held power over their residents once they emigrated.[32] The newly formed United Nations promulgated the idea in the aftermath of World War II when it drafted the Universal Declaration of Human Rights. Article 13 of the declaration asserts that everyone has the right to move and reside within the borders of each country and echoes the 1928 assertion of the United States that people have the right "to leave any country, including their own, and to return to their country."[33] The United States was a signatory to the declaration when it was passed by the United Nations General Assembly on December 10, 1948, upholding immigration not only as a right of its own citizens but also as a universal right. These were early indications that the United States was limited in what it could do about men who emigrated to resist the draft or to desert the military.

In 1952 the U.S. Congress passed the Immigration and Nationality Act, more commonly known as the McCarran-Walter Act, revising U.S. immigration policy into the form it held throughout the Vietnam War era and into the twenty-first century. McCarran-Walter requires that U.S. citizens carry a passport when they leave and reenter the United States, but it allows the president to make exceptions. One exception to this rule throughout the second half of the twentieth century was travel to Canada and Mexico, as well as to most of the rest of the Western Hemisphere.[34] (The exception to the exception was travel to Cuba, which was nearly impossible for U.S. citizens in the second half of the twentieth century, after the United States imposed sanctions on the country in 1961 for having adopted a Communist government.[35])

In 1958 a study of tourism and foreign travel called for by President Dwight D. Eisenhower continued to confirm and extol the U.S. government's liberal attitude toward travel by its citizens. The study noted Eisenhower's emphasis on the importance of international travel, observed that travel by Americans was of cultural benefit both to travelers and their hosts, and suggested that travel could help bring capitalism to developing countries. The report concluded that the freedom to travel was "a unique instrument of friendly, peaceful communication among the nations and the peoples of the earth," or what the historians Nancy L. Green and François Weil have more recently characterized as "a form of diffuse ambassadorship—the spread of civilization or the avant-garde of investment abroad."[36]

Passports do more than facilitate the travel of citizens outside their home country. They also provide a way for nations to control people within their boundaries. People become dependent on the state for an identity, which the sociologist John Torpey says "they can escape only with difficulty and which may significantly shape their access to various spaces."[37] With such control over identity, states can then monopolize "the legitimate means of movement" of people within its borders, the result being "to deprive people of the freedom to move across certain spaces and to render them dependent on states and the state system for the authorization to do so."[38]

Among the reasons states seek to control movement of people is for state-building activities. Significant among such activities are extracting military service, facilitating law enforcement, and controlling "brain drain" of trained workers.[39] Conditions along the U.S.-Canada border in the 1960s and 1970s complicate Torpey's theory, however. The U.S. government's view that nations held no power over their expatriates kept it from being able to extract military service from tens of thousands of male émigrés during the Vietnam War era. Further, it allowed for an exodus of men who had been trained to be soldiers but who took the skills they had acquired from the U.S. military out of the country with them, as well as that of well-educated men and women who moved from the United States to Canada for myriad reasons, not all of which were related to the war.

A third purpose of passports, beyond facilitating travel outside of one's home country and controlling movement of people within a county's borders, is to make the distinction between citizen and noncitizen knowable and therefore enforceable, in order to protect people of a place from other people whose identity is uncertain, a practice that evolved in late nineteenth-century Europe.[40] The passport system evolved in such a way after World War I that nations, by issuing them to their citizens and requiring them of noncitizens upon entry to the country, were simply adhering to and responding to the norms of a "cooperating 'international society.'"[41] Americans entering Canada did not need passports in the twentieth century, so we can surmise that Canada did not feel strongly compelled enough to protect its own people from Americans, seeing Americans instead as capable, if not highly desirable, residents. In its search for young, educated, English-speaking immigrants, Canada refused to extradite American draft resisters and military deserters, which reinforced the lack of control the United States had over people who had left it. Therefore, the right to restrict the access of Americans to Canada was held not by the United States but by Canada, which asserted its sovereignty by accepting Americans into the country and protecting them there, even over the protests of the U.S. government. In this situation, there was no "cooperating international society."

Passport-free travel by U.S. citizens to Western Hemisphere destinations continued throughout the rest of the twentieth century but came to an end on June 1, 2009. The commission investigating the September 11, 2001, terrorist attacks on the United States observed that the minimal identification required for non–U.S. citizens to enter the United States left the country vulnerable to terrorism. The Intelligence Reform and Terrorism Prevention Act of 2004 required the U.S. Departments of Homeland Security and State to require passports (or allowable substitutions such as passport cards, enhanced drivers licenses, "trusted traveler" cards, or merchant marine, military, or American Indian identification documents) for all persons entering or leaving the United States, including U.S. citizens.[42]

The use of passports has a checkered history in U.S. emigration. Passports were not in standard use worldwide until the early twentieth century, but the U.S. government had encouraged its citizens to carry them for decades. The lack of passport requirements to travel from the United States to nearly all Western Hemisphere destinations is an exception to most histories of the passport and points to the special circumstances that U.S. émigrés to Canada exploited in their search for relief from military obligation during the Vietnam War.

A REGULAR PAYCHECK IN A COLD COUNTRY

Americans have left the United States from the moment it became a nation. By the 1960s U.S. citizens could be sure that their government supported their right to travel, with the added encouragement that no passport was necessary to go to and to return from nearly all Western Hemisphere countries. Transportation in the second half of the twentieth century could easily take Americans many places. Trains and buses would convey them, but only on routes and schedules determined by transit companies. After automobiles became more commonly available and affordable, people could drive themselves wherever and whenever they wanted to go: to places trains and buses would not take them and to places where they could escape their working-class lives, and on a schedule and at a speed that trains and buses could not accommodate.[43] The United States had two neighbors to which automobile drivers and their passengers easily could go—Mexico and Canada. Mexico had a warmer climate and was a less expensive place to live, but it was more culturally and linguistically different from the United States than was Canada. Still, Mexico lingered in the imaginations of some as a place to immigrate.

For example, consider the dilemma Jack Todd faced when he decided to desert from the U.S. Army in December 1969. He had been stationed at Fort Lewis, Washington, 135 miles (220 kilometers) from the Canadian border. After boot camp, he spent part of his time on leave in San Diego, only a few miles from Mexico. As he recalled in his memoirs, "I never felt the urge to go to Canada. I always wanted to go to Mexico. Books do that to you. You read, you want to be there: Malcolm Lowry's *Under the Volcano,* Graham Greene's *The Power and the Glory.* Mexico is exotic, but still close enough to the U.S. that you can get the baseball scores. Mexico is warm, Canada is cold. Mexico is cheap, Canada is—well, I don't know what Canada is, but I assume it isn't cheap. If I have to live underground, Mexico is as good as Canada—better, because it's warmer and cheaper."[44]

Todd ended up in Mexico and found himself on a beach where he struck up a conversation with a graduate student from the University of California–Berkeley, who worked with a group that helped deserters and resisters go to Canada. When she learned why he was in Mexico, she revealed the major difference between Mexico and Canada for men in his situation, beseeching him, "You can't stay here.... The Mexicans will extradite you for sure. But first they'll put you in a Mexican jail. Nobody told you that?" She added, "You know you can work in Canada.... Pierre Trudeau changed the rules. Deserters can work legally in Canada. As long as you have a college education and you can get a job, it shouldn't be a problem." Accordingly Todd reversed the trajectory of his self-exile and headed north to Canada, realizing that "Mexico was a pleasant fantasy.... If Canada is a sure thing, then I'm going to Canada. Better a regular paycheck in a cold country than hunger and dysentery in a Mexican jail."[45]

If Todd had read Arlo Tatum and Joseph S. Tuchinsky's 1969 *Guide to the Draft,* he would have been advised that men were indeed being returned to the United States from Mexico.[46] Likewise, the American Deserters Committee's pamphlet "Travel to a Foreign Country" warned émigrés, "DO NOT go to Mexico or other parts of Latin America."[47] It was difficult to secure a work permit in Mexico, so many who exiled themselves there eventually ended up returning to the United States or moved to another country if they were not extradited from Mexico first.[48]

Canada was a place to which Americans of various races, religions, occupational groups, and economic classes moved for nearly two centuries. Such a reputation, along with similarities in culture and language and proximity to the United States, caused Canada to loom large in the minds of Americans, not simply as a friendly neighboring country or a pleasant place to visit but also as an alternative to, or refuge from, the United States. In this era, 80 percent of Americans traveling out of the country went to Canada.[49] Much travel literature describing Canada for U.S. audiences assured them that Canada was familiar, welcoming, friendly, nearby, accessible, and easy to enter, especially due to the relaxed passport laws. Such travel literature served double duty for both tourists and for potential emigrants.

Draft resisters, military deserters, and other Vietnam War–era émigrés from the United States to Canada recognized that Canada was a place to which they could move and enjoy a life similar to that which they had in the United States, but where they could avoid social conditions to which they objected, and where U.S. laws would not apply to them. These Americans were unique in that they constituted a large emigration group on the leading edge of a model of transnational citizenship in an era when nations' grips on their residents were relaxing. Young Americans worked to survive and to carve out spaces for themselves in the world while resisting their country's attempts to enforce standards of citizenship built on models of nationhood that dated to the nineteenth century.

Americans uncomfortable with life in the United States often needed to be reassured that they could leave the country. As Richard Paterak, who emigrated to Canada in the late 1960s, observed, it was "in the nature of American life" that aid groups were necessary to show American men how to resist the military draft because "America has indoctrinated its young so well that the thought of emigration is extraordinary."[50] An article in an October 1968 issue of *U.S. News and World Report* echoed this, describing Canadian asylum in the words of one person providing such aid: "Some come filled with anxiety and expect to be caught up in some sort of cloak-and-dagger operation. They often are a little turned off when we tell them to relax, and when we point out that there is nothing illegal in Canada about what they are doing."[51] Tourist information published in periodical literature and travel guides encouraged Americans to go to Canada, especially leading up to Canada's 1967 centennial celebration. Vietnam War–era draft advice literature discussing immigration to Canada mentioned that the sparsely populated country was interested in attracting immigrants, that Canadian immigration officials would "treat people fairly" and were "business-like or sympathetic toward Americans rather than hostile," and that Canadian people generally would be friendly and welcoming.[52] Not surprisingly, residents of the northern United States, who were only hours away from Canada via various forms of transportation, were more likely to immigrate to Canada than their southern compatriots. (See the appendix.)

In the Vietnam War era many people expressed, through religion, their conviction in a higher moral calling by not participating in, or by aiding those who resisted participation in, the Vietnam War. Even in this religious expression, the state was not entirely escapable. Americans sometimes emigrated on religious grounds when the Selective Service System (SSS) rejected their applications for conscientious objector status. Many religion-based Canadian immigrant aid groups sought not only to aid émigrés but to influence the government of Canada to have liberal policies concerning émigrés.

Many late adolescents of the late 1960s and early 1970s genuinely wanted postsecondary degrees, often appealing to more universal, cosmopolitan ideals in their pursuit of them. Once again the state was not inescapable in such efforts. Young American men had to prove their standing as good students to the SSS in order to receive a deferment from military service to attend universities. If they failed to be good students—or when they succeeded in graduating—they became eligible for the draft. Men with serious interest in pursuing undergraduate and graduate degrees and who could not be assured of deferment from the draft often could attend school in Canada in a university system that very closely resembled that of the United States.

Accessibility, favorable passport and immigration laws, receptive religious groups, and postsecondary educational opportunities directed Americans who were out of options in the United States over the border to Canada. Through the extreme action of expatriation, Americans pointed to their distaste for the requirement that young men subject themselves to military conscription as a condition of U.S. citizenship. Their movement was only accelerated when Canada actively sought them as new residents and potential citizens.

BLURRING THE BORDER

The geographic indistinguishableness of the United States and Canada serves to blur the border between them, something that has been apparent to many people, with nineteenth-century Loyalists, mid-nineteenth-century travelers on the Underground Railroad, agricultural émigrés of the late nineteenth and early twentieth centuries, and draft resisters and military deserters of the Vietnam War era among the most notable groups. If we consider the Western or "civic" model of the nation described by Anthony D. Smith, in which nations have compact, well-defined territories, where "people and territory must ... belong to each other," and where "terrain and people have exerted mutual, and beneficial, influence over several generations," we can see how such a model does not hold up well for the United States and Canada.[53] Scholars must be careful in their application of European-based theories of nation, citizenship, and immigration to North American examples. As the third- and second-largest countries in area in the world, each sprawling across six time zones, the United States and Canada are not compact, but are generally well-defined.[54] The primary boundary that divides the two countries in their wests is the forty-ninth parallel, a straight line that ignores mountain ranges, watersheds, and ecosystems. Further, natural water boundaries, such as the Great Lakes and the St. Lawrence River in their easts, that could divide the two countries actually serve to unite them, with the two countries having negotiated several treaties in order to share them peacefully, while other waterways pass between them, oblivious to human-determined boundaries.[55] Likewise, in many places, roads continue from one side of the border to the other, with—in the twentieth century—minimal checkpoints at the border and, as we have noted, passports not necessary for Canadians and Americans to visit one another's countries.

Smith further cited such factors as "genealogy and presumed descent ties, popular mobilization, vernacular languages, customs and traditions" as elements that describe ethnic constructions of nations.[56] With such a definition, the United States and Canada once again seem more like one nation, not two. Americans and Canadians largely share ancestral ties: they were founded by the same European settler societies, share English as the primary language of their people, and share customs and traditions derived from their history as former colonies of Britain. While each country has its own economy, those economies are inextricably connected, with each country acting as the other's largest trading partner.[57]

Other aspects of Smith's definition of a nation do hold up regarding the sovereignty of the United States and Canada. The two countries share history as former colonies of Great Britain, though those histories took divergent paths in the late eighteenth century. Canada remained a colony of Britain for ninety more years and did not gain absolute control over its own constitution until 1982. While there are many similarities in the culture of the two countries because of their shared history and language and Canadians' great interest in mass culture of U.S. origin, the Canadian government has long taken measures, legal and fiscal, to protect and promote culture created in Canada.

The Canadian parliamentary system, borrowed from Britain, certainly distinguishes Canada from the United States. The latter has regularly scheduled elections, most of its officials hold office for predetermined amounts of time, and there is greater separation of executive and legislative branches. Both systems are effective, but the two governments operate independently from the other. Indeed, it was the independent thinking of the Canadian government that allowed U.S. émigrés to move easily to Canada during the Vietnam War era.

The United States and Canada certainly are not one nation, but their sovereignty frequently has been blurred throughout their histories and certainly was during the 1960s and 1970s. The point here is not to determine whether the United States and Canada were the same nation, or even whether Canada was the country most similar to the United States, but rather to assert that the two countries were similar enough that emigrants from one country could move to the other with a relatively minimal disruption in their lives.

A NORTH AMERICAN LANDSCAPE OF EMIGRATION

Studying the United States as a sending nation of emigrants, rather than as a receiving nation of immigrants, is to observe a reversal of the traditional perspective of U.S. immigration history. It recognizes that foreign audiences can help tell the history of the United States and that ideas and institutions— entities without "clear national identities"—contribute to that history. It also recognizes that U.S. residents, ideas, and institutions may not be "distinctly American." They may have originated somewhere else and could continue elsewhere.[58] Further, because a person can only be in one place at a time, it is important to look at immigration from the point of view of the individual. Focusing on movement from the perspective of the individual proposes a new paradigm of the history of the movement of people of the United States as one of the history of emigration, that is, leaving the United States, rather than that of the history of immigration, or arrivals there. When an émigré makes the choice to move, he or she must deal with various restrictions and regulations with which they can either willingly comply or willfully ignore. The latter scenario transforms their movement—their emigration— into something akin to an escape. This inverts Mae Ngai's observations on the sovereignty of nations, because it is the émigré who determines his or her own national membership for the sake of his or her self-preservation.[59]

Attention to the emigrant acknowledges that individuals move not randomly but to specific places at specific times. While it is important that their country of destination is open to them, because immigration is a national policy issue, it is the specific place to which émigrés move in that country that is most crucial to them. Upon their arrival in a new country, émigrés concentrate on the small portion of their new world upon which they can exert control: their households, workplaces, and communities.[60] In the 1960s and 1970s, tourist literature and communication with immigrant aid and draft resistance groups helped U.S. émigrés decide where to move in Canada, whether it was to a rural area, where they could get "back to the land," to a metropole, or somewhere in between. For this reason, the historian Arif Dirlik suggested leaving the concept of nation out of the equation when considering the "ethnic and diasporic spaces" defined by immigrants and asserted that "translocal" is a better term than "transnational" to describe that space. Translocal space undermines the "unity and homogeneity" of the nation and may even outlast it.[61] Although Dirlik did not articulate it, the idea of the translocal gives greater agency to émigrés to determine the conditions of the spaces to which they move. As they recognize local variables in laws, economic opportunities, and social customs, they search for those places that present the best possible combination of those variables to warrant a change of location. The qualities of a particular place are of greater concern to an émigré than are the qualities of a particular country.

Attention to the emigrant also acknowledges that a person's emotional and intellectual background complicates their lives in such a way that people who move can at once be natives, immigrants, and exiles, depending on the extent to which they want to be conscious of any or all of those identities.[62] The notion of *fuite en avant,* the French phrase meaning, literally, "fleeing ahead" or, more figuratively, an uncalculated, headlong rush into a new situation, is therefore not so much falling into a completely unknown space but, rather, movement to a space not readily understood or recognized by others. The space *is* knowable and definable by the emigrant. Just because you do not know *where* you are going does not mean you do not want to go and that you cannot attain that which you seek in another place.

Further complicating the sense of place that émigrés experienced in North America is the unique context of the United States–Canada border, with its porousness and the similarity of cultures on either side of it. The opportunity to be outside the United States and therefore outside the reach of law enforcement concerning draft and military laws, yet still live in a familiar North American culture, created a stunningly unique place for Vietnam War–era draft resisters and military deserters to move.

Victor Konrad and Heather N. Nicol have recognized what they call "third spaces" created by the unique context of the U.S.-Canada border, seeing them intriguingly as "'neither here nor there'" but that "they are indeed physically and territorially 'somewhere,'" even if they are "invisible from a geographical perspective."[63] Konrad and Nicol see such spaces as accommodating trade, such as the 1994 North American Free Trade Agreement (NAFTA) between Canada, the United States, and Mexico.[64] Yet for all the attention paid to trade ties across the U.S.-Canada border, Konrad and Nicol maintain that cultural relations provide the "critical infrastructure for political economies."[65] Cultural relations between countries, more so than trade relations, point to spaces through which or into which émigrés can move, hence the relative comfort U.S. émigrés found in Canada after their move there.

Seeing immigrant-defined places as translocal or third spaces can explain the lack of patriotism and the lack of allegiance to the United States that émigrés could have demonstrated by service in the U.S. military. It could also explain the lack of connection to Canada felt by many Americans who went there, with many expressing an affinity for something beyond the nation. We do well to pay attention to the landscapes described by the movement of Vietnam War–era émigrés from the United States to Canada. While their movement was undoubtedly motivated by the disadvantages and advantages posed by residency in the two nations, émigrés carved out a space in which they could live their lives the way they wanted. They were able to enjoy the economic perquisites of life in North America, continued to use the English language in their day-to-day lives, experienced minimal disruption in their cultural, if not social, life, and avoided the disruption of military service. That they had to move from one country to another to accomplish this is inescapable, but the space they made for themselves was essentially local. They transferred their lives from one place, where they had experienced conditions that were not entirely to their liking, to another place, where they found conditions more sustainable.

The governments of the United States and Canada, long aware of the commonalities of their postcolonial North American societies, have often contributed to the blurring of the border between their countries. In the past two centuries the two countries have maintained a relatively unguarded border that generally has allowed for the easy flow of people over it. Kwame Appiah observed that everyone is required to "accept the political arrangements of their birthplace" unless they can persuade another country to admit them, and it follows that someone else will prescribe new political arrangements in the émigrés' new domiciles.[66] After all, the traditional paradigm of modern immigration holds that the movement of people is over borders—from one nation to another.

By recognizing migration on the scale of the individual, we acknowledge that immigrants have the ability to perceive differences in places and to negotiate the arrangements for living in them. Rather than seeing immigrants as moving from one country to another, we do better to see them as moving from one place to another, or from one home to a new home. Home is ideally the place where one feels satisfied and safe. When that home feels threatened, people assert the modern human right of emigration and take on the burden of moving themselves to a new home in a new place.

Vietnam War–era emigrants from the United States to Canada witnessed a confluence of three historical conditions that came together in a unique way in the 1960s and 1970s: the possibility of emigration, the strong links between the United States and Canada, and Vietnam's struggle for autonomy. In studying their emigrations—great in number, but short in distance—we challenge two paradigms of immigration in U.S. history. The first is that people do not leave the United States. They do. We should listen to their stories. That which they reject about the United States can tell us much about that nation in particular and much about nations of the late twentieth and early twenty-first centuries in general. Further, the collective stories of emigrants from the United States over the sweep of history of the past two centuries fills a gap in U.S. history. Reclaiming the stories of U.S. émigrés who might otherwise disappear from U.S. history helps us better contextualize the United States in world history.

The second is that we need to pay much closer attention to the individual and the local in immigration history. The nation-state model of citizenship does not work well in this history because the nation endeavors to impose an order on all who occupy a defined geographical space. Attention to the concepts of globalism, cosmopolitanism, ethnic identities, natural rights, and statelessness erode the idea of the nation-state but still do not arrive at an individual's motivation to leave a place that is not comfortable as a home. Ultimately it is the individual who decides for him- or herself to leave, either out of conviction or compulsion. The individual presents him- or herself at the border of another country to declare interest in entering it and to exit the United States—to enter the seeming terra incognita that lies outside the geographical imagination of many Americans. For emigrants, the world does not begin and end at a nation's boundaries. It begins in new homes in a multitude of places beyond the nation.

ACKNOWLEDGMENTS

The topic of this book came to me more than three decades before I realized that I had witnessed some of it. In 1968 I was a little boy in the back seat of a blue, four-door Ford Fairlane, riding north through Michigan with my parents and brother on our way to Canada. My first encounter with Canada, the town of Sault Ste. Marie, Ontario, did not seem particularly foreign, but the border crossing to get there, along with the trip west on the Trans-Canada Highway, along the north shore of Lake Superior, were eye-opening experiences for a six-year-old from the middle of a Midwestern state. The signs I saw—various flags, large distances between places, accents, vocabulary, spelling, variations on foods and drinks—seemed minor, but I knew that they meant *something*. The trip was seminal in my appreciation of Canada. A curiosity has stayed with me all those years and has long defined how I look at the culture and history of my own country, the United States.

In the early twenty-first century, on my umpteenth trip to Canada but my first research trip there as a graduate student in history, pursuing some of my interests in immigration to Canada, I found myself on the same highway as in 1968, in the front seat this time, driving, but my thoughts wandered back to those of the little boy in the back seat more than thirty years before. Out of the window from time to time the boy saw young men hitchhiking, with suitcases or bundles of belongings in tow, also heading north, also apparently on their way to Canada. The boy heard murmurs of recognition from his parents in the front seat.

It dawned on me, three decades later, what the boy saw and what his parents were talking about. A few weeks later, I asked my parents, on their front porch, who those men were. Mom and Dad confirmed that they were likely draft resisters—young American men resisting military service in the Vietnam War era by going north to Canada. These young men had apparently been living in the back of my mind all these years. I know now that there surely must have been some women among them. Maybe these memories explained my pacifism. Perhaps they explained my lifelong interest in Canada. After all, why was I always looking for reasons to go there?[1] Why did I never, as a friend once suggested I might, get tired of reading about Canada? Why have I thrived for so long with the tension of living in the United States while always dreaming of Canada? Does this explain my long-standing interest in immigration to Canada from the United States?

I have been captivated for so long—consciously or unconsciously—by those young émigré American men, only a generation older than me. I hope I can do justice to them by bringing them out of the back seat of my mind, off of the road, out of the countries between which they moved and in which they lived, and into this book where their story will be heard. I would not be in a position to tell their story were it not for the kindness and generosity of many people and institutions. First of all, I extend my thanks to the employees of libraries and archives who helped me by identifying collections I should view and who brought them to me for use in reading rooms from Vancouver to Boston to Atlanta to Ottawa. Thanks also to the many people working behind the scenes at Indiana University and Indiana State University libraries and many other libraries across North America to fulfill the dozens of interlibrary loan requests I submitted to them.

Travel to use archival collections in North America is not inexpensive. I could not have afforded to have taken the many trips it required to collect information had it not been for the support of the Indiana State University Department of History, the Indiana University Department of History, the Indiana University Graduate and Professional Student Organization, the Society for Historians of American Foreign Relations, and the Gerald R. Ford Foundation.

The Association for Canadian Studies in the United States, the Organization for the History of Canada, the Organization of American Historians, and the Immigration and Ethnic History Society provided funding for me to travel to their conferences to present early versions of portions of this book. I am likewise grateful for funding from the Indiana State University Department of History, the Indiana State University College of Arts and Sciences, and Franklin College of Indiana for funding to present later portions of this book in various conferences in the United States, Canada, and France.

The basis of this book was my doctoral dissertation in the Department of History at Indiana University. I am particularly grateful to Claude A. Clegg III, who helped me frame questions for my research, who became my adviser, and who steered me through qualifying exams, a dissertation proposal, and the dissertation itself. I have always felt lucky to have worked with such an incredible gentleman and scholar. I thank him profusely.

Eric Sandweiss, Matt Guterl, Ed Linenthal, and John Bodnar of my dissertation committee collectively helped me find my way toward becoming a historian. Individually they lavished me with time and attention, each showing me paths that led me to the work that I present on the following pages. Their questions echoed in my head in archival reading rooms and in library stacks and helped me articulate questions about how and why Americans leave. My thanks also to professors Ellen Dwyer, Stephen Stein, and Pedro Machado, in whose courses I did work that made its way into this book. My gratitude extends also to David Thelen, Joanne Meyerowitz, David Pace, Maria Bucur, Beverly Stoeltje, and Larry Friedman, who also indulged me in ideas that show up here. Susan Armeny taught me much about historical writing that I endeavor to practice every day.

Many friends and colleagues looked at draft versions of this book and gave me ideas to make it easier to understand and read. I am particularly grateful to Fritz Lieber, Mike Nelson, Jane Crisler, Kathryn Fuller, and Tony Rotundo. Mike Nelson in particular helped me carve a massive manuscript into chapters. He and Brian Smith steered me toward software to help me create a map. Thanks also to Wallace Daniel and Patricia Cornett, who worked with me on an essay published in the *Journal of Church and State* that forms part of chapter 3, and Heather Fryer, Erika Kuhlman, and Robbie Lieberman, who worked with me on an essay published in the journal *Peace and Change* that forms part of chapter 5. Keith Eberly and Phil Guerty at the Organization of American Historians' *Magazine of History* provided advice on what became portions of chapters 1 and 2. Chad Parker, Donna Drucker, Steve Andrews, Jeremy Rapport, and Deborah Cohn also provided guidance on early writing. Jane Guskin and Fred Barnhart found primary documents for me in the dust of their institutions. Lillian Fuller, Deb Hutton, Mitzi Lewison, Marianne Mitchell, Laura Plummer, Lislott and John Richardson, Alex Tanford, and Norita and Sonny Varkalis provided much support over the many years. Colleagues in the Indiana State University Department of History have given me the underpinnings and camaraderie for a career as a historian and educator. I am beyond grateful for all of this help. Thanks also to Nicole Solano of, and the anonymous readers for, Rutgers University Press for shepherding me through the publication of this book, and to Angela Piliouras and Michelle Asakawa of Westchester Publishing Services for their cheerful help in polishing this manuscript.

My thanks also to friends Canadian, American, Canadian American, and American Canadian who gave me places to stay and provided hospitality while I conducted research and did writing: Amy Flint, Mike Flint, Robin Milhausen and Steve Jett, Peter Varns and Brian O'Connor, Dan Haataja, Alex Cruz, and Fern Bayer. Cathy Freebairn graciously loaned me one of her family's historic cabins in northern Michigan for several weeks for a writing retreat. It was inspiring to write a few feet away from one of the paths that many people have taken on their way out of the United States to Canada.

My parents, Don and Kaye, demonstrated an early interest in history to me and my brothers Terry and Patrick and instilled in us a strong appreciation of travel, logic, and investigation. I hope those qualities are reflected in this book. I am forever grateful to them for helping me get off on the right foot in this life. I would not be a good cat dad if I were to fail to acknowledge the lessons in patience, perseverance, and fidelity provided by many gray, calico, orange, black-and-white, and black felines.

Most of all, my thanks to my friend and my partner Fritz Lieber, who has stuck with me through thick and through thin, through the last year of an undergraduate degree and through three graduate degrees, and who became my husband soon after the federal government of the United States became willing to recognize our decades-long relationship. I have been so lucky to have found someone with whom I can talk so easily and about so much and with whom I can travel through this world. That this book would emerge from the pencils, pens, papers, books, and conversations in our home is no surprise and no miracle. He reminded me that Sigmund Freud said that love and work are the cornerstone of our humanness and essential to our mental health.[2] Indeed, Fritz, as we have loved and worked every day over the many, many years, you have driven me crazy and kept me sane. Thank you for all of it.

APPENDIX

Rate of Population Moving to Canada, by State, 1966–1972

State	Total emigrants to Canada, 1966–1972	Population, 1970	Emigrants per 100,000 population	Rank
Alabama	332	3,444,165	9.6	51
Alaska	618	300,382	205.7	6
Arizona	1,148	1,770,900	64.8	22
Arkansas	273	1,923,295	14.2	48
California	22,394	19,953,134	112.2	17
Colorado	3,224	2,207,259	146.1	9
Connecticut	3,079	3,031,709	101.6	18
Delaware	299	548,104	54.6	29
District of Columbia	301	756,510	39.8	37
Florida	2,389	6,789,443	35.2	38
Georgia	810	4,589,575	17.6	47
Hawai'i	440	768,561	57.2	27
Idaho	1,506	712,567	211.3	5
Illinois	6,891	11,113,976	62.0	24
Indiana	2,205	5,193,669	42.5	36
Iowa	1,370	2,824,376	48.5	33
Kansas	1,127	2,246,578	50.2	31
Kentucky	671	3,218,706	20.8	43
Louisiana	835	3,641,306	22.9	42
Maine	1,760	992,048	177.4	8
Maryland	1,858	3,922,399	47.4	34
Massachusetts	6,973	5,689,170	122.6	15
Michigan	11,161	8,875,083	125.8	14
Minnesota	3,338	3,804,971	87.7	19

(continued)

State	Total emigrants to Canada, 1966–1972	Population, 1970	Emigrants per 100,000 population	Rank
Mississippi	240	2,216,912	10.8	49
Missouri	1,480	4,676,501	31.6	40
Montana	2,351	694,409	338.6	1
Nebraska	786	1,483,493	53.0	30
Nevada	680	488,738	139.1	10
New Hampshire	1,000	737,681	135.6	11
New Jersey	4,673	7,168,164	65.2	21
New Mexico	599	1,016,000	59.0	25
New York	21,084	18,236,967	115.6	16
North Carolina	1,034	5,082,059	20.3	44
North Dakota	799	617,761	129.3	13
Ohio	5,947	10,652,017	55.8	28
Oklahoma	1,248	2,559,229	48.8	32
Oregon	5,572	2,091,385	266.4	3
Pennsylvania	5,437	11,793,909	46.1	35
Rhode Island	724	946,725	76.5	20
South Carolina	254	2,590,516	9.8	50
South Dakota	418	665,507	62.8	23
Tennessee	723	3,923,687	18.4	45
Texas	3,852	11,196,730	34.4	39
Utah	1,401	1,059,273	132.3	12
Vermont	789	444,330	177.6	7
Virginia	1,436	4,648,494	30.9	41
Washington	9,723	3,409,169	285.2	2
West Virginia	320	1,744,237	18.3	46
Wisconsin	2,597	4,417,731	58.8	26
Wyoming	729	332,416	219.3	4
Not stated	269			
TOTAL	151,167	203,211,926	74.4	

SOURCES: Emigration figures from M. G. Clark (Director General, Foreign Service) to J. S. Nutt (Director General, Bureau of Western Hemisphere Affairs, Department of External Affairs), May 22, 1974, "Immigration from the United States by State of Last Permanent Residence, Calendar Years, 1966–1970," file 5850-3-637, vol. 1251, "Selection & Processing—General Series—Immigration from United States," Records of the Immigration Branch (RG 76), Library and Archives Canada, Ottawa, Ontario. "Immigration from the United States by State of Last Permanent Residence, Calendar Years, 1971–1972," ibid. Population figures for 1970 from table 8: "Population of the United States and Puerto Rico: 1790 to 1970," U.S. Bureau of the Census, *1970 Census of the Population*, vol. 1: *Characteristics of the Population*, part A: *Number of Inhabitants* (Washington, DC: U.S. Government Printing Office, 1972), 148.

NOTES

INTRODUCTION

1. Fern Bayer, comp., "Chronology of the Life of David W. Diamond," 2005, vol. 1, [p. 2], David W. Diamond fonds (R11554), Library and Archives Canada, Ottawa, Ontario.

2. Bayer, "Chronology of the Life of David W. Diamond," [pp. 3–5].

3. "Mon. April 7, 1975," p. 2, folder "Diamond, David W.—'Synapse; A Deserter's Diary'—Typescript, 2 of 5, 1975," vol. 2, David W. Diamond fonds.

4. Atossa Araxia Abrahamian, *The Cosmopolites: The Coming of the Global Citizen* (New York: Columbia Global Reports, 2015), 9–10. The philosopher Kwame Anthony Appiah suggests another definition: "a rejection of the conventional view that every civilized person belonged to *a* community among communities." Kwame Anthony Appiah, *Cosmopolitanism: Ethics in a World of Strangers* (New York: Norton, 2006), xiv. Appiah traces this idea to the Cynics of the fourth century BCE, who distinguished a cosmopolitan from a citizen (politēs), the latter owing loyalty to a specific city (polis). Ibid. In the context of this study, the term "city" or "community" applies to the United States in general, however ungainly those terms might be when applied to a nation of 203 million people (in 1970) and 3.8 million square miles of territory.

5. "Jan. 1, 1975 Wed.," p. 2, folder "Diamond, David W.—'Synapse; A Deserter's Diary'—Typescript, 1 of 5," vol. 2, David W. Diamond fonds.

6. Rick Thome in Charles Hillinger, "War Resisters in Canada: They're Doing More Than Just Waiting," *Los Angeles Times,* June 4, 1972.

7. Michael Warsh in Alan Haig-Brown, *Hell No We Won't Go: Vietnam Draft Resisters in Canada* (Vancouver: Raincoast, 1996), 17.

8. Don Gayton, "Do Draft Dodgers Like Me Need a Monument?," *Tyee* (Vancouver, BC), October 5, 2004, http://thetyee.ca/Views/2004/10/05/DraftDogerMonument/.

9. Anonymous, survey returned to AMEX/Canada office, September 28, 1973 (Whaletown, BC), folder 4, "Questionnaire to exiles, 1973," box 1, AMEX/Canada Records, 1968–1977 (Mss. 736), Wisconsin Historical Society, Madison.

10. Anonymous, survey returned to AMEX/Canada office, September 6, [1973] (Drumheller, AB), folder 4, "Questionnaire to exiles, 1973," box 1, AMEX/Canada Records; Anonymous, survey returned to AMEX/Canada office, September 7, [1973] (Ottawa), ibid.

11. Michael Schaub, survey returned to AMEX/Canada office, September 6, [1973] (Toronto), folder 4, "Questionnaire to exiles, 1973," box 1, AMEX/Canada Records.

12. J. Chuckman, survey returned to AMEX/Canada office, August 30, [1973] (London, ON), folder 4, "Questionnaire to exiles, 1973," box 1, AMEX/Canada Records.

13. Interview 9, folder 4, "Research by Bob Eyers, 1967, on American Draft Exiles, Questionnaire Results," box 9, Renée Kasinsky fonds, Rare Books and Special Collections, Irving K. Barber Learning Centre, University of British Columbia, Vancouver, Canada.

14. Bill King (Toronto) to Gerald Ford (Washington, DC) [fall 1974] (photocopy), p. 2, folder 11, "Vietnam Veterans Against the War, 1971–1975," box 8, AMEX/Canada Records.

15. Gérard Pelletier, *The October Crisis*, trans. Joyce Marshall (Toronto: McClelland & Stewart, 1971), 197–205; Renée G. Kasinsky, *Refugees from Militarism: Draft-Age Americans in Canada* (1976; Totowa, NJ: Littlefield, Adams, 1978), 135–137. For background on the shift in the national mood of Canada in the late 1960s, see Pierre Berton, *1967: The Last Good Year* (Toronto: Doubleday, 1997), esp. 314–325; and Gary R. Miedema, *For Canada's Sake: Public Religion, Centennial Celebrations, and the Re-making of Canada in the 1960s* (Montréal: McGill-Queen's University Press, 2005).

16. Toronto Anti-Draft Programme, *Manual for Draft-Age Immigrants to Canada*, 6th ed. (Toronto: Toronto Anti-Draft Programme, 1971), 45; "Emigration to Canada under the War Measures Act" (news release) [late 1970], folder 10, "DCIC operations—News releases and broadsides," box 1, Draft Counseling and Information Center, Madison, Wisconsin, Records, 1968–1974 (Mss. 442), Wisconsin Historical Society; Charles Hillinger, "Crackdown under Canadian War Act Hits Draft Dodgers," *Los Angeles Times*, November 8, 1970. For a comprehensive study on Canadian groups that aided Vietnam War–era U.S. draft resisters, see Jessica Squires, *Building Sanctuary: The Movement to Support Vietnam War Resisters in Canada, 1965–73* (Vancouver: UBC Press, 2013).

17. John Hagan, *Northern Passage: American Vietnam War Resisters in Canada* (Cambridge, MA: Harvard University Press, 2001), 141, 147; James Dickerson, *North to Canada: Men and Women against the Vietnam War* (Westport, CT: Praeger, 1999), 68–69.

18. Myra MacPherson, *Long Time Passing: Vietnam and the Haunted Generation*, new ed. (Bloomington: Indiana University Press, 2001), 554; Amy J. Rutenberg, *Rough Draft: Cold War Military Manpower Policy and the Origins of Vietnam-Era Draft Resistance* (Ithaca, NY: Cornell University Press, 2019), 159, 173, 183–184. See also Frank Kusch, *All American Boys: Draft Dodgers in Canada from the Vietnam War* (Westport, CT: Praeger, 2001), 76–80; Lawrence M. Baskir and William A. Strauss, *Chance and Circumstance: The Draft, the War, and the Vietnam Generation* (New York: Vintage, 1978), 120, 125; and Squires, *Building Sanctuary*, 40–41, 173–174.

19. Baskir and Strauss, *Chance and Circumstance*, 8; MacPherson, *Long Time Passing*, 25. Amy J. Rutenberg notes that the Department of Defense did not keep records about the socioeconomic status of conscriptees during the Vietnam War, nor did it use "Hispanic" as a racial identifier until 1978; therefore "most available evidence" about the conscription, service, and deaths of those groups "is either anecdotal or backfilled from later studies." Rutenberg, *Rough Draft*, 165–167, quote 167.

20. Dorothee Schneider, "The United States Government and the Investigation of European Emigration in the Open Door Era," in *Citizenship and Those Who Leave: The Politics of Emigration and Expatriation*, ed. Nancy L. Green and François Weil, 195 (Urbana: University of Illinois Press, 2007); John R. Wennersten, *Leaving America: The New Expatriate Generation* (Westport, CT: Praeger, 2008).

21. This book is macro in scope and does not consider any specific places in depth. There is certainly room for histories of specific communities of draft resisters and military deserters in Canada, such as Kathleen Rodgers, *Welcome to Resisterville: American Dissidents in British Columbia* (Vancouver: UBC Press, 2015).

CHAPTER 1   ESCAPING OVER THE BORDER

1. Renée G. Kasinsky estimated that men between the ages of 15 and 24 who gained landed immigrant status in Canada between 1965 and 1975 numbered 40,350. Men were not required to register for the draft until age 18, however. Renée G. Kasinsky, *Refugees from Militarism: Draft-Age Americans in Canada* (1976; Totowa, NJ: Littlefield, Adams, 1978), 294. David S. Surrey cited estimates of the émigré population ranging from 15,000 to 100,000. David S. Surrey, *Choice of Conscience: Vietnam Era Military and Draft Resisters in Canada* (New York: Praeger, 1982), 5. James Dickerson speculated that as many as 500,000 men *and women* went to Canada during the Vietnam War era. James Dickerson, *North to Canada: Men and Women against the Vietnam War* (Westport, CT: Praeger, 1999), xiii. In 2001 the sociologist and legal scholar John Hagan used Canadian census data on U.S. immigration to, emigration from, and length of residency in Canada to estimate that 52,669 people (25,865 men and 26,804 women) went to Canada between 1965 and 1974. John Hagan, *Northern Passage: American Vietnam War Resisters in Canada* (Cambridge, MA: Harvard University Press, 2001), 3, 241. The historian David S. Churchill speculated that 250,000 Americans immigrated between 1966 and 1976. David S. Churchill, "Draft Resisters, Left Nationalism, and the Politics of Anti-Imperialism," *Canadian Historical Review* 93 (June 2012), 228n1. For an extended discussion of the number of people who went to Canada during this exodus, see Joseph Jones, *Contending Statistics: The Numbers for U.S. Vietnam War Resisters in Canada* (Vancouver: Quarter Sheaf, 2005).

2. Uniform Code of Military Justice, *U.S. Statutes at Large* 64 (1950): 135, codified at *U.S. Code* 10 § 885.

3. Robert Kanigel, *Eyes on the Street: The Life of Jane Jacobs* (New York: Knopf, 2016), 279–280, quote 280.

4. Robin Folvik, "'They Followed Their Men into Canada?': American Women in Canada during the Vietnam War Era" (conference paper, New World Coming: The Sixties and the Shaping of Global Consciousness, Kingston, Ontario, Canada, June 16, 2007); Lara Campbell, "'Women United against the War': Gender Politics, Feminism, and Vietnam Draft Resistance in Canada," in *New World Coming: The Sixties and the Shaping of Global Consciousness,* ed. Karen Dubinsky et al., 339–346 (Toronto: Between the Lines, 2009).

5. As used here, citizenship is the civil, legal, political, and socioeconomic rights and duties that demonstrate a person's connections to a nation, as well as proof the person has renounced allegiance to other nations. Anthony D. Smith, *National Identity* (Reno: University of Nevada Press, 1991), 10, 118.

6. Myra MacPherson, *Long Time Passing: Vietnam and the Haunted Generation,* new ed. (Bloomington: Indiana University Press, 2001), 25–26, 554.

7. In the new system, a potential immigrant needed to be assessed at least 50 out of 100 points by an immigration or visa official to be admitted to the country. A draft-age man with a high school diploma and the ability to speak, read, and write English would automatically earn 27 points: 12 for the number of years of education he had completed, 10 for being between eighteen and thirty-five years of age, and 5 for his language skills. He could earn an additional point for each year of postsecondary education, and as many as 30 more points depending on his occupational skills, demand for his occupation in Canada, and

any written guarantees for a job upon his arrival in Canada. Officers could also award up to 5 points if the potential immigrant had a relative in Canada, up to 5 points for the ability to speak, read, and write French, and up to 15 points at his or her discretion. "Schedule A: Norms for Assessment of Independent Applicants, New. P.C. 1967–1616, Aug. 16, 1967," in *Office Consolidation of the Immigration Act, R.S.C., 1952, c. 325, as amended by 1966–67, cc. 25, 90, 1967–68, cc. 1, 37; Immigration Regulations, Part I, made by P.C. 1962–86, as amended by P.C. 1966–525, P.C. 1967–1616* (Ottawa: Queen's Printer and Controller of Stationery, 1968). An annotated list of the regulations appeared in the *Manual for Draft-Age Immigrants to Canada.* See, for example, Toronto Anti-Draft Programme, *Manual for Draft-Age Immigrants to Canada,* 6th ed. (Toronto: Toronto Anti-Draft Programme, 1971), 56–61. David S. Churchill observed that the discretionary points wielded by the immigration officer could make or break a potential immigrant's case for entering Canada. See David S. Churchill, "An Ambiguous Welcome: Vietnam Draft Resistance, the Canadian State and Cold War Containment," *Social History | Histoire sociale* 37 (May 2004), 5. For an assessment of the points system, see Garth Stevenson, *Building Nations from Diversity: Canadian and American Experience Compared* (Montréal: McGill-Queen's University Press, 2014), 174–175.

8. "Statement by the Honourable Allan MacEachen to the House of Commons, Thursday, May 22/69," pp. 3–4, file IM5650–1, part 1, vol. 1208, Records of the Immigration Branch (RG 76), Library and Archives Canada, Ottawa, Ontario. Emphasis in the original. See also Canada, House of Commons Debates, May 22, 1969, p. 8930 (Allan MacEachen [Minister of Manpower and Immigration]). For press accounts of Canadian government policy, see Lewis Seale, "Deserters Will Be Eligible for Status As Immigrants," *Globe and Mail* (Toronto), May 23, 1969; Jay Walz, "Canada to Admit Any U.S. Deserter," *New York Times,* May 23, 1969; and Gerald Waring, "Canada Eases Deserters' Entry," *Washington Post,* May 23, 1969.

9. Adam M. McKeown, *Melancholy Order: Asian Migration and the Globalization of Borders* (New York: Columbia University Press, 2008), 43.

10. Roger Daniels, *Coming to America: A History of Immigration and Ethnicity in American Life* (New York: HarperCollins, 1990), 111.

11. "Table Ad1-2—U.S. immigrants and emigrants: 1820–1998" and "Table Ad1072-1075—Deportable aliens located, and aliens expelled: 1892–1998," *Historical Statistics of the United States,* millennial edition online, http://hsus.cambridge.org (accessed October 18, 2022).

12. "Table Ad80-81—Emigrants from the United States to Canada: 1881–1998," *Historical Statistics of the United States* (accessed October 18, 2022).

13. Richard Sutch in Sam Roberts, "A Book for People Who Love Numbers," *New York Times,* February 22, 2006.

14. Claude A. Clegg III, *The Price of Liberty: African Americans and the Making of Liberia* (Chapel Hill: University of North Carolina Press, 2004).

15. Eugene C. Harter, *The Lost Colony of the Confederacy* (College Station: Texas A&M University Press, 2000); Matthew Pratt Guterl, *American Mediterranean: Southern Slaveholders in the Age of Emancipation* (Cambridge, MA: Harvard University Press, 2008).

16. John Herd Thompson and Stephen J. Randall, *Canada and the United States: Ambivalent Allies,* 4th ed. (Athens: University of Georgia Press, 2008), 15, 351n7. See also Ninette

Kelley and Michael Trebilcock, *The Making of the Mosaic: A History of Canadian Immigration Policy* (Toronto: University of Toronto Press, 1998), 36–43.

17. Robin W. Winks, *The Blacks in Canada: A History,* 2nd ed. (Montréal: McGill-Queen's University Press, 1997), xiv, 24–60; Maya Jasanoff, *Liberty's Exiles: American Loyalists in the Revolutionary World* (New York: Knopf, 2011), [23,] 357–358; Christopher G. Anderson, *Canadian Liberalism and the Politics of Border Control, 1867–1967* (Vancouver: University of British Columbia Press, 2012), 33; Stevenson, *Building Nations from Diversity,* 34–36.

18. Winks, *Blacks in Canada,* 114–141.

19. On the end of slavery in the British Empire, see Winks, *Blacks in Canada,* 111; Kelley and Trebilcock, *Making of the Mosaic,* 52; and Thompson and Randall, *Canada and the United States,* 20. Much of Winks's *Blacks in Canada* is concerned with the movement of Blacks—enslaved people, formerly enslaved people, and the never enslaved—from the United States to Canada from 1815 to 1870. Winks, *Blacks in Canada,* 142–270. See Anderson, *Canadian Liberalism and the Politics of Border Control,* 33–34. On the exodus of enslaved people to Mexico, see Alice L. Baumgartner, *South to Freedom: Runaway Slaves to Mexico and the Road to the Civil War* (New York: Basic Books, 2020).

20. Pekka Hämäläinen, *Lakota America: A New History of Indigenous Power* (New Haven, CT: Yale University Press, 2019), 254–256, 373; Thompson and Randall, *Canada and the United States,* 50–51; Joseph Manzione, *"I Am Looking to the North for My Life": Sitting Bull, 1876–1881* (Salt Lake City: University of Utah Press, 1991).

21. Thompson and Randall, *Canada and the United States,* 80–81; Kelley and Trebilcock, *Making of the Mosaic,* 124–125, 78; Winks, *Blacks in Canada,* 300–307; Anderson, *Canadian Liberalism and the Politics of Border Control,* 60.

22. Thompson and Randall, *Canada and the United States,* 52; Kelley and Trebilcock, *Making of the Mosaic,* 79–80, 125; Anderson, *Canadian Liberalism and the Politics of Border Control,* 219n10.

23. Henri Lefebvre, *Everyday Life in the Modern World,* trans. Sacha Rabinovich (New York: Harper & Row, 1971), 147–148, 150. The phrase *fuite en avant* first came to me in a European travelogue by the Canadian writer Taras Grescoe. See Taras Grescoe, *The End of Elsewhere: Travels among the Tourists* (London: Serpent's Tail, 2004), 85–86.

24. "Series A385-416—Immigration to Canada by country of last permanent residence, 1956 to 1976," in F. H. Leacy, ed. *Historical Statistics of Canada,* 2nd ed. (Ottawa: Statistics Canada, 1983).

25. Daniel Yankelovich, Inc., *The Changing Values on Campus: Political and Personal Attitudes of Today's College Students; A Survey for the JDR 3rd Fund* (New York: Washington Square, 1972), 87; "Gallup Finds 12% Want to Quit U.S.," *New York Times,* March 21, 1971; M. A. Farber, "Pessimism Voiced in Student Study," *New York Times,* April 11, 1972.

26. "Table Ad80-81—Emigrants from the United States to Canada: 1881–1998."

27. "These Americans Call City 'Home,'" *Financial Post* (Toronto) 59 (August 21, 1965), 41; Jon Ruddy, "Calgaryanks," *Macleans* 79 (September 3, 1966), 18–20, 25–26; Kay Bartlett, "More Americans Move to Canada," *Washington Post,* May 25, 1969; Michael Cope, "'The American Middle Class Looking to Canada'—Rubbish!," *Executive* (Don Mills, ON) 11 (September 1969), 21; Edward Cowan, "Americans Move to Canada in Record Numbers," *New York Times,* January 1, 1970; Eugene Griffin, "Americans Who Migrate to Canada," *Chicago Tribune,* April 30, 1974.

28. Cowan, "Americans Move to Canada in Record Numbers"; Donald W. Townson, "The Americans Are Coming! The Americans Are Coming!," *Business Quarterly* (London, ON) 35 (Winter 1970), 82; "Immigration from the U.S.A.," *World Affairs* (Toronto) 35 (February 1970), 10; [James C. Jones,] "Canada's Other U.S. Immigrants," *Newsweek* 77 (May 24, 1971), 38, 43; William Borders, "Canada Drawing More Americans," *New York Times,* November 11, 1973; "Why More Americans Are Leaving These Shores," *U.S. News and World Report* 77 (August 26, 1974), 41–42.

29. Barry Ashley in Hedley Burrell, "New Trend in Migration: 40,000 Are Quitting U.S.," *Washington Post,* October 19, 1970.

30. Al Finkel in Karl Fleming, "How the Exiles View the Issue," *Newsweek* 79 (January 17, 1972), 25.

31. Aerlyn Weissman in Valerie Miner Johnson, "American Women in Canada: A Young U.S. Immigrant and Her Friends Discover the Canadian Dream," *Chatelaine* 46 (May 1973), 112.

32. Norman Forman in Burrell, "New Trend in Migration."

33. Cowan, "Americans Move to Canada in Record Numbers."

34. Jon Ruddy, "The Americans Who Voted with Their Feet," *Maclean's* 82 (March 1969), 29; Marlene Nadle, "Exiles in Canada: The New Lost Generation," *Village Voice* 20 (February 24, 1975), 28; Johnson, "American Women in Canada," 110; "And What Happened to All Those Brilliant Americans?," *Saturday Night* 92 (October 1977), 14.

35. Art Seidenbaum, "Vietnam Evasion Vancouver Style: A Refugee Report," *Los Angeles Times,* September 30, 1968.

36. Charlie Argast in "An Indiana Family Leaves the U.S. for Keeps," *Life* 69 (July 17, 1970), 42, 42A–42B, 43–45, quote 42B.

37. Gary Dunford in Bartlett, "More Americans Move to Canada"; Jim Wilson in Karl Fleming, "America's Sad Young Exiles," *Newsweek* 77 (February 15, 1971), 29.

38. George A. Cohon in "Seeking a Better Life in Canada," *Business Week,* April 21, 1973, 86–87.

39. Art Green in "And What Happened to All Those Brilliant Americans?," 14–15, quote 15. Emphasis in the original. See also Nadle, "Exiles in Canada," 28–31.

40. Mary Anne Duffy in Johnson, "American Women in Canada," 110.

41. Ruddy, "Americans Who Voted with Their Feet," 29, 31; John Gray, "How Seven Families Really Got Away from It All," *Maclean's* 74 (October 7, 1961), 98.

42. Tom Lawrence in Fleming, "America's Sad Young Exiles," 29.

43. Frederick Jackson Turner, *The Significance of the Frontier in American History* (New York: Henry Holt, 1921), http://www.gutenberg.org/ebooks/22994.

44. Gray, "How Seven Families Really Got Away from It All," 33–35, 94, 96–98; Robert Hunter, "Green Power," *Maclean's* 81 (May 1968), 13–15, 84–88; Bartlett, "More Americans Move to Canada"; Cope, "'American Middle Class Looking to Canada'—Rubbish!," 21; Cowan, "Americans Move to Canada in Record Numbers"; "Indiana Family Leaves the U.S. for Keeps," 42B; "Why More Americans Are Leaving These Shores," 41.

45. Roger Davies in Alan Haig-Brown, *Hell No We Won't Go: Vietnam Draft Resisters in Canada* (Vancouver: Raincoast, 1996), 124.

46. Bill Postl in Bob Lundegaard, "Resisters' Dilemma: Come Home or Stay Home?" *Minneapolis Tribune,* September 17, 1972.

47. H. W. Thompson in Ruddy, "Americans Who Voted with Their Feet," 29.

48. Richard L. Killmer and Charles P. Lutz, *The Draft and the Rest of Your Life* (Minneapolis: Augsburg Publishing House, 1972), 73.

49. Percy Rowe, *Percy Rowe's Travel Guide to Canada: A Complete Guide to Every Province* (Richmond Hill, ON: Simon & Schuster, 1973), 2. See also Chris Turner, "On Strawberry Hill," *Walrus* 4 (September 2007), 68–73.

50. Bob Proctor, interview with author, Indianapolis, IN, September 22, 2004, tape recording in author's possession.

51. Mark Vonnegut, *The Eden Express: A Memoir of Madness* (1975; New York: Seven Stories Press, 2002), 28. For an extended study of British Columbia as a destination for U.S. military service resisters, see Kathleen Rodgers, *Welcome to Resisterville: American Dissidents in British Columbia* (Vancouver: UBC Press, 2015).

52. Abbie Hoffman, *Steal This Book* (1971; New York: Four Walls Eight Windows, 2002), xxi, 42–43.

53. On Canadian involvement in the International Control Commission, see Robert Bothwell, *Alliance and Illusion: Canada and the World, 1945–1984* (Vancouver, UBC Press, 2007), 195–211. The extent of Canada's neutrality during the Vietnam War was the subject of much debate. See Andrew Preston, "Balancing War and Peace: Canadian Foreign Policy and the Vietnam War, 1961–1965," *Diplomatic History* 27 (January 2003), 73–111; Charles Taylor, *Snow Job: Canada, the United States, and Vietnam (1954 to 1973)* (Toronto: Anansi, 1974); Douglas A. Ross, *In the Interests of Peace: Canada and Vietnam, 1954–1973* (Toronto: University of Toronto Press, 1984); Edelgard E. Mahant and Graeme S. Mount, *An Introduction to Canadian-American Relations* (Toronto: Methuen, 1984), 210–213; J. L. Granatstein and Norman Hillmer, *For Better or for Worse: Canada and the United States to the 1990s* (Toronto: Copp Clark Pitman, 1991), 230; and Bothwell, *Alliance and Illusion*, 212–236.

54. Ross, *In the Interests of Peace*, 303; Preston, "Balancing War and Peace," 73.

55. Ross, *In the Interests of Peace*, 304–305, 307; Mahant and Mount, *Introduction to Canadian-American Relations*, 211–213; Thompson and Randall, *Canada and the United States*, 221–222.

56. Ross, *In the Interests of Peace*, 305–308.

57. Hagan, *Northern Passage*, 65, 187; Lawrence M. Baskir and William A. Strauss, *Chance and Circumstance: The Draft, the War, and the Vietnam Generation* (New York: Vintage, 1978), 174; Thompson and Randall, *Canada and the United States*, 215; "Statement by the Honourable Allan MacEachen to the House of Commons, Thursday, May 22/69."

58. Robert Mann, *A Grand Delusion: America's Descent into Vietnam* (New York: Basic Books, 2001), 66–68; Fredrik Logevall, *The Origins of the Vietnam War* (Harlow, England: Longman, 2001), 17–18.

59. Logevall, *Origins of the Vietnam War*, 19–37.

60. Michael S. Foley, *Confronting the War Machine: Draft Resistance during the Vietnam War* (Chapel Hill: University of North Carolina Press, 2003), 36; George Q. Flynn, *The Draft, 1940–1973* (Lawrence: University Press of Kansas, 1993), 88–109.

61. U.S. Department of Veterans Affairs, Office of Public Affairs, "America's Wars," November 2012," https://www.va.gov/opa/publications/docs/Americas_Wars_Fact_Sheet.doc; Lester H. Brune and Richard Dean Burns, *America and the Indochina Wars, 1945–1990: A Bibliographical Guide* (Claremont, CA: Regina, 1992), 184.

62. Stephen Minot, "On Aiding and Abetting: The Anguish of Draft Counseling," *Harper's Magazine* 237 (September 1968), 47–50, quote 49.

63. Turner, "On Strawberry Hill," 73.

64. Foley, *Confronting the War Machine*, 13.

65. Hagan, *Northern Passage*, 18–21.

66. Foley, *Confronting the War Machine*, 45, 94–95, 100, 170.

67. John W. Perry (Bronx, NY) to Vancouver Committee [to Aid American War Objectors,] [November 1969], p. 1, folder 2, "Correspondence—VCAAWO," box 1, Renée Kasinsky fonds, Rare Books and Special Collections, Irving K. Barber Learning Centre, University of British Columbia, Vancouver, Canada.

68. Interview with Jack Colhoun, pp. 3–4, folder "Jack Colhoun," box 17, "Interview Transcripts A–C," Michael Maclear fonds (Accession no. 2004.005), Media Commons Archives, John P. Roberts Research Library, University of Toronto, Ontario, Canada.

69. Interview with David Harris, pp. 30–31, folder "Jack David Harris," box 18, "Interview Transcripts D–H," Michael Maclear fonds.

70. "Why I Resist" (mimeograph), folder 1, "Draft Resistence [*sic*] 1968 correspondence, newspaper articles, misc. draft forms," box 1, Samuel J. Steiner Fonds (Hist. Mss. 1.138), Mennonite Archives of Ontario, Conrad Grebel University College, Milton Good Library, University of Waterloo, Ontario, Canada; "SSS Report of Oral Information," April 23, 1968, folder 10, "Draft 1967–74 misc. documents," ibid.; "Five Picket As 30 Leave for Service," *Youngstown Indicator*, April 23, 1968, folder 10, "Draft 1967–74 misc. documents," ibid.

71. Richard Moore III, *Richard: Portrait of a Vietnam War Resister* (San Francisco: Richard Moore III, 1987), part 2, p. 4.

72. "Tues Jun. 17, 1975," pp. 1–2, folder "Diamond, David W.—'Synapse; A Deserter's Diary'—Typescript, 3 of 5, 1975," vol. 2, David W. Diamond fonds (R11554), Library and Archives Canada; "October 30, 1975 Thurs.," p. 2, folder "Diamond, David W.—'Synapse; A Deserter's Diary'—Typescript, 4 of 5, 1975," ibid.

73. Diane Francis in Dickerson, *North to Canada*, 10.

74. These reasons were mentioned in various files in the folder "Master Case File," box 6, Robert J. Horn Papers, Gerald R. Ford Presidential Library, Ann Arbor, Michigan.

75. "Interview with draft dodger from Toronto communal house," n.d., p. 15, folder 9, "Interview with Draft Dodger from Toronto Communal House," box 4, Renée Kasinsky fonds.

76. "26, July 1975 Sat.," folder "Diamond, David W.—'Synapse; A Deserter's Diary'—Typescript, 4 of 5, 1975," vol. 2, David W. Diamond fonds.

77. [December 1972], p. 72 (December 1972) (typewritten, original), box 2, folder P55, 3rd Canadian Journal, 1972 (April)–1973 (April), Steve Trimm Papers (DG 232), Swarthmore College Peace Collection, McCabe Library, Swarthmore College, Swarthmore, Pennsylvania.

78. "Political Criminals Continue the Struggle in Canada," *Rebel* 1 (March–April 1968), 2, 15, 16.

79. Robert W. Bars (Providence, RI) to Goldie Josephy (Ottawa), February 24, 1968, file 6, "Ottawa Committee for Peace and Liberation—Correspondence with and concerning U.S. Draft Evader Immigration to Canada, 1968," vol. 9, Goldie Josephy fonds (R4460), Library and Archives Canada.

80. Students for a Democratic Society, *Port Huron Statement* (1962), https://en.wiki source.org/wiki/Port_Huron_Statement (accessed October 16, 2022).

81. Students for a Democratic Society, *Port Huron Statement*.

82. Joel P. Rhodes, *The Voice of Violence: Performative Violence as Protest in the Vietnam Era* (Westport, CT: Praeger, 2001), 1.

83. Vonnegut, *Eden Express*, 82.

84. Flynn, *Draft*, 183–184.

85. Flynn, *Draft*, 172; William S. White, "Drafting College Men Might Thin Ranks of Those Slandering Cause," *Los Angeles Times*, September 2, 1965.

86. Flynn, *Draft*, 180.

87. Flynn, *Draft*, 240.

88. Selective Service Act of 1948, Public Law 759, 80th Cong., 2d sess. (June 24, 1948), section 6(g); Military Selective Service Act of 1971, Public Law 129, 92d Cong., 2d sess. (September 28, 1971), section 6(g)(2).

89. Paul Ketterer (Madison, WI) to J. McRee Elrod (Vancouver, BC), April 4, 1968, folder 2, "Incoming Correspondence (1968), A–L," box 1, J. McRee Elrod fonds, University Archives, University of British Columbia Library.

90. Joseph E. Capizzi, "Selective Conscientious Objection in the United States," *Journal of Church and State* 38 (Spring 1996), 339–363; John M. Swomley Jr., "Conscience and the Draft," *Christian Century* 84 (June 28, 1967), 833–835; James H. Smylie, "American Religious Bodies, Just War, and Vietnam," *Journal of Church and State* 11 (Autumn 1969), 383–408.

91. Patrick Grady in Dickerson, *North to Canada*, 129.

92. Stephen Eaton Hume in Haig-Brown, *Hell No We Won't Go*, 72.

93. Baskir and Strauss, *Chance and Circumstance*, 57, 78–79; *United States v. Seeger*, 380 U.S. 163 (1965); *Welsh v. United States*, 398 U.S. 333 (1970).

94. Flynn, *Draft*, 257–258.

95. Flynn, *Draft*, 200.

96. Foley, *Confronting the War Machine*, 39–40.

97. Flynn, *Draft*, 257–258; U.S. Selective Service System, "Induction Statistics," https://www.sss.gov/history-and-records/induction-statistics/ (accessed October 18, 2022).

98. Betty Vetter, ed., *Draft Facts for Graduates and Graduate Students* (Washington, DC: Scientific Manpower Commission, 1968), 3, 10; Scientific Manpower Commission, *The Draft Lottery and You* (Washington, DC: Scientific Manpower Commission, 1970), 2; "New Draft Policy to Cut Graduate School Enrollment," in *U.S. Draft Policy and Its Impact, July 1968* (Washington, DC: Congressional Quarterly Service, 1968), 1–4; Flynn, *Draft*, 202, 205, 221–222.

99. Vetter, *Draft Facts for Graduates and Graduate Students*, 10–11.

100. Rhodri Jeffreys-Jones, *Peace Now!: American Society and the Ending of the Vietnam War* (New Haven, CT: Yale University Press, 1999), 76–77.

101. Flynn, *Draft*, 171.

102. Vetter, *Draft Facts for Graduates and Graduate Students*, 7–9; Flynn, *Draft*, 200.

103. Scientific Manpower Commission, *Draft Lottery and You*, 2–3.

104. John Burns, "The Draft Lesson That Sends Americans to Canada's Grad Schools," *Globe and Mail* (Toronto), May 11, 1968; Krista Maeots, "Canadian Universities—The American Way," *Ottawa Citizen*, November 13, 1968.

105. Flynn, *Draft*, 180.

106. U.S. Department of the Army, Medical Services, *Standards of Medical Fitness* (1960; Washington, DC: U.S. Government Printing Office, 1974), ¶2–21, ¶2–22, ¶2–9b, ¶2–35aa, ¶2–7, ¶2–28a(2), ¶2–39a(2), ¶2–31b(2); "Rx for Draft Dodging," 42–43.

107. U.S. Department of the Army, Medical Services, *Standards of Medical Fitness*, ¶2–33a(1), ¶2–34a(3), ¶2–34a(6), ¶2–34a(4)–(5), ¶2–34a(1), ¶2–34b.

108. U.S. Department of the Army, Medical Services, *Standards of Medical Fitness*, ¶2–34a(2).

109. Flynn, *Draft*, 116, 182, 193.

110. Foley, *Confronting the War Machine*, 100, 104–105; *U.S. Draft Policy and Its Impact, July 1968*, 1; Flynn, *Draft*, 206–207.

111. Flynn, *Draft*, 208; MacPherson, *Long Time Passing*, 25–26, 554. See also "Rx for Draft Dodging," *Newsweek* 76 (August 3, 1970), 43.

112. Flynn, *Draft*, 246–249; Foley, *Confronting the War Machine*, 339; "ABC's of Draft by Lottery," *U.S. News and World Report* 67 (December 15, 1969), 33–35.

113. U.S. Selective Service System, "Vietnam Lotteries," https://www.sss.gov/history -and-records/vietnam-lotteries/ (accessed October 16, 2022).

114. Vetter, *Draft Facts for Graduates and Graduate Students*, 6, 3, 4, 5; Amy J. Rutenberg, *Rough Draft: Cold War Military Manpower Policy and the Origins of Vietnam-Era Draft Resistance* (Ithaca, NY: Cornell University Press, 2019), 167–168.

115. Scientific Manpower Commission, *Draft Lottery and You*, inside back cover.

116. Flynn, *Draft*, 180–181.

117. Flynn, *Draft*, 180.

118. Foley, *Confronting the War Machine*, 39, 59–60, 149–150; Flynn, *Draft*, 184.

119. *Oestereich v. Selective Service System Local Board No. 11*, 393 U.S. 233 (1968); *Gutknecht v. United States*, 396 U.S. 295 (1970); *Breen v. Selective Service Board No. 16*, 396 U.S. 460 (1970). See also Foley, *Confronting the War Machine*, 328–331; Flynn, *Draft*, 250–251; Richard E. Rubenstein, "We're Unfair to Draft-Card Burners," *Saturday Evening Post* 239 (February 12, 1966), 10, 15; and "No Draft as Discipline," *Time* 95 (February 9, 1970), 43.

120. On U.S. deserters in Sweden, see Carl-Gustaf Scott, "Swedish Sanctuary of American Deserters during the Vietnam War: A Facet of Social Democratic Domestic Politics," *Scandinavian Journal of History* 26, no. 2 (2001), 123–142; Carl-Gustaf Scott, "'Sweden Might Be a Haven, but It's Not Heaven': American War Resisters in Sweden during the Vietnam War," *Immigrants and Minorities: Historical Studies in Ethnicity, Migration, and Diaspora* 33, no. 3 (2015), 205–230; John Cooney and Dana Spitzer, "'Hell, No, We Won't Go!,'" *Trans-action* 6 (September 1969), 55; "Deserters in Sweden: Fourteen Black Ex-GIs Find Refuge from Vietnam War," *Ebony* 23 (August 1968), 120–122; Lucinda Franks, *Waiting Out a War: The Exile of Private John Picciano* (New York: Coward, McCann & Geoghegan, 1974); and Terry Whitmore with Richard Weber, *Memphis—Nam—Sweden: The Story of a Black Deserter* (1971; Jackson: University Press of Mississippi, 1997). For an extensive study of U.S. deserters in Europe, see Paul Benedikt Glatz, *Vietnam's Prodigal Heroes: American Deserters, International Protest, European Exile, and Amnesty* (Lanham, MD: Lexington, 2021).

121. Baskir and Strauss, *Chance and Circumstance*, 5.

122. Flynn, *Draft*, 277–279.

CHAPTER 2   THE WELCOME MAT IS SPREAD ALL ALONG THE BORDER

1. Arlo Tatum and Joseph S. Tuchinsky, *Guide to the Draft* (Boston: Beacon, 1969), vii.

2. David Suttler, *IV-F: A Guide to Medical, Psychiatric, and Moral Unfitness Standards for Military Induction* (New York: Grove, 1970).

3. Andrew O. Shapiro and John M. Striker, *Mastering the Draft: A Comprehensive Guide for Solving Draft Problems* (Boston: Little, Brown, 1970).

4. Scientific Manpower Commission, *The Draft Lottery and You* (Washington, DC: Scientific Manpower Commission, 1970), quote inside back cover.

5. See, for example, Arlo Tatum, ed., *Handbook for Conscientious Objectors*, 10th ed. (Philadelphia: Central Committee for Conscientious Objectors, 1969). Publication statistics for the handbook come from Robert A. Seeley, *Handbook for Conscientious Objectors*, 13th ed. (Philadelphia: Central Committee for Conscientious Objectors, 1982), back of title page.

6. Richard L. Killmer and Charles P. Lutz, *The Draft and the Rest of Your Life* (Minneapolis: Augsburg Publishing House, 1972).

7. American Friends Service Committee, "If the Army Is Not Your Bag!" [booklet], (Philadelphia: American Friends Service Committee, 1968); American Friends Service Committee, "Something's Happening Here to the Draft" [brochure], (Philadelphia: American Friends Service Committee, 1968). The name of the leaflet was a reference to lyrics of the popular song "For What It's Worth (Hey, What's That Sound)," recorded by the rock group Buffalo Springfield, written by group member Stephen Stills and released in early 1967. The song had been appropriated by the counterculture because it was inspired by demonstrations in 1966 against a curfew for people under eighteen years of age in Hollywood, California. See Danny Hajek, "A Thousand People in the Street: 'For What It's Worth' Captured Youth in Revolt," *Morning Edition*, National Public Radio, February 20, 2019, https://www.npr.org/2019/02/20/693790065/buffalo-springfield-for-what-its-worth-american-anthem.

8. Abbie Hoffman, *Steal This Book* (1971; New York: Four Walls Eight Windows, 2002), 191, 193.

9. Hoffman, *Steal This Book*, 303–304.

10. "The Draft . . . or What? Choices for Spring Graduates," *U.S. News and World Report* 68 (March 30, 1970), 80–81.

11. "The Draft: Retain? Reform? Or Abolish?," *Senior Scholastic* 94 (May 2, 1969), 5–6.

12. Circulation figures from the Magazine Advertising Bureau of the Magazine Publishers Association. See Luman H. Long, ed., *The World Almanac and Book of Facts*, 1971 ed. (New York: Newspaper Enterprise Association, 1970), 174.

13. "The Draft: How to Beat It without Really Trying," *Time* 91 (March 15, 1968), 15–16.

14. "Rx for Draft Dodging," *Newsweek* 76 (August 3, 1970), 42–43; "Beating the Draft, 1970 Style," *Newsweek* 76 (November 9, 1970), 27–28.

15. "Beating the Draft, 1970 Style," 28; "Rx for Draft Dodging," 42; "The Draft: How to Beat It without Really Trying," 15; Noel Perrin, "Our Far-Flung Correspondents: Dartmouth '70 and the War," *New Yorker* 46 (July 18, 1970), 55.

16. Douglas S. Looney, "How to Help Your Son Face the Draft," *Better Homes and Gardens* 48 (November 1970), 30.

17. Long, *World Almanac and Book of Facts*, 174.

18. "Beating the Draft, 1970 Style," 28.

19. Roger Rapoport, "The Magical Mystery Great Lakes Express," *Esquire* 70 (September 1968), 84.

20. "Canada: Escape Hatch for U.S. Draft Resisters," *U.S. News and World Report* 61 (September 26, 1966), 61–62; "For Americans: An Easier Life in Canada," *U.S. News and World Report* 65 (October 28, 1968), 64. Passports were not required for U.S. citizens to leave or enter the United States until June 1, 2009. See "Passport requirement; Definitions," *Code of Federal Regulations*, title 22, sec. 53.1, September 20, 2022, https://www.ecfr.gov (accessed October 2, 2022).

21. Jack Kerouac, *On the Road* (1957; New York: Penguin, 1991), 129, 135.

22. Marie-Françoise Lanfant, "Introduction," trans. Alison Steele and Nelson Graburn, in *International Tourism: Identity and Change*, ed. Marie-Françoise Lanfant, John B. Allcock, and Edward M. Bruner, 1–6 (Thousand Oaks, CA: Sage, 1995).

23. Marie-Françoise Lanfant, "International Tourism: Internationalization and the Challenge to Identity," trans. John B. Allcock, in *International Tourism*, ed. Lanfant, Allcock, and Bruner, 33–34.

24. John A. Jakle, *The Tourist: Travel in Twentieth-Century North America* (Lincoln: University of Nebraska Press, 1985), xii, 2; John A. Jakle and Keith A. Sculle, *Motoring: The Highway Experience in America* (Athens: University of Georgia Press, 2008), 217, 220.

25. Jakle, *Tourist*, 10, 305.

26. Jakle, *Tourist*, 305.

27. Karen Dubinsky, *The Second Greatest Disappointment: Honeymooning and Tourism at Niagara Falls* (New Brunswick, NJ: Rutgers University Press, 1999), 214, 180, 178–179. See also Karen Dubinsky, "'Everybody Likes Canadians': Canadians, Americans, and the Post–World War II Travel Boom," in *Being Elsewhere: Tourism, Consumer Culture, and Identity in Modern Europe and North America*, ed. Shelley Baranowski and Ellen Furlough, 320–347 (Ann Arbor: University of Michigan Press, 2001).

28. Dubinsky, "'Everybody Likes Canadians,'" 342.

29. Dubinsky, "'Everybody Likes Canadians,'" 332, 345n62.

30. Michael Dawson, *Selling British Columbia: Tourism and Consumer Culture, 1890–1970* (Vancouver: UBC Press, 2004), 155–156.

31. Ninette Kelley and Michael Trebilcock, *The Making of the Mosaic: A History of Canadian Immigration Policy* (Toronto: University of Toronto Press, 1998), 369–370; Freda Hawkins, *Canada and Immigration: Public Policy and Public Concern*, 2nd ed. (Kingston: McGill-Queen's University Press, 1988), 387–388; Charles A. White, "Immigration Laws: Should We Loosen or Tighten?," *Canada and the World* 38 (January 1973), 4.

32. [Winnipeg Committee to Assist War Objectors,] "On Sending Potential Immigrants to Canada" (memo), p. 2, folder 8, "DCIC operations & other memos," box 1, Draft Counseling and Information Center, Madison, Wisconsin, Records, 1968–1974 (Mss. 442), Wisconsin Historical Society, Madison. Emphasis in the original.

33. See, for example, Toronto Anti-Draft Programme, *Manual for Draft-Age Immigrants to Canada*, 6th ed. (Toronto: Toronto Anti-Draft Programme, 1971), 52.

34. William Stadiem, *Jet Set: The People, the Planes, the Glamour, and the Romance in Aviation's Glory Years* (New York: Ballantine, 2014), ix–xiii. In 1958, 4,578,568 passengers

arrived in Canada on commercial foreign and domestic flights. In 1972, 18,079,859 passengers arrived. See "Series T195–198. Canadian commercial aviation activity, 1946 to
1975," in F. H. Leacy, ed., *Historical Statistics of Canada*, 2nd ed. (Ottawa: Statistics Canada, 1983).

35. "Statement by the Honourable Allan MacEachen to the House of Commons, Thursday, May 22/69" (photocopy), pp. 3–4 file IM5650–1, part 1, vol. 1208, Records of the
Immigration Branch (RG 76), Library and Archives Canada, Ottawa, Ontario.

36. Daniel J. Boorstin, *The Image: A Guide to Pseudo-events in America* (1961; New York:
Vintage, 1992), 116, in Jakle, *Tourist*, 17.

37. John Bodnar, *The Transplanted: A History of Immigrants in Urban America* (Bloomington: Indiana University Press, 1985), 54, 209.

38. Bill Katz, *Magazines for Libraries* (New York: Bowker, 1969), 195.

39. Patricia P. Coleman, "Just across the Border," *Scholastic Teacher* 86 (April 15, 1965), 8, 9.

40. William H. Bristow, "Happy Hundred!," *Scholastic Teacher* 90 (February 10, 1967), 13;
Lucy Jonckheere, "The One Hundredth Year: Canada Celebrates Birthday," ibid., 18.

41. Franklin S. Gross, "Canada: An Exciting Teaching Opportunity," *Scholastic Teacher*
90 (February 10, 1967), 16. Emphasis in the original.

42. Lord Thomson of Fleet, "The Birthday Party Upstairs," *Saturday Review* 50 (January 7, 1967), 62, 64.

43. [untitled magazine text,] *Seventeen* 28 (May 1969), 137.

44. "Teen Travel Talk," *Seventeen* 28 (May 1969), 237. This advice appears to have been
quoted almost directly from the Canadian government publication *So You're Going to
Canada* (Ottawa: Canadian Government Travel Bureau, 1970[?]), 1.

45. Air Canada advertisement, *Seventeen* 28 (May 1969), 34.

46. John Hagan, *Northern Passage: American Vietnam War Resisters in Canada* (Cambridge, MA: Harvard University Press, 2001), 241.

47. V. S. Pritchett, "Canada: Land of Contrast and Diversity," *Reader's Digest* 86 (April 1965),
204–205. The article was condensed from *Holiday* magazine in "an entire issue devoted to
Canada" as V. S. Pritchett, "Across the Vast Land," *Holiday* 35 (April 1964), 52–69, 184–189.

48. Pritchett, "Canada," 204.

49. Robert A. Liston, *Young Americans Abroad* (New York: Julian Messer, 1971), 19.

50. Robert S. Kane, *Canada A to Z* (Garden City, NY: Doubleday, 1964), 29; Len Hilts,
Explore Canada (Chicago: Rand McNally, 1972), iv.

51. Mark Satin, ed., *Manual for Draft-Age Immigrants to Canada*, 2nd ed. (Toronto:
Toronto Anti-Draft Programme/House of Anansi, 1968), 9; Mark Satin, ed., *Manual for
Draft-Age Immigrants to Canada*, 3rd ed. (Toronto: Toronto Anti-Draft Programme/NTO
Press, 1969), 9; Mark Satin, ed., *Manual for Draft-Age Immigrants to Canada*, 4th rev. ed.
(Toronto: Toronto Anti-Draft Programme, 1969), 13; Byron Wall, ed., *Manual for Draft-
Age Immigrants to Canada*, 5th ed. (Toronto: House of Anansi, 1970), 6.

52. Hilts, *Explore Canada*, iii.

53. *So You're Going to Canada*, back of title page.

54. Howard Cohen and Charles Greene, *Young Person's Guide to Canada* (New York:
Collier, 1971), 74, 137, 2, xviii.

55. Stuart Henderson, "Off the Streets and into the Fortress: Experiments in Hip Separatism
at Toronto's Rochdale College, 1968–1975," *Canadian Historical Review* 92 (March 2011), 117.

56. Henderson, "Off the Streets and into the Fortress," 124–125.

57. Henderson, "Off the Streets and into the Fortress," 116.

58. Henderson, "Off the Streets and into the Fortress," 118, 132.

59. Wall, *Manual for Draft-Age Immigrants to Canada,* 86.

60. Tri-fold brochure to attract residents [n.d., ca. March 1969], folder "Misc. publications, Aug. 69–Feb. 70," box 5, "Publications and misc. essays," Rochdale College Collection (Ms. Coll. 184), Thomas Fisher Rare Book Library, University of Toronto, Ontario, Canada. Emphasis in the original. Sergeant Preston was a fictitious officer in the Royal Canadian Mounted Police appearing in radio and television shows of the 1930s through 1950s who often worked in Canada's Arctic north.

61. *What Every American Tourist Should Know about Canada* (Vancouver: Doug Smith, 1967), 3, 23, 35.

62. Stanley R. Tupper and Douglas L. Bailey, *Canada and the United States—The Second Hundred Years* (New York: Hawthorne, 1967), 143, 146. Published in Canada as *One Continent—Two Voices: The Future of Canada/U.S. Relations* (Toronto: Clarke, Irwin & Company Limited, 1967).

63. Ted Kosoy, *A Guide for Travellers in Canada* (New York: Hastings House, 1973), 18, 19.

64. Norman Reader and Jerome E. Klein, *Canada* (Blauvelt, NY: Educational Press, 1967), 11, 19.

65. David Rideout and Ray Amiro, *Handbook Canada* (Toronto: Transglobular Functions, 1972), 66–67, 210–214.

66. Mopsy Strange Kennedy and Steven D. Stark, eds., *Let's Go: The Student Guide to the United States and Canada, 1972–73* (New York: Dutton, 1972), 649, 659, 699–700.

67. Stuart Roche, ed., *The Toronto Survival Manual: A Practical Guide to Better Living and Psychological Survival for Young People Who Have Just Left Home* (Toronto: n.p., 1970). Brian J. Grieveson, ed., *Toronto Survival Guide* (Toronto: Church of the Holy Trinity, 1973), 2. For more on U.S. émigrés' adaptation to, and activism in, Toronto, particularly in the city's alternative and intentional communities, including the anti–Vietnam War movement and movements for sexual liberation, feminism, alternative schools, and day care centers, see David S. Churchill, "American Expatriates and the Building of Alternative Social Space in Toronto, 1965–1977," *Urban History Review | Revue d'histoire urbaine* 39 (Autumn 2010), 31–44.

68. Volkmar Richter, "Canada," in United States National Student Travel Association, *Student Travel in America,* 340 (New York: Pyramid, 1968).

69. Max Braithwaite, *Canada: Wonderland of Surprises* (New York: Dodd, Mead, 1967), 7–8, 62.

70. Benedict Anderson, *Imagined Communities: Reflections on the Origin and Spread of Nationalism,* rev. ed. (1991; New York: Verso, 2006), 7.

71. Randy William Widdis, "Migration, Borderlands, and National Identity: Directions for Research," in John J. Bukowczyk et al., *Permeable Border: The Great Lakes Basin as Transnational Region, 1650–1990,* 155 (Pittsburgh: University of Pittsburgh Press, 2005).

72. Among the two other border states, New York ranked sixteenth and Minnesota nineteenth. Nonborder states in the first quartile were Oregon (third), Wyoming (fourth), Colorado (ninth), Nevada (tenth), and Utah (twelfth). This information is based on a statistical analysis in which the number of immigrants from each state to Canada from 1966 to 1972 was divided by the population of the state in 1970. See appendix for state-by-state statistics. Emi-

gration figures from M. G. Clark (Director General, Foreign Service) to J. S. Nutt (Director General, Bureau of Western Hemisphere Affairs, Department of External Affairs), May 22, 1974, "Immigration from the United States by State of Last Permanent Residence, Calendar Years, 1966–1970," file 5850-3-637, vol. 1251, "Selection & Processing—General Series—Immigration from United States," Records of the Immigration Branch (RG 76), Library and Archives Canada, Ottawa, Ontario. "Immigration from the United States by State of Last Permanent Residence, Calendar Years, 1971–1972," ibid. Population figures for 1970 from Table 8: "Population of the United States and Puerto Rico: 1790 to 1970," U.S. Bureau of the Census, *1970 Census of the Population*, vol. 1: *Characteristics of the Population*, part A: *Number of Inhabitants* (Washington, DC: U.S. Government Printing Office, 1972), 148.

73. Interview with Howie and Cathy Prince, p. 7 (p. 83), folder "Deserter Interview Transcripts 1970s," box 3, Sallie Marx Papers (DG 270), Swarthmore College Peace Collection, McCabe Library, Swarthmore College, Swarthmore, Pennsylvania.

74. Tom Engelhardt in Christian G. Appy, *Patriots: The Vietnam War Remembered from All Sides* (New York: Viking, 2003), 272.

75. Interview with Bill [Wittmeyer], n.d., folder 11, "Interview with Bill, Vietnam Vet., Montreal," box 3, Renée Kasinsky fonds, Rare Books and Special Collections, Irving K. Barber Learning Centre, University of British Columbia, Vancouver, Canada.

76. Jack Todd, *The Taste of Metal: A Deserter's Story* (Toronto: HarperPerennial, 2001), 131, 132.

77. John Bentley Mays, *Emerald City: Toronto Visited* (Toronto: Viking, 1994), xvi, xxi.

78. Mark Satin in Harry F. Rosenthal, "Canada Increasingly Draft Dodgers' Haven," *Los Angeles Times*, June 2, 1968.

79. Dick Perrin with Tim McCarthy, *G.I. Resister: The Story of How One American Soldier and His Family Fought the War in Vietnam* (Victoria, BC: Trafford, 2001), 117–118.

80. John Cooney and Dana Spitzer, "'Hell, No, We Won't Go!,'" *Trans-action* 6 (September 1969), 62. Renée L. Kasinsky, a graduate student in the School of Criminology at the University of California–Berkeley, wrote to the editors of *Trans-action* to dispute Cooney's and Spitzer's view that those exiled in Canada were simply protesting U.S. involvement in Vietnam: "The political protests of exiles extends much deeper.... Although leaving the country was precipitated by the immediate necessity to escape the draft and the U.S. military, the decision usually involved a more total reaction against an authoritarian system directly endangering their autonomous existence." Renée L. Kasinsky, letter to the editor, *Trans-action* 7 (February 1970), 10, 61–62, quote 10.

81. Bill Davidson, "'Hell, No, We Won't Go!,'" *Saturday Evening Post* 241 (January 27, 1968), 22.

82. Oliver Clausen, "Boys without a Country," *New York Times Magazine* (May 21, 1967), 95. Clausen was on the staff of the *Globe and Mail*, a major Canadian newspaper based in Toronto.

83. "Table Ad80–81—Emigrants from the United States to Canada: 1881–1998," *Historical Statistics of the United States*, millennial edition online, http://hsus.cambridge.org (accessed October 18, 2022).

84. Benedict Anderson saw that newspaper reading "made it possible for rapidly growing numbers of people to think about themselves, and to relate themselves to others, in profoundly new ways." Anderson, *Imagined Communities*, 36.

85. The historian John McMillian contends however, that "many New Leftists never bothered to read daily newspapers, at least not when they wanted to know what was going on in their own milieu." John McMillian, *Smoking Typewriters: The Sixties Underground Press and the Rise of Alternative Media in America* (New York: Oxford University Press, 2011), 4.

86. "Canada: Escape Hatch for U.S. Draft Resisters," *U.S. News and World Report* 61 (September 26, 1966), 62; John M. Swomley Jr., "Draft Exiles in Canada," *Christian Century* 85 (October 30, 1968), 1371.

87. Edmond Taylor, "Draft Resisters in Canada," *Reporter* 38 (May 2, 1968), 21.

88. Clausen, "Boys without a Country," 98, 99, 101, 104.

89. Stewart Alsop, "The Need to Hate," *Newsweek* 76 (July 27, 1970), 80.

90. Gail Cameron, "Why 'Good' Sons Become Draft Dodgers," *Ladies' Home Journal* 84 (August 1967), 94.

91. Cooney and Spitzer, "'Hell, No, We Won't Go!,'" 57.

92. Cameron, "Why 'Good' Sons Become Draft Dodgers," 92.

93. "Canada: Escape Hatch for U.S. Draft Resisters," 61.

94. Stewart Alsop, "They Can't Go Home Again," *Newsweek* 76 (July 20, 1970), 88.

95. Clausen, "Boys without a Country," 25, 96.

96. Alsop, "Need to Hate," 80.

97. Satin, *Manual for Draft-Age Immigrants to Canada*, 2nd ed., 23; Satin, *Manual for Draft-Age Immigrants to Canada*, 3rd ed., 23; Satin, *Manual for Draft-Age Immigrants to Canada*, 4th rev. ed., 35; Wall, *Manual for Draft-Age Immigrants to Canada*. 5th ed., 24; Toronto Anti-Draft Programme, *Manual for Draft-Age Immigrants to Canada*, 6th ed., 73.

98. Clausen, "Boys without a Country," 106; "For Americans." 64.

99. Hoffman, *Steal This Book*, 196.

100. Alexander Ross Society, "Notes on Immigrating to Canada, March 1970" (mimeograph), p. 3, folder 6, "Alexander Ross Society," box 1, Canadian Student Social and Political Organizations, [ca. 1966]–1977 (Collection RC0217), William Ready Division of Archives and Research Collections, Mills Memorial Library, McMaster University, Hamilton, Ontario, Canada.

101. Clausen, "Boys without a Country," 94, 96, 101, 104.

102. Oliver Clausen, letter to the editor, *New York Times Magazine* (July 2, 1967), 2.

103. Cooney and Spitzer, "'Hell, No, We Won't Go!,'" 54, 58.

104. Kasinsky, letter to the editor, 61.

105. Dana L. Spitzer, letter to the editor, *Trans-action* 7 (February 1970), 62.

106. Davidson, "'Hell, No, We Won't Go!'" 24, 23.

107. John Poppy, "The Draft: Hazardous to Your Health?," *Look* 33 (August 12, 1969), 32–33.

108. Leonard Loschen, letter to the editor, *Saturday Evening Post* 241 (March 9, 1968), 4.

109. Joan Baez in Clausen, "Boys without a Country," 104. See also Interview with Jack David Harris, folder "Jack David Harris," box 18, "Interview Transcripts D–H," Michael Maclear fonds (Accession no. 2004.005), Media Commons Archives, John P. Robarts Research Library, University of Toronto.

110. Clausen, "Boys without a Country," 104.

111. Mark Satin, letter to the editor, *New York Times Magazine* (July 2, 1967), 2.

112. Swomley, "Draft Exiles in Canada," 1372.

113. Cameron, "Why 'Good' Sons Become Draft Dodgers," 96, 98. Emphasis in the original.

114. Cooney and Spitzer, "'Hell, No, We Won't Go!,'" 62, 61, 62.

115. Taylor, "Draft Resisters in Canada," 20.

116. Davidson, "'Hell, No, We Won't Go!'" 24; Stuart Byczynski in ibid.

117. Taylor, "Draft Resisters in Canada," 20.

118. Stan Pietlock in Alsop, "Need to Hate," 80.

119. Mrs. Lynch Steiner, letter to the editor, *Newsweek* 76 (August 31, 1970), 5.

120. Pietlock in Alsop, "Need to Hate," 80. For an analysis of *AMEX/Canada,* particularly the difficulty editors had in incorporating the wide range of experiences of U.S. émigrés in Canada, see Jay Young, "Defining a Community in Exile: Vietnam War Resister Communication and Identity in *AMEX,* 1968–1973," *Social History | Histoire sociale* 44 (May 2011), 115–146.

121. Davidson, "'Hell, No, We Won't Go!'" 26.

122. "The Draft: How the Resisters Fare," *Time* 92 (September 20, 1968), 54, 59; "The Draft: Retain? Reform? Or Abolish?," 6; "Stiffer Penalties for Draft Resisters?," *Senior Scholastic* 94 (May 2, 1969), 10–11; "Is Defiance of Draft Growing?," *U.S. News and World Report* 66 (May 5, 1969), 13; "The Chances of Being Drafted Now," *U.S. News and World Report* 68 (June 8, 1970), 25–26; and Looney, "How to Help Your Son Face the Draft," 30.

123. Oscar Handlin, in his 1952 Pulitzer Prize–winning study *The Uprooted,* asserted that the immigration of Europeans to the United States in the nineteenth century forced émigrés to face "the enormous compulsion of working out new relationships, new meaning to their lives, often under harsh and hostile environments," adding that "the immigrants lived in crisis because they were uprooted. . . . Before the new [roots] were established, the immigrant existed in an extreme fashion." Oscar Handlin, *The Uprooted,* 2nd ed. (Boston: Little, Brown, 1990), 5, 6.

124. Davidson, "'Hell, No, We Won't Go!'" 21; Michael Miller in ibid., 24.

125. "For Americans," 64.

126. Clausen, "Boys without a Country," 25.

127. Alsop, "Need to Hate," 80.

128. Taylor, "Draft Resisters in Canada," 21.

129. Clausen, "Boys without a Country," 100.

130. "For Americans," 64.

131. Cooney and Spitzer, "'Hell, No, We Won't Go!,'" 57.

132. See, for example, Wall, *Manual for Draft-Age Immigrants to Canada,* 76–77, 5–6, 33–35.

133. Robert D. Katz and Naomi Wall, "Jobs Are Available," in *Manual for Draft-Age Immigrants to Canada,* 2nd ed., ed. Satin, 68.

134. Robert D. Katz, "'Discrimination against Immigrants Is Strictly Prohibited,'" in *Manual for Draft-Age Immigrants to Canada,* 2nd ed., 2; Robert D. Katz, "'Discrimination against Immigrants Is Strictly Prohibited,'" in *Manual for Draft-Age Immigrants to Canada,* 3rd ed., ed. Satin, 2; Robert D. Katz, "'Discrimination against Immigrants Is Strictly Prohibited,'" in *Manual for Draft-Age Immigrants to Canada,* 4th rev. ed., ed. Satin, 3.

135. Satin, *Manual for Draft-Age Immigrants to Canada,* 2nd ed., 84–86.

136. Satin, *Manual for Draft-Age Immigrants to Canada*, 3rd ed., 66–67 (essay), 84–86 (list); Satin, *Manual for Draft-Age Immigrants to Canada*, 4th rev. ed., 78–80 (essay), 96–98 (list); Wall, *Manual for Draft-Age Immigrants to Canada*, 5th ed., 76–77 (essay), 101–103 (list).

137. Toronto Anti-Draft Programme, *Manual for Draft-Age Immigrants to Canada*, 6th ed., 7.

138. Toronto Anti-Draft Programme, *Manual for Draft-Age Immigrants to Canada*, 6th ed., 15.

139. Killmer and Lutz, *Draft and the Rest of Your Life*, 72–79, quotes 77–78, 73, 78.

140. Leslie S. Rothenberg, *The Draft and You: A Handbook on Selective Service* (Garden City, NY: Anchor, 1968), 227–228.

141. Hoffman, *Steal This Book*, 194–197, quotes 194–195, 197.

142. Tatum and Tuchinsky, *Guide to the Draft*, 229–236, quotes 230, 232.

143. Tatum and Tuchinsky, *Guide to the Draft*, 237–245, quote 244–245.

144. Arlo Tatum, ed., *Handbook for Conscientious Objectors*, 10th ed. (Philadelphia: Central Committee for Conscientious Objectors, 1969), 56; Arlo Tatum, ed., *Handbook for Conscientious Objectors*, 12th ed. (Philadelphia: Central Committee for Conscientious Objectors, 1972), 42–44.

145. Mike Wittels, *Advice for Conscientious Objectors in the Armed Forces*, 2nd ed. (San Francisco: CCCO–Western Region, 1972); Mike Wittels, *Advice for Conscientious Objectors in the Armed Forces*, 3rd ed. (Philadelphia: Central Committee for Conscientious Objectors, 1975). "Emigration to Canada: Notes for Draft-Age Men, December 1969," pp. 1, 5, folder "CCCO Draft Counselor's Manual," box 1, Robert P. Tabak Papers, 1968–1985 (M86–086), Wisconsin Historical Society.

146. "Immigration to Canada and Its Relation to the Draft and the Military, September 1971," quote p. 1, folder "CCCO Draft Counselor's Manual," box 1, Robert P. Tabak Papers.

147. "Going to Canada: A Personal Account, July 1970," folder 8, "DCIC operations & other memos," box 1, Draft Counseling and Information Center, Madison, Wisconsin, Records.

148. Winnipeg Committee to Assist War Objectors, "Canada As an Alternative" [1971,] [p. 1], folder 2, "Conscientious Objection—Canada information, 1967–1971," box 2, American Friends Service Committee, Madison, Wisconsin, Area Committee: Records, 1964–1974 (Mss. 886), Wisconsin Historical Society.

149. Both Kenneth Fred Emerick and John Hagan guessed that a third of the resisters they encountered had access to the *Manual for Draft-Age Immigrants to Canada*. Kenneth Fred Emerick, *War Resisters Canada: The World of the American Military-Political Refugees* (Knox, PA: Knox, Pennsylvania Free Press, 1972), 101; Hagan, *Northern Passage*, 77–78. *Manual for Draft-Age Immigrants to Canada* was mentioned in Vietnam War–era magazine articles, including Cooney and Spitzer, "'Hell, No, We Won't Go!,'" 56–57; Swomley, "Draft Exiles in Canada," 1371; and Taylor, "Draft Resisters in Canada," 21. It was cited in the CCCO (Central Committee for Conscientious Objectors) memos "Emigration to Canada: Notes for Draft-Age Men, December, 1969" and "Going to Canada: A Personal Account, July 1970." Further, it was mentioned in Hoffman, *Steal This Book*, 303; Roger Neville Williams, *The New Exiles: American War Resisters in Canada* (New York: Liver-

ight, 1971), 66; and Emerick, *War Resisters Canada*. Forty years after its first publication, editors of the House of Anansi called the manual their best-selling publication, estimating that nearly 100,000 copies were sold. See James Adams, "'The Big Guys Keep Being Surprised by Us,'" *Globe and Mail* (Toronto), October 20, 2007.

150. The *Manual for Draft-Age Immigrants to Canada* was preceded by a less comprehensive, pocket-sized mimeographed publication. See Toronto Anti-Draft Programme and Student Union for Peace Action, *Escape to Freedom: Immigration to Canada as an Alternative to the Draft* (Toronto: SUPA Anti-Draft Programme, 1967).

151. "*Manual for Draft-Age Immigrants to Canada*, bulk sales records," item 7, box 2, "TADP intake records, sales records, stationery, and other materials," Jack Pocock Memorial Collection (Ms. Coll. 331), Thomas Fisher Rare Book Library, University of Toronto.

152. "Toronto Anti-Draft Programme," mission statement, [ca. 1970] (mimeograph), folder 7, "Mission statements, incl. drafts, and descr. of *Manual*," box 13, "Lobbying and public relations," Jack Pocock Memorial Collection.

153. Howard Sacks, *Manual for Draft-Age Americans in Europe* (London: War Resisters' International, 1968). Updates were Howard Sacks, *Addendum to Manual for Draft-Age Americans in Europe* (London: War Resisters' International, 1969); and Howard D. Sacks, *Manual for Draft-Age Americans in Europe (Second Addendum)* (London: War Resisters' International, 1971).

154. *American Deserters* [booklet] (London: War Resisters' International, [1968]), 16–20, quote 18.

155. American Friends Service Committee, "Is Immigration to Canada the Answer?" [n.d.], folder 2, "Conscientious Objection—Canada information, 1967–1971," box 2, American Friends Service Committee, Madison, Wisconsin, Area Committee: Records.

156. Satin, *Manual for Draft-Age Immigrants to Canada*, 2nd ed., 44–50 (US and Canadian centers); Satin, *Manual for Draft-Age Immigrants to Canada*, 3rd ed., 44–45 (Canadian centers only); Satin, *Manual for Draft-Age Immigrants to Canada*, 4th rev. ed., 58–59 (Canadian centers only); Wall, *Manual for Draft-Age Immigrants to Canada*, 5th ed., 46–53; Toronto Anti-Draft Programme, *Manual for Draft-Age Immigrants to Canada*, 6th ed., 41–46 (Canadian centers only).

157. Bob Tabak, Draft Counselor, to Dave Pufall (Ashland, WI), May 14, 1970, folder 1, "Correspondence—Draft advice, 1970," box 1, Draft Counseling and Information Center, Madison, Wisconsin, Records.

158. Robert Turner (Oshkosh, WI) to Wisconsin Draft Resistance Union (Madison, WI) [February 1968,] folder 2, "Correspondence," box 1, Wisconsin Draft Resistance Union, Records, 1967–1969 (Mss. 382), Wisconsin Historical Society; Joe Chandler to Turner, March 2, 1968 (carbon copy), ibid. Emphasis in the original.

159. "Papers" referred to such documents as birth certificates, high school and college transcripts, passports, marriage certificates, and letters of references that would have helped a person make a good application for landed immigrant status. J. Richard Ranidazzo (Burlington, VT) to Goldie Josephy, February 23, 1968, file 6, "Ottawa Committee for Peace and Liberation—Correspondence with and concerning U.S. Draft Evader Immigration to Canada, 1968," vol. 9, Goldie Josephy fonds (R4460), Library and Archives Canada, Ottawa, Ontario; Josephy to Ranidazzo, [late] February 1968 (carbon copy), ibid.

160. Jake Goldberg (New York, NY) to Josephy, n.d. [early September 1967], file 5, "Ottawa Committee for Peace and Liberation—Correspondence with U.S. Draft Evaders, Immigration to Canada, 1967–1968," vol. 9, Goldie Josephy fonds; Josephy to Goldberg, September 9, 1967 (carbon copy), ibid.

161. Michael Mark (Minneapolis) to Josephy, September 30, 1967, Goldie Josephy fonds; Josephy to Mark, October 3, 1967 (carbon copy), ibid.

162. William McGowan (Philadelphia) to Josephy, March 18, 1968, file 6, "Ottawa Committee for Peace and Liberation—Correspondence with and concerning U.S. Draft Evader Immigration to Canada, 1968," Goldie Josephy fonds; Josephy to McGowan, March 22, 1968 (carbon copy), ibid.

163. Arthur Fried (Park Forest, IL) to Josephy, February 27, 1968, Goldie Josephy fonds; Josephy to Fried, March 4, 1968 (carbon copy), ibid.

164. Robert W. Bars (Providence, RI) to Josephy, February 24, 1968, Goldie Josephy fonds; Josephy to Bars, February 28, 1968 (carbon copy), ibid.

165. Lynn and David Millard (Yellow Springs, OH) to Josephy, February 18, 1968, Goldie Josephy fonds; Josephy to Lynn and David Millard, February 23, 1968 (carbon copy), ibid.

166. Richard Braswell (Memphis) to Josephy, February 8, 1968, Goldie Josephy fonds; Josephy to Braswell, February 23, 1968 (carbon copy), ibid.

167. Dave Hughey (Columbia, MO) to Mark Satin, March 12, 1968, [pp. 1–2], box 1, folder 22, "Letters to TADP, 1968, from potential immigrants," Mark Satin Papers (Ms. Coll. 629), Thomas Fisher Rare Book Library, University of Toronto.

168. [name illegible] to Toronto Anti-Draft Programme, February 20, 1968, box 1, folder 21, "Letters to TADP, 1968, from potential immigrants," Mark Satin Papers.

169. J. McRee Elrod, letter to the editor, Christian Century 85 (March 6, 1968), 303; J. McRee Elrod, letter to the editor, New York Review of Books 10 (February 29, 1968), 35.

170. Phung Duc Minh (Berkeley, CA) to [North Shore Unitarian Church Social Action Committee], May 4, 1972, folder 6, "Correspondence (1972)," box 1, J. McRee Elrod fonds, University of British Columbia Archives, Irving K. Barber Learning Centre, University of British Columbia, Vancouver, Canada.

171. Nguyen Tinh Thong (Berkeley, CA) to J. McRee Elrod, August 14, 1972, J. McRee Elrod fonds.

CHAPTER 3   RELIGION AND POLITICS AT THE BORDER

1. Robert Gardner, Coordinator, Ministry to Draft Age Immigrants, "Canadian Council of Churches—National Council of Churches–U.S.A., Finance and Interpretation Committee on American Refugees in Canada, Meeting of 10 May 1971, Admiral's Club, Metropolitan Airport, Detroit Michigan" (mimeograph), p. 3, folder 13, "Ministry to Draft-Age Immigrants to Canada, 1971," box 21, Jack Pocock Memorial Collection (Ms. Coll. 331), Thomas Fisher Rare Book Library, University of Toronto, Ontario, Canada.

2. For discussions of U.S.-Canadian tensions over draft resisters and military deserters, see Edelgard E. Mahant and Graeme S. Mount, An Introduction to Canadian-American Relations (Toronto: Methuen, 1984), 216–217; "US Deserters in Canada," in Canadian

Annual Review for 1969, ed. John Saywell, 211–212 (Toronto: University of Toronto Press, 1970); and "Questions and Answers following Prime Minister Trudeau's Address to the National Press Club, March 25, 1969," in *Canadian-American Summit Diplomacy, 1923–1973: Selected Speeches and Documents*, ed. Roger Frank Swanson, 281–282 (Toronto: McClelland & Stewart, 1975).

3. Canadian Council of Churches and National Council of Churches, Joint Consultation on Pastoral Service with U.S. Draft-Age Emigrants in Canada, "A Report to Churches and Synagogues of the United States and Canada, December 3, 1969" (mimeograph), p. 2, folder "Canada—(Deserters), 1969–1971," box 6, National Council for Universal and Unconditional Amnesty Records, 1964–1978 (M 80-391), Wisconsin Historical Society, Madison.

4. John Hagan, *Northern Passage: American Vietnam War Resisters in Canada* (Cambridge, MA: Harvard University Press, 2001), 187.

5. William Westfall, "Voices from the Attic: The Canadian Border and the Writing of American Religious History," in *Retelling U.S. Religious History*, ed. Thomas A. Tweed, 197 (Berkeley: University of California Press, 1997). Emphasis in the original.

6. "Dissent in Canada," *Christian Century* 84 (June 14, 1967), 772–773. On J. Raymond Hord's remark, see Allen Spraggett, "Church Killed Draft-Dodger Aid, Feared Collections Would Drop—Official," *Toronto Daily Star*, September 30, 1967; and Ross H. Munro, "Emerging Conflict and Tension in a Divided United Church," *Globe and Mail* (Toronto), September 30, 1967.

7. "A Harvest of Hatred," *Christianity Today* 16 (April 28, 1972), 25. For a comparison of the two main nondenominational religious periodicals in the United States during this era, see David E. Settje, "'Sinister' Communists and Vietnam Quarrels: The *Christian Century* and *Christianity Today* Respond to the Cold and Vietnam Wars," *Fides et Historia* 32 (Winter–Spring 2000), 81–97.

8. Toronto Anti-Draft Programme, "Quarterly Report to the Accountability Committee—Canadian Council of Churches" [October 1–December 4, 1971,] p. 1, folder 15, "Ministry to Draft-Age Immigrants to Canada, 1971," box 21, "Canadian Council of Churches and other anti-war religious groups," Jack Pocock Memorial Collection.

9. Michael Carley, Committee to Aid American War Objectors, Vancouver, to Accountability Committee, Canadian Council of Churches, Toronto, September 1, 1971 (mimeograph), folder 2, "Accountability Committee—Reports from other anti-draft organizations," box 21, "Canadian Council of Churches and other anti-war religious groups," Jack Pocock Memorial Collection.

10. Louise M. Swift, Treasurer, Alexander Ross Society, Edmonton, to Canadian Council of Churches, September 15, 1971 (mimeograph), folder 3, "Accountability Committee—Reports from other anti-draft organizations," box 21, "Canadian Council of Churches and other anti-war religious groups," Jack Pocock Memorial Collection.

11. J. Patrick Cook, Co-ordinator, and Tim Mahoney, Treasurer, Winnipeg Committee to Assist War Objectors to Accountable Committee, Canadian Council of Churches, March 1, 1972 (mimeograph), p. 2, folder 14, "Ministry to Draft-Age Immigrants to Canada, 1971," box 21, "Canadian Council of Churches and other anti-war religious groups," Jack Pocock Memorial Collection.

12. American Refugee Service, Montréal, "Report to the Canadian Council of Churches on the Winter Quarter, 1972," March 12, 1972, p. 3, folder 14, "Ministry to Draft-Age Immigrants

to Canada, 1971," box 21, "Canadian Council of Churches and other anti-war religious groups," Jack Pocock Memorial Collection.

13. Mark Satin to Friends, November 1967 (mimeographed form letter), folder 2, "Conscientious Objection—Canada information, 1967–1971," box 2, American Friends Service Committee, Madison, Wisconsin, Area Committee: Records, 1964–1974 (Mss. 886), Wisconsin Historical Society.

14. American Refugee Service of Montréal, "Quarterly report, Jan. to March 1973," folder 4, "Accountability Committee—Reports from other anti-draft organizations," box 2, American Friends Service Committee, Madison, Wisconsin, Area Committee: Records, 1964–1974; American Refugee Service, Montréal, "Report to the Canadian Council of Churches on the Winter Quarter, 1972," p. 1, March 12, 1972, folder 14, "Ministry to Draft-Age Immigrants to Canada, 1971," box 21, "Canadian Council of Churches and other anti-war religious groups," Jack Pocock Memorial Collection; Toronto Anti-Draft-Programme, "Quarterly Report to the Accountability Committee—Canadian Council of Churches" [October 1–December 4, 1971,] p. 1, folder 15, "Ministry to Draft-Age Immigrants to Canada, 1971," box 21, "Canadian Council of Churches and other anti-war religious groups," ibid.

15. Fred Judson and Dawn Wright, Victoria Committee to Aid War Resisters, to [Accountability Committee, Canadian Council of Churches,] August 28, 1971 (mimeograph), folder 3, "Accountability Committee—Reports from other anti-draft organizations," box 21, "Canadian Council of Churches and other anti-war religious groups," Jack Pocock Memorial Collection.

16. Carley, Committee to Aid American War Objectors, Vancouver, to Accountability Committee, Canadian Council of Churches, Toronto, September 1, 1971, folder 2, "Accountability Committee—Reports from other anti-draft organizations," box 21, "Canadian Council of Churches and other anti-war religious groups," Jack Pocock Memorial Collection.

17. Ron Goodridge, Co-Ordinator and Tim Maloney, Social Worker, Winnipeg Committee to Assist War Objectors to Accountability Committee, Canadian Council of Churches, Toronto, September 1, 1971 (mimeograph), folder 3, "Accountability Committee—Reports from other anti-draft organizations," box 21, "Canadian Council of Churches and other anti-war religious groups," Jack Pocock Memorial Collection.

18. R. Eric Stine [Nova Scotia Committee to Aid American War Objectors], to Bob [Robert Gardner, Co-ordinator, Ministry to U.S. Draft Age Immigrants in Canada, Canadian Council of Churches], September 20, 1971, folder 3, "Accountability Committee—Reports from other anti-draft organizations," box 21, "Canadian Council of Churches and other anti-war religious groups," Jack Pocock Memorial Collection.

19. Gardner, "Canadian Council of Churches—National Council of Churches–U.S.A., Finance and Interpretation Committee on American Refugees in Canada, Meeting of 10 May 1971, Admiral's Club, Metropolitan Airport, Detroit Michigan," folder 13, "Ministry to Draft-Age Immigrants to Canada, 1971," box 21, "Canadian Council of Churches and other anti-war religious groups," Jack Pocock Memorial Collection; "Canadian Council of Churches Statement of Ministry to U.S. Draft Age Immigrants for the Year Ended December 31, 1970," ibid.; Canadian Council of Churches Ministry to U.S. Draft Age Immigrants in Canada, "Sources of Major Financial Contributions—1971," folder 16,

"Ministry to Draft-Age Immigrants to Canada, 1971," box 21, "Canadian Council of Churches and other anti-war religious groups," ibid. For a book-length treatment of CAL-CAV, see Mitchell K. Hall, *Because of Their Faith: CALCAV and Religious Opposition to the Vietnam War* (New York: Columbia University Press, 1990).

20. Patricia Clarke, "Robert Gardner: Why a War Veteran Helps War Resisters," *United Church Observer* 33 (June 1971), 6.

21. "World Council Asks Assistance for Draft Exile Work," *Christian Century* 87 (August 5, 1970), 934.

22. "Legal Brutality and the Anguish of Separation," *Christian Century* 88 (January 6, 1971), 5–6. Emphasis in the original.

23. J. Robert Nelson, "No Utopia in Ethiopia," *Christian Century* 88 (February 17, 1971), 215.

24. Richard L. Killmer, Robert S. Lecky, and Debrah S. Wiley, *They Can't Go Home Again: The Story of America's Political Refugees* (Philadelphia: Pilgrim Press, 1971), 36.

25. For the text of a resolution passed by the Canadian Council of Churches on March 21, 1972, see Press release, Canadian Council of Churches, March 22, 1972 (mimeograph), folder 2, "1972," box 17, "Correspondence, ephemera, notes," Jack Pocock Memorial Collection.

26. Barrie Doyle, "Federal Aid to Religion?: 'Good Samaritan' State," *Christianity Today* 17 (November 10, 1972), 50.

27. Clarke, "Robert Gardner," 6; "Canadian Council Names Director to Aid U.S. Draft Evaders," *Christian Century* 88 (January 13, 1971), 38; "T.O. Has Its Own Dodger Chaplain," *Amex: The American Expatriate in Canada* 2 (no. 7, 1970), 8. On indignation, see Robert Gardner, "Repatriation: Sell-Out or Social Work," *AMEX/Canada* 3 (January–February 1972), 30.

28. Robert Gardner, "A Canadian Perspective: Amnesty When?," *New Republic* 165 (December 25, 1971), 12. Gardner, "Repatriation," 30–31; Gardner, "Canadian Perspective," 12. For an early manuscript of Gardner's position paper, see "Repatriation: Sell-out or Social Work? A Position Paper Prepared by Robert Gardner, Coordinator, Canadian Council of Churches, Ministry to Draft Age Immigrants, 26 October 1971," folder 13, "Ministry to Draft-Age Immigrants to Canada, 1971," box 21, "Canadian Council of Churches and other anti-war religious groups," Jack Pocock Memorial Collection.

29. Gardner, "Repatriation," 30–31.

30. Gardner, "Repatriation," 30. In the mid-1980s, former U.S. president Richard M. Nixon described the United States as suffering from "Vietnam syndrome," the sense that the country should not get involved in the affairs of other countries and that the United States lacked "confidence in [its] ability to wield power effectively." Richard Nixon, *No More Vietnams* (New York: Arbor House, 1985), 22.

31. Gardner, "Repatriation," 31.

32. *The Canadian Encyclopedia*, 2nd ed., "United Church of Canada" (Edmonton: Hurtig, 1988); "Table 5.20—Principal religious denominations of the population, 1951 and 1961, and preliminary figures for 1971," *Canada Year Book 1973: An Annual Review of Economic, Social, and Political Developments in Canada* (Ottawa: Information Canada, 1973), 215–216.

33. Phyllis D. Airhart, "'As Canadian as Possible under the Circumstances': Reflections on the Study of Protestantism in North America," in *New Directions in American Religious History*, ed. Harry S. Stout and D. G. Hart, 116–137 (New York: Oxford University Press, 1997).

34. Ron Graham, *God's Dominion: A Skeptic's Quest* (Toronto: McClelland & Stewart, 1990), 222, quoted in Airhart, "'As Canadian as Possible under the Circumstances,'" 127.

35. Pierre Berton, *The Comfortable Pew: A Critical Look at Christianity and the Religious Establishment in the New Age* (1964; Philadelphia: Lippincott, 1965), xxvii; William Kilbourn, ed., *The Restless Church: A Response to* The Comfortable Pew (Philadelphia: Lippincott, 1966); Gary R. Miedema, *For Canada's Sake: Public Religion, Centennial Celebrations, and the Re-making of Canada in the 1960s* (Montréal: McGill-Queen's University Press, 2005), 37–38.

36. On the publication of *The Comfortable Pew,* see Berton, *Comfortable Pew,* x.

37. *Why the Sea Is Boiling Hot: A Symposium on the Church and the World* (Toronto: Ryerson, 1965), 57.

38. *Why the Sea Is Boiling Hot,* iv, 54, 53, 54, quote iv.

39. *Why the Sea Is Boiling Hot,* 54, quote 56–57.

40. Donald Evans, ed., *Peace, Power, and Protest* (Toronto: Ryerson, 1967), v–vi, 3.

41. Donald Evans, "Ten Principles for Foreign Policy," in *Peace, Power, and Protest,* 35.

42. Donald Evans, "A Reasonable Scream of Protest," in *Peace, Power, and Protest,* 6.

43. Evans, "Ten Principles for Foreign Policy," 32. Emphasis in the original.

44. Evans, "Reasonable Scream of Protest," 2; Evans, "Ten Principles for Foreign Policy," 36.

45. Evans, "Ten Principles for Foreign Policy," 29–31, 17, 21. Emphasis in the original.

46. Jeanne Wayling, "The Swingingest Church in Town," *United Church Observer* 31 (June 1, 1969), 18, 20. The haven came in the form of a forty-bed hostel created by removing ten rows of pews, with the organizer of the hostel observing, "This is really the traditional role of the church—the sanctuary." See Volkmar Richter, "Church Pews Removed for Draft Dodger Bunks," *Toronto Daily Star,* July 18, 1968.

47. Frank Chamberlain, "The Surprising New Ways They Spend Church Money," *United Church Observer* 31 (October 15, 1969), 28–30.

48. "Resolution on the Church and American Draft Resistors, Passed by the Executive of the Board of Evangelism and Social Service on Thursday, September 21st, 1967" (mimeograph), file 10, "American draft resisters, publications, clippings, 1968–1969," box 43, United Church of Canada [hereafter UCC] Board of Evangelism and Social Service fonds (fonds F510), United Church of Canada Archives, Toronto, Ontario, Canada.

49. For statistics on the number of U.S. expatriates living in Canada in 1967, see Hagan, *Northern Passage,* 241.

50. "United Church statement on the church and American draft resistors, Sept. 28, 1967" (mimeograph), file 1, "Draft resisters, anti," box 43, United Church of Canada Board of Evangelism and Social Service fonds. See also Allen Spraggett, "Church Killed Draft-Dodger Aid, Feared Collections Would Drop—Official," *Toronto Daily Star,* September 30, 1967.

51. J. Soderling (Clarkson, ON) to E. E. Long, Secretary of the General Council, United Church of Canada, September 27, 1967 (carbon copy), [p. 1], file 1, "Draft resisters, anti," box 43, United Church of Canada Board of Evangelism and Social Service fonds.

52. H. A. Lee (Port Credit, ON) to J. Raymond Hord, September 28, 1967, file 1, "Draft resisters, anti," box 43, UCC Board of Evangelism and Social Service fonds.

53. Doug Orchard (Haileybury, ON) to Hord, September 27, [1967], [p. 1], file 1, "Draft resisters, anti," box 43, UCC Board of Evangelism and Social Service fonds.

54. R. C. Patterson (Markham, ON) to United Church Board of Evangelism and Social Service, September 27, 1967, file 1, "Draft resisters, anti," box 43, UCC Board of Evangelism and Social Service fonds.

55. W. G. Rivers (Fonthill, ON) to Hord, October 22, 1967, file 1, "Draft resisters, anti," box 43, UCC Board of Evangelism and Social Service fonds.

56. D. M. Sennett (Port Credit, ON) to Hord, September 27, 1967, [p. 1], file 1, "Draft resisters, anti," box 43, UCC Board of Evangelism and Social Service fonds.

57. R. J. Hauser (Ottawa) to Hord, September 30, 1967, [p. 1], file 1, "Draft resisters, anti," box 43, UCC Board of Evangelism and Social Service fonds.

58. Wray Hagerman, Clerk of Session, Applewood United Church (Cooksville, ON), to Hord, October 2, 1967, file 1, "Draft resisters, anti," box 43, UCC Board of Evangelism and Social Service fonds; I. L. (Mrs. W. I.) Reid (Brampton, ON) to Hord, September 26, 1967, [p. 1], ibid.

59. Cassius Clay was Muhammad Ali, a three-time world heavyweight boxing champion who refused to be inducted into the U.S. military in 1967 because of his Muslim beliefs and opposition to the Vietnam War. D. L. Aiton (Oakville, ON) to Hord, October 8, 1967, file 1, "Draft resisters, anti," box 43, UCC Board of Evangelism and Social Service fonds.

60. Jean (Mrs. B. E.) Conquergood (Toronto) to Hord, September 27, 1967, file 1, "Draft resisters, anti," box 43, UCC Board of Evangelism and Social Service fonds.

61. MacGregor W. Sinclair (Toronto) to the Board of Evangelism and Social Service, September 26, 1967, p. 2, file 1, "Draft resisters, anti," box 43, UCC Board of Evangelism and Social Service fonds. Emphasis in the original.

62. "How You Vote on Viet Nam," *United Church Observer* 30 (March 15, 1968), 16.

63. George D. Watt, St. Paul's United Church (Oakville, ON) to Hord, September 27, 1967, [p. 1], file 1, "Draft resisters, anti," box 43, UCC Board of Evangelism and Social Service fonds.

64. Andrew Stevens (Toronto) to the editor, *Toronto Daily Star,* September 30, 1967.

65. Claude de Mestral, "Canadian Christians Primed for Ministry to U.S. Draft 'Refugees,'" *Christian Century* 88 (January 20, 1971), 73.

66. Orchard to Hord, October 14, [1967], [p. 1], file 1, "Correspondence re American draft resisters in Canada, 1967–1971," box 44, "American draft resisters in Canada, 1967–1971," UCC Board of Evangelism and Social Service fonds.

67. W. H. Tester (St. Catherines, ON) to the Board of Evangelism and Social Service, October 1, 1967, file 1, "Draft resisters, anti," box 43, UCC Board of Evangelism and Social Service fonds.

68. Hord to Tester, October 4, 1967 (carbon copy), file 1, "Draft resisters, anti," box 43, UCC Board of Evangelism and Social Service fonds.

69. Hord to Donald W. Laing, Regina Presbytery, Saskatchewan Conference, United Church (Regina, SK), October 13, 1967 (carbon copy), [p. 1], file 1, "Draft resisters, anti," box 43, UCC Board of Evangelism and Social Service fonds.

70. See, for example, Rev. Charlie Fox (Toronto) to Hord, October 30, 1967, file 2, "Draft resisters, pro, 1967–1970," box 43, UCC Board of Evangelism and Social Service fonds.

71. Eva Sanderson, vice chairman, Canadian Peace Congress (Toronto) to the United Church General Council (copy sent to Hord), October 16, 1967, file 2, "Draft resisters, pro, 1967–1970," box 43, UCC Board of Evangelism and Social Service fonds.

72. Claire (Mrs. Leo) Agranone (Toronto) to Hord, October 16, 1967, [p. 2], file 2, "Draft resisters, pro, 1967–1970," box 43, UCC Board of Evangelism and Social Service fonds. Emphasis in the original.

73. Bev Johnston, Grace Church (Saskatoon, SK) to Hord, October 19, 1967, [p. 1], file 2, "Draft resisters, pro, 1967–1970," box 43, UCC Board of Evangelism and Social Service fonds.

74. (Mrs.) Edna Burnett, (Mrs.) Ruby Rapsey, (Mrs.) Jean Foster, and (Mrs.) Ruby Brown (Toronto) to W. C. Lockhart, Moderator, United Church of Canada, October 16, 1967, [p. 1], file 2, "Draft resisters, pro, 1967–1970," box 43, UCC Board of Evangelism and Social Service fonds.

75. Rev. Ronald R. Clark (Macklin, ON) to Hord, October 13, 1967, file 10, "American draft resisters, publications, clippings, 1968–1969," box 43, UCC Board of Evangelism and Social Service fonds.

76. Harold Barker (Scarborough, ON) to Hord, October 15, 1967, file 2, "Draft resisters, pro, 1967–1970," box 43, UCC Board of Evangelism and Social Service fonds.

77. Edna (Mrs. Lorne) Hahn (Toronto) to Hord, October 16, 1967, file 2, "Draft resisters, pro, 1967–1970," box 43, UCC Board of Evangelism and Social Service fonds.

78. Bruce Cameron, South Nanaimo Combined Congregation of the United Church of Canada (Nanaimo, BC), to Hord, October 27, 1967, file 2, "Draft resisters, pro, 1967–1970," box 43, UCC Board of Evangelism and Social Service fonds.

79. Ross E. Readhead, Minister, Paisley Memorial United Church (Guelph, ON), to Hord, October 12, 1967, file 2, "Draft resisters, pro, 1967–1970," box 43, UCC Board of Evangelism and Social Service fonds.

80. Rev. G. M. Paterson (Downsview, ON) to Hord, October 7, 1967, file 3, "Correspondence re: position of Ray Hord on American draft resisters, 1967," box 43, UCC Board of Evangelism and Social Service fonds.

81. Alex Cowan, Canadian Bible Society (Toronto), to Hord, October 24, 1967, [pp. 1, 2], file 2, "Draft resisters, pro, 1967–1970," box 43, UCC Board of Evangelism and Social Service fonds.

82. K. Teddy Smits (Toronto), to Hord, October 18, 1967, [p. 2], file 2, "Draft resisters, pro, 1967–1970," box 43, UCC Board of Evangelism and Social Service fonds.

83. "D-Dodgers," United Church Observer 29 (November 1, 1967), 40. See also Robert Marjoribanks, "Draft Dodgers: What Makes Them Run?," United Church Observer 30 (September 1, 1968), 15. For coverage of this debate in a U.S. religious journal, see "Via the Underground to Canada," Christian Century 84 (November 1, 1967), 1388–1389; and John M. Swomley Jr., "Draft Exiles in Canada," Christian Century 85 (October 30, 1968), 1372.

84. "D-Dodgers," 11, 40. For the full text of the General Council's statement, see "News release, United Church statement on the church and American Draft resisters, Sept. 28, 1967" (mimeograph), file 1, "Draft resisters, anti," box 43, UCC Board of Evangelism and Social Service fonds.

85. T. R. Haythorne, letter to editor, United Church Observer 29 (December 15, 1967), 4.

86. "Via the Underground to Canada," 1389.

87. For press coverage of Paul VI's statement, see "Pope Rebukes Draft Dodging in Peace Bid," *Chicago Tribune*, December 16, 1967; "Pope's Message Assails Draft Evaders," *Washington Post*, December 16, 1967; Robert C. Doty, "Pontiff Sets Jan. 1 As a 'Day of Peace,'" *New York Times*, December 16, 1967; and "Pope Urges World Peace Day Jan. 1," *Los Angeles Times*, December 16, 1967.

88. Marjoribanks, "Draft Dodgers," 12, 14, quote 15.

89. John C. Lott, "'You Cannot Christianize War,'" *United Church Observer* 32 (March 15, 1970), 16–17, 25, 40, quotes 25, 40. Ellipses in the original. Lott's piece was originally a sermon given at the Ottawa Mennonite Church in September 1969. It first appeared in print as John C. Lott, "The Christian, His Country, His Conscience: An Apology for Non-cooperation," *Canadian Mennonite* 17 (October 24, 1969), 6, 8.

90. Virginia Cunningham, "Our Son, the Deserter," *United Church Observer* 33 (November 1970), 29.

91. Marjoribanks, "Draft Dodgers," 12.

92. Patricia Clarke, "Parliament Makes the Laws," *United Church Observer* 31 (June 15, 1969), 10.

93. "How You Vote on Viet Nam," *United Church Observer* 30 (March 15, 1968), 18; James R. Mutchmor, "The World around Us: Ontario," *Christian Century* 86 (May 14, 1969), 692.

94. Carmen Guild in Marjoribanks, "Draft Dodgers," 15.

95. Hagan, *Northern Passage*, 65.

96. The historian Bruce Douville avers that "the United Church's actions were progressive, controversial, and activist, but they cannot be construed as *explicitly* antiwar." Emphasis in the original. Bruce Douville, *The Uncomfortable Pew: Christianity and the New Left in Toronto* (Montréal: McGill-Queen's University Press, 2021), 168.

CHAPTER 4   "KNOWLEDGE HAS NO NATIONAL CHARACTER"

1. "Tues Jun. 17, 1975," p. 1, folder "Diamond, David W.—'Synapse; A Deserter's Diary'—Typescript, 3 of 5, 1975," David W. Diamond fonds (R11554), Library and Archives Canada, Ottawa, Ontario.

2. "March 4, 1975 Tues.," pp. 1–2, folder "Diamond, David W.—'Synapse; A Deserter's Diary'—Typescript, 2 of 5, 1975," David W. Diamond fonds. "II-S" was the Selective Service classification for a deferment for continuing college students.

3. "March 4, 1975 Tues.," p. 2.

4. "Table Bc523–536—Enrollment in institutions of higher education, by sex, enrollment status, and type of institution: 1869–1995," *Historical Statistics of the United States*, millennial edition online, http://hsus.cambridge.org (accessed October 18, 2022).

5. George Q. Flynn, *The Draft, 1940–1973* (Lawrence: University Press of Kansas, 1993), 39–42, 79.

6. "Table Bc523–536—Enrollment in institutions of higher education, by sex, enrollment status, and type of institution: 1869–1995," *Historical Statistics of the United States*.

7. Flynn, *Draft*, 107, 142; Executive Order no. 10,292, *Code of Federal Regulations*, title 3 (1949–1953), 808–810.

8. Flynn, *Draft*, 199.

9. Flynn, *Draft*, 200.

10. Flynn, *Draft*, 180, 184, 199, 311n29; Lawrence M. Baskir and William A. Strauss, *Chance and Circumstance: The Draft, the War, and the Vietnam Generation* (New York: Vintage, 1978), 23; Michael S. Foley, *Confronting the War Machine: Draft Resistance during the Vietnam War* (Chapel Hill: University of North Carolina Press, 2003), 39–40.

11. Betty Vetter, ed., *Draft Facts for Graduates and Graduate Students* (Washington, DC: Scientific Manpower Commission, 1968), 3, 10; Scientific Manpower Commission, *The Draft Lottery and You* (Washington, DC: Scientific Manpower Commission, 1970), 2; "New Draft Policy to Cut Graduate School Enrollment," in *U.S. Draft Policy and Its Impact, July 1968*, 1–2 (Washington, DC: Congressional Quarterly Service, 1968); Flynn, *Draft*, 221–222. Vetter, *Draft Facts for Graduates and Graduate Students*, 10–11.

12. "March 3, 1975," p. 2, folder "Diamond, David W.—'Synapse; A Deserter's Diary'—Typescript, 2 of 5, 1975," vol. 2, David W. Diamond fonds.

13. "March 3, 1975," p. 2, folder "Diamond, David W.—'Synapse; A Deserter's Diary'—Typescript, 2 of 5, 1975," vol. 2, pp. 2, 1, David W. Diamond fonds.

14. "April 2, 1975 Wed.," p. 1, folder "Diamond, David W.—'Synapse; A Deserter's Diary'—Typescript, 2 of 5, 1975," vol. 2, David W. Diamond fonds.

15. Fern Bayer, comp., "Chronology of the Life of David W. Diamond," 2005 [pp. 2–3], vol. 1, David W. Diamond fonds.

16. Erik H. Erikson, *Identity: Youth and Crisis* (New York: Norton, 1968), 156–158; Laurence Steinberg, *Adolescence*, 11th ed. (New York: McGraw-Hill Education, 2017), 220–221.

17. Jacob L. Orlofsky, James E. Marcia, and Ira M. Lesser, "Ego Identity Status and the Intimacy versus Isolation Crisis of Young Adulthood," *Journal of Personality and Social Psychology* 27 (August 1973), 212.

18. "March 4, 1975 Tues.," p. 2, folder "Diamond, David W.—'Synapse; A Deserter's Diary'—Typescript, 2 of 5, 1975," vol. 2, David W. Diamond fonds.

19. Richard Moore III, *Richard: Portrait of a Vietnam War Resister* (San Francisco: Richard Moore III, 1987), part 2, p. 4.

20. Lawrence Kohlberg and Carol Gilligan, "The Adolescent as a Philosopher: The Discovery of the Self in a Postconventional World," *Dædalus* 100 (Fall 1971), 1067–1068.

21. Daniel Yankelovich, Inc., *The Changing Values on Campus: Political and Personal Attitudes of Today's College Students; A Survey for the JDR 3rd Fund* (New York: Washington Square, 1972), 92, 94.

22. Daniel Yankelovich, Inc., *Changing Values on Campus*, 107, 109, 108–109.

23. George H. Gallup, *The Gallup Poll: Public Opinion, 1935–1971* (New York: Random House, 1972), 3:2249.

24. Folders 6–11, "Questionnaires," box 1, Renée Kasinsky fonds, Rare Books and Special Collections, Irving K. Barber Learning Centre, University of British Columbia, Vancouver, Canada; folders 2-1–2-5, "Questionnaires," box 2, ibid.; Renée G. Kasinsky, *Refugees from Militarism: Draft-Age Americans in Canada* (1976; Totowa, NJ: Littlefield, Adams, 1978), 10, 273–280.

25. [Questionnaire responses from #24GM,] folder 7, "Questionnaires," box 1, Renée Kasinsky fonds; "Interview—Steve Wohl, political resister, June 1969, Montreal, #24GM," pp. 1–2, 9, 13, folder 14, box 3, ibid.

26. [Questionnaire responses from #18GV,] folder 7, "Questionnaires," box 1, Renée Kasinsky fonds.

27. Herbert Ford (Bethlehem, PA) to Goldie Josephy (Ottawa), February 22, 1968, file 6, "Ottawa Committee for Peace and Liberation—Correspondence with and concerning U.S. Draft Evader Immigration to Canada, 1968," vol. 9, Goldie Josephy fonds (R4460), Library and Archives Canada.

28. Steven C. Wood (New Orleans) to Josephy (Ottawa), March 5, 1968, file 6, "Ottawa Committee for Peace and Liberation—Correspondence with and concerning U.S. Draft Evader Immigration to Canada, 1968," vol. 9, Goldie Josephy fonds.

29. Joel Kestenbaum (Brooklyn, NY) to Josephy (Ottawa), March 21, 1968, file 6, "Ottawa Committee for Peace and Liberation—Correspondence with and concerning U.S. Draft Evader Immigration to Canada, 1968," vol. 9, Goldie Josephy fonds.

30. John W. Perry (Bronx, NY) to Vancouver Committee to Aid American War Objectors [late 1969?], folder 2, "Correspondence—VCAAWO," box 1, Renée Kasinsky fonds.

31. Canada. Department of Manpower and Immigration, *Admission of University Students to Canada* (Ottawa: Information Canada, 1971), 1, 17.

32. Mark Satin, ed., *Manual for Draft-Age Immigrants to Canada,* 2nd ed. (Toronto: Toronto Anti-Draft Programme/House of Anansi, 1968), 70–76; Mark Satin, ed., *Manual for Draft-Age Immigrants to Canada,* 3rd ed. (Toronto: Toronto Anti-Draft Programme/NTO Press, 1969), 70–76; Mark Satin, ed., *Manual for Draft-Age Immigrants to Canada,* 4th rev. ed. (Toronto: Toronto Anti-Draft Programme, 1969), 82–88; Byron Wall, ed., *Manual for Draft-Age Immigrants to Canada.* 5th ed. (Toronto: House of Anansi, 1970), 79–89.

33. Toronto Anti-Draft Programme, *Manual for Draft-Age Immigrants to Canada,* 6th ed. (Toronto: Toronto Anti-Draft Programme, 1971).

34. Arlo Tatum and Joseph S. Tuchinsky, *Guide to the Draft* (Boston: Beacon, 1969), 240.

35. [Central Committee for Conscientious Objectors,] "Immigration to Canada and Its Relation to the Draft and Military, September 1971," p. 6, folder "CCCO Draft Counselor's Manual, box 1, Robert P. Tabak Papers, 1968–1985 (M86-086), Wisconsin Historical Society, Madison; "Session IV: Emigration to Canada," *Handbook for Training Draft Counselors, 1970,* by Gene Hooyman and Paul Frazier, p. 1, folder 4, box 2, Draft Counseling and Information Center, Madison, Wisconsin, Records, 1968–1974, Wisconsin Historical Society, Madison.

36. "Series A125–163. Origins of the population, census dates, 1871 to 1971," in F. H. Leacy, ed., *Historical Statistics of Canada,* 2nd ed. (Ottawa: Statistics Canada, 1983).

37. *Expo 67 guide officiel | Expo 67 Official Guide* (Toronto: Maclean-Hunter, 1967), 308–310, 311, 330–331, 334, 347–349, 322–326, 332–333, 299–302, quote 299; Bryan D. Palmer, *Canada's 1960s: The Ironies of Identity in a Rebellious Era* (Toronto: University of Toronto Press, 2009), 425–429.

38. Pierre Berton, *1967: The Last Good Year* (Toronto: Doubleday Canada, 1997), 62.

39. Oliver Clausen, "Boys without a Country," *New York Times Magazine* (May 21, 1967), 104.

40. Greg Donaghy, "Minding the Minister: Pearson, Martin, and American Policy in Asia, 1963–1967," in *Pearson: The Unlikely Gladiator,* ed. Norman Hillmer, 136 (Montréal: McGill-Queen's University Press, 1999).

41. Douglas A. Ross, *In the Interests of Peace: Canada and Vietnam, 1954–1973* (Toronto: University of Toronto Press, 1984), 258; Lester B. Pearson, "Address of Prime Minister Pearson at Temple University's Founder's Dinner of the General Alumni Association (on

Receiving the University's Second World Peace Award), Philadelphia, Pennsylvania, April 2, 1965," in *Canadian-American Summit Diplomacy, 1923–1973: Selected Speeches and Documents*, ed. Roger Frank Swanson, 251–254 (Toronto: McClelland & Stewart, 1975).

42. Robert Bothwell, *Alliance and Illusion: Canada and the World, 1945–1984* (Vancouver, UBC Press, 2007), 225–226.

43. Greg Donaghy, *Tolerant Allies: Canada and the United States, 1963–1968* (Montréal: McGill-Queen's University Press, 2002), 130; Edelgard E. Mahant and Graeme S. Mount, *An Introduction to Canadian-American Relations* (Toronto: Methuen, 1984), 212; J. L. Granatstein and Norman Hillmer, *For Better or for Worse: Canada and the United States to the 1990s* (Toronto: Copp Clark Pitman, 1991), 231; John English, *The Worldly Years: The Life of Lester Pearson*, vol. 2, *1949–1972* (Toronto: Knopf, 1992), 364; John Herd Thompson and Stephen J. Randall, *Canada and the United States: Ambivalent Allies*, 4th ed. (Athens: University of Georgia Press, 2008), 219.

44. Charles Ritchie, "The Day the President of the United States Struck Fear and Trembling into the Heart of Our PM," *Maclean's* 87 (January 1974), 42. See also Charles Ritchie, *Storm Signals: More Undiplomatic Diaries, 1962–1971* (Toronto: Macmillan, 1983), 80–83. Analyses of U.S.-Canadian relations during the Vietnam War era often mention the Temple University speech and the Camp David encounter. See Ross, *In the Interests of Peace*, 258–275; Mahant and Mount, *Introduction to Canadian-American Relations*, 212; Victor Levant, *Quiet Complicity: Canadian Involvement in the Vietnam War* (Toronto: Between the Lines, 1986), 196–198; Granatstein and Hillmer, *For Better or for Worse*, 231; English, *Worldly Years*, 2:362–364; Edelgard Mahant and Graeme S. Mount, *Invisible and Inaudible in Washington: American Policies toward Canada* (Vancouver: UBC Press, 1999), 56; David S. Patterson, ed., *Foreign Relations of the United States, 1964–1968*, vol. 12, *Western Europe* (Washington, DC: U.S. Government Printing Office, 2001), 695; Donaghy, *Tolerant Allies*, 128–131; James Laxer, *The Border: Canada, the U.S., and Dispatches from the 49th Parallel* (Toronto: Doubleday, 2003), 273–274; Bothwell, *Alliance and Illusion*, 225–227; Andrew Preston, "Balancing War and Peace: Canadian Foreign Policy and the Vietnam War, 1961–1965," *Diplomatic History* 27 (January 2003), 73–74; and Thompson and Randall, *Canada and the United States*, 218–220.

45. Donaghy, "Minding the Minister," 138; Lester B. Pearson, *Mike: The Memoirs of the Right Honorable Lester B. Pearson, PC, CC, OM, OBE, MA, LLD*, vol. 3, *1957–1968* (Toronto: University of Toronto Press, 1973), 137–147.

46. Thompson and Randall, *Canada and the United States*, 221–222; Bothwell, *Alliance and Illusion*, 233–235; Ross, *In the Interests of Peace*, 299–303.

47. Luke Stewart, "'Hell, They're Your Problem, Not Ours': Draft Dodgers, Military Deserters, and Canada–United States Relations in the Vietnam War Era," *Études canadiennes | Canadian Studies*, no. 85 (2018), 72; Bothwell, *Alliance and Illusion*, 233–235.

48. Bothwell, *Alliance and Illusion*, 227–228.

49. Stewart, "'Hell, They're Your Problem, Not Ours,'" 72.

50. Royal Commission on National Development in the Arts, Letters, and Sciences, *1949–1951*, *Report* (Ottawa: Cloutier, 1951), xvii. For an extended study of the Massey Commission, see Paul Litt, *The Muses, the Masses, and the Massey Commission* (Toronto: University of Toronto Press, 1992). See also Mike Gasher, "From Sacred Cows to White Elephants: Cultural Policy under Siege," *Canadian Issues* 19 (1997), 18–29; Karen A. Fin-

lay, *The Force of Culture: Vincent Massey and Canadian Sovereignty* (Toronto: University of Toronto Press, 2004), 210–237; Zoë Druick, *Projecting Canada: Government Policy and Documentary Film at the National Film Board of Canada* (Montréal: McGill-Queen's University Press, 2007), 90–100; and Ryan Edwardson, *Canadian Content: Culture and the Quest for Nationhood* (Toronto: University of Toronto Press, 2008), 51–77.

51. Jeffrey Cormier, *The Canadianization Movement: Emergence, Survival, and Success* (Toronto: University of Toronto Press, 2004), 5.

52. Royal Commission on National Development in the Arts, Letters, and Sciences, *Report*, 271.

53. Royal Commission on National Development, *Report*, 16–17.

54. Royal Commission on National Development, *Report*, 354–355.

55. Thompson and Randall, *Canada and the United States*, 199, 197, 202.

56. Thompson and Randall, *Canada and the United States*, 210–212; George Grant, *Lament for a Nation: The Defeat of Canadian Nationalism* (1965; Toronto: McClelland & Stewart, 1970), 25–36.

57. Grant, *Lament for a Nation*, 90, 91, 8, quotes 68, 72.

58. Grant, *Lament for a Nation*, 12, 20–24.

59. Grant, *Lament for a Nation*, 86–87.

60. For discussions of the impact of George Grant's *Lament for a Nation* on nationalism in Canada, see Charles Taylor, *Radical Tories: The Conservative Tradition in Canada* (Toronto: Anansi, 1982), 148–157; English, *Worldly Years*, 2:253–256; Donaghy, *Tolerant Allies*, 167–168; Laxer, *Border*, 284; Cormier, *Canadianization Movement*, 76; and Edwardson, *Canadian Content*, 136–137.

61. A. W. Purdy, ed., *The New Romans: Candid Canadian Opinions of the U.S.* (Edmonton: Hurtig, 1968), i, iv. Emphasis in the original. See also John Manning, "Why Anti-Americanism Haunts the Forty-Ninth Parallel," *Texas Quarterly* 15 (Autumn 1972), 98; and William M. Baker, "The Anti-American Ingredient in Canadian History," *Dalhousie Review* 53 (Spring 1973), 71–72.

62. Stephen Clarkson, ed., *An Independent Foreign Policy for Canada?* (Toronto: McClelland & Stewart, 1968), xi.

63. Clarkson, *Independent Foreign Policy for Canada?*, xi.

64. Ian Lumsden, ed., *Close the 49th Parallel etc.: The Americanization of Canada* (Toronto: University of Toronto Press, 1970), book jacket.

65. John H. Redekop, ed., *The Star Spangled Beaver* (Toronto: Peter Martin Associates, 1971), [ix].

66. Ramsay Cook, *The Maple Leaf Forever: Essays on Nationalism and Politics in Canada* (Toronto: Macmillan, 1971), 184.

67. Frank Underhill in Dalton C. Camp, "Canadian-American Interdependence: How Much?," *Canadian Forum* 48 (February 1969), 243.

68. James Laxer, "The Student Movement and Canadian Independence," *Canadian Dimension* 6 (August–September 1969), 27–28.

69. Robert Fulford, "The New Anti-Americanism," *Saturday Night* 85 (May 1970), 11.

70. Robert Fulford, "Cut Off from Our Own Reality," *Saturday Night* 86 (February 1971), 7–8, quote 7.

71. J. L. Granatstein, "The Arrival of the Anti-American Americans: The Vietnam War and Draft Dodgers," in *Yankee Go Home?: Canadians and Anti-Americanism*, 170–191 (Toronto: Harper Collins, 1996).

72. Ron Lambert, "Concerning Frying Pans and Fires," in Toronto Anti-Draft Programme, ed., *Manual for Draft-Age Immigrants to Canada*, 6th ed., 32–40, quote 36.

73. Cormier, *Canadianization Movement*, 19.

74. Edwardson, *Canadian Content*, 139.

75. Cormier, *Canadianization Movement*, 9, 87, 48.

76. Cormier, *Canadianization Movement*, 48, 204n54.

77. Cormier, *Canadianization Movement*, 7.

78. Edwardson, *Canadian Content*, 150–151.

79. Cormier, *Canadianization Movement*, 19, 87.

80. Melville H. Watkins, "Education in the Branch Plant Economy," *Canadian Dimension* 6 (October–November 1969), 39.

81. "Series W340–348. Full-time university enrolment, by sex, Canada and by province, selected years, 1920 to 1975," in *Historical Statistics of Canada*, ed. Leacy.

82. Cormier, *Canadianization Movement*, 46, 87.

83. "Series W519–532. Operating and capital expenditures of universities, by source of funds, Canada, selected years, 1920 to 1974," in *Historical Statistics of Canada*, ed. Leacy.

84. "Series W475–485. Full-time university teachers, Canada and by province, selected years, 1920 to 1975," in *Historical Statistics of Canada*, ed. Leacy.

85. Cormier, *Canadianization Movement*, 19; Edwardson, *Canadian Content*, 151, 167.

86. "Series W504–512. Degrees awarded by Canadian universities and colleges, by sex, Canada, selected years, 1831 to 1973," in *Historical Statistics of Canada*, ed. Leacy.

87. In 1960, 10,575 scholars earned doctorates in the United States. In 1970, 32,107 earned doctorates. The average number of doctorates earned in U.S. universities from 1960 to 1970 was over 19,000 a year. "Table Bc568–587—Degrees conferred by institutions of higher education, by degree and sex: 1869–1994," *Historical Statistics of the United States* (accessed October 18, 2022).

88. Edwardson, *Canadian Content*, 167. For criticism of the lack of advertising, see James Steele, "Item 3: Article by Steele in the *Toronto Daily Star*, June 18, 1969," in *The Struggle for Canadian Universities: A Dossier*, ed. Robin Mathews and James Steele, 64–67 (Toronto: New Press, 1969); Committee of Concern, Graduate English Association, University of Toronto to Faculty Members, March 31, 1969, in *Struggle for Canadian Universities*, ed. Mathews and Steele, 177–179; and J. Laurence Black, "Americans in Canadian Universities II," *Laurentian University Review* 2 (June 1969), 109–110.

89. Cormier, *Canadianization Movement*, 66–67.

90. Laxer, "Student Movement and Canadian Independence," 27. For more on the influx of U.S. academics to Canada, see Michael Butler and David Shugarman, "Canadian Nationalism, Americanization, and Scholarly Values," *Journal of Canadian Studies* 5 (August 1970), 12–28; Manning, "Why Anti-Americanism Haunts the Forty-Ninth Parallel," 98; and William M. Baker, "The Anti-American Ingredient in Canadian History," *Dalhousie Review* 53 (Spring 1973), 72.

91. "Memorandum to C.U.A.S.A. on De-Canadianization, and Five Motions," in *Struggle for Canadian Universities*, ed. Mathews and Steele, 15–20. For a discussion of Carleton's

consideration of the memorandum, see Cormier, *Canadianization Movement*, 24–26. For Mathews's and Steele's account of the internal debate at Carleton, see *Struggle for Canadian Universities*, ed. Mathews and Steele, 3–4, 13–14; and Robin Mathews, "The Americanization of Canadian Universities," *Canadian Dimension* 5 (February 1969), 15–16, 53.

92. "Memorandum to C.U.A.S.A. on De-Canadianization, and Five Motions," 17.

93. Bruce McFarlane and Dennis Forcese, "Item 5: Petition circulated by Professors McFarlane and Forcese," in *Struggle for Canadian Universities*, ed. Mathews and Steele, 23–24.

94. Mathews and Steele, *Struggle for Canadian Universities*.

95. Robin Mathews and James Steele, "The Problem: A Statement by the Editors," in *Struggle for Canadian Universities*, ed. Mathews and Steele, 3–4.

96. Mathews and Steele, "Problem," 4.

97. Robin Mathews, "The Americanization of Canada Means Precisely the Takeover of Canadian Culture by U.S. Citizens," *Saturday Night* 86 (May 1971), 21.

98. Pauline Jewett, "Who's Being Hired to Teach in Our Universities? Foreigners, Mostly. We Used to Be Short of Qualified Canadians. Now We're Turning Out Many More of Them; but We Don't Give Them Jobs," *Maclean's* 82 (March 1969), 10. Pauline Jewett was the first woman to be president of a Canadian university, holding the post at Simon Fraser University in Burnaby, British Columbia, from 1974 to 1978. She also was chancellor of Carleton University in Ottawa from 1990 until her death in 1992.

99. Watkins, "Education in the Branch Plant Economy," 37, 39.

100. Charles F. Doran and James Patrick Sewell, "Anti-Americanism in Canada?," *Annals of the American Academy of Political and Social Science*, no. 497 (May 1988), 113. This phenomenon is akin to the "creole pioneers" Benedict Anderson described in *Imagined Communities*. Creoles, or descendants of Europeans born in the Western Hemisphere, were limited in their job aspirations because of their place of birth. Benedict Anderson, *Imagined Communities: Reflections on the Origin and Spread of Nationalism*, rev. ed. (1991; New York: Verso, 2006), 56–58.

101. Howard H. Lentner, "Canada and U.S. (2) / Mosaic, Melting Pot—Both Myths," *Toronto Daily Star*, August 20, 1970, in *Americanization*, ed. Hugh Innis, 11–14 (Toronto: McGraw-Hill Ryerson, 1972).

102. Watkins, "Education in the Branch Plant Economy," 38.

103. Lewis Hertzman, "Americans in Canadian Universities I," *Laurentian University Review* 2 (June 1969), 108.

104. Mathews, "Americanization of Canada Means Precisely the Takeover of Canadian Culture by U.S. Citizens," 21.

105. H. Blair Neatby, "Item 17: C.B.C. broadcast by Professor Neatby, January 2, 1969," in *Struggle for Canadian Universities*, ed. Mathews and Steele, 44.

106. G. C. Andrew, "Item 26: Letter to Miss Marya Hardman from Dr. Andrew, February 4, 1969," in *Struggle for Canadian Universities*, ed. Mathews and Steele, 60–61.

107. Herbert Lefcourt, letter to the editor, *Saturday Night* 86 (December 1970), 3.

108. Bernard H. Gustin, "Item 1: Letter in *The Globe and Mail* from Professor Gustin, Published May 30, 1969," in *Struggle for Canadian Universities*, ed. Mathews and Steele, 123–125.

109. Natalie [Zemon] Davis in Valerie Miner Johnson, "What It's Like to Be an American Professor in Canada and Discover the Canadians Aren't So Happy to Have You Here,"

Saturday Night 86 (April 1971), 21. See also William C. Latta Jr., letter to the editor, *Saturday Night* 86 (June 1971), 2.

110. David J. O'Brien, "An American Professor Answers Back," *Weekend Magazine*, March 29, 1969, in *Struggle for Canadian Universities*, ed. Mathews and Steele, 73. O'Brien was a professor of history at Loyola College in Montréal, since 1974 part of Concordia University. See also Neatby, "Item 17," 43–44; Canada, *House of Commons Debates* (May 29, 1969), pp. 9243 (Mark Rose, MP), in *Struggle for Canadian Universities*, ed. Mathews and Steele, 83; and Barbara Pentland (Vancouver) to James Steele, May 25, 1969, in ibid., 172. After World War II the government of the province of Québec took steps to shift from a rural, Catholic Church–oriented society to one that that was more industrial and secular. In the early 1960s a strong provincial government promised to make the Québécois "maîtres chez nous," or, "masters of our house," and that it would no longer tolerate the colonial status it felt the province had within Canada. The government secularized and modernized the provincial educational system, developed a strong welfare system, was closely involved with the development of both public and private enterprise, and created a bureaucracy to preserve and encourage French-Canadian culture and the French language. J. M. Bumsted and Michael C. Bumsted, *A History of the Canadian Peoples*, 5th ed. (Don Mills, ON: Oxford University Press, 2016), 460–462.

111. National Conference of Canadian Universities in Litt, *Muses, the Masses, and the Massey Commission*, 158.

112. Robin Mathews, "The U.S. Draft Dodger in Canada Is Part of U.S. Imperialism in Canada," *Amex: The American Expatriate in Canada* 2 (June 1970), 24–25.

113. Laxer, "Student Movement and Canadian Independence," 30.

114. Thompson and Randall, *Canada and the United States*, 224.

115. Richard Lemm, e-mail message to author, May 27, 2007.

116. Stephen Eaton Hume in Alan Haig-Brown, *Hell No, We Won't Go: Vietnam Draft Resisters in Canada* (Vancouver: Raincoast, 1996), 73.

117. Edward Cowan, "More in U.S. Pick Canada for Study," *New York Times*, April 14, 1968; Kenneth Dent (Toronto) to Allan MacEachen (Minister of Manpower and Immigration, Ottawa), April 30, 1969, file IM 5660–2, pt. 5, box 726, Records of the Immigration Branch (RG 76), Library and Archives Canada; Lemm, e-mail message to author, May 27, 2007.

118. Robert Adolph, "Reflections of a New Canadian Professor," *Canadian Dimension* 7 (October–November 1970), 43.

119. Clausen, "Boys without a Country," 106, 104.

120. Roger Williams, "Go North Young Man: The New Exodus," *New Republic* 162 (May 16, 1970), 16.

121. John Cooney and Dana Spitzer, "'Hell, No, We Won't Go!,'" *Trans-action* 6 (September 1969), 55.

122. Bayer, "Chronology of the Life of David W. Diamond," 2005 [pp. 6–8], vol. 1, David W. Diamond fonds.

123. "Oct. 11, 1984, Thurs.," p. 1, box 1, folder "Diamond, David W.—Untitled diary, 3 of 3, 1984," David W. Diamond fonds.

124. "Oct. 11, 1984, Thurs.," p. 2.

125. Ken Hull, "'Open Arms' to Draft Dodgers: Students to Offer Invitations," *Windsor* (Ontario) *Star,* March 22, 1967; "Anti-draft Group Loses: U. of W. Committee, Down, Not Out," *Windsor* (Ontario) *Star,* March 30, 1967.

126. Andrew Szende, "Toronto Students Vote to Help U.S. Draft Dodgers," *Toronto Daily Star,* September 22, 1967.

127. University of Toronto, Faculty Committee on Vietnam, "Statement on Draft Resisters" (press release, mimeograph), December 1, 1967, folder 11, "Record Series Group 4—Exile Group Publications: Toronto, Montreal," box 7, Renée Kasinsky fonds.

128. K. Peter et al. (Simon Fraser University, Burnaby, British Columbia) to Pierre Trudeau (Prime Minister, Ottawa), March 28, 1969 (photocopy), p. 2 file IM 5660-2, vol. 4, box 726, Records of the Immigration Branch. United Nations, "Universal Declaration of Human Rights," https://www.un.org/en/about-us/universal-declaration-of-human-rights (accessed October 18, 2022).

129. "Interview—Steve Wohl, political resister, June 1969, Montreal, #24GM," p. 13, folder 14, box 3, Renée Kasinsky fonds.

130. Dick Perrin with Tim McCarthy, *G.I. Resister: The Story of How One American Soldier and His Family Fought the War in Vietnam* (Victoria, BC: Trafford, 2001), 133.

131. Christopher Clausen, "An Army of One," *American Scholar* 72 (Autumn 2003), 58.

132. [Questionnaire responses from #59GV,] folder 11, "Questionnaires," pp. 5–6, box 1, Renée Kasinsky fonds; [Questionnaire responses from #105GO], folder 4, "Questionnaires," pp. 6–7, box 2, ibid.

133. Cormier, *Canadianization Movement,* 68.

134. Edwardson, *Canadian Content,* 216; Cormier, *Canadianization Movement,* 186–190.

135. Edwardson, *Canadian Content,* 216–217.

136. Dominion Bureau of Statistics, Education Division, Higher Education Section, *Survey of Higher Education, Part II: Degrees, Staff, and Summary, 1963-64-1968-69* (Ottawa: Queen's Printer, 1966–1970); Dominion Bureau of Statistics, Education Division, Student Information Section, *Survey of Higher Education, Part I: Fall Enrolment in Universities and Colleges, 1969-70* (Ottawa: Queen's Printer, 1970); Statistics Canada, Education Division, Student Information Section, *Fall Enrolment in Universities and Colleges, 1970-71* (Ottawa: Information Canada, 1972); Statistics Canada. Education, Science, and Culture Division, Student Information Section, *Fall Enrolment in Universities and Colleges, 1971-72* (Ottawa: Information Canada, 1973); Statistics Canada, Education, Science, and Culture Division, Post-secondary Education Section, *Fall Enrolment in Universities, 1972-73-1973-74-1975-1976* (Ottawa: Statistics Canada, 1976–1977); Statistics Canada, Education, Science, and Culture Division, Post-Secondary Education Section, *Universities: Enrolment and Degrees, 1976-1977* (Ottawa: Statistics Canada, 1978–1979).

137. Statistics Canada, *Fall Enrolment in Universities and Colleges, 1970-71; Fall Enrolment in Universities and Colleges, 1971-72;* and *Fall Enrolment in Universities, 1972-73-1973-74-1975-1976;* Statistics Canada, Education, Science, and Culture Division, Post-Secondary Education Section, *Universities: Enrolment and Degrees, 1976-1979* (Ottawa: Statistics Canada, 1978–1981).

138. Kasinsky, *Refugees from Militarism,* 260–261; John Hagan, *Northern Passage: American Vietnam War Resisters in Canada* (Cambridge, MA: Harvard University Press, 2001), 163.

139. "Jan. 1, 1975 Wed.," pp. 1–2, folder "Diamond, David W.—'Synapse; A Deserter's Diary'—Typescript, 1 of 5, 1975," vol. 2, David W. Diamond fonds. Diamond often commented on his life in exile. For example, in a March 31, 1975, entry he said, "I don't hate home and in fact I would much prefer living in the states now than I would living here. I just sort of live here, but I don't really participate in the life of the place." "Mon. March 31, 1975," pp. 1–2, folder "Diamond, David W.—'Synapse; A Deserter's Diary'—Typescript, 2 of 5, 1975," ibid. In a New Year's Eve entry in 1975, he observed, "Odd though it may seem, I have always considered myself a patriot in a solid believing sort of way. . . . Canada is alright but it isn't home. The people don't walk, talk, drink, or think the way I do; which means I spend much of my time alone even when I'm with others." "Dec. 31, 1975 Wed.," folder "Diamond, David W.—'Synapse; A Deserter's Diary'—Typescript, 5 of 5, 1975," ibid.

140. "Mon. March 31, 1975," pp. 1–2, folder "Diamond, David W.—'Synapse; A Deserter's Diary'—Typescript, 2 of 5, 1975," David W. Diamond fonds.

141. "Jan. 1, 1975 Wed.," p. 1, folder "Diamond, David W.—'Synapse: A Deserter's Diary'—Typescript, 1 of 5, 1975," David W. Diamond fonds.

142. Bayer, "Chronology of the Life of David W. Diamond," [pp. 11–13, 15], vol. 1, David W. Diamond fonds.

CHAPTER 5   "THESE ARE THE THINGS YOU GAIN IF YOU MAKE OUR COUNTRY YOUR COUNTRY"

1. See Hugh Ll. Keenleyside, *Canada and the United States: Some Aspects of the History of the Republic and the Dominion* (New York: Knopf, 1929), xi.

2. Lauren McKinsey and Victor Konrad, *Borderland Reflections: The United States and Canada* (Orono, ME: Borderlands Project, 1989), iii.

3. Douglas Coupland, *Souvenir of Canada* (Vancouver: Douglas & McIntyre, 2002), 33.

4. John J. Bukowczyk, "The Production of History, the Becoming of Place," in *Permeable Border: The Great Lakes Basin as Transnational Region, 1650–1990*, by John J. Bukowczyk et al., 7 (Pittsburgh: University of Pittsburgh Press, 2005); John Herd Thompson and Stephen J. Randall, *Canada and the United States: Ambivalent Allies*, 4th ed. (Athens: University of Georgia Press, 2008), 334.

5. Porter Fox, *Northland: A 4,000-Mile Journey along America's Forgotten Border* (New York: Norton, 2018), xiv–xv.

6. James Laxer, *The Border: Canada, the U.S., and Dispatches from the 49th Parallel* (Toronto: Doubleday, 2003), 110.

7. Ninette Kelley and Michael Trebilcock, *The Making of the Mosaic: A History of Canadian Immigration Policy* (Toronto: University of Toronto Press, 1998), 369–370; Freda Hawkins, *Canada and Immigration: Public Policy and Public Concern*, 2nd ed. (Kingston: McGill-Queen's University Press, 1988), 387–388; Freda Hawkins, *Critical Years in Immigration: Canada and Australia Compared* (Montréal: McGill-Queen's University Press, 1991), 45. See also "Immigration to Canada in 1967," *Labour Gazette* 68 (May 1968), 290. *Labour Gazette* was the official journal of the Canadian Department of Labour. On the uniqueness of the Canadian law, see Charles A. White, "Immigration Laws: Should We Loosen

or Tighten?," *Canada and the World* 38 (January 1973), 4; and Heward Grafftey, "'Special' Immigrants Now Manpower Dilemma," *Canadian Business* 46 (October 1973), 98.

8. White, "Immigration Laws," 4; "Memorandum: Passports for American Immigrants," July 25, 1968, p. 1, file IM5660–1, part 4, vol. 1210, Records of the Immigration Branch (RG 76), Library and Archives Canada, Ottawa, Ontario.

9. "Schedule A: Norms for Assessment of Independent Applicants, New. P.C. 1967–1616, Aug. 16, 1967," in *Office Consolidation of the Immigration Act, R.S.C., 1952, c. 325, as amended by 1966–67, cc. 25, 90, 1967–68, cc. 1, 37; Immigration Regulations, Part I, made by P.C. 1962–86, as amended by P.C. 1966–525, P.C. 1967–1616* (Ottawa: Queen's Printer and Controller of Stationery, 1968). An annotated list of the regulations appeared in the *Manual for Draft-Age Immigrants to Canada.* See, for example, Toronto Anti-Draft Programme, *Manual for Draft-Age Immigrants to Canada,* 6th ed. (Toronto: Toronto Anti-Draft Programme, 1971), 56–62.

10. Canada, *House of Commons Debates* (December 2, 1966), pp. 10666–10667; ibid. (December 12, 1966), pp. 10982–10983; ibid. (March 9, 1967), pp. 13761–13762; ibid. (March 19, 1969), p. 6818; ibid. (April 16, 1969), p. 7584; ibid. (June 2, 1969), pp. 9329–9330.

11. "A Note on the Handling of Draft-Age Americans Who Apply for Entry to Canada" (mimeograph), [1967], pp. 3, 14, 18–20, 25, folder 8, "A Note on the Handling of Draft-Age Americans Who Apply for Entry to Canada," box 8, Renée Kasinsky fonds, Rare Books and Special Collections, Irving K. Barber Learning Centre, University of British Columbia, Vancouver, Canada. Immigrant aid groups in Vancouver, Toronto, and Montréal compiled the note as a brief submitted to Jean Marchand, minister of immigration, and Pierre Trudeau, prime minister. See Renée G. Kasinsky, *Refugees from Militarism: Draft-Age Americans in Canada* (1976; Totowa, NJ: Littlefield, Adams, 1978), 112–115; Clive Cocking, "How Did the Canadian Mounties Develop Their Unfortunate Habit of Deporting People They Don't Happen to Like?," *Saturday Night* 85 (June 1970), 28–30; and letter (Vancouver, WA) to Central Processing Office, Immigration (Ottawa), December 5, 1968 (photocopy), file IM5655-1-1, part 4, vol. 1209, Records of the Immigration Branch. On veterans working as immigration agents, see "Note on the Handling of Draft-Age Americans Who Apply for Entry to Canada," 19; and Harry Trimborn, "U.S. Deserters Create Controversy in Canada," *Los Angeles Times,* March 16, 1969. On refugees, see Kelley and Trebilcock, *Making of the Mosaic,* 363–365; and Hawkins, *Canada and Immigration,* 439n51.

12. For the codified version of this law, see Immigration Act, *Revised Statutes of Canada, 1970,* c. I-2, s. 57 (g)(ii)–(iv).

13. "Statement by the Honourable Allan MacEachen to the House of Commons, Thursday, May 22/69," p. 3, file IM5650–1, part 1, vol. 1208, Records of the Immigration Branch.

14. "Statement by the Honourable Allan MacEachen to the House of Commons," pp. 3–4.

15. Peter C. Connolly (Ottawa) to William G. Egan (Pierrefonds, Québec), July 16, 1969, p. 2 (carbon copy), file IM5660–2, part 13, vol. 726, Records of the Immigration Branch. Connolly was an assistant to MacEachen. The letter was a form letter used in responding to comments sent to MacEachen concerning his May 22, 1969, announcement.

16. See "Draft Dodgers and Deserters," March 18, 1969, p. 2, file IM5655-1-1, part 4, vol. 1209, Records of the Immigration Branch. For more on the debate among Canadian government officials about the admissibility of U.S. émigrés to Canada in light of shared U.S. and Canadian security concerns resulting from student movement and anti–Vietnam War protests

of the era, see David S. Churchill, "An Ambiguous Welcome: Vietnam Draft Resistance, the Canadian State, and Cold War Containment," *Social History | Histoire sociale* 37 (May 2004), 1–26.

17. Richard Nixon, "A Conversation with the President," Interview with Dan Rather of the Columbia Broadcasting System, January 2, 1972, *Public Papers of the Presidents of the United States: Containing the Public Messages, Speeches, and Statements of the President: Richard Nixon, 1972* (Washington, DC: U.S. Government Printing Office, 1974), 17; Richard Nixon in "Amnesty for the War Exiles?," *Newsweek* 79 (January 17, 1972), 19.

18. Richard Nixon, "The President's News Conference of August 29, 1972," *Public Papers of the Presidents of the United States . . . 1972*, 836.

19. On mockery, see Richard Nixon, "Radio Address on the American Veteran, October 22, 1972," *Public Papers of the Presidents of the United States . . . 1972*, 1007. On fairness, see Richard Nixon, "Remarks at Albuquerque, New Mexico, November 4, 1972," ibid., 1061. On insult, see Richard Nixon, "The President's News Conference of March 2, 1973," *Public Papers of the Presidents of the United States: Containing the Public Messages, Speeches, and Statements of the President: Richard Nixon, 1973* (Washington, DC: U.S. Government Printing Office, 1975), 155.

20. Richard Nixon, "Remarks at Greensboro, North Carolina, November 4, 1972," *Public Papers of the Presidents of the United States . . . 1972*, 1118–1119. See also Richard Nixon, "Informal Exchange of Remarks in Mantua Corners, Ohio, October 28, 1972," ibid., 1061.

21. Nixon, "President's News Conference of March 2, 1973," 155.

22. Richard Nixon, "The President's News Conference of January 31, 1973," *Public Papers of the Presidents of the United States . . . 1973*, 55–56, quotes 56. For press accounts of Nixon's stance, see "Nixon Firm in Opposing Draft Dodgers' Amnesty," *Chicago Tribune*, February 1, 1973; "Nixon's Nix on Amnesty," ibid.; George Lardner Jr., "Nixon Rejects Amnesty for Deserters," *Washington Post*, February 1, 1973; "Amnesty Ruled Out for Draft Dodgers," *Toronto Star*, February 1, 1973; and Haynes Johnson, "Peace Fires Amnesty Issue," *Toronto Star*, February 4, 1973.

23. Hawkins, *Canada and Immigration*, 387; Hawkins, *Critical Years in Immigration*, 45–46; Kelley and Trebilcock, *Making of the Mosaic*, 369, 545n125. On the rate of arrivals to Canada, see Hugh Winsor, "'Crisis' Caused Arbitrary Cutoff of Immigration Flow, Andras Concedes," *Globe and Mail* (Toronto), April 6, 1973. Robert Andras was minister of manpower and immigration in Canada from late November 1972 to September 1976.

24. "Statement by the Honourable Bryce Mackasey, Minister of Manpower and Immigration, June 22, 1972, 'New Measures to Expedite Immigration Inquiry Cases'" (press release) (photocopy), pp. [1–2], folder 5, "Immigration statements, 1968–1974," box 6, "Counseling materials—Canadian legal publications," Jack Pocock Memorial Collection (Ms. Coll. 331), Fisher Rare Book Library, University of Toronto, Ontario, Canada.

25. Ministry of Manpower and Immigration, press release, November 3, 1972 (mimeograph), folder 4, "Subject files, Amnesty—Hearings & Briefings, 1975," box 11, AMEX/Canada Records, 1968–1977 (Mss. 736), Wisconsin Historical Society, Madison; Eugene Griffin, "Canada Curbs on Immigrants Hit Deserters," *Chicago Tribune*, November 11, 1972; Eugene Griffin, "Canada Gives Illegal Aliens a New Chance," *Chicago Tribune*, July 9, 1973; Hawkins, *Canada and Immigration*, 387; Hawkins, *Critical Years in Immigration*, 46–47; Kelley and Trebilcock, *Making of the Mosaic*, 369–371.

26. Department of Manpower and Immigration, *Highlights from the Green Paper on Immigration and Population* (Ottawa: Information Canada, 1975), 23; Jennifer Lewington, "Huge Backlog of Appeals for Immigration on Hand," *Financial Post* (Toronto), November 18, 1972; John Beaufoy, "Immigration Backlog Turns Newcomers into Residents," *Globe and Mail* (Toronto), February 20, 1973; Grafftey, "'Special' Immigrants Now Manpower Dilemma," 98.

27. Griffin, "Canada Curbs on Immigrants Hit Deserters"; Don Shannon, "Canada Makes It Easier on U.S. Deserters," *Los Angeles Times*, August 15, 1973.

28. Ministry of Manpower and Immigration, press release, November 3, 1972 (mimeograph), folder 4, "Subject files, Amnesty—Hearings & Briefings, 1975," box 11, AMEX/Canada Records; Hawkins, *Canada and Immigration*, 387; Hawkins, *Critical Years in Immigration*, 46–47; Kelley and Trebilcock, *Making of the Mosaic*, 369–371.

29. "Canadian Immigration Procedures Closed," (Midwest Committee for Draft Counseling) *Draft Counselor's Newsletter*, no. 9 ([November or December] 1972), 3.

30. *House of Commons Debates*, June 20, 1973, pp. 4952, 4950.

31. *House of Commons Debates*, June 20, 1973, p. 4956.

32. *House of Commons Debates*, June 20, 1973, p. 4956. Workers at the Toronto Anti-Draft Programme noted the vulnerability of U.S. émigrés in Canada in late 1972 and concurred with Lincoln M. Alexander, asserting in an internal memo that "the public backlash against immigration during the election was not directed at war resisters but at blacks immigrating from the West Indies and Asians immigrating from India and other places—we simply got caught in the racist backlash when everything was stopped." Dick Brown, Toronto Anti-Draft Programme, to Stan [Pietlock?], December 8, 1972, [p. 1], folder 1, "TADP statements and lobbying," box 13, "Lobbying and public relations," Jack Pocock Memorial Collection. Statistical data shows that the national origin of immigrants to Canada did indeed shift from the mid-1960s to 1972. The percentage of immigrants to Canada in 1965 who arrived from Europe was 73.5 percent (107,816), from Africa 2.2 percent (3,196), from Asia 8.0 percent (11,684), from Central and South America 1.8 percent (2,676), and from the West Indies 2.1 percent (3,095). By 1972, those numbers had shifted to Europe 42.0 percent (51,293), Africa 6.8 percent (8,308), Asia 19.1 percent (23,325), Central and South America 4.6 percent (5,691), and the West Indies 6.7 percent (8,234). See "Series A385–416—Immigration to Canada by country of last permanent residence, 1956 to 1976," in F. H. Leacy, ed. *Historical Statistics of Canada*, 2nd ed. (Ottawa: Statistics Canada, 1983).

33. Immigrant Workers United Front, "Let's Unite against the Repressive Immigration Laws" (flyer), [May 1973], folder 5, "Immigration to Canada," box 11, "Subject Files," AMEX/Canada Records; Committee against the Racist Immigration Policy, "End Racist Immigration Policy" (flyer), [1972], ibid.; AMEX/Canada, "To: Those interested in immigration to Canada" (news release), [1973], ibid.

34. Dee Knight, "New Immigration Rules: New Restrictions on Non-immigrant Visitors," *AMEX/Canada* 3 (January–February 1973), 11; Committee against the Racist Immigration Policy, "End Racist Immigration Policy."

35. Carolyn Kline and Frank Dingman, Co-chairmen, Quaker Social Concerns Committee of Vancouver, to Pierre Trudeau, May 8, 1973 (photocopy), pp. [1–2], folder 12, "Correspondence, press releases and notes," box 14, "Canadian Adjustment of Status Program," Jack Pocock Memorial Collection.

36. Marjorie Hyer, "Canada Offers Status to COs," *Washington Post*, August 8, 1973.

37. Ministry of Manpower and Immigration, "If you were in Canada by November 30, 1972, and have remained here since, as a visitor or without legal status, we're going to give you until midnight, October 15, 1973 to make our country your country" (poster) (Ottawa: Ministry of Manpower and Immigration, [1973]); "If you were in Canada by November 30, 1972, and have remained here since, as a visitor or without legal status, these are the things you gain if you make our country your country" (advertisement), *Globe and Mail* (Toronto), September 11, 1973. For press accounts, see Dick Brown, "New Immigration Law Opens Door for 60 Days," *AMEX/Canada* 4 (July–August 1973), 28–29; "Immigration: 30,000 People Take Advantage of Government Mop-Up Program in First 30 Days," *AMEX/Canada* 4 (September–October 1973), 31–32; Griffin, "Canada Gives Illegal Aliens a New Chance"; Hyer, "Canada Offers Status to COs"; Shannon, "Canada Makes It Easier on U.S. Deserters"; Terrence Belford, "400 Step Forward Daily, Seek Legal Landed Status," *Globe and Mail* (Toronto), September 7, 1973; William Borders, "Canada Is Offering Amnesty to Illegal Immigrants," *New York Times,* September 9, 1973; Eugene Griffin, "Canadian Amnesty Running Out, Yank Draft Evaders Face Deportation," *Chicago Tribune,* October 14, 1973; and Barbara Young, "Canada Gives Welcome to Lots of People Who Were There All Along," *Wall Street Journal* (New York), October 15, 1973. See also Kasinsky, *Refugees from Militarism,* 200–205; Hawkins, *Canada and Immigration,* 387–388; Hawkins, *Critical Years in Immigration,* 47–50; and Kelley and Trebilcock, *Making of the Mosaic,* 370–371.

38. On the blocking of potential immigrants, see Henry Aubin, "Illegal Immigrants Fear 'Amnesty,'" *Montreal Gazette,* September 1, 1973. On the relaxed standard for immigration, see Robert Andras to Trudeau, August 30, 1973, p. 2, file 5660–1, part 7, vol. 1210, Records of the Immigration Branch. For the Andras interview, see Toronto Anti-Draft Programme, press release, August 6, 1973 [p. 1], folder 9, "Press release, August 6, 1973," box 14, "Canadian Adjustment of Status Program," Jack Pocock Memorial Collection. For the Andras press release, see Robert Andras in Canadian Coalition of War Objectors, press release, July 31, 1973 (mimeograph), p. 2, folder 4, "Subject files, Amnesty—Hearings & Briefings, 1975," box 11, AMEX/Canada Records. See also Grafftey, "'Special' Immigrants Now Manpower Dilemma," 98; and Dick Brown, "Grace Period for Immigrants Affects 1,200 at U of T," *Varsity* (Toronto), September 12, 1973. U of T was the University of Toronto. *The Varsity* was its campus newspaper.

39. AMEX/Canada, "Canada Now Closed to War Resisters Because of New Immigration Rules" (press release), January 4, 1973, folder 5, "Subject files, Immigration to Canada, Nov. 1972–Feb. 1974," box 11, AMEX/Canada Records; Borders, "Canada Is Offering Amnesty to Illegal Immigrants."

40. Canadian Coalition of War Resistors, news release, July 31, 1973 (mimeograph), folder 12, "Correspondence, press releases, and notes," box 14, "Canadian Adjustment of Status Program, 1972–1973," Jack Pocock Memorial Collection.

41. Dick Brown, Toronto Anti-Draft Programme, to Nancy Johnson, CFPL-TV (London, Ontario), September 11, 1973, folder 23, "Advertising correspondence and notes," box 14, "Canadian Adjustment of Status Program, 1972–1973," Jack Pocock Memorial Collection; Canadian Coalition of War Resistors, news release, September 17, 1973 (photocopy), file 5660–1, part 7, vol. 1210, Records of the Immigration Branch; "Personal service contract between Dennis Hayward and the Canadian Coalition of War Objectors dated

Aug. 9, 1973" (photocopy), folder 26, "Bus promotion," box 14, "Canadian Adjustment of Status Program, 1972–1973," Jack Pocock Memorial Collection.

42. Jessica Squires, *Building Sanctuary: The Movement to Support Vietnam War Resisters in Canada, 1965–73* (Vancouver: UBC Press, 2013), 214–215; Norman Hartley, "Ethnic 'Mediators' Recruited to Encourage More Illegal Immigrants," *Globe and Mail* (Toronto), September 22, 1973.

43. Toronto Anti-Draft Programme, "Sixty Days of Grace: Your Last Chance, Aug. 15, 1973 through Oct. 15, 1973" (manual), folder 16, "Correspondence, press releases, and notes," box 14, "Canadian Adjustment of Status Program, 1972–1973," Jack Pocock Memorial Collection. [Toronto Anti-Draft Programme,] "Unlanded War Exile? This Could Be Your Last Chance! You May Apply for Landed Immigrant Status until Oct. 15, but It's Not That Simple (No Government Ever Is)" (poster), folder 11–7, "Dissent in Society," box 11, Goldie Josephy fonds (R4460), Library and Archives Canada. [Toronto Anti-Draft Programme,] "Corrections to the Sixth Edition of 'Manual for Draft-Age Immigrants to Canada' (July 1973)," folder 6, "Manual for Draft-Age Immigrants to Canada, 6th edition—Corrections," box 2, ibid. Emphasis in the original.

44. T.E.F. Honey (General Secretary, Canadian Council of Churches), undated form letter (mimeograph), folder 12, "Correspondence, press releases, and notes," box 14, "Canadian Adjustment of Status Program, 1972–1973," Jack Pocock Memorial Collection. Ironically, six years earlier, Joan Baez had strongly advocated that men go to jail to oppose the draft rather than go to Canada. The journalist Oliver Clausen quoted Baez as saying, "These kids can't fight the Vietnam madness by holing up in Canada. What they're doing is opting out of the struggle at home. That's where they should go, even if only to fill the jails." Baez's husband, David Harris, did just that, serving twenty-three months in prison. See Joan Baez in Oliver Clausen, "Boys without a Country," *New York Times Magazine* (May 21, 1967), 104.

45. Folder P62, Coming Out of Hiding, 1973 (October), box 3, Steve Trimm Papers (DG 232), Swarthmore College Peace Collection, McCabe Library, Swarthmore College, Swarthmore, Pennsylvania.

46. United Church of Canada, "United Church supports government olive branch to illegal immigrants," news release, August 1, 1973 (mimeograph), [p. 1], folder 12, "Correspondence, press releases, and notes," box 14, "Canadian Adjustment of Status Program, 1972–1973," Jack Pocock Memorial Collection.

47. Chick Judd, Emergencies Ministries, National Council of Churches, to Members of the Steering Committee of the National Council for Universal and Unconditional Amnesty, August 15, 1973 (mimeograph), p. 2, folder 11, "Amnesty—National Council of Churches, 1972–1975," box 7, Vietnam Veterans Against the War Records, 1967–2006 (Mss. 370), Wisconsin Historical Society; [National Council of Churches,] "Sample 'Letter to the Editor,'" [1973] (mimeograph), folder 1, "Amnesty for Draft Resisters and Deserters, 1971–1973," box 1, United Methodist Office for the United Nations, Reference File, 1966–1976 (Mss. 541), Wisconsin Historical Society.

48. "If you were in Canada by November 30, 1972, and have remained here since, as a visitor or without legal status, these are the things you gain if you make our country your country" (advertisement); "If you were in Canada by November 30, 1972, and have remained here since, as a visitor or without legal status, we're going to give you until midnight, October 15, 1973 to make our country your country" (poster).

49. Robert Andras to Trudeau, August 30, 1973 (carbon copy), file 5660–1, part 7, vol. 1210, Records of the Immigration Branch; United Nations, High Commissioner for Refugees, *The 1951 Convention Relating to the Status of Refugees and Its 1967 Protocol,* September 2011, https://www.unhcr.org/en-us/about-us/background/4ec262df9/1951-convention-relating -status-refugees-its-1967-protocol.html.

50. Laurence Martin et al., Vancouver Committee to Aid American War Objectors, to Robert Andras, Minister of Manpower and Immigration, October 1, 1973 (mimeograph), pp. [1–2], folder 1, "TADP statements and lobbying," box 13, "Lobbying and public relations," Jack Pocock Memorial Collection.

51. Canadian Coalition of War Resistors, news release, September 17, 1973 (photocopy), file 5660–1, part 7, vol. 1210, Records of the Immigration Branch. See also "Immigration 'Grace Period' Ends, No Extension," *AMEX/Canada* 4 (November–December 1973), 21.

52. Hawkins, *Critical Years in Immigration,* 49.

53. President's Commission on an All-Volunteer Armed Force, *The Report of the President's Commission on an All-Volunteer Armed Force* (Washington, DC: U.S. Government Printing Office, 1970), 5–6.

54. President's Commission on an All-Volunteer Armed Force, *Report,* 6.

55. President's Commission on an All-Volunteer Armed Force, *Report,* 9–10.

56. President's Commission on an All-Volunteer Armed Force, *Report,* 14; Beth Bailey, "The Army in the Marketplace: Recruiting an All-Volunteer Force," *Journal of American History* 94 (June 2007), 52–53.

57. William C. Westmoreland in Bailey, "Army in the Marketplace," 59.

58. Bailey, "Army in the Marketplace," 57–61; quote 60.

59. Bailey, "Army in the Marketplace," 62.

60. Bailey, "Army in the Marketplace," 50.

61. House Subcommittee on Courts, Civil Liberties, and the Administration of Justice of the Committee on the Judiciary, *Hearings on H.R. 236, H.R. 674, H.R. 2167, H.R. 3100, H.R. 5195, H.R. 10979, H.R. 10980, H.R. 13001, H. Con. Res. 144, and H. Con. Res. 385 relating to Amnesty,* 93rd Cong., 2nd Sess., 1974.

62. Robert F. Froehlke in House Subcommittee on Courts, Civil Liberties, and the Administration of Justice of the Committee on the Judiciary, *Hearings,* 373.

63. House Subcommittee on Courts, Civil Liberties, and the Administration of Justice of the Committee on the Judiciary, *Hearings,* 29–36, 533–559, quote 535.

64. Mrs. Beverly Joynt (Chuluota, FL) to Robert F. Froehlke, March 7, 1974, folder 1, "Amnesty Correspondence, 1974," box 5, Robert F. Froehlke Papers, 1968–1974 (M2002–164), Wisconsin Historical Society.

65. Melton P. Young (Lakewood, NJ) to Froehlke, March 12, 1974, folder 6, "Amnesty Correspondence, 1974," box 4, Robert F. Froehlke Papers. See also Samuel E. Hayes (Spruce Creek, PA) to Froehlke, March 12, 1974, ibid.

66. William J. Egan (Omaha, NE) to Froehlke, March 12, 1974, folder 6, "Amnesty Correspondence, 1974," box 4, Robert F. Froehlke Papers.

67. Carroll Kilpatrick, "Ford to Consider Conditional Amnesty," *Washington Post,* August 20, 1974; "Ford's Proposal Fails to Please Veterans, Amnesty Activists," *Chicago Tribune,* August 20, 1974; "Amnesty Reaction Is Mixed," *Washington Post,* August 21, 1974;

Gerald R. Ford, *A Time to Heal: The Autobiography of Gerald R. Ford* (New York: Harper & Row, 1979), 141; Robert T. Hartmann, *Palace Politics: An Inside Account of the Ford Years* (New York: McGraw-Hill, 1980), 209–215.

68. Gerald Ford, "Remarks to the Veterans of Foreign Wars Annual Convention, Chicago, Illinois, August 19, 1974," *Public Papers of the Presidents of the United States. Gerald Ford. Containing the Public Messages, Speeches, and Statements of the President, August 9 to December 31, 1974* (Washington, DC: U.S. Government Printing Office, 1975), 24–25. Emphasis in the original.

69. "VFW Votes against Conditional Amnesty," *Chicago Defender*, August 21, 1974; "VFW Votes Solid 'No' to Amnesty Proposal," *Los Angeles Times*, August 21, 1974.

70. Gerald Ford, "Remarks Announcing a Program for the Return of Vietnam Era Draft Evaders and Military Deserters, September 16, 1974," *Public Papers of the Presidents of the United States . . . August 9 to December 31, 1974*, 136–137; Gerald Ford, "Proclamation 4313, Announcing a Program for the Return of Vietnam Era Draft Evaders and Military Deserters, September 16, 1974," ibid., 138–140.

71. Presidential Clemency Board, *Report to the President* (Washington, DC: U.S. Government Printing Office, 1975), 23–29; Presidential Clemency Board, "The Presidential Clemency Program: What Is It? How Does It Work?," December 11, 1974 (mimeograph), folder "Fact Sheet—PCB," box 4, Robert J. Horn Papers, Gerald R. Ford Presidential Library, Ann Arbor, Michigan. On the lack of support, see Interview with Charles Goodell, February 27, 1985, pp. 6–7, William A. Syers Interview Transcripts, 1984–1985, Gerald R. Ford Presidential Library.

72. Presidential Clemency Board, *Report to the President*, xii.

73. "Presidential Clemency Board Case Summary, Case Number: 74-127-WMA-M," folder "Case Summaries 101–125," box 11, "Presidential Clemency Board Case Summaries," Charles Goodell Papers, 1974–77, Gerald R. Ford Presidential Library.

74. "Presidential Clemency Board Case Summary, Case Number: 74-649-RGF-M," folder "Case Summaries 551–650," box 12, "Presidential Clemency Board Case Summaries," Charles Goodell Papers.

75. "Presidential Clemency Board Case Summary, Case Number: 1914-VRH-C," folder "Case Summaries 1801–2000," box 13, "Presidential Clemency Board Case Summaries," Charles Goodell Papers.

76. "Presidential Clemency Board Case Summary, Case Number: 2293-BWF-C," folder "Case Summaries 2001–2600," box 13, "Presidential Clemency Board Case Summaries," Charles Goodell Papers.

77. "Presidential Clemency Board Case Summary, Case Number: 6631-OVH-C," folder "Case Summaries 6001–7000," box 14, "Presidential Clemency Board Case Summaries," Charles Goodell Papers.

78. "Presidential Clemency Board Case Summary, Case Number: 1187-HFJ-C," folder "Case Summaries 1101–1200," box 13, "Presidential Clemency Board Case Summaries," Charles Goodell Papers.

79. Presidential Clemency Board, *Report to the President*, xi.

80. John Hagan, *Northern Passage: American Vietnam War Resisters in Canada* (Cambridge, MA: Harvard University Press, 2001), 161–164; David S. Surrey, *Choice of Conscience: Vietnam Era Military and Draft Resisters in Canada* (New York: Praeger, 1982), 167–168; Lawrence M.

Baskir and William A. Strauss, *Chance and Circumstance: The Draft, the War, and the Vietnam Generation* (New York: Knopf, 1978), 212–213, 215–222, 224–225, 232–235.

81. See Michael S. Foley, *Confronting the War Machine: Draft Resistance during the Vietnam War* (Chapel Hill: University of North Carolina Press, 2003), 94–95, 105, 170–171, 292.

82. "An Urgent Plea from Exiled War Resisters" (advertisement), *New York Times*, August 25, 1974.

83. Gerry Condon in "Veterans Critical," *Washington Post*, September 17, 1974. See also Don Sellar, "War Resisters' First Reactions Negative," *Christian Science Monitor* (Boston), September 18, 1974.

84. Charles Stimac in William Borders, "Most Draft Evaders and Deserters in Canada Reject Ford's Amnesty Plan," *New York Times*, January 26, 1975. See also MacPherson, *Long Time Passing*, 371–373.

85. Richard Moore (Burnaby, British Columbia) to NCUUA Members, September 17, 1974, p. 1, folder "Correspondence by state/country—Canada," box 16, National Council for Universal and Unconditional Amnesty Records, 1964–1978 (M 80-391), Wisconsin Historical Society.

86. Jack D. Kaufman in Jay Mathews, "U.S. Amnesty Job Program Faltering," *Washington Post*, January 25, 1975.

87. "A Veteran" (Baltimore, MD) to Goodell, received October 31, 1974, folder "Correspondence without Return Addresses," box 4, Robert J. Horn Papers.

88. Norman Lewis (Lake George, NY) to the editor, *Toronto Star*, September 28, 1974.

89. Robert F. Drinan, "Additional Views of Mr. Drinan," in House Subcommittee on Courts, Civil Liberties, and the Administration of Justice of the Committee on the Judiciary, *Report on the Presidential Clemency Program*, 94th Cong., 1st Sess., 1975, 15–16.

90. Andrew Young, "Mass Transportation and Amnesty," in Congressional Black Caucus, "Position Statements Presented to the President of the United States," August 21, 1974, p. 69, folder "Black Caucus—Meeting with the President, Aug. 1974: Position Statements," box 4, "Subject File," Stanley S. Scott Papers (1969) 1971–1977, Gerald R. Ford Presidential Library. Scott was special assistant to the president for minority affairs.

91. Tommy J. Keith (Rogers, AR) to Theodore C. Marrs, November 11, 1974, folder "Amnesty—Public Opinion Mail (1)," box 2, "General Subject File," Theodore C. Marrs Files, 1974–76, Gerald R. Ford Presidential Library.

92. Vernon E. Jordan Jr. in Paul Delaney, "Urban League Head Asks U.S. to Grant Total Amnesty to Veterans of Vietnam," *New York Times*, July 28, 1975. See also Gerry Condon, "Outrage, but No Surprise: How the Pardon Looks to U.S. Exiles in Canada," *Los Angeles Times*, September 17, 1974.

93. James Dickerson, *North to Canada: Men and Women against the Vietnam War* (Westport, CT: Praeger, 1999), 142–146.

94. James R. Schlesinger and William B. Saxbe to Gerald Ford, August 30, 1974 (mimeograph), p. 4, folder "Amnesty—White House Meetings, 8/74–9/74," box 2, John O. Marsh Files, Gerald R. Ford Presidential Library. James Reston Jr. (Washington, DC) to Philip Buchen, September 2, 1974, p. 2, folder "Amnesty—Public Opinion Mail, 8/74–9/74," ibid. See also Alfred B. Fitt, "Amnesty," *New York Times Magazine*, September 8, 1974, 15–16.

95. "Statement of William Meis, Draft Resister, Outlining His Rejection of Ford's Amnesty Plan, Clemency Board Bldg., Washington, D C, Monday, September 20, 1974, 10:30 a.m.,"

folder 8, "Magazine organization and production, William Meis, 1974–1975," box 1, "Magazine Organization and Production," AMEX/Canada Records. See also Diane Henry, "Jail Term Risked by Draft Evader," *New York Times*, October 1, 1974.

96. John Alberts in "Veterans Critical."

97. Emil M. Deutsch (Buckeye, AZ) to Goodell, October 16, 1974 (photocopy), folder "Correspondence (2)," box 2, Charles Goodell Papers.

98. Stimac in Eleanor Randolph, "Amnesty Plan Foes Rally Here," *Chicago Tribune*, September 23, 1974; Mark Davies in James Elsener, "Ford Offer Met Coolly in Canada," *Chicago Tribune*, September 17, 1974; Jack Colhoun, "'Earned Re-entry' a Sham: Full of Inequities and Traps," *AMEX/Canada* 5 (October 1974), 8.

99. Bill King to Ford, [Fall 1974], (photocopy), p. 3, folder 11, "Sympathetic organizations, Vietnam Veterans Against the War, 1971–1975," box 8, AMEX/Canada Records.

100. "Statement of Henry Schwarzschild," in Senate Subcommittee on Administrative Practice and Procedure of the Committee on the Judiciary, *Clemency Practices and Procedures*, 93rd Cong., 2nd Sess., 1974, pp. 71–72; Henry Schwarzschild (Project on Amnesty, American Civil Liberties Union) to Jack [John O.] Marsh (Counselor to the President), September 4, 1974 (telegram), folder "Amnesty—Public Opinion Mail, 8/74–9/74," box 2, John O. Marsh Files.

101. Mary McGrory, "An Unfinished War at Home," *Chicago Tribune*, February 5, 1975.

102. Reston to Buchen, September 2, 1974, p. 2, folder "Amnesty—Public Opinion Mail, 8/74–9/74," box 2, John O. Marsh Files.

103. See the NCUUA's suggestions for an amnesty bill to be passed by the U.S. Congress, which listed forty-one sections of the U.S. Code that the organization believed would automatically qualify a person for amnesty, if the law were broken between January 1, 1961, and April 30, 1975. National Council for Universal and Unconditional Amnesty, "Summary: NCUUA Draft Amnesty Bill," [1975?], folder 6, "National Committee for Universal and Unconditional Amnesty—Amnesty correspondence, 1975," box 6, AMEX/Canada Records.

104. National Council for Universal and Unconditional Amnesty, "Urgent Memo to All Contacts," September 17, 1974, folder 2, "National Committee for Universal and Unconditional Amnesty—General correspondence, 1973–1977," box 6, AMEX/Canada Records.

105. National Council for Universal and Unconditional Amnesty, "Have You Heard the Joke about President Ford's Clemency Program?" (pamphlet) (New York: National Council for Universal and Unconditional Amnesty, 1974); National Council for Universal and Unconditional Amnesty, "Amnesty for Vets Too!" (booklet) (New York: National Council for Universal and Unconditional Amnesty, [1976]); *NCUUA Amnesty Update* (April 1974–August 1977).

106. See many of these statements collected in National Interreligious Service Board for Conscientious Objectors, Amnesty Information Service, *Religious Statements on Amnesty* (Washington, DC: National Interreligious Service Board for Conscientious Objectors, 1974).

107. Delton Franz, Director, Mennonite Central Committee Peace Section, Washington Office, and Ralph Smeltzer, Director, Washington Office, Church of the Brethren (Washington, DC) to Marsh, September 12, 1974, folder "Amnesty—Public Opinion Mail (1)," box 2, "General Subject File," Theodore C. Marrs Files.

108. "AFSC Statement on Amnesty and the Ford Earned Re-entry Program, 17 September 1974," *L & C News* 1 (October 1974). *L & C News* was a "newsletter for lawyers & counselors, laypeople & clergy, concerned with amnesty, conscription, draft and military counseling and related issues," published by the Miami, Florida, office of the American Friends Service Committee during the Vietnam War era.

109. William P. Thompson, Stated Clerk, United Presbyterian Church (New York, NY) to Marsh, August 21, 1974, folder "Amnesty—Public Opinion Mail, 8/74–9/74," box 2, John O. Marsh Files.

110. Interview with Charles Goodell, February 27, 1985, p. 6, William A. Syers Interview Transcripts.

111. A. R. Burns to Goodell, [1974?] (postcard, photocopy), folder "Correspondence without Return Addresses," box 4, Robert J. Horn Papers; C. R. McMillan (Miami, FL) to Marrs (special assistant to President Gerald Ford), December 19, 1974, folder "Amnesty—Public Opinion Mail (1)," box 2, "General Subject File," Theodore C. Marrs Files; James Andrews (Bean Station, TN) to Goodell, January 30, 1975, folder "Correspondence (3)," box 2, "Presidential Clemency Board Subject File," Charles Goodell Papers; Mrs. Clarence Gardiner (East Point, GA) to Froehlke, March 13, 1974, folder 1, "Amnesty Correspondence, 1974," box 5, Robert F. Froehlke Papers; Mrs. Linn Hopkinson (Herkimer, NY) to Froehlke, March 17, 1974, folder 6, "Amnesty Correspondence, 1974," box 4, ibid.

112. See folders "Amnesty—Return of Military Medals and Certificates by Veterans in Protest against the Amnesty Program" (1)–(3), box 2, "General Subject File," Theodore C. Marrs Files; especially Anthony Fasano (Forest Hills, NY) to Ford, September 17, 1974, folder "Amnesty—Return of Military Medals and Certificates by Veterans in Protest against the Amnesty Program (2)," ibid. There is further irony associated with the items that were a part of these protests. Unique among U.S. presidential libraries, materials from the Ford presidency are housed in two separate places. The letters that accompanied medals and certificates returned by disgruntled veterans are housed in the Gerald R. Ford Presidential Library in Ann Arbor, Michigan, while the medals and certificates themselves are stored 130 miles (220 kilometers) away at the Gerald R. Ford Presidential Museum in Grand Rapids, Michigan.

113. This quote comes from a standard reply sent by Ford's campaign office during the 1976 presidential campaign. See folder "Correspondence—Topics—Amnesty," box B74, "Administrative Office: Correspondence Topical File," President Ford Committee Campaign Records, 1975–76, Gerald R. Ford Presidential Library. See also Richard R. Kiernan (New York, NY) to Froehlke, March 11, 1974, folder 1, "Amnesty Correspondence, 1974," box 5, Robert F. Froehlke Papers; and Lawrence L. Gruman (Minister, First Congregational Church) (Madison, WI) to Froehlke, [1974], ibid.

114. Carol Bernstein Ferry and W. H. Ferry (Scarsdale, NY) to Goodell, August 24, 1974, folder "Correspondence (1)," box 2, "Presidential Clemency Board Subject File," Charles Goodell Papers. See also Paul Deats (professor of social ethics, School of Theology, Boston University) to Ford, August 22, 1974, folder "Amnesty—Public Opinion Mail, 8/74–9/74," box 2, John O. Marsh Files.

115. Lee Sherman Dreyfuss to Froehlke, March 15, 1974, folder 1, "Amnesty Correspondence, 1974," box 5, Robert F. Froehlke Papers.

116. Earl Martin et al. (Billings, MT) to Ford, September 21, 1974, folder "Amnesty—Return of Military Medals and Certificates by Veterans in Protest against the Amnesty Program (1)," box 2, "General Subject File," Theodore C. Marrs Files.

117. F. E. Foster (East Cleveland, OH) to Froehlke, [1974], folder 1, "Amnesty Correspondence, 1974," box 5, Robert F. Froehlke Papers.

118. C. Donald O'Donnell (Springfield, IL) to Senator Robert Taft, March 14, 1974 (carbon copy), folder 6, "Amnesty Correspondence, 1974," box 4, Robert F. Froehlke Papers; "Blanket Amnesty Is Unjust," *San Diego Union,* March 17, 1974; John J. Stang (National Commander-in-Chief, Veterans of Foreign Wars) to Ford, June 4, 1975 (telegram, photocopy), folder "Public Opinion Mail (3)," box 2, "General Subject File," Theodore C. Marrs Files; Samuel D. Lyons (Montgomery, AL) to Ford, September 19, 1974, folder "Amnesty—Return of Military Medals and Certificates by Veterans in Protest against the Amnesty Program (2)," box 2, "General Subject File," ibid. See also Burns to Goodell, [1974?]; "A War Widow" (New York, NY) to Goodell, September 27, 1974, folder "Correspondence without Return Addresses," box 4, Robert J. Horn Papers; and Mrs. O. Jensen (Westmont, IL), letter to the editor, *Chicago Tribune,* August 25, 1974.

119. Charles F. Foster (San Antonio, TX) to The Headquarters, The President Ford Campaign, September 13, 1976, folder "Correspondence—Topics—Amnesty," box B74, "Administrative Office: Correspondence Topical File," President Ford Committee Campaign Records.

120. Benedict Anderson, *Imagined Communities: Reflections on the Origin and Spread of Nationalism,* rev. ed. (1991; New York: Verso, 2006), 7.

121. John B. Currie (Boston) to Goodell, September 27, 1974, folder "Correspondence without Return Addresses," box 4, Robert J. Horn Papers. See also Glen D. Condron (Claude H. Montgomery Post No. 58, Department of Nebraska, Veterans of Foreign Wars, Valley, NE) to Froehlke, March 10, 1974, folder 6, "Amnesty Correspondence, 1974," box 4, Robert F. Froehlke Papers; H. L. Reynolds (Atlanta, GA) to Jack Colhoun, [1974?], p. 2, folder 5, "Hate mail," box 4, "Correspondence," AMEX/Canada Records; Mrs. Harold G. Tyson (Springfield, MA) to [AMEX/Canada,] August 23, [1974], ibid.; George D. Conrad (Harrisonburg, VA) to Ford, September 4, 1974 (photocopy), p. 1, folder "Amnesty—Public Opinion Mail, 8/74–9/74," box 2, John O. Marsh Files; and Agnes Murvin (Los Angeles) to Marrs, folder "Amnesty—Public Opinion Mail (2), box 2, "General Subject File," Theodore C. Marrs Files; (Miss) René Collins (Studio City, CA) to Froehlke, March 24, 1974, p. 1, ibid.

122. Arthur C. Grafflin (Sewickley, PA) to Colhoun (Toronto), September 18, 1974, p. 1, folder 5, "Hate mail," box 4, "Correspondence," AMEX/Canada Records.

123. Mrs. Abel Cailloued [?] to Gerry Condon, September 17, 1974, folder 5, "Hate mail," box 4, "Correspondence," AMEX/Canada Records. Emphasis in the original.

124. Mrs. Anton B. Dunker (Godfrey, IL) to Froehlke (March 14, 1974), folder 6, "Amnesty Correspondence, 1974," box 4, Robert F. Froehlke Papers. Emphasis in the original.

125. Suzanne Reynolds to [AMEX/Canada], September 18, 1974, folder 5, "Hate mail," box 4, "Correspondence," AMEX/Canada Records. For an analysis of the gender politics of draft resisters in Canada during the Vietnam War, see Lara Campbell, "'The Moral Grandeur of Fleeing to Canada': Masculinity and the Gender Politics of American Draft Dodgers during the Vietnam War," in *Making Men, Making History: Canadian Masculinities*

across Time and Place, ed. Peter Gossage and Robert Rutherdale, 347–363 (Vancouver: UBC Press, 2018).

126. Conrad to Ford, September 4, 1974, p. 2, folder "Amnesty—Public Opinion Mail, 8/74–9/74," box 2, John O. Marsh Files; Grafflin to Colhoun, September 18, 1974, p. 1, ibid.

127. M. V. Smith and Family (Daytona Beach, FL) to Froehlke, March 14, 1974, folder 6, "Amnesty Correspondence, 1974," box 4, Robert F. Froehlke Papers.

128. Grafflin to Colhoun, September 18, 1974, p. 1, folder 5, "Hate mail," box 4, "Correspondence," AMEX/Canada Records.

129. Henry Schwarzschild in James Coates, "'Losers' Win Clemency for Amnesty Plan," *Chicago Tribune,* February 2, 1975.

130. VISTA, or Volunteers in Service to America, was a Great Society program of the Lyndon B. Johnson administration. It placed volunteers in low-income communities for one year to provide support for a variety of programs. Reston to Buchen, September 2, 1974, p. 1, folder "Amnesty—Public Opinion Mail, 8/74–9/74," box 2, John O. Marsh Files.

131. Press release, Toronto Anti-Draft Programme, [early 1975], folder 5, "'Media,'" box 13, "Lobbying and public relations," Jack Pocock Memorial Collection.

132. Sylvia G. Lisnoff (West Warwick, RI) to Goodell, September 17, 1974, p. 1, folder "Correspondence (1)," box 2, "Presidential Clemency Board Subject File," Charles Goodell Papers.

133. Goodell to Ford, memorandum, [January 1, 1975], p. 4, folder "Memoranda—President and White House Staff," box 8, Charles Goodell Papers.

134. "Loophole for Deserters," *New York Times,* September 20, 1974; Phil Stanford, "By Almost Any Standard, the Amnesty Plan Isn't Working," *New York Times,* October 27, 1974.

135. "Table Cb24-27—Unemployment rates: 1940–2003," *Historical Statistics of the United States,* millennial edition online, http://hsus.cambridge.org (accessed October 18, 2022).

136. Horace Wendall (Hartford, CT) to [AMEX/Canada], August 23, 1974, folder 5, "Hate mail," box 4, "Correspondence," AMEX/Canada Records. See also Sheldon R. Shepard (Cheyenne, WY) to Marrs, February 15, 1975, folder "Amnesty—Public Opinion Mail (1)," box 2, "General Subject File," Theodore C. Marrs Files. For press accounts, see Jay Mathews, "U.S. Amnesty Job Program Faltering," *Washington Post,* January 25, 1975; Nancy Hicks, "Amnesty Plan Ends with Few Signed Up," *New York Times,* April 1, 1975; and Jon Nordheimer, "60% of Deserters Leave Amnesty Service," *New York Times,* September 15, 1975.

137. Gerald Ford, "Statement Announcing Extension of the Program for the Return of Vietnam Era Draft Evaders and Military Deserters. January 30, 1975," *Public Papers of the Presidents of the United States. Gerald Ford. Containing the Public Messages, Speeches, and Statements of the President. 1975,* vol. 1, *January 1 to July 17, 1975* (Washington, DC: U.S. Government Printing Office, 1977), 134–135. On the same day, Ford signed Proclamation 4345 and Executive Order 11837 to extend the clemency to March 1, 1975. Gerald Ford, "Statement Announcing Final Extension of the Program for the Return of Vietnam Era Draft Evaders and Military Deserters. February 28, 1975," ibid., 305. Later, Ford signed Proclamation 4353 and Executive Order 11842 to extend the clemency to March 31, 1975. See Gerald R. Ford, "Proclamation 4353—Program for the Return of Vietnam Era Draft Evaders and Military Deserters," February 28, 1975, The American Presidency Project, https://www.presidency.ucsb.edu/documents/proclamation-4353-program-for-the-return

-vietnam-era-draft-evaders-and-military-deserters; Gerald R. Ford, "Executive Order 11842—Amending Executive Order Nos. 11803 and 11837 to Further Extend the Period for Application for Clemency Board Review of Certain Convictions and Military Service Discharges," February 28, 1975, The American Presidency Project, https://www.presidency.ucsb .edu/documents/executive-order-11842-amending-executive-order-nos-11803-and-11837 -further-extend-the. For descriptions of President Gerald Ford's clemency program and reactions to it, see Hagan, *Northern Passage*, 161–164; Surrey, *Choice of Conscience*, 167–168; and Baskir and Strauss, *Chance and Circumstance*, 212–213, 215–222, 224–225, 232–235.

138. The Presidential Clemency Board welcomed approximately 90,000 applications from servicemen given bad discharges for going AWOL (13,589, or 15 percent applied) and approximately 8,700 applications from convicted draft offenders (1,879, or 22 percent applied). The board also asked the U.S. Department of Justice to consider applications from 4,522 draft offenders (706, or 16 percent applied). These unconvicted draft offenders could have their prosecutions dropped, thereby avoiding imprisonment and the stigma of a felony conviction. The board also asked the Department of Defense to consider applications from "fugitive offenders," i.e., men who had gone AWOL (5,555, or 55 percent applied). These men could qualify for an Undesirable Discharge, which kept them from a Bad Conduct or Dishonorable Discharge and possible imprisonment. Presidential Clemency Board, *Report to the President*, xi–xiii.

139. Sellar, "War Resisters' First Reactions Negative"; Jon Nordheimer, "Deserters in Canada Face Agony of Decision-Making on Amnesty Issue," *Chicago Tribune*, September 26, 1974; Coates, "'Losers' Win Clemency for Amnesty Plan."

140. MacPherson, *Long Time Passing*, 349; Baskir and Strauss, *Chance and Circumstance*, 222.

141. See, for example, Vernon E. Jordan Jr., "The Amnesty Issue," *Chicago Defender*, November 15, 1975, 8.

142. Gerald Ford, "Exchange with Reporters in Vail, Colorado, December 29, 1976," *Public Papers of the Presidents of the United States. Gerald Ford. Containing the Public Messages, Speeches, and Statements of the President. 1976–77*, vol. 3, *July 10, 1976 to January 20, 1977* (Washington, DC: U.S. Government Printing Office, 1979), 2878n1; Gerald Ford, "Letter to Mrs. Philip A. Hart on Amnesty for Vietnam-Era Draft Evaders and Deserters, January 19, 1977," ibid., 2967–2968.

143. Laura E. Hart (Waltham, MA) to Jimmy Carter, January 20, 1977 (photocopy), folder JL 1 1/20/77–2/28/77, box JL-1, Carter White House Central Files, 1977–1981; Series: White House Central Files Subject File, 1977–1981 (Collection JC-WHCF), Jimmy Carter Presidential Library, Atlanta, Georgia.

144. "Amnesty Program: Fall '76," *NCUUA Amnesty Update*, no. 10 (Fall 1976), 3.

145. Gold Star parents have lost children in military service. Kovic's approach to the convention podium was re-created in the last scene of Oliver Stone's 1989 Academy Award–winning film *Born on the Fourth of July*, based on Kovic's memoir of the same name. *Born on the Fourth of July*, dir. Oliver Stone (1989); Ron Kovic, *Born on the Fourth of July* (New York: McGraw-Hill, 1976).

146. Fritz Efaw in Hagan, *Northern Passage*, 173–174.

147. "1976 Democratic Party Platform," July 12, 1976, The American Presidency Project, https://www.presidency.ucsb.edu/documents/1976-democratic-party-platform;

David E. Rosenbaum, "Democrats Adopt a Platform Aimed at Uniting Party," *New York Times,* June 16, 1976, 6; Jonathan Alter, *His Very Best: Jimmy Carter, A Life* (New York: Simon & Schuster, 2020), chap. 18.

148. Jules Witcover, "Jimmy Carter: The Candidate on the Issues: An Interview," *Washington Post,* March 21, 1976. Carter's characterization of the reluctance of Georgians to move to Canada was accurate. For every 100,000 Georgians, only 17.6 immigrated to Canada in the 1966–1972 period. This was less than one-quarter the national average of 74.4 per 100,000 (see appendix). Carter also mentioned poor and Black soldiers in an interview in *Playboy* magazine. See "*Playboy* Interview: Jimmy Carter: A Candid Conversation with the Democratic Candidate for the Presidency," *Playboy* 23 (November 1976), 71, 74.

149. Hal Bruno, "Carter Meets the Questions," *Newsweek* 87 (February 2, 1976), 18.

150. "*Playboy* Interview," 71.

151. R. D. Smith in "A Georgian Becomes V.F.W.'s Commander," *New York Times,* August 21, 1976.

152. Jules Witcover, *Marathon: The Pursuit of the Presidency, 1972–1976* (New York: Viking, 1977), 526; Peter G. Bourne, *Jimmy Carter: A Comprehensive Biography from Plains to Postpresidency* (New York: Scribner, 1997), 341. See also "Carter Says He'll Pardon Viet Evaders in 1st Week," *Los Angeles Times,* August 24, 1976; Michael Coakley, "Legionnaires Jeer Carter Vow to Pardon Viet Draft Resisters," *Chicago Tribune,* August 25, 1976; and James T. Wooten, "Legionnaires Boo Carter on Pardon for Draft Defiers," *New York Times,* August 25, 1976.

153. "Mr. Carter Speaks Out," *New York Times,* August 26, 1976.

154. Douglas E. Kneeland, "Dole Attacks Carter on Pardon for Draft Evaders," *New York Times,* August 26, 1976; Bourne, *Jimmy Carter,* 341.

155. Jimmy Carter in "Presidential Campaign Debate of September 23, 1976," *Public Papers of the Presidents of the United States . . . 1976–77,* vol. 3, 2291, 2292. Carter made similar statements throughout his campaign for the presidency. See Jimmy Carter Presidential Campaign, "Jimmy Carter on Vietnam Pardon" [1976] (mimeograph), folder 4, "Subject file, Amnesty—Carter and the Vietnam pardon, May 1976–March 1977," box 10, "Subject files," AMEX/Canada Records. Gerald Ford in "Presidential Campaign Debate of September 23, 1976," 2291.

156. Jimmy Carter, "Presidential Proclamation of Pardon. Proclamation 4483. January 21, 1977: Granting Pardon for Violations of the Selective Service Act, August 4, 1964 to March 28, 1973," *Public Papers of the President of the United States. Jimmy Carter. 1977,* vol. 1, *January 20 to June 24, 1977* (Washington, DC: U.S. Government Printing Office, 1977), 5; Jimmy Carter, "Executive Order Relating to Proclamation of Pardon. Executive Order 11967. January 21, 1977: Relating to Violations of the Selective Service Act, August 4, 1964 to March 28, 1973," ibid., 6. For discussions of Jimmy Carter's amnesty, see Hagan, *Northern Passage,* 175–176; Surrey, *Choice of Conscience,* 168–169; Baskir and Strauss, *Chance and Circumstance,* 227–232; and Frank Kusch, *All American Boys: Draft Dodgers in Canada from the Vietnam War* (Westport, CT: Praeger, 2001), 121–125.

157. Claiborne Pell to Carter, January 21, 1977, folder JL 1 1/20/77–2/28/77, box JL-1, "Judicial-Legal Matters, Executive, JL 1/20/77–8/31/77 through Executive, JL 1 1/20/77–2/28/77," Carter White House Central Files.

158. Francis T. Mauser (New York, NY) to Carter, January 24, 1977, folder JL 1 1/20/77–2/28/77, box JL-1, "Judicial-Legal Matters, Executive, JL 1/20/77–8/31/77 through Exec-

utive, JL 1 1/20/77–2/28/77," Carter White House Central Files. Second ellipses in the original. See also Theodore R. Johnson Jr. (Costa Mesa, CA) to Carter, January 23, 1977, ibid.; Ed Claus (Keene, NH) to Carter, January 27, 1977, folder JL 1 1/20/77–1/20/81, box JL-2, ibid.; and Margot Schuetze (Rochester, NY) to Margaret Costanza, January 20, 1977, ibid.

159. Roger Chapman (Mitchellville, MD), letter to the editor, *Washington Post,* January 29, 1977.

160. "Vets Blast Carter's Pardon," *Chicago Tribune,* January 22, 1977.

161. New Hampshire House of Representatives, "House Resolution No. 4," folder JL 1 1/20/77–2/28/77, box JL-1 "Judicial-Legal Matters, Executive, JL 1/20/77–8/31/77 through Executive, JL 1 1/20/77–2/28/77," Carter White House Central Files.

162. Oklahoma House of Representatives, "A Resolution Urging the President of the United States to Refrain from Granting a Pardon to Deserters from the Viet Nam War; and Directing Distribution" (photocopy), folder "JL 1 3/1/77–8/31/77," box JL-2 "Judicial-Legal Matters, Executive, JL 1 3/1/77–8/31/77 through Executive, JL 1-1 1/20/77–10/31/78," Carter White House Central Files.

163. *A resolution to express the sense of the Senate in opposition to a general Presidential pardon by proclamation or executive order of Vietnam era draft evaders,* S Res. 40, 95th Cong., 1st sess. (January 18, 1977); "Carter Pardons Draft Resisters," *Congress and the Nation* (Washington, DC: Congressional Quarterly, 1981), 5:181.

164. Mrs. G. D. Pirani, letter to the editor, *Commercial Appeal* (Memphis), January 26, 1977.

165. Grant W. McCombs (Laguna, CA) to Jody Powell, January 21, 1977, folder JL 1 1/20/77–1/20/81, box JL-2, Carter White House Central Files.

166. R. D. Smith in Mary Hladky, "Georgia VFW Opens Drive to Amend Carter's Pardon," *Atlanta Constitution,* January 24, 1977.

167. Charles J. Reynolds (National Security Chairman, Thirteenth District Council, The Ohio American Legion, Cleveland) to Mary Rose Oakar (member, U.S. House of Representatives, Cleveland), March 8, 1977 (photocopy), folder JL 2, 1/20/77–3/31/77, box JL-3, Carter White House Central Files.

168. Carter to John Wayne (Beverly Hills, CA), January 31, 1977, folder JL 1 1/20/77–2/28/77, box JL-1, "Judicial-Legal Matters, Executive, JL 1/20/77–8/31/77 through Executive, JL 1 1/20/77–2/28/77," Carter White House Central Files.

169. "Amnesty Options," *New Republic* 175 (December 25, 1976), 5. See also Lee Lescaze, "Deserters Seek Carter Pardon with No Strings," *Washington Post,* December 5, 1976; Joe Jones, "Carter Should Sign Blanket Pardon and Help His 'Least Brethren,'" *Los Angeles Times,* December 26, 1976; and Larry and Lenna Mae Cara (Wilmington, OH) to Carter, December 29, 1976 (photocopy), folder 4, "Subject file, Amnesty—Carter and the Vietnam Pardon, 1976–1977," box 10, "Subject files," AMEX/Canada Records.

170. Jimmy Carter Presidential Campaign, "Jimmy Carter on Vietnam Pardon" [1976] (mimeograph), AMEX/Canada Records.

171. "*Playboy* Interview," 71. See also Lescaze, "Deserters Seek Carter Pardon with No Strings."

172. Baskir and Strauss, *Chance and Circumstance,* 8–10.

173. Leon White in Major Robinson, "Carter's Pardons Called Slap in Face to Black Vets," *New York Amsterdam News,* January 29, 1977.

174. Charles B. Rangel to Carter, January 26, 1977 (photocopy), folder JL 1 1/20/77–2/28/77, box JL-1, Carter White House Central Files.

175. Peter Salerno Jr. (Louisville, KY) to Brothers and Sisters, January 28, 1977, folder 9, "Staff activities, International Conference of Veterans and War Resisters (Jan. 1977)," box 2, AMEX/Canada Records.

176. Jeff Sallot, "Deserters Call Carter Plan Too Little, Too Late and a Sham," *Washington Post,* February 1, 1977. For other press coverage, see Austin Scott, "Reaction to the Pardon Runs Gamut from Joy to Outrage," *Washington Post,* January 22, 1977; Stef Donev, "Draft Evaders Want Broader Pardon," *Chicago Tribune,* January 23, 1977; and Jeff Sallot, "Draft Evaders, Deserters Protest Carter Pardon," *Washington Post,* January 30, 1977.

177. Veterans Caucus of the International Conference of War Resisters and Veterans, "Open Letter to President Carter," January 28–30, 1977, folder 5, "Condon, Gerry, 1975," box 10, "Subject files," AMEX/Canada Records. See also Carol Oppenheim, "War Evaders Plan Protests at White House," *Chicago Tribune,* January 31, 1977; and Joan Elbert, "'Universal and Unconditional,'" *Christian Century* 94 (February 16, 1977), 134–135. See also Baskir and Strauss, *Chance and Circumstance,* 231–232.

178. "Presentation by Louise Ransom, Affiliate Director of NCUUA, N.Y. and Gold Star Parent for Amnesty, International Conference of Veterans and War Resisters, Lord Simcoe Hotel, Toronto, Canada, January 29–30, 1977" (mimeograph), p. 1, folder 9, "Staff activities, International Conference of Veterans and War Resisters (Jan. 1977)," box 2, AMEX/Canada Records. For more on the NCUUA's criticism of Carter's program, see "Our Work Continues: Report on the NCUUA Conference on New Directions, June 10–12, 1977, Milwaukee," *NCUUA Amnesty Update,* no. 12 (July–August 1977), 3–5; and "Carter's Amnesty Two-Step," ibid., 10–15.

179. Presentation by Pat Simon, Coordinator of Gold Star Parents for Amnesty, International Conference of Veterans and War Resisters, Lord Simcoe Hotel, Toronto, Canada, January 29–30, 1977" (mimeograph), p. 1, folder 9, "Staff activities, International Conference of Veterans and War Resisters (Jan. 1977)," box 2, AMEX/Canada Records.

180. Patricia Schroeder to Carter, January 28, 1977 (photocopy), p. 1 folder JL 1 1/20/77–2/28/77, box JL-1, Carter White House Central Files.

181. Robert C. Macek (Buffalo, NY) to Robert J. Lipshutz (Counsel to the President), February 11, 1977 (photocopy), pp. 5, 3, folder "Pardon, etc., Vietnam War, 1–2/77 [CF, O/A 121]," box 41, "Panama Canal Zone through Peanut Oil Sale 1977," Records of the White House Office of Counsel to the President, 1977–1981; Series: Robert J. Lipshutz Files, 1977–1979 (Collection JC-COUNSL), Jimmy Carter Presidential Library.

182. Phil Jordan (special assistant to the Attorney General) to Midge Costanza, memorandum on meeting with Amnesty Coalition, February 14, 1977, p. 3, folder "[Vietnam Amnesty Coalition] 2/77 [O/A 5771]," box 10, Records of the Office of the Assistant for Public Liaison, 1977–1981; Series: Margaret Costanza Files, 1977–1978 (Collection JC-PUBLIAIS), Jimmy Carter Presidential Library.

183. Office of Assistant Secretary of Defense (Public Affairs), "Detailed Application Procedures for Program for Review of Vietnam-Era Discharges" (press release), April 5, 1977 (photocopy), folder "Pardon, etc., Vietnam War, 3/77–10/78 [CF, o/A 121]," box 41, "Panama Canal Zone through Peanut Oil Sale, 1977," Robert J. Lipshutz Files. For press coverage,

see Charles Mohr, "Most Deserters Will Be Eligible for Upgrading," *New York Times*, April 2, 1977; Charles Mohr, "Mr. Carter Spoke Softly, Effectively on Discharges," *New York Times*, April 3, 1977; and Lee Lescaze, "Deserters Wary about Pentagon Discharge Offer," *Washington Post*, May 30, 1977.

184. The U.S. Immigration and Naturalization Service (INS) recorded only 381 entries by draft resisters and military deserters into the United States from January 21, 1977, when Carter announced amnesty for draft resisters, until June 1, 1978, when it stopped keeping records on those returning exiles. Of the 381, only 114 said they planned to remain in the United States and 267 planned only to visit. See "Record-Keeping Ended for Vietnam Deserters," *New York Times*, March 5, 1979.

185. Stuart E. Eizenstat (Assistant to the President for Domestic Affairs and Policy) to Clarence E. Miller (member, U.S. House of Representatives, Ohio), May 12, 1979 (photocopy), folder JL 1 5/1/78–8/31/1979, box JL-2, Carter White House Central Files; *An Act to Deny Entitlement to Veterans' Benefits to Certain Persons Who Would Otherwise Become So Entitled Solely by Virtue of the Administrative Upgrading under Temporarily Revised Standards of Other Than Honorable Discharges from Service during the Vietnam Era*, Public Law 95-126, *U.S. Statutes at Large* 91 (1977), 1106–1109.

186. Jimmy Carter, *Keeping Faith: Memoirs of a President* (New York: Bantam, 1982), 482–483. Jimmy Carter, "Proclamation 4771—Registration under the Military Selective Service Act," July 2, 1980, last reviewed August 15, 2016, https://www.archives.gov/federal-register/codification/proclamations/04771.html.

187. Jimmy Carter, "Vietnam Veterans Memorial Bill, Remarks on Signing S.J. Res. 119 into Law, July 1, 1980," *Public Papers of the Presidents of the United States: Jimmy Carter, 1980–81*, vol. 2, *May 24 to September 26, 1980* (Washington, DC: U.S. Government Printing Office, 1982), 1268; Carter, "Presidential Campaign Debate of September 23, 1976," 2291–2292.

188. Carter, *Keeping Faith*; Jimmy Carter, *White House Diary* (New York: Farrar, Straus & Giroux, 2010), xiv; Jimmy Carter, *A Full Life: Reflections at Ninety* (New York: Simon & Schuster, 2015), 118.

189. Hagan, *Northern Passage*, 242.

CHAPTER 6 AMERICAN VIETNAM WAR–ERA ÉMIGRÉS AND THE BLURRING OF BORDERS

1. Susan Kollin has suggested that beyond conservation of space, placing Alaska and Hawai'i out of context on national maps "demonstrates a denial of empire by reducing evidence of the nation's imperialist past." Conversely, not including Canada on maps as a sovereign nation between the continental United States and Alaska conceals the late nineteenth-century failure of the United States to control more of the North American continent. The U.S. purchase of Alaska in 1867 accelerated Britain's efforts to create a nation out of its North American colonies north of the forty-ninth parallel in an attempt to thwart U.S. attempts to annex British Columbia and other territory. Susan Kollin, *Nature's State: Imagining Alaska as the Last Frontier* (Chapel Hill: University of North Carolina Press, 2001), 8, 7, 180n16.

2. Benedict Anderson, *Imagined Communities: Reflections on the Origin and Spread of Nationalism*, rev. ed. (1991; New York: Verso, 2006), 175.

3. Martin W. Lewis and Kären E. Wigen, *The Myth of Continents: A Critique of Metageography* (Berkeley: University of California Press, 1997), 11.

4. J. H. Andrews, "Introduction: Meaning, Knowledge, and Power in the Map Philosophy of J. B. Harley," in J. B. Harley, *The New Nature of Maps: Essays in the History of Cartography*, ed. Paul Laxton, 23–25; quotes 25 (Baltimore: Johns Hopkins University Press, 2001).

5. Kwame Anthony Appiah, "Citizenship in Theory and Practice: A Response to Charles Kesler," in *Immigration and Citizenship in the Twenty-first Century*, ed. Noah M. J. Pickus, 41 (Lanham, MD: Rowman & Littlefield, 1998).

6. Lewis and Wigen, *Myth of Continents*, 11.

7. Anthony D. Smith, *National Identity* (Reno: University of Nevada Press, 1991), 176.

8. Adam M. McKeown, *Melancholy Order: Asian Migration and the Globalization of Borders* (New York: Columbia University Press, 2008), 95–96.

9. Atossa Araxia Abrahamian, *The Cosmopolites: The Coming of the Global Citizen* (New York: Columbia Global Reports, 2015), 12.

10. Mae M. Ngai, *Impossible Subjects: Illegal Aliens and the Making of Modern America* (Princeton, NJ: Princeton University Press, 2004), 10, 11.

11. Ngai, *Impossible Subjects*, 11–12, quote 11.

12. Michael Howard, *The Invention of Peace: Reflections on War and International Order* (New Haven, CT: Yale University Press, 2000), 99–100; Andreas Fahrmeir, *Citizenship: The Rise and Fall of a Modern Concept* (New Haven, CT: Yale University Press, 2007), 231; Dimitry Kochenov, *Citizenship* (Cambridge, MA: MIT Press, 2019), 191.

13. "Table 1: The abolition of military conscription around the world," in Kochenov, *Citizenship*, 162–163; "Field Listing—Military service age and obligation," in U.S. Central Intelligence Agency, *The World Factbook*, https://www.cia.gov/the-world-factbook/field/military-service-age-and-obligation/ (accessed October 18, 2022).

14. Derek Heater, *A Brief History of Citizenship* (Edinburgh: Edinburgh University Press, 2004), 140–142. Heater cites T. H. Marshall and T. Bottomore, *Citizenship and Social Class* (Concord, MA: Pluto, 1992).

15. Kochenov, *Citizenship*, 166–167; McKeown, *Melancholy Order*, 350.

16. Heater, *Brief History of Citizenship*, 140, 143.

17. Heater, *Brief History of Citizenship*, 143–145. For more on the ways that transnational corporations transcend nation-states, see Masao Miyoshi, "A Borderless World?: From Colonialism to Transnationalism and the Decline of the Nation-State," in *Global/Local: Cultural Production and the Transnational Imaginary*, ed. Rob Wilson and Wimal Dissanayake, 91–97 (Durham, NC: Duke University Press, 1996).

18. Smith, *National Identity*, 175–176.

19. Linda K. Kerber, "Toward a History of Statelessness in America," in *Legal Borderlands: Law and the Construction of American Borders*, ed. Mary L. Dudziak and Leti Volpp, 138 (Baltimore: Johns Hopkins University Press, 2006).

20. Abrahamian, *Cosmopolites*, 16–17. Abrahamian reminds us that in the twenty-first century, "citizenship can be bought, sold, renounced, and revoked," the number of refugees is at a very high level, and "cross-border trade and technology have diluted the ties

between citizens, strengthened bonds between geographical strangers, and revealed a fresh layer of arbitrariness to our national allegiances," adding that "if the nation is being called into question as a result of globalizing technology, trade, and crisis, it makes perfect sense for our connection and allegiance to the nation to be challenged too." Abrahamian, *Cosmopolites*, 152, 156.

21. On extended border patrols of the U.S. government in the early twenty-first century, see Daniel Kanstroom, *Deportation Nation: Outsiders in American History* (Cambridge, MA: Harvard University Press, 2007), 12–14.

22. Aristide R. Zolberg, *A Nation by Design: Immigration Policy in the Fashioning of America* (Cambridge, MA: Harvard University Press, 2006), 45–49; McKeown, *Melancholy Order*, 27.

23. Nancy L. Green, "The Politics of Exit: Reversing the Immigration Paradigm," *Journal of Modern History* 77 (June 2005), 270; Alan Taylor, *The Civil War of 1812: American Citizens, British Subjects, Irish Rebels, and Indian Allies* (New York: Knopf, 2010), 101–106.

24. Craig Robertson, *The Passport in America: The History of a Document* (New York: Oxford University Press, 2010), 142.

25. Green, "Politics of Exit," 287. See also McKeown, *Melancholy Order*, 24–25.

26. "General instructions in regard to passports, June 1, 1888," in *The American Passport: Its History and a Digest of Laws, Rulings, and Regulations Governing Its Issuance by the Department of State*, 169 (Washington, DC: U.S. Government Printing Office, 1898). For an analysis of the evolution of immigration law in the United States, see John Torpey, *The Invention of the Passport: Surveillance, Citizenship, and the State* (New York: Cambridge University Press, 2000), 93–103.

27. [Richard] Olney, Secretary [of State], to President [Grover Cleveland], February 8, 1897, in *American Passport*, 169–170.

28. Executive Order no. 2,285, *A Compilation of the Messages and Papers of the Presidents* (New York: Bureau of National Literature, 1916), 18:8169–8170.

29. *An act to prevent in time of war departure from or entry into the United States contrary to the public safety*, Public Law 154, *U.S. Statutes at Large* 40 (1917–1919), 559; Robertson, *Passport in America*, 187–188.

30. *An act to regulate further the entry of aliens into the United States*, Public Law 79, *U.S. Statutes at Large* 41 (1919–1921), 353–354.

31. Torpey, *Invention of the Passport*, 117–118.

32. McKeown, *Melancholy Order*, 339.

33. United Nations, "Universal Declaration of Human Rights," https://www.un.org/en/about-us/universal-declaration-of-human-rights (accessed October 18, 2022).

34. *Immigration and Nationality Act of 1952*, Public Law 82-414, *U.S. Statutes at Large* 66 (1952), 190–191.

35. U.S. Department of State, "Dept. Reg. 108-456," *Federal Register* 26 (January 19, 1961), 482–483. See also Zolberg, *Nation by Design*, 316–318.

36. Clarence B. Randall, *International Travel: Report to the President of the United States* (Washington, DC: U.S. Government Printing Office, 1958), iii, 3, 1–2, quote iii. See also U.S. Department of State, Passport Office, *The United States Passport: Past, Present, Future* (Washington, DC: U.S. Government Printing Office, 1976), iii; Nancy L. Green and François Weil,

"Introduction," in *Citizenship and Those Who Leave: The Politics of Emigration and Expatriation,* ed. Nancy L. Green and François Weil, 2 (Urbana: University of Illinois Press, 2007).

37. Torpey, *Invention of the Passport,* 4.

38. Torpey, *Invention of the Passport,* 4.

39. Torpey, *Invention of the Passport,* 6–7. See also Kerber, "Toward a History of Statelessness in America," 140; and Robert Wiebe, "Framing U.S. History: Democracy, Nationalism, and Socialism," in *Rethinking American History in a Global Age,* ed. Thomas Bender, 239 (Berkeley: University of California Press, 2002).

40. Torpey, *Invention of the Passport,* 2, 7. See also Fahrmeir, *Citizenship,* 46–50.

41. Torpey, *Invention of the Passport,* 3, 8, 9, quote 3. See also McKeown, *Melancholy Order,* 1–3, 13. In asserting this method of organizing modern states, Torpey argued against Benedict Anderson's theory of nations as "imagined communities," saying that authorizing and regulating the movement of people "has been intrinsic to the very construction of state since the rise of absolutism in modern Europe" and adding that identifying persons is essential to that process; therefore, "the notion of national communities must be codified in documents rather than merely 'imagined.'" See Torpey, *Invention of the Passport,* 6; and Anderson, *Imagined Communities.*

42. *The 9/11 Commission Report: Final Report of the National Commission on Terrorist Attacks upon the United States* (New York: Norton, 2004), 387–389. From 2004 to 2009 the Western Hemisphere Travel Initiative (WHTI) required increasingly more identification to enter the United States—even for U.S. citizens. As of June 1, 2009, it would be "unlawful for a citizen of the United States . . . to enter or depart, or attempt to enter or depart, the United States, without a valid U.S. passport." See "Passport requirement; Definitions," *Code of Federal Regulations,* title 22, sec. 53.1, September 20, 2022, https://www.ecfr.gov.

43. John A. Jakle, *The Tourist: Travel in Twentieth-Century North America* (Lincoln: University of Nebraska Press, 1985), xii, 2; John A. Jakle and Keith A. Sculle, *Motoring: The Highway Experience in America* (Athens: University of Georgia Press, 2008), 217, 220.

44. Jack Todd, *The Taste of Metal: A Deserter's Story* (Toronto: HarperPerennial, 2001), 109.

45. Todd, *Taste of Metal,* 114–115.

46. Arlo Tatum and Joseph S. Tuchinsky, *Guide to the Draft* (Boston: Beacon, 1969), 231–232.

47. American Deserters Committee, "Travel to a Foreign Country" (pamphlet) (mimeograph), folder 10, "Canada," box 2, Draft Counseling and Information Center, Madison, Wisconsin, Records, 1968–1974 (Mss. 442), Wisconsin Historical Society. Emphasis in the original.

48. Lawrence M. Baskir and William A. Strauss, *Chance and Circumstance: The Draft, the War, and the Vietnam Generation* (New York: Vintage, 1978), 174, 180.

49. Karen Dubinsky, *The Second Greatest Disappointment: Honeymooning and Tourism at Niagara Falls* (New Brunswick, NJ: Rutgers University Press, 1999), 178–179.

50. Richard Paterak in Alice Lind, *We Won't Go: Personal Accounts of War Objectors* (Boston: Beacon, 1968), 113.

51. "For Americans: An Easier Life in Canada," *U.S. News and World Report* 65 (October 28, 1968), 64.

52. Winnipeg Committee to Assist War Objectors, "Canada As an Alternative" [1971,] [p. 1], folder 2, "Conscientious Objection—Canada information, 1967–1971," box 2,

American Friends Service Committee, Madison, Wisconsin, Area Committee: Records, 1964–1974 (Mss. 886), Wisconsin Historical Society.

53. Smith, *National Identity,* 9.

54. Total area is defined as "the sum of all land and water areas delimited by international boundaries and/or coastlines." See "Country Comparisons—Area," in U.S. Central Intelligence Agency, *World Factbook,* https://www.cia.gov/the-world-factbook/field/area/country-comparison (accessed October 18, 2022).

55. Given that one-third of the boundary between the United States and Canada is formed by water, and that many other waterways and watersheds traverse that boundary, it should be no surprise that the two countries have cooperated on their use. Shared possession of the Great Lakes between the United States and Canada dates to the Treaty of Paris (1783) that ended the War for American Independence. The Rush-Bagot Treaty (1817) demilitarized interior waterways of North America, including the Great Lakes and Lake Champlain. Shared use of the Great Lakes was assured by the Webster-Ashburton Treaty (1842). The Boundary Waters Treaty (1909) created the International Joint Commission, which has a watchdog role over shared waterways. The 2,200-mile-long (3,500-kilometer-long) Great Lakes St. Lawrence Seaway, constructed and shared by the two countries, has been in use since 1958. See John Herd Thompson and Stephen J. Randall, *Canada and the United States: Ambivalent Allies,* 4th ed. (Athens: University of Georgia Press, 2008), 76, 15, 23, 31, 75–76, 198. John J. Bukowczyk, "The Production of History, the Becoming of Place," in *Permeable Border: The Great Lakes Basin as Transnational Region, 1650–1990,* by John J. Bukowczyk et al., 2 (Pittsburgh: University of Pittsburgh Press, 2005).

56. Smith, *National Identity,* 12.

57. In 1969, 72.5 percent of Canadian imports came from the United States while 70.9 percent of Canadian exports went to the United States. See "Table 2.—Trade of Canada with Commonwealth and Preferential Countries, and Other Countries, 1956–70," *Canada Year Book 1972: Statistical Annual of the Resources, Demography, Institutions, and Social and Economic Conditions of Canada* (Ottawa: Statistics Canada, 1972), 1072.

58. David Thelen, "Of Audiences, Borderlands, and Comparisons: Toward the Internationalization of American History," *Journal of American History* 79 (September 1992), 436.

59. Green, "Politics of Exit," 288–289. Ngai, *Impossible Subjects,* 11.

60. John Bodnar, *The Transplanted: A History of Immigrants in Urban America* (Bloomington: Indiana University Press, 1985), 209.

61. Arif Dirlik, "Performing the World: Reality and Representation in the Making of World Histor(ies)," *Journal of World History* 16 (December 2005), 397.

62. Orm Øverland, "Visions of Home: Exiles and Immigrants," in *The Dispossessed: An Anatomy of Exile,* ed. Peter I. Rose, 8, 22 (Amherst: University of Massachusetts Press, 2005).

63. Victor Konrad and Heather N. Nicol, *Beyond Walls: Re-inventing the Canada–United States Borderlands* (Burlington, VT: Ashgate, 2008), 289.

64. On July 1, 2020, the United States–Mexico–Canada Agreement (USMCA) replaced the North American Free Trade Agreement (NAFTA).

65. Konrad and Nicol, *Beyond Walls,* 291.

66. Appiah, "Citizenship in Theory and Practice," 41.

ACKNOWLEDGMENTS

1. The writer C. S. Giscombe has caused me to think about my propensity for travel to and in Canada. In his 2000 memoirs he observed, as can I, "I've always, all my life, been going on into Canada, going up to Canada, over into Canada," and asked, as can I, "Why was I always running to Canada when I had some time, crossing that border to touch the big otherness?" C. S. Giscombe, *Into and Out of Dislocation* (New York: North Point, 2000), 15, 126.

2. Fritz Lieber (Bloomington, IN) to Don Maxwell (Carp Lake, MI), May 14, 2008. In the author's possession.

BIBLIOGRAPHY

PRIMARY SOURCES

Manuscript Collections

Gerald R. Ford Presidential Library (Ann Arbor, Michigan)
   Charles Goodell Papers, 1974–77
   Robert J. Horn Papers
   Theodore C. Marrs Files, 1974–76
   John O. Marsh Files
   President Ford Committee Campaign Records, 1975–76
   Stanley S. Scott Papers, (1969) 1971–1977
   William A. Syers Interview Transcripts, 1984–1985

Jimmy Carter Presidential Library (Atlanta, Georgia)
   Carter White House Central Files, 1977–1981; Series: White House Central Files Subject File, 1977–1981 (Collection JC-WHCF)
   Records of the Office of the Assistant for Public Liaison, 1977–1981; Series: Margaret Costanza Subject Files, 1977–1978 (Collection JC-PUBLIAS)
   Records of the White House Office of Counsel to the President, 1977–1981; Series: Robert J. Lipshutz Files, 1977–1979 (Collection JC-COUNSL)

Library and Archives Canada (Ottawa, Ontario)
   David W. Diamond fonds (R11554)
   Goldie Josephy fonds (R4460)
   Records of the Immigration Branch (RG 76)

McMaster University, Mills Memorial Library, William Ready Division of Archives and Research Collections (Hamilton, Ontario, Canada)
   Canadian Student Social and Political Organizations, [ca. 1966–]1977 (Collection RC0217)

Swarthmore College, McCabe Library, Swarthmore College Peace Collection (Swarthmore, Pennsylvania)
   Sallie Marx Papers (DG 270)
   Steve Trimm Papers (DG 232)

Texas Tech University, The Vietnam Center & Sam Johnson Vietnam Archive (https://www.vietnam.ttu.edu/)
   Douglas Pike Collection

United Church of Canada Archives (Toronto, Ontario)
   United Church of Canada Board of Evangelism and Social Service fonds (fonds F510)

University of British Columbia, Irving K. Barber Learning Centre, Rare Books and Special Collections (Vancouver, Canada)
   Renée Kasinsky fonds

University of British Columbia, Irving K. Barber Learning Centre, University Archives
(Vancouver, Canada)
  J. McRee Elrod fonds
University of Toronto, John P. Robarts Research Library, Media Commons Archives
(Ontario, Canada)
  Michael Maclear fonds (Accession no. 2004.005)
University of Toronto, Thomas Fisher Rare Book Library (Ontario, Canada)
  Jack Pocock Memorial Collection (Ms. Coll. 331)
  Mark Satin Papers (Ms. Coll. 629)
  Rochdale College Collection (Ms. Coll. 184)
University of Waterloo, Conrad Grebel University College, Milton Good Library, Men-
nonite Archives of Ontario (Waterloo, Ontario, Canada)
  Samuel J. Steiner Fonds (Hist. Mss. 1.138)
Wisconsin Historical Society (Madison, Wisconsin)
  American Friends Service Committee, Madison, Wisconsin, Area Committee: Rec-
ords, 1964–1974 (Mss. 886)
  AMEX/Canada Records, 1968–1977 (Mss. 736)
  Draft Counseling and Information Center, Madison, Wisconsin, Records, 1968–1974
(Mss. 442)
  National Council for Universal and Unconditional Amnesty Records, 1964–1978
(M 80-391)
  Robert F. Froehlke Papers, 1968–1974 (M2002–164)
  Robert P. Tabak Papers, 1968–1985 (M86-086)
  United Methodist Office for the United Nations, Reference File, 1966–1976 (Mss. 541)
  Vietnam Veterans Against the War Records, 1967–2006 (Mss. 370)
  Wisconsin Draft Resistance Union, Records, 1967–1969 (Mss. 382)

Oral History Interview
Bob Proctor, Indianapolis, IN, September 22, 2004.

Personal Communication
Richard Lemm, e-mail message to author, May 27, 2007.

BOOKS AND ARTICLES

"1976 Democratic Party Platform." July 12, 1976. The American Presidency Project.
https://www.presidency.ucsb.edu/documents/1976-democratic-party-platform.
"ABC's of Draft by Lottery." U.S. News and World Report 67 (December 15, 1969), 33–35.
Abrahamian, Atossa Araxia. The Cosmopolites: The Coming of the Global Citizen. New
York: Columbia Global Reports, 2015.
Adams, James. "'The Big Guys Keep Being Surprised by Us,'" Globe and Mail (Toronto),
October 20, 2007.
Adolph, Robert. "Reflections of a New Canadian Professor." Canadian Dimension 7
(October–November 1970), 39–43.

"AFSC Statement on Amnesty and the Ford Earned Re-entry Program, 17 September 1974." *L & C News* 1 (October 1974).

Airhart, Phyllis D. "'As Canadian as Possible under the Circumstances': Reflections on the Study of Protestantism in North America." In *New Directions in American Religious History,* edited by Harry S. Stout and D. G. Hart, 116–137. New York: Oxford University Press, 1997.

Alsop, Stewart. "The Need to Hate." *Newsweek* 76 (July 27, 1970), 80.

———. "They Can't Go Home Again." *Newsweek* 76 (July 20, 1970), 88.

Alter, Jonathan. *His Very Best: Jimmy Carter, A Life.* New York: Simon & Schuster, 2020.

American Deserters. London: War Resisters' International, [1968].

American Friends Service Committee. "If the Army Is Not Your Bag!" [booklet]. Philadelphia: American Friends Service Committee, 1968.

———. "Something's Happening Here to the Draft" [brochure]. Philadelphia: American Friends Service Committee, 1968.

"Amnesty for the War Exiles?" *Newsweek* 79 (January 17, 1972), 19–20, 23–24, 26.

"Amnesty Options." *New Republic* 175 (December 25, 1976), 3–5.

"Amnesty Program: Fall '76." *NCUUA Amnesty Update,* no. 10 (Fall 1976), 3.

"And What Happened to All Those Brilliant Americans?" *Saturday Night* 92 (October 1977), 14, 17.

Anderson, Benedict. *Imagined Communities: Reflections on the Origin and Spread of Nationalism.* rev. ed. 1991. Reprint, New York: Verso, 2006.

Anderson, Christopher G. *Canadian Liberalism and the Politics of Border Control, 1867–1967.* Vancouver: University of British Columbia Press, 2012.

Andrew, G. C. "Item 26: Letter to Miss Marya Hardman from Dr. Andrew, February 4, 1969." In *The Struggle for Canadian Universities: A Dossier,* edited by Robin Mathews and James Steele, 60–61. Toronto: New Press, 1969.

Andrews, J. H. "Introduction: Meaning, Knowledge, and Power in the Map Philosophy of J. B. Harley." In J. B. Harley, *The New Nature of Maps: Essays in the History of Cartography,* edited by Paul Laxton, 1–32. Baltimore: Johns Hopkins University Press, 2001.

Appiah, Kwame Anthony. "Citizenship in Theory and Practice: A Response to Charles Kesler." In *Immigration and Citizenship in the Twenty-first Century,* edited by Noah M. J. Pickus, 41–48. Lanham, MD: Rowman & Littlefield, 1998.

———. *Cosmopolitanism: Ethics in a World of Strangers.* New York: Norton, 2006.

Appy, Christian G. *Patriots: The Vietnam War Remembered from All Sides.* New York: Viking, 2003.

Arendt, Hannah. *The Origins of Totalitarianism.* New York: Harcourt Brace Jovanovich, 1951.

Ascoli, Max. "Farewell to Our Readers." *Reporter* 38 (June 13, 1968), 18.

Bailey, Beth. "The Army in the Marketplace: Recruiting an All-Volunteer Force." *Journal of American History* 94 (June 2007), 47–74.

Baker, William M. "The Anti-American Ingredient in Canadian History." *Dalhousie Review* 53 (Spring 1973), 57–77.

Baskir, Lawrence M., and William A. Strauss. *Chance and Circumstance: The Draft, the War, and the Vietnam Generation.* New York: Vintage, 1978.

Baumgartner, Alice L. *South to Freedom: Runaway Slaves to Mexico and the Road to the Civil War*. New York: Basic Books, 2020.

"Beating the Draft, 1970 Style." *Newsweek* 76 (November 9, 1970), 27–28.

Berton, Pierre. *1967: The Last Good Year*. Toronto: Doubleday, 1997.

———. *The Comfortable Pew: A Critical Look at Christianity and the Religious Establishment in the New Age*. Philadelphia: Lippincott, 1965.

Black, J. Laurence. "Americans in Canadian Universities II." *Laurentian University Review* 2 (June 1969), 109–110.

Bodnar, John. *The Transplanted: A History of Immigrants in Urban America*. Bloomington: Indiana University Press, 1985.

Boorstin, Daniel J. *The Image: A Guide to Pseudo-events in America*. 1961. Reprint, New York: Vintage, 1992.

Born on the Fourth of July. dir. Oliver Stone. 1989.

Bothwell, Robert. *Alliance and Illusion: Canada and the World, 1945–1984*. Vancouver: UBC Press, 2007.

Bourne, Peter G. *Jimmy Carter: A Comprehensive Biography from Plains to Postpresidency*. New York: Scribner, 1997.

Braithwaite, Max. *Canada: Wonderland of Surprises*. New York: Dodd, Mead, 1967.

Brewin, John. "Deserter Dodging." *Canadian Forum* 49 (May 1969), 30–31.

Brinkley, Douglas. *Gerald R. Ford*. New York: Times Books, 2007.

Bristow, William H. "Happy Hundred!" *Scholastic Teacher* 90 (February 10, 1967), 13.

Brown, Dick. "New Immigration Law Opens Door for 60 Days." *AMEX/Canada* 4 (July–August 1973), 28–29.

Brune, Lester H., and Richard Dean Burns. *America and the Indochina Wars, 1945–1990: A Bibliographical Guide*. Claremont, CA: Regina, 1992.

Bruno, Hal. "Carter Meets the Questions." *Newsweek* 87 (February 2, 1976), 18–19.

Bukowczyk, John J. "The Production of History, the Becoming of Place." In John J. Bukowczyk et al., *Permeable Border: The Great Lakes Basin as Transnational Region, 1650–1990*, 1–9. Pittsburgh: University of Pittsburgh Press, 2005.

Bumsted, J. M., and Michael C. Bumsted. *A History of the Canadian Peoples*. 5th ed. Don Mills, ON: Oxford University Press, 2016.

Cameron, Gail. "Why 'Good' Sons Become Draft Dodgers." *Ladies' Home Journal* 84 (August 1967), 72–73, 92, 94, 96, 98–100.

Camp, Dalton C. "Canadian-American Interdependence: How Much?" *Canadian Forum* 48 (February 1969), 242–244.

Campbell, Lara. "'The Moral Grandeur of Fleeing to Canada': Masculinity and the Gender Politics of American Draft Dodgers during the Vietnam War." In *Making Men, Making History: Canadian Masculinities across Time and Place*, edited by Peter Gossage and Robert Rutherdale, 347–363. Vancouver: UBC Press, 2018.

———. "'Women United against the War': Gender Politics, Feminism, and Vietnam Draft Resistance in Canada." In *New World Coming: The Sixties and the Shaping of Global Consciousness*, edited by Karen Dubinsky et al., 339–346. Toronto: Between the Lines, 2009.

"Canada." *Issues & Actions: Newsletter of Clergy and Laymen Concerned About Vietnam* (August 1, 1969), 4–5.

"Canada: Escape Hatch for U.S. Draft Resisters." *U.S. News and World Report* 61 (September 26, 1966), 61–62.

"Canadian Council Names Director to Aid U.S. Draft Evaders." *Christian Century* 88 (January 13, 1971), 38.

The Canadian Encyclopedia. 2nd ed. Edmonton: Hurtig, 1988.

"Canadian Immigration Procedures Closed" (Midwest Committee for Draft Counseling) *Draft Counselor's Newsletter,* no. 9 ([November or December] 1972), 3.

Capizzi, Joseph E. "Selective Conscientious Objection in the United States." *Journal of Church and State* 38 (Spring 1996), 339–363.

Carter, Jimmy. *A Full Life: Reflections at Ninety.* New York: Simon & Schuster, 2015.

———. *Keeping Faith: Memoirs of a President.* New York: Bantam, 1982.

———. *White House Diary.* New York: Farrar, Straus & Giroux, 2010.

"Carter Pardons Draft Resisters." *Congress and the Nation.* Washington, DC: Congressional Quarterly, 1981, 5:181.

"Carter's Amnesty Two-Step." *NCUUA Amnesty Update,* no. 12 (July–August 1977), 10–15.

Chamberlain, Frank. "The Surprising New Ways They Spend Church Money." *United Church Observer* 31 (October 15, 1969), 28–30.

"The Chances of Being Drafted Now." *U.S. News and World Report* 68 (June 8, 1970), 25–26.

"The Christian and Viet Nam: A Reader-Opinion Poll." *United Church Observer* 29 (February 1, 1968), 4.

Churchill, David S. "An Ambiguous Welcome: Vietnam Draft Resistance, the Canadian State, and Cold War Containment." *Social History | Histoire sociale* 37 (May 2004), 1–26.

———. "American Expatriates and the Building of Alternative Social Space in Toronto, 1965–1977." *Urban History Review | Revue d'histoire urbaine* 39 (Autumn 2010), 31–44.

———. "Draft Resisters, Left Nationalism, and the Politics of Anti-Imperialism." *Canadian Historical Review* 93 (June 2012), 227–260.

Clarke, Patricia. "Parliament Makes the Laws." *United Church Observer* 31 (June 15, 1969), 10.

———. "Robert Gardner: Why a War Veteran Helps War Resisters." *United Church Observer* 33 (June 1971), 6–7.

Clarkson, Stephen, ed. *An Independent Foreign Policy for Canada?* Toronto: McClelland & Stewart, 1968.

Clausen, Christopher. "An Army of One." *American Scholar* 72 (Autumn 2003), 51–61.

Clausen, Oliver. "Boys without a Country." *New York Times Magazine* (May 21, 1967), 25, 94–101, 104–105.

———. Letter to the editor. *New York Times Magazine* (July 2, 1967), 2.

Clegg, Claude A., III. *The Price of Liberty: African Americans and the Making of Liberia.* Chapel Hill: University of North Carolina Press, 2004.

Cocking, Clive. "How Did the Canadian Mounties Develop Their Unfortunate Habit of Deporting People They Don't Happen to Like?" *Saturday Night* 85 (June 1970), 28–30.

Cohen, Howard, and Charles Greene. *Young Person's Guide to Canada.* New York: Collier, 1971.

Coleman, Patricia P. "Just across the Border." *Scholastic Teacher* 86 (April 15, 1965), 8–9.

Colhoun, Jack. "'Earned Re-entry' a Sham: Full of Inequities and Traps." *AMEX/Canada* 5 (October 1974), 8–10.

Cook, Ramsay. *The Maple Leaf Forever: Essays on Nationalism and Politics in Canada.* Toronto: Macmillan, 1971.

Cooney, John, and Dana Spitzer. "'Hell, No, We Won't Go!'" *Trans-action* 6 (September 1969), 53–62.

Cope, Michael. "'The American Middle Class Looking to Canada'—Rubbish!" *Executive* (Don Mills, ON) 11 (September 1969), 18, 21.

Cormier, Jeffrey. *The Canadianization Movement: Emergence, Survival, and Success.* Toronto: University of Toronto Press, 2004.

Coupland, Douglas. *Souvenir of Canada.* Vancouver: Douglas & McIntyre, 2002.

Cunningham, Virginia. "Our Son, the Deserter." *United Church Observer* 33 (November 1970), 29.

"D-Dodgers." *United Church Observer* 29 (November 1, 1967), 11, 40.

Daniel Yankelovich, Inc. *The Changing Values on Campus: Political and Personal Attitudes of Today's College Students; A Survey for the JDR 3rd Fund.* New York: Washington Square, 1972.

Daniels, Roger. *Coming to America: A History of Immigration and Ethnicity in American Life.* New York: HarperCollins, 1990.

Davidson, Bill. "'Hell, No, We Won't Go!'" *Saturday Evening Post* 241 (January 27, 1968), 21–26.

Dawson, Michael. *Selling British Columbia: Tourism and Consumer Culture, 1890–1970.* Vancouver: UBC Press, 2004.

de Mestral, Claude. "Canadian Christians Primed for Ministry to U.S. Draft 'Refugees.'" *Christian Century* 88 (January 20, 1971), 73.

"Deserters in Sweden: Fourteen Black Ex-GIs Find Refuge from Vietnam War." *Ebony* 23 (August 1968), 120–122.

Dickerson, James. *North to Canada: Men and Women against the Vietnam War.* Westport, CT: Praeger, 1999.

Dirlik, Arif. "Performing the World: Reality and Representation in the Making of World Histor(ies)." *Journal of World History* 16 (December 2005), 391–410.

"Dissent in Canada." *Christian Century* 84 (June 14, 1967), 772–773.

Donaghy, Greg. "Minding the Minister: Pearson, Martin, and American Policy in Asia, 1963–1967." In *Pearson: The Unlikely Gladiator*, edited by Norman Hillmer, 131–149. Montréal: McGill-Queen's University Press, 1999.

———. *Tolerant Allies: Canada and the United States, 1963–1968.* Montréal: McGill-Queen's University Press, 2002.

Doran, Charles F., and James Patrick Sewell. "Anti-Americanism in Canada?" *Annals of the American Academy of Political and Social Science*, no. 497 (May 1988), 105–119.

Douville, Bruce. *The Uncomfortable Pew: Christianity and the New Left in Toronto.* Montréal: McGill-Queen's University Press, 2021.

Doyle, Barrie. "Federal Aid to Religion?: 'Good Samaritan' State." *Christianity Today* 17 (November 10, 1972), 50–51.

"The Draft: How the Resisters Fare." *Time* 92 (September 20, 1968), 54, 59.

"The Draft: How to Beat It without Really Trying." *Time* 91 (March 15, 1968), 15–16.

"The Draft: Retain? Reform? Or Abolish?" *Senior Scholastic* 94 (May 2, 1969), 4–9.

"The Draft . . . or What? Choices for Spring Graduates." *U.S. News and World Report* 68 (March 30, 1970), 80–81.

Druick, Zoë. *Projecting Canada: Government Policy and Documentary Film at the National Film Board of Canada.* Montréal: McGill-Queen's University Press, 2007.

Du Bois, W. E. Burghardt. *The Souls of Black Folk.* 1903. Reprint, New York: Signet, 1995.

Dubinsky, Karen. "'Everybody Likes Canadians': Canadians, Americans, and the Post–World War II Travel Boom." In *Being Elsewhere: Tourism, Consumer Culture, and Identity in Modern Europe and North America,* edited by Shelley Baranowski and Ellen Furlough, 320–347. Ann Arbor: University of Michigan Press, 2001.

———. *The Second Greatest Disappointment: Honeymooning and Tourism at Niagara Falls.* New Brunswick, NJ: Rutgers University Press, 1999.

Edwardson, Ryan. *Canadian Content: Culture and the Quest for Nationhood.* Toronto: University of Toronto Press, 2008.

Elbert, Joan. "'Universal and Unconditional.'" *Christian Century* 94 (February 16, 1977), 134–135.

Elrod, J. McRee. Letter to the editor. *Christian Century* 85 (March 6, 1968), 303.

———. Letter to the editor. *New York Review of Books* 10 (February 29, 1968), 35.

Emerick, Kenneth Fred. *War Resisters Canada: The World of the American Military-Political Refugees.* Knox, PA: Knox, Pennsylvania Free Press, 1972.

English, John. *The Worldly Years: The Life of Lester Pearson.* Vol. 2, *1949–1972.* Toronto: Knopf, 1992.

Erikson, Erik H. *Identity: Youth and Crisis.* New York: Norton, 1968.

Evans, Donald. "A Reasonable Scream of Protest." In *Peace, Power, and Protest,* edited by Donald Evans, 1–13. Toronto: Ryerson, 1967.

———. "Ten Principles for Foreign Policy." In *Peace, Power, and Protest,* edited by Donald Evans, 14–40. Toronto: Ryerson, 1967.

———, ed. *Peace, Power, and Protest.* Toronto: Ryerson, 1967.

Expo 67 guide officiel | Expo 67 Official Guide. Toronto: Maclean-Hunter, 1967.

Fahrmeir, Andreas. *Citizenship: The Rise and Fall of a Modern Concept.* New Haven, CT: Yale University Press, 2007.

Finlay, Karen A. *The Force of Culture: Vincent Massey and Canadian Sovereignty.* Toronto: University of Toronto Press, 2004.

Fitt, Alfred B. "Amnesty." *New York Times Magazine* (September 8, 1974), 27, 96–97.

Fleming, Karl. "America's Sad Young Exiles." *Newsweek* 77 (February 15, 1971), 28–30.

———. "How the Exiles View the Issue." *Newsweek* 79 (January 17, 1972), 24–25.

Flynn, George Q. *The Draft, 1940–1973.* Lawrence: University Press of Kansas, 1993.

Foley, Michael S. *Confronting the War Machine: Draft Resistance during the Vietnam War.* Chapel Hill: University of North Carolina Press, 2003.

Folvik, Robin. "'They Followed Their Men into Canada?': American Women in Canada during the Vietnam War Era." Conference paper, New World Coming: The Sixties and the Shaping of Global Consciousness, Kingston, ON, Canada, June 16, 2007.

"For Americans: An Easier Life in Canada." *U.S. News and World Report* 65 (October 28, 1968), 64.

Ford, Gerald R. *A Time to Heal: The Autobiography of Gerald R. Ford*. New York: Harper & Row, 1979.

Fox, Porter. *Northland: A 4,000-Mile Journey along America's Forgotten Border*. New York: Norton, 2018.

Franks, Lucinda. *Waiting Out a War: The Exile of Private John Picciano*. New York: Coward, McCann & Geoghegan, 1974.

Fulford, Robert. "Cut Off from Our Own Reality." *Saturday Night* 86 (February 1971), 7–8.

———. "General Perspectives on Canadian Culture." *American Review of Canadian Studies* 3 (Spring 1973), 115–121.

———. "The New Anti-Americanism." *Saturday Night* 85 (May 1970), 11.

Gallup, George H. *The Gallup Poll: Public Opinion, 1935–1971*. New York: Random House, 1972.

Gardner, Robert. "A Canadian Perspective: Amnesty When?" *New Republic* 165 (December 25, 1971), 12–13.

———. "Repatriation: Sell-Out or Social Work." *AMEX/Canada* 3 (January–February 1972), 30–31.

Gasher, Mike. "From Sacred Cows to White Elephants: Cultural Policy under Siege." *Canadian Issues* 19 (1997), 18–29.

Gayton, Don. "Do Draft Dodgers Like Me Need a Monument?" *Tyee* (Vancouver, BC), October 5, 2004. http://thetyee.ca/Views/2004/10/05/DraftDogerMonument/.

Giscombe, C. S. *Into and Out of Dislocation*. New York: North Point, 2000.

Glatz, Paul Benedikt. *Vietnam's Prodigal Heroes: American Deserters, International Protest, European Exile, and Amnesty*. Lanham, MD: Lexington, 2021.

Grafftey, Heward. "'Special' Immigrants Now Manpower Dilemma." *Canadian Business* 46 (October 1973), 98.

Granatstein, J. L. "The Arrival of the Anti-American Americans: The Vietnam War and Draft Dodgers." In *Yankee Go Home?: Canadians and Anti-Americanism*, 170–191. Toronto: Harper Collins, 1996.

Granatstein, J. L., and Norman Hillmer. *For Better or for Worse: Canada and the United States to the 1990s*. Toronto: Copp Clark Pitman, 1991.

Grant, George. *Lament for a Nation: The Defeat of Canadian Nationalism*. 1965. Reprint, Toronto: McClelland & Stewart, 1970.

Gray, John. "How Seven Families Really Got Away from It All." *Maclean's* 74 (October 7, 1961), 33–35, 94, 96–98.

Green, Nancy L. "The Politics of Exit: Reversing the Immigration Paradigm." *Journal of Modern History* 77 (June 2005), 263–289.

Green, Nancy L., and François Weil. "Introduction." In *Citizenship and Those Who Leave: The Politics of Emigration and Expatriation*, edited by Nancy L. Green and François Weil, 1–9. Urbana: University of Illinois Press, 2007.

Grescoe, Taras. *The End of Elsewhere: Travels among the Tourists*. London: Serpent's Tail, 2004.

Grieveson, Brian J., ed. *Toronto Survival Guide*. Toronto: Church of the Holy Trinity, 1973.

Gross, Franklin S. "Canada: An Exciting Teaching Opportunity." *Scholastic Teacher* 90 (February 10, 1967), 16.

Gustin, Bernard H. "Item 1: Letter in *The Globe and Mail* from Professor Gustin, Published May 30, 1969." In *The Struggle for Canadian Universities: A Dossier,* edited by Robin Mathews and James Steele, 123–125. Toronto: New Press, 1969.

Guterl, Matthew Pratt. *American Mediterranean: Southern Slaveholders in the Age of Emancipation.* Cambridge, MA: Harvard University Press, 2008.

Hagan, John. "Cause and Country: The Politics of Ambivalence and the American Vietnam War Resistance in Canada." *Social Problems* 48 (May 2001), 168–184.

———. *Northern Passage: American Vietnam War Resisters in Canada.* Cambridge, MA: Harvard University Press, 2001.

Haig-Brown, Alan. *Hell No We Won't Go: Vietnam Draft Resisters in Canada.* Vancouver: Raincoast, 1996.

Hajek, Danny. "A Thousand People in the Street: 'For What It's Worth' Captured Youth in Revolt." *Morning Edition,* National Public Radio, February 20, 2019. https://www.npr.org/2019/02/20/693790065/buffalo-springfield-for-what-its-worth-american-anthem.

Hall, Mitchell K. *Because of Their Faith: CALCAV and Religious Opposition to the Vietnam War.* New York: Columbia University Press, 1990.

Hämäläinen, Pekka. *Lakota America: A New History of Indigenous Power.* New Haven, CT: Yale University Press, 2019.

Handlin, Oscar. *The Uprooted.* 2nd ed. Boston: Little, Brown, 1990.

Harter, Eugene C. *The Lost Colony of the Confederacy.* College Station: Texas A&M University Press, 2000.

Hartmann, Robert T. *Palace Politics: An Inside Account of the Ford Years.* New York: McGraw-Hill, 1980.

"A Harvest of Hatred." *Christianity Today* 16 (April 28, 1972), 25–26.

Hawkins, Freda. *Canada and Immigration: Public Policy and Public Concern.* 2nd ed. Kingston: McGill-Queen's University Press, 1988.

———. *Critical Years in Immigration: Canada and Australia Compared.* Montréal: McGill-Queen's University Press, 1991.

Haythorne, T. R. Letter to editor. *United Church Observer* 29 (December 15, 1967), 4.

Heater, Derek. *A Brief History of Citizenship.* Edinburgh: Edinburgh University Press, 2004.

Henderson, Stuart. "Off the Streets and into the Fortress: Experiments in Hip Separatism at Toronto's Rochdale College, 1968–1975." *Canadian Historical Review* 92 (March 2011), 107–133.

Hertzman, Lewis. "Americans in Canadian Universities I." *Laurentian University Review* 2 (June 1969), 107–108.

Hilts, Len. *Explore Canada.* Chicago: Rand McNally, 1972.

Hoffman, Abbie. *Steal This Book.* 1971. Reprint, New York: Four Walls Eight Windows, 2002.

Hopkins, Charles H. *The Rise of the Social Gospel in American Protestantism.* New Haven, CT: Yale University Press, 1940.

"How You Vote on Viet Nam." *United Church Observer* 30 (March 15, 1968), 16–18, 46.

Howard, Michael. *The Invention of Peace: Reflections on War and International Order.* New Haven, CT: Yale University Press, 2000.

Hunter, Robert. "Green Power." *Maclean's* 81 (May 1968), 13–15, 84–88.

"Immigration: 30,000 People Take Advantage of Government Mop-Up Program in First 30 Days." *AMEX/Canada* 4 (September–October 1973), 31–32.

"Immigration from the U.S.A." *World Affairs* (Toronto) 35 (February 1970), 10.

"Immigration 'Grace Period' Ends, No Extension." *AMEX/Canada* 4 (November–December 1973), 21.

"Immigration to Canada in 1967." *Labour Gazette* 68 (May 1968), 290.

"An Indiana Family Leaves the U.S. for Keeps." *Life* 69 (July 17, 1970), 42, 42A–42B, 43–45.

Innis, Hugh, ed. *Americanization*. Toronto: McGraw-Hill Ryerson, 1972.

"Is Defiance of Draft Growing?" *U.S. News and World Report* 66 (May 5, 1969), 13.

Jakle, John A. *The Tourist: Travel in Twentieth-Century North America*. Lincoln: University of Nebraska Press, 1985.

Jakle, John A., and Keith A. Sculle. *Motoring: The Highway Experience in America*. Athens: University of Georgia Press, 2008.

Jasanoff, Maya. *Liberty's Exiles: American Loyalists in the Revolutionary World*. New York: Knopf, 2011.

Jeffreys-Jones, Rhodri. *Peace Now!: American Society and the Ending of the Vietnam War*. New Haven, CT: Yale University Press, 1999.

Jewett, Pauline. "Who's Being Hired to Teach in Our Universities? Foreigners, Mostly. We Used to Be Short of Qualified Canadians. Now We're Turning Out Many More of Them; but We Don't Give Them Jobs." *Maclean's* 82 (March 1969), 10.

Johnson, R. Charles. *Don't Sit in the Draft*. Occidental, CA: Nolo, 1980.

Johnson, Valerie Miner. "American Women in Canada: A Young U.S. Immigrant and Her Friends Discover the Canadian Dream." *Chatelaine* 46 (May 1973), 48, 110, 112, 114–115.

———. "What It's Like to Be an American Professor in Canada and Discover the Canadians Aren't So Happy to Have You Here." *Saturday Night* 86 (April 1971), 20–22.

Jonckheere, Lucy. "The One Hundredth Year: Canada Celebrates Birthday." *Scholastic Teacher* 90 (February 10, 1967), 18–19.

[Jones, James C.] "Canada's Other U.S. Immigrants." *Newsweek* 77 (May 24, 1971), 38, 43.

Jones, Joseph. *Contending Statistics: The Numbers for U.S. Vietnam War Resisters in Canada*. Vancouver: Quarter Sheaf, 2005.

Kane, Robert S. *Canada A to Z*. Garden City, NY: Doubleday, 1964.

Kanigel, Robert. *Eyes on the Street: The Life of Jane Jacobs*. New York: Knopf, 2016.

Kanstroom, Daniel. *Deportation Nation: Outsiders in American History*. Cambridge, MA: Harvard University Press, 2007.

Kasinsky, Renée G. *Refugees from Militarism: Draft-Age Americans in Canada*. 1976. Reprint, Totowa, NJ: Littlefield, Adams, 1978.

Kasinsky, Renée L. Letter to the editor. *Trans-action* 7 (February 1970), 10, 61–62.

Katz, Bill. *Magazines for Libraries*. New York: Bowker, 1969.

Keenleyside, Hugh Ll. *Canada and the United States: Some Aspects of the History of the Republic and the Dominion*. New York: Knopf, 1929.

Kelley, Ninette, and Michael Trebilcock. *The Making of the Mosaic: A History of Canadian Immigration Policy*. Toronto: University of Toronto Press, 1998.

Kennedy, Mopsy Strange, and Steven D. Stark, eds. *Let's Go: The Student Guide to the United States and Canada, 1972–73*. New York: Dutton, 1972.

Kerber, Linda K. "Toward a History of Statelessness in America." In *Legal Borderlands: Law and the Construction of American Borders*, edited by Mary L. Dudziak and Leti Volpp, 135–157. Baltimore: Johns Hopkins University Press, 2006.

Kerouac, Jack. *On the Road*. 1957. Reprint, New York: Penguin, 1991.

Kilbourn, William, ed. *The Restless Church: A Response to* The Comfortable Pew. Philadelphia: Lippincott, 1966.

Killmer, Richard L., and Charles P. Lutz. *The Draft and the Rest of Your Life*. Minneapolis: Augsburg Publishing House, 1972.

Killmer, Richard L., Robert S. Lecky, and Debrah S. Wiley. *They Can't Go Home Again: The Story of America's Political Refugees*. Philadelphia: Pilgrim Press, 1971.

Knight, Dee Charles. "New Immigration Rules: New Restrictions on Non-immigrant Visitors." *AMEX/Canada* 3 (January–February 1973), 10–11.

Kochenov, Dimitry. *Citizenship*. Cambridge, MA: MIT Press, 2019.

Kohlberg, Lawrence, and Carol Gilligan. "The Adolescent as a Philosopher: The Discovery of the Self in a Postconventional World." *Dædalus* 100 (Fall 1971), 1051–1086.

Kollin, Susan. *Nature's State: Imagining Alaska as the Last Frontier*. Chapel Hill: University of North Carolina Press, 2001.

Konrad, Victor, and Heather N. Nicol. *Beyond Walls: Re-inventing the Canada–United States Borderlands*. Burlington, VT: Ashgate, 2008.

Kosoy, Ted. *A Guide for Travellers in Canada*. New York: Hastings House, 1973.

Kovic, Ron. *Born on the Fourth of July*. New York: McGraw-Hill, 1976.

Kroeker, Wally. "Canadian Council: Is Anybody Listening?" *Christianity Today* 17 (January 5, 1973), 49.

Kusch, Frank. *All American Boys: Draft Dodgers in Canada from the Vietnam War*. Westport, CT: Praeger, 2001.

Lambert, Ron. "Concerning Frying Pans and Fires." In *Manual for Draft-Age Immigrants to Canada*, 6th ed., 32–40. Toronto: Toronto Anti-Draft Programme, 1971.

Lanfant, Marie-Françoise. "International Tourism: Internationalization and the Challenge to Identity." Translated by John B. Allcock. In *International Tourism: Identity and Change*, edited by Marie-Françoise Lanfant, John B. Allcock, and Edward M. Bruner, 24–43. Thousand Oaks, CA: Sage, 1995.

———. "Introduction." Translated by Alison Steele and Nelson Graburn. In *International Tourism: Identity and Change*, edited by Marie-Françoise Lanfant, John B. Allcock, and Edward M. Bruner, 1–23. Thousand Oaks, CA: Sage, 1995.

Latta, William C., Jr. Letter to the editor. *Saturday Night* 86 (June 1971), 2.

Laxer, James. *The Border: Canada, the U.S., and Dispatches from the 49th Parallel*. Toronto: Doubleday, 2003.

———. "The Student Movement and Canadian Independence." *Canadian Dimension* 6 (August–September 1969), 27–34, 69–70.

Lefcourt, Herbert. Letter to the editor. *Saturday Night* 86 (December 1970), 3.

Lefebvre, Henri. *Everyday Life in the Modern World*. Translated by Sacha Rabinovich. New York: Harper & Row, 1971.

"Legal Brutality and the Anguish of Separation." *Christian Century* 88 (January 6, 1971), 5–6.

Lentner, Howard H. "Canada and U.S. (2) / Mosaic, Melting Pot—Both Myths." *Toronto Daily Star*, August 20, 1970. In *Americanization*, edited by Hugh Innis, 11–14. Toronto: McGraw-Hill Ryerson, 1972.

Levant, Victor. *Quiet Complicity: Canadian Involvement in the Vietnam War*. Toronto: Between the Lines, 1986.

Lewis, Martin W., and Kären E. Wigen. *The Myth of Continents: A Critique of Metageography*. Berkeley: University of California Press, 1997.

Lind, Alice. *We Won't Go: Personal Accounts of War Objectors*. Boston: Beacon, 1968.

Liston, Robert A. *Young Americans Abroad*. New York: Julian Messer, 1971.

Litt, Paul. *The Muses, the Masses, and the Massey Commission*. Toronto: University of Toronto Press, 1992.

Logevall, Fredrik. *The Origins of the Vietnam War*. Harlow, England: Longman, 2001.

Long, Luman H., ed. *The World Almanac and Book of Facts*. 1971 ed. New York: Newspaper Enterprise Association, 1970.

Looney, Douglas S. "How to Help Your Son Face the Draft." *Better Homes and Gardens* 48 (November 1970), 30.

Loschen, Leonard. Letter to the editor. *Saturday Evening Post* 241 (March 9, 1968), 4.

Lott, John C. "The Christian, His Country, His Conscience: An Apology for Noncooperation." *Canadian Mennonite* 17 (October 24, 1969), 6, 8.

———. "'You Cannot Christianize War.'" *United Church Observer* 32 (March 15, 1970), 16–17, 25, 40.

Lumsden, Ian, ed. *Close the 49th Parallel etc.: The Americanization of Canada*. Toronto: University of Toronto Press, 1970.

MacLure, Millar. Letter to the editor. *Saturday Night* 86 (July 1971), 2.

MacPherson, Myra. *Long Time Passing: Vietnam and the Haunted Generation*. New ed. Bloomington: Indiana University Press, 2001.

Mahant, Edelgard, and Graeme S. Mount. *Invisible and Inaudible in Washington: American Policies toward Canada*. Vancouver: UBC Press, 1999.

Mahant, Edelgard E., and Graeme S. Mount. *An Introduction to Canadian-American Relations*. Toronto: Methuen, 1984.

Mann, Robert. *A Grand Delusion: America's Descent into Vietnam*. New York: Basic Books, 2001.

Manning, John. "Why Anti-Americanism Haunts the Forty-Ninth Parallel." *Texas Quarterly* 15 (Autumn 1972), 93–99.

Manzione, Joseph. *"I Am Looking to the North for My Life": Sitting Bull, 1876–1881*. Salt Lake City: University of Utah Press, 1991.

Marjoribanks, Robert. "Draft Dodgers: What Makes Them Run?" *United Church Observer* 30 (September 1, 1968), 12–15.

Marshall, T. H., and T. Bottomore. *Citizenship and Social Class*. Concord, MA: Pluto, 1992.

Mathews, Robin. "The Americanization of Canada Means Precisely the Takeover of Canadian Culture by U.S. Citizens." *Saturday Night* 86 (May 1971), 20–22.

———. "The Americanization of Canadian Universities." *Canadian Dimension* 5 (February 1969), 15–16, 53.

———. "Opinion: On Draft Dodging and U.S. Imperialism in Canada." *Canadian Dimension* 6 (February–March 1970), 10–11.

———. "The U.S. Draft Dodger in Canada Is Part of U.S. Imperialism in Canada." *Amex: The American Expatriate in Canada* 2 (June 1970), 24–25.

Mathews, Robin, and James Steele. "The Problem: A Statement by the Editors." In *The Struggle for Canadian Universities: A Dossier,* edited by Robin Mathews and James Steele, 1–11. Toronto: New Press, 1969.

Mathews, Robin, and James Steele, eds. *The Struggle for Canadian Universities: A Dossier.* Toronto: New Press, 1969.

Mays, John Bentley. *Emerald City: Toronto Visited.* Toronto: Viking, 1994.

McFarlane, Bruce, and Dennis Forcese. "Item 5: Petition Circulated by Professors McFarlane and Forcese." In *The Struggle for Canadian Universities: A Dossier,* edited by Robin Mathews and James Steele, 23–24. Toronto: New Press, 1969.

McKeown, Adam M. *Melancholy Order: Asian Migration and the Globalization of Borders.* New York: Columbia University Press, 2008.

McKinsey, Lauren, and Victor Konrad. *Borderland Reflections: The United States and Canada.* Orono, ME: Borderlands Project, 1989.

McMillian, John. *Smoking Typewriters: The Sixties Underground Press and the Rise of Alternative Media in America.* New York: Oxford University Press, 2011.

"Memorandum to C.U.A.S.A. on De-Canadianization, and Five Motions." In *The Struggle for Canadian Universities: A Dossier,* edited by Robin Mathews and James Steele, 15–20. Toronto: New Press, 1969.

Miedema, Gary R. *For Canada's Sake: Public Religion, Centennial Celebrations, and the Remaking of Canada in the 1960s.* Montréal: McGill-Queen's University Press, 2005.

Minot, Stephen. "On Aiding and Abetting: The Anguish of Draft Counseling." *Harper's Magazine* 237 (September 1968), 47–50.

Miyoshi, Masao. "A Borderless World?: From Colonialism to Transnationalism and the Decline of the Nation-State." In *Global/Local: Cultural Production and the Transnational Imaginary,* edited by Rob Wilson and Wimal Dissanayake, 78–106. Durham, NC: Duke University Press, 1996.

Moore, Richard, III. *Richard: Portrait of a Vietnam War Resister.* San Francisco: Richard Moore III, 1987.

Morgan, Allen. *Dropping Out in 3/4 Time.* New York: Seabury, 1972.

Mutchmor, James R. "The World around Us: Ontario." *Christian Century* 86 (May 14, 1969), 690, 692.

Nadle, Marlene. "Exiles in Canada: The New Lost Generation." *Village Voice* 20 (February 24, 1975), 28–31.

National Council for Universal and Unconditional Amnesty. "Amnesty for Vets Too!" New York: National Council for Universal and Unconditional Amnesty, 1976.

———. "Have You Heard the Joke about President Ford's Clemency Program?" New York: National Council for Universal and Unconditional Amnesty, 1974.

National Interreligious Service Board for Conscientious Objectors. Amnesty Information Service. *Religious Statements on Amnesty.* Washington, DC: National Interreligious Service Board for Conscientious Objectors, 1974.

Neatby, H. Blair. "Item 17: C.B.C. broadcast by Professor Neatby, January 2, 1969." In *The Struggle for Canadian Universities: A Dossier,* edited by Robin Mathews and James Steele, 42–44. Toronto: New Press, 1969.

Nelson, J. Robert. "No Utopia in Ethiopia." *Christian Century* 88 (February 17, 1971), 214–216.

"New Draft Policy to Cut Graduate School Enrollment." In *U.S. Draft Policy and Its Impact, July 1968*, 1–2. Washington, DC: Congressional Quarterly Service, 1968.

Ngai, Mae M. *Impossible Subjects: Illegal Aliens and the Making of Modern America.* Princeton, NJ: Princeton University Press, 2004.

Nixon, Richard. *No More Vietnams.* New York: Arbor House, 1985.

"No Draft as Discipline." *Time* 95 (February 9, 1970), 43.

O'Brien, David J. "An American Professor Answers Back." *Weekend Magazine,* March 29, 1969. In *The Struggle for Canadian Universities: A Dossier,* edited by Robin Mathews and James Steele, 72–74. Toronto: New Press, 1969.

Orlofsky, Jacob L., James E. Marcia, and Ira M. Lesser. "Ego Identity Status and the Intimacy versus Isolation Crisis of Young Adulthood." *Journal of Personality and Social Psychology* 27 (August 1973), 211–219.

"Our Work Continues: Report on the NCUUA Conference on New Directions, June 10–12, 1977, Milwaukee." *NCUUA Amnesty Update,* no. 12 (July–August 1977), 3–5.

Øverland, Orm. "Visions of Home: Exiles and Immigrants." In *The Dispossessed: An Anatomy of Exile,* edited by Peter I. Rose, 7–26. Amherst: University of Massachusetts Press, 2005.

Palmer, Bryan D. *Canada's 1960s: The Ironies of Identity in a Rebellious Era.* Toronto: University of Toronto Press, 2009.

Pearson, Lester B. "Address of Prime Minister Pearson at Temple University's Founder's Dinner of the General Alumni Association (on Receiving the University's Second World Peace Award), Philadelphia, Pennsylvania, April 2, 1965." In *Canadian-American Summit Diplomacy, 1923–1973: Selected Speeches and Documents,* edited by Roger Frank Swanson, 251–254. Toronto: McClelland & Stewart, 1975.

———. *Mike: The Memoirs of the Right Honorable Lester B. Pearson, PC, CC, OM, OBE, MA, LLD.* Vol. 3: *1957–1968.* Toronto: University of Toronto Press, 1973.

Pelletier, Gérard. *The October Crisis.* Translated by Joyce Marshall. Toronto: McClelland & Stewart, 1971.

Perrin, Dick, with Tim McCarthy. *G.I. Resister: The Story of How One American Soldier and His Family Fought the War in Vietnam.* Victoria, BC: Trafford, 2001.

Perrin, Noel. "Our Far-Flung Correspondents: Dartmouth '70 and the War." *New Yorker* 46 (July 18, 1970), 53–58.

"*Playboy* Interview: Jimmy Carter: A Candid Conversation with the Democratic Candidate for the Presidency." *Playboy* 23 (November 1976), 63–64, 66, 68–71, 74, 77, 81, 84, 86.

"Political Criminals Continue the Struggle in Canada." *Rebel* (Montréal) 1 (March–April 1968), 2, 15–16.

Poppy, John. "The Draft: Hazardous to Your Health?" *Look* 33 (August 12, 1969), 32–34.

Preston, Andrew. "Balancing War and Peace: Canadian Foreign Policy and the Vietnam War, 1961–1965." *Diplomatic History* 27 (January 2003), 73–111.

Pritchett, V. S. "Across the Vast Land." *Holiday* 35 (April 1964), 52–69, 184–189.

———. "Canada: Land of Contrast and Diversity." *Reader's Digest* 86 (April 1965), 200–202, 204–205, 207–208, 210.

Purdy, A. W., ed. *The New Romans: Candid Canadian Opinions of the U.S.* Edmonton: Hurtig, 1968.

"Questions and Answers following Prime Minister Trudeau's Address to the National Press Club, March 25, 1969." In *Canadian-American Summit Diplomacy, 1923–1973: Selected Speeches and Documents,* ed. Roger Frank Swanson, 281–282. Toronto: McClelland & Stewart, 1975.

"Quick Quiz on Articles in this Issue." *Senior Scholastic* 94 (May 2, 1969), 31.

Rapoport, Roger. "The Magical Mystery Great Lakes Express." *Esquire* 70 (September 1968), 84.

Reader, Norman, and Jerome E. Klein. *Canada.* Blauvelt, NY: Educational Press, 1967.

Readers' Guide to Periodical Literature. New York: H. W. Wilson, March 1965–February 1971.

Redekop, John H., ed. *The Star Spangled Beaver.* Toronto: Peter Martin Associates, 1971.

Rhodes, Joel P. *The Voice of Violence: Performative Violence as Protest in the Vietnam Era.* Westport, CT: Praeger, 2001.

Richter, Volkmar. "Canada." In United States National Student Travel Association. *Student Travel in America,* 340–352. New York: Pyramid, 1968.

Rideout, David, and Ray Amiro. *Handbook Canada.* Toronto: Transglobular Functions, 1972.

Ritchie, Charles. "The Day the President of the United States Struck Fear and Trembling into the Heart of Our PM." *Maclean's* 87 (January 1974), 34–35, 40, 42.

———. *Storm Signals: More Undiplomatic Diaries, 1962–1971.* Toronto: Macmillan, 1983.

Robertson, Craig. *The Passport in America: The History of a Document.* New York: Oxford University Press, 2010.

Roche, Stuart, ed. *The Toronto Survival Manual: A Practical Guide to Better Living and Psychological Survival for Young People Who Have Just Left Home.* Toronto: n.p., 1970.

Rodgers, Kathleen. *Welcome to Resisterville: American Dissidents in British Columbia.* Vancouver: UBC Press, 2015.

Ross, Douglas A. *In the Interests of Peace: Canada and Vietnam, 1954–1973.* Toronto: University of Toronto Press, 1984.

Rothenberg, Leslie S. *The Draft and You: A Handbook on Selective Service.* Garden City, NY: Anchor, 1968.

Rowe, Percy. *Percy Rowe's Travel Guide to Canada: A Complete Guide to Every Province.* Richmond Hill, ON: Simon & Schuster, 1973.

Rubenstein, Richard E. "We're Unfair to Draft-Card Burners." *Saturday Evening Post* 239 (February 12, 1966), 10, 15.

Ruddy, Jon. "The Americans Who Voted with Their Feet." *Maclean's* 82 (March 1969), 27–32.

———. "Calgaryanks." *Maclean's* 79 (September 3, 1966), 18–20, 25–26.

Rutenberg, Amy J. *Rough Draft: Cold War Military Manpower Policy and the Origins of Vietnam-Era Draft Resistance.* Ithaca, NY: Cornell University Press, 2019.

"Rx for Draft Dodging." *Newsweek* 76 (August 3, 1970), 42–43.

Sacks, Howard. *Addendum to Manual for Draft-Age Americans in Europe.* London: War Resisters' International, 1969.

———. *Manual for Draft-Age Americans in Europe.* London: War Resisters' International, 1968.

Sacks, Howard D. *Manual for Draft-Age Americans in Europe (Second Addendum)*. London: War Resisters' International, 1971.

Satin, Mark. Letter to the editor. *New York Times Magazine* (July 2, 1967), 2.

Satin, Mark, ed. *Manual for Draft-Age Immigrants to Canada*. 2nd ed. Toronto: Toronto Anti-Draft Programme/House of Anansi, 1968.

———. *Manual for Draft-Age Immigrants to Canada*. 3rd ed. Toronto: Toronto Anti-Draft Programme/NTO Press, 1969.

———. *Manual for Draft-Age Immigrants to Canada*. 4th rev. ed. Toronto: Toronto Anti-Draft Programme, 1969.

Saywell, John. *Quebec 70: A Documentary Narrative*. Toronto: University of Toronto Press, 1971.

Schneider, Dorothee. "The United States Government and the Investigation of European Emigration in the Open Door Era." In *Citizenship and Those Who Leave: The Politics of Emigration and Expatriation*, edited by Nancy L. Green and François Weil, 195–210. Urbana: University of Illinois Press, 2007.

Scientific Manpower Commission. *The Draft Lottery and You*. Washington, DC: Scientific Manpower Commission, 1970.

Scott, Carl-Gustaf. "'Sweden Might Be a Haven, but It's Not Heaven': American War Resisters in Sweden during the Vietnam War." *Immigrants and Minorities: Historical Studies in Ethnicity, Migration, and Diaspora* 33, no. 3 (2015), 205–230.

———. "Swedish Sanctuary of American Deserters during the Vietnam War: A Facet of Social Democratic Domestic Politics." *Scandinavian Journal of History* 26, no. 2 (2001), 123–142.

"Seeking a Better Life in Canada." *Business Week* (April 21, 1973), 86–87.

Seeley, Robert A. *Handbook for Conscientious Objectors*. 13th ed. Philadelphia: Central Committee for Conscientious Objectors, 1982.

Settje, David E. "'Sinister' Communists and Vietnam Quarrels: The *Christian Century* and *Christianity Today* Respond to the Cold and Vietnam Wars." *Fides et Historia* 32 (Winter–Spring 2000), 81–97.

Shapiro, Andrew O., and John M. Striker. *Mastering the Draft: A Comprehensive Guide for Solving Draft Problems*. Boston: Little, Brown, 1970.

Shugarman, David. "Canadian Nationalism, Americanization, and Scholarly Values." *Journal of Canadian Studies* 5 (August 1970), 12–28.

Smith, Anthony D. *National Identity*. Reno: University of Nevada Press, 1991.

Smylie, James H. "American Religious Bodies, Just War, and Vietnam." *Journal of Church and State* 11 (Autumn 1969), 383–408.

So You're Going to Canada. Ottawa: Canadian Government Travel Bureau, 1970[?].

Spitzer, Dana L. Letter to the editor. *Trans-action* 7 (February 1970), 62.

Squires, Jessica. *Building Sanctuary: The Movement to Support Vietnam War Resisters in Canada, 1965–73*. Vancouver: UBC Press, 2013.

Stadiem, William. *Jet Set: The People, the Planes, the Glamour, and the Romance in Aviation's Glory Years*. New York: Ballantine, 2014.

Steele, James. "Item 3: Article by Steele in the *Toronto Daily Star*, June 18, 1969." In *The Struggle for Canadian Universities: A Dossier*, edited by Robin Mathews and James Steele, 64–67. Toronto: New Press, 1969.

Steinberg, Laurence. *Adolescence*. 11th ed. New York: McGraw-Hill Education, 2017.

Steiner, Lynch, Mrs. Letter to the editor. *Newsweek* 76 (August 31, 1970), 5.

Stevenson, Garth. *Building Nations from Diversity: Canadian and American Experience Compared*. Montréal: McGill-Queen's University Press, 2014.

Stewart, Luke. "'Hell, They're Your Problem, Not Ours': Draft Dodgers, Military Deserters and Canada–United States Relations in the Vietnam War Era." *Études canadiennes | Canadian Studies*, no. 85 (2018), 67–96.

"Stiffer Penalties for Draft Resisters?" *Senior Scholastic* 94 (May 2, 1969), 10–11.

Students for a Democratic Society. *Port Huron Statement*. 1962. Accessed October 16, 2022. https://en.wikisource.org//wiki/Port_Huron_Statement.

Surrey, David S. *Choice of Conscience: Vietnam Era Military and Draft Resisters in Canada*. New York: Praeger, 1982.

Suttler, David. *IV-F: A Guide to Medical, Psychiatric, and Moral Unfitness Standards for Military Induction*. New York: Grove, 1970.

Swomley, John M., Jr. "Conscience and the Draft." *Christian Century* 84 (June 28, 1967), 833–835.

———. "Draft Exiles in Canada." *Christian Century* 85 (October 30, 1968), 1370–1372.

Tai, Chong-Soo, Erick J. Peterson, and Ted Robert Gurr. "Internal versus External Sources of Anti-Americanism: Two Comparative Studies." *Journal of Conflict Resolution* 17 (September 1973), 455–488.

Tatum, Arlo, ed. *Handbook for Conscientious Objectors*. 10th ed. Philadelphia: Central Committee for Conscientious Objectors, 1969.

———. *Handbook for Conscientious Objectors*. 12th ed. Philadelphia: Central Committee for Conscientious Objectors, 1972.

Tatum, Arlo, and Joseph S. Tuchinsky. *Guide to the Draft*. Boston: Beacon, 1969.

Taylor, Alan. *The Civil War of 1812: American Citizens, British Subjects, Irish Rebels, and Indian Allies*. New York: Knopf, 2010.

Taylor, Charles. *Radical Tories: The Conservative Tradition in Canada*. Toronto: Anansi, 1982.

———. *Snow Job: Canada, the United States, and Vietnam (1954 to 1973)*. Toronto: Anansi, 1974.

Taylor, Edmond. "Draft Resisters in Canada." *Reporter* 38 (May 2, 1968), 20–21.

"Teen Travel Talk." *Seventeen* 28 (May 1969), 237.

"Their Own Thing." *Newsweek* 72 (November 25, 1968), 98, 100.

Thelen, David. "Of Audiences, Borderlands, and Comparisons: Toward the Internationalization of American History." *Journal of American History* 79 (September 1992), 432–462.

Thompson, John Herd, and Stephen J. Randall. *Canada and the United States: Ambivalent Allies*. 4th ed. Athens: University of Georgia Press, 2008.

Thomson, Lord, of Fleet. "The Birthday Party Upstairs." *Saturday Review* 50 (January 7, 1967), 60, 62, 64, 69.

"T.O. Has Its Own Dodger Chaplain." *Amex: The American Expatriate in Canada* 2, no. 7 (1970), 8.

Todd, Jack. *The Taste of Metal: A Deserter's Story*. Toronto: HarperPerennial, 2001.

Toronto Anti-Draft Programme, ed. *Manual for Draft-Age Immigrants to Canada*. 6th ed. Toronto: Toronto Anti-Draft Programme, 1971.

Toronto Anti-Draft Programme and Student Union for Peace Action. *Escape to Freedom: Immigration to Canada as an Alternative to the Draft.* Toronto: SUPA Anti-Draft Programme, 1967.

Torpey, John. *The Invention of the Passport: Surveillance, Citizenship, and the State.* New York: Cambridge University Press, 2000.

Townson, Donald W. "The Americans Are Coming! The Americans Are Coming!" *Business Quarterly* (London, ON) 35 (Winter 1970), 82–83.

Trudeau, Pierre E. "Address of Prime Minister Trudeau to the National Press Club, March 25, 1969." In *Canadian-American Summit Diplomacy, 1923–1973: Selected Speeches and Documents,* edited by Roger Frank Swanson, 278–283. Toronto: McClelland & Stewart, 1975.

Tupper, Stanley R., and Douglas L. Bailey. *Canada and the United States—The Second Hundred Years.* New York: Hawthorne, 1967.

———. *One Continent—Two Voices: The Future of Canada/U.S. Relations.* Toronto: Clarke, Irwin, 1967.

Turner, Chris. "On Strawberry Hill." *Walrus* 4 (September 2007), 68–73.

Turner, Frederick Jackson. *The Significance of the Frontier in American History.* New York: Henry Holt, 1921. http://www.gutenberg.org/ebooks/22994.

United Nations. "Universal Declaration of Human Rights." Accessed October 18, 2022. https://www.un.org/en/about-us/universal-declaration-of-human-rights.

United Nations High Commissioner for Refugees. *The 1951 Convention Relating to the Status of Refugees and Its 1967 Protocol,* September 2011. https://www.unhcr.org/en-us/about-us/background/4ec262df9/1951-convention-relating-status-refugees-its-1967-protocol.html.

"US Deserters in Canada." In *Canadian Annual Review for 1969,* edited by John Saywell, 211–212. Toronto: University of Toronto Press, 1970.

U.S. Draft Policy and Its Impact, July 1968. Washington, DC: Congressional Quarterly Service, 1968.

Vetter, Betty, ed. *Draft Facts for Graduates and Graduate Students.* Washington, DC: Scientific Manpower Commission, 1968.

"Via the Underground to Canada." *Christian Century* 84 (November 1, 1967), 1388–1389.

Vonnegut, Mark. *The Eden Express: A Memoir of Madness.* 1975. Reprint, New York: Seven Stories Press, 2002.

Wall, Byron, ed. *Manual for Draft-Age Immigrants to Canada.* 5th ed. Toronto: House of Anansi, 1970.

Watkins, Melville H. "Education in the Branch Plant Economy." *Canadian Dimension* 6 (October–November 1969), 37, 39.

Wayling, Jeanne. "The Swingingest Church in Town." *United Church Observer* 31 (June 1, 1969), 18–20.

Wennersten, John R. *Leaving America: The New Expatriate Generation.* Westport, CT: Praeger, 2008.

Westfall, William. "Voices from the Attic: The Canadian Border and the Writing of American Religious History." In *Retelling U.S. Religious History,* edited by Thomas A. Tweed, 181–199. Berkeley: University of California Press, 1997.

What Every American Tourist Should Know about Canada. Vancouver: Doug Smith, 1967.

White, Charles A. "Immigration Laws: Should We Loosen or Tighten?" *Canada and the World* 38 (January 1973), 3–4.

Whitmore, Terry, with Richard Weber. *Memphis—Nam—Sweden: The Story of a Black Deserter.* 1971. Reprint, Jackson: University Press of Mississippi, 1997.

"Why More Americans Are Leaving These Shores." *U.S. News and World Report* 77 (August 26, 1974), 41–43.

Why the Sea Is Boiling Hot: A Symposium on the Church and the World. Toronto: Ryerson, 1965.

Widdis, Randy William. "Migration, Borderlands, and National Identity: Directions for Research." In John J. Bukowczyk et al., *Permeable Border: The Great Lakes Basin as Transnational Region, 1650–1990,* 152–174. Pittsburgh: University of Pittsburgh Press, 2005.

Wiebe, Robert. "Framing U.S. History: Democracy, Nationalism, and Socialism." In *Rethinking American History in a Global Age,* edited by Thomas Bender, 236–249. Berkeley: University of California Press, 2002.

Williams, Roger. "Go North Young Man: The New Exodus." *New Republic* 162 (May 16, 1970), 15–16.

Williams, Roger Neville. *The New Exiles: American War Resisters in Canada.* New York: Liveright, 1971.

Winks, Robin W. *The Blacks in Canada: A History.* 2nd ed. Montréal: McGill-Queen's University Press, 1997.

Witcover, Jules. *Marathon: The Pursuit of the Presidency, 1972–1976.* New York: Viking, 1977.

Wittels, Mike. *Advice for Conscientious Objectors in the Armed Forces.* 2nd ed. San Francisco: CCCO–Western Region, 1972.

———. *Advice for Conscientious Objectors in the Armed Forces.* 3rd ed. Philadelphia: Central Committee for Conscientious Objectors, 1975.

"World Council Asks Assistance for Draft Exile Work." *Christian Century* 87 (August 5, 1970), 934.

Young, Jay. "Defining a Community in Exile: Vietnam War Resister Communication and Identity in *AMEX,* 1968–1973." *Social History | Histoire sociale* 44 (May 2011), 115–146.

Zolberg, Aristide R. *A Nation by Design: Immigration Policy in the Fashioning of America.* Cambridge, MA: Harvard University Press, 2006.

CANADIAN GOVERNMENT PUBLICATIONS

Canada Year Book 1972: Statistical Annual of the Resources, Demography, Institutions, and Social and Economic Conditions of Canada. Ottawa: Statistics Canada, 1972.

Canada Year Book 1973: An Annual Review of Economic, Social, and Political Developments in Canada. Ottawa: Information Canada, 1973.

Department of Manpower and Immigration. *Admission of University Students to Canada.* Ottawa: Information Canada, 1971.

Dominion Bureau of Statistics. Education Division. Higher Education Section. *Survey of Higher Education, Part II: Degrees, Staff, and Summary, 1963–64–1968–69.* Ottawa: Queen's Printer, 1966–1970.

———. Education, Science, and Culture Division. Post-secondary Education Section. *Fall Enrolment in Universities, 1972–73–1973–74–1975–76.* Ottawa: Statistics Canada, 1976–1977.

————. Education, Science, and Culture Division. Student Information Section. *Fall Enrolment in Universities and Colleges, 1971–72*. Ottawa: Information Canada, 1973.

————. Student Information Section. *Survey of Higher Education, Part I: Fall Enrolment in Universities and Colleges, 1969–70*. Ottawa: Queen's Printer, 1970.

————. *Universities: Enrolment and Degrees, 1976–1979*. Ottawa: Statistics Canada, 1978–1981.

Leacy, F. H., ed. *Historical Statistics of Canada*. 2nd ed. Ottawa: Statistics Canada, 1983.

Royal Commission on National Development in the Arts, Letters, and Sciences, 1949–1951. *Report*. Ottawa: Cloutier, 1951.

Statistics Canada. Education Division. Student Information Section. *Fall Enrolment in Universities and Colleges, 1970–71*. Ottawa: Information Canada, 1972.

CANADIAN STATUTES AND PARLIAMENTARY DEBATES

Canada. *House of Commons Debates*. 1966–1969.

————. *House of Commons Debates* (May 29, 1969), pp. 9243 (Mark Rose, MP). In *The Struggle for Canadian Universities: A Dossier*, edited by Robin Mathews and James Steele, 78–83. Toronto: New Press, 1969.

Immigration Act, Revised Statutes of Canada 1970, c. I-2, s. 57 (g)(ii)–(iv).

Office Consolidation of the Immigration Act, R.S.C., 1952, c. 325, as amended by 1966–67, cc. 25, 90, 1967–68, cc. 1, 37; Immigration Regulations, Part I, made by P.C. 1962–86, as amended by P.C. 1966–525, P.C. 1967–1616 . . . . Ottawa: Queen's Printer and Controller of Stationery, 1968.

UNITED STATES CONGRESSIONAL PUBLICATIONS

House of Representatives. Subcommittee on Courts, Civil Liberties, and the Administration of Justice of the Committee on the Judiciary. *Hearings on H.R. 236, H.R. 674, H.R. 2167, H.R. 3100, H.R. 5195, H.R. 10979, H.R. 10980, H.R. 13001, H. Con. Res. 144, and H. Con. Res. 385 relating to Amnesty*, 93rd Cong., 2nd Sess., 1974.

————. *Report on the Presidential Clemency Program*, 94th Cong., 1st Sess., 1975.

Senate. Subcommittee on Administrative Practice and Procedure of the Committee on the Judiciary. *Clemency Practices and Procedures*, 93rd Cong., 2nd Sess., 1974.

UNITED STATES GOVERNMENT PUBLICATIONS

The American Passport: Its History and a Digest of Laws, Rulings, and Regulations Governing Its Issuance by the Department of State. Washington, DC: U.S. Government Printing Office, 1898.

Historical Statistics of the United States, millennial edition online. Accessed October 18, 2022. http://hsus.cambridge.org.

The 9/11 Commission Report: Final Report of the National Commission on Terrorist Attacks upon the United States. New York: Norton, 2004.

Patterson, David S., ed. *Foreign Relations of the United States, 1964–1968*, vol. 12: *Western Europe*. Washington, DC: U.S. Government Printing Office, 2001.

Presidential Clemency Board. *Report to the President.* Washington, DC: U.S. Government Printing Office, 1975.

President's Commission on an All-Volunteer Armed Force. *The Report of the President's Commission on an All-Volunteer Armed Force.* Washington, DC: U.S. Government Printing Office, 1970.

Randall, Clarence B. *International Travel: Report to the President of the United States.* Washington, DC: U.S. Government Printing Office, 1958.

U.S. Bureau of the Census. *1970 Census of Population.* Vol. 1: *Characteristics of the Population,* part 1, *United States Summary.* Washington, DC: U.S. Government Printing Office, 1973.

———. *Statistical Abstract of the United States, 1970.* Washington, DC: U.S. Department of Commerce, 1970.

U.S. Central Intelligence Agency. *The World Factbook.* Accessed October 18, 2022. https://www.cia.gov/the-world-factbook.

U.S. Department of the Army. Medical Services. *Standards of Medical Fitness.* 1960. Washington, DC: U.S. Government Printing Office, 1974.

U.S. Department of State. "Dept. Reg. 108–456." *Federal Register* 26 (January 19, 1961), 482–483.

———. Passport Office. *The United States Passport: Past, Present, Future.* Washington, DC: U.S. Government Printing Office, 1976.

U.S. Department of Veterans Affairs. Office of Public Affairs, "America's Wars." November 2012. https://www.va.gov/opa/publications/docs/Americas_Wars_Fact_Sheet .doc.

U.S. Selective Service System. "Induction Statistics." Accessed October 18, 2022. https://www.sss.gov/history-and-records/induction-statistics/.

———. "The Vietnam Lotteries." Accessed October 18, 2022. https://www.sss.gov /history-and-records/vietnam-lotteries/.

UNITED STATES LAWS AND STATUTES

An Act to Deny Entitlement to Veterans' Benefits to Certain Persons Who Would Otherwise Become So Entitled Solely by Virtue of the Administrative Upgrading under Temporarily Revised Standards of Other Than Honorable Discharges from Service during the Vietnam Era . . ." Public Law 95-126. *U.S. Statutes at Large* 91 (1977), 1106–1109.

An Act to Prevent in Time of War Departure from or Entry into the United States Contrary to the Public Safety, Public Law 154. *U.S. Statutes at Large* 40 (1917–1919), 559.

An Act to Regulate Further the Entry of Aliens into the United States, Public Law 79. *U.S. Statutes at Large* 41 (1919–1921), 353–354.

Immigration and Nationality Act of 1952, Public Law 82-414. *U.S. Statutes at Large* 66 (1952), 190–191.

Military Selective Service Act of 1971, Public Law 129. 92d Cong., 2d sess. (September 28, 1971), section 6(g)(2).

"Passport requirement; Definitions." *Code of Federal Regulations,* title 22, sec. 53.1, September 20, 2022. https://www.ecfr.gov.

UNITED STATES PRESIDENTIAL PAPERS, PROCLAMATIONS, AND EXECUTIVE ORDERS

Carter, Jimmy. "Proclamation 4771—Registration under the Military Selective Service Act." July 2, 1980. Last reviewed August 15, 2016. https://www.archives.gov/federalregister /codification/proclamations/04771.html.

Executive Order no. 2,285. *A Compilation of the Messages and Papers of the Presidents.* New York: Bureau of National Literature, 1916, 18:8169–8170.

Executive Order no. 10,292. *Code of Federal Regulations,* title 3 (1949–1953), 808–810.

Ford, Gerald R. "Executive Order 11842—Amending Executive Order Nos. 11803 and 11837 to Further Extend the Period for Application for Clemency Board Review of Certain Convictions and Military Service Discharges." February 28, 1975. The American Presidency Project, https://www.presidency.ucsb.edu/documents/executive -order-11842-amending-executive-order-nos-11803-and-11837-further-extend-the.

———. "Proclamation 4353—Program for the Return of Vietnam Era Draft Evaders and Military Deserters." February 28, 1975. The American Presidency Project, https:// www.presidency.ucsb.edu/documents/proclamation-4353-program-for-the-return -vietnam-era-draft-evaders-and-military-deserters.

Public Papers of the Presidents of the United States: Containing the Public Messages, Speeches, and Statements of the President: Richard Nixon, 1972. Washington, DC: U.S. Government Printing Office, 1974.

Public Papers of the Presidents of the United States: Containing the Public Messages, Speeches, and Statements of the President: Richard Nixon, 1973. Washington, DC: U.S. Government Printing Office, 1975.

Public Papers of the Presidents of the United States. Gerald Ford. Containing the Public Messages, Speeches, and Statements of the President, August 9 to December 31, 1974. Washington, DC: U.S. Government Printing Office, 1975.

Public Papers of the Presidents of the United States. Gerald Ford. Containing the Public Messages, Speeches, and Statements of the President. 1975. Vol. 1: January 1 to July 17, 1975. Washington, DC: U.S. Government Printing Office, 1977.

Public Papers of the Presidents of the United States. Gerald Ford. Containing the Public Messages, Speeches, and Statements of the President. 1976–77. Vol. 3: July 10, 1976 to January 20, 1977. Washington, DC: U.S. Government Printing Office, 1979.

Public Papers of the Presidents of the United States. Jimmy Carter, 1977. Vol. 1: January 20 to June 24, 1977. Washington, DC: U.S. Government Printing Office, 1977.

Public Papers of the Presidents of the United States: Jimmy Carter, 1980–81. Vol. 2: May 24 to September 26, 1980, Washington, DC: U.S. Government Printing Office, 1982.

UNITED STATES SUPREME COURT CASES

Breen v. Selective Service Board No. 16, 396 U.S. 460 (1970).

Gutknecht v. United States, 396 U.S. 295 (1970).

Oestereich v. Selective Service System Local Board No. 11, 393 U.S. 233 (1968).

United States v. Seeger, 380 U.S. 163 (1965).

Welsh v. United States, 398 U.S. 333 (1970).

NEWSPAPERS

Atlanta Constitution	*Montreal Gazette*
Chicago Defender	*New York Amsterdam News*
Chicago Tribune	*New York Times*
Christian Science Monitor (Boston)	*Ottawa Citizen*
Commercial Appeal (Memphis)	*Toronto Daily Star*
Financial Post (Toronto)	*Varsity* (Toronto)
Globe and Mail (Toronto)	*Wall Street Journal* (New York)
Los Angeles Times	*Washington Post*
Minneapolis Tribune	*Windsor* (Ontario) *Star*

INDEX

Page numbers in italics refer to figures and tables.

ABOUT THE AUTHOR

DONALD W. MAXWELL is assistant professor of history at Indiana State University, where he teaches courses on U.S. and world history. His PhD is from Indiana University–Bloomington. Having always lived in the center of a state in the center of the country, he is fascinated with borders.

Available titles in the War Culture series